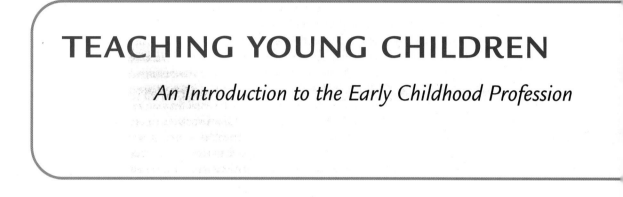

# TEACHING YOUNG CHILDREN

## *An Introduction to the Early Childhood Profession*

Join us on the web at

**EarlyChildEd.delmar.com**

# TEACHING YOUNG CHILDREN

*An Introduction to the Early Childhood Profession*

## SECOND EDITION

**MARGARET B. PUCKETT**
*Texas Wesleyan University*

**DEBORAH DIFFILY**
*Southern Methodist University*

**THOMSON**

**DELMAR LEARNING**

Australia   Canada   Mexico   Singapore   Spain   United Kingdom   United States

**THOMSON**

**DELMAR LEARNING**

**Teaching Young Children**
**An Introduction to the Early Childhood Profession, Second Edition**
Margaret B. Puckett   Deborah Diffily

**Vice President, Career Education SBU:**
Dawn Gerrain

**Director of Editorial:**
Sherry Gomoll

**Acquisitions Editor:**
Erin J. O'Connor

**Editorial Assistant:**
Ivy Ip

**Director of Production:**
Wendy A. Troeger

**Production Editor:**
Joy Kocsis

**Technology Project Manager:**
Joseph Saba

**Director of Marketing:**
Donna J. Lewis

**Channel Manager:**
Nigar Hale

**Composition:**
Carlisle Communications, Inc.

For permission to use material from this text or product, contact us by
Tel   (800) 730-2214
Fax   (800) 730-2215
www.thomsonrights.com

Library of Congress Cataloging-in-Publication Data

Puckett, Margaret B.
    Teaching young children: an introduction to the early childhood profession / Margaret B. Puckett, Deborah Diffily.—2nd ed.
        p. cm.
    Includes bibliographical references (p. ) and index.
    ISBN 1-4018-2583-4
    1. Early childhood teachers. 2. Early childhood teachers—United States. 3. Early childhood education. 4. Child development. 5. Teaching-Vocational guidance—United States. I. Diffily, Deborah. II. Title.

LB1775.6.P83 2004
372.21—dc21                                    2003048910

**NOTICE TO THE READER**

## Dedication

*This book is dedicated to all of the early childhood education students we've watched grow from well-intentioned novices into knowledgeable early childhood educators. Initially, many chose this field simply because they loved young children. Now, after years of continued study and practical experience, they have become professional educators who make a difference in the lives of young children and their families every day.*

# CONTENTS

# APPENDIXES

# PREFACE

Academic and social emphasis on early childhood education in recent years has occasioned an unprecedented awareness of the need for, and importance of, a knowledgeable and skilled early childhood workforce. The early childhood care and education profession has from its earliest history endeavored to describe and promote the best possible child-rearing and education experiences for infants and young children. Two important contemporary bodies of research and scholarship undergird the material presented in this second edition of *Teaching Young Children: An Introduction to the Early Childhood Profession.*

The first is the dramatically enlightening neurobiological research that informs the practitioner's views of how early experiences can influence brain growth and neurological development during a child's formative years. The types and frequency of early experiences have been shown to influence, in positive or negative ways, long-term outcomes for child development. This has implications for all adults who care for and interact with infants and young children. Early childhood educators have an ethical responsibility to learn about child growth and development and make studied and wise decisions regarding pedagogy and their relationships with young children and their families.

The second body of research that has emerged from similar earlier studies is the growing data (and, we might add, affirmation of extant literature) on what constitutes quality early childhood education. From this emerging and affirming research, we have extrapolated a set of guiding principles for early care and education from infancy through the primary grades. More and more children at earlier and earlier ages are being cared for and provided early education experiences by adults other than their parents. A major emphasis in this research is on the caregiver/educator. The success of early care and education experiences rests with the knowledge, skills, and dispositions of the adults who provide care and education opportunities and who interact with children and their families regularly.

This text employs a contextualized approach; that is, the principles of quality early childhood education are frequently described and analyzed through the use of vignettes, case studies, and stories to illustrate the professional early childhood educator's roles, responsibilities, and interactions with children and families. Through these examples, the reader is introduced to both the child development and pedagogical aspects of early care and education. The construct of developmentally appropriate practice is explored in the context of constructivist and ecological perspectives. Throughout this text, we draw upon historical and contemporary research as well as on our own experiences as parents, as early childhood educators in child care and in private and public schools, and as teachers of early childhood educators.

An introduction to the profession necessarily evokes appreciation for the thinkers, philosophers, scholars, researchers, and advocates who have guided thought, practice, and policy relating to children and families over the years. The attempt is made throughout this text to bring to life the names and personalities of a few of history's great philosophers and scholars whose contributions continue to influence early childhood philosophy, research, and practice today. In addition, contemporary scholars and leaders are presented in biographical sketches with overviews of their contributions to the field of early childhood education.

The text is divided into four parts:

    I. Foundations of Early Childhood Education
    II. Information That Informs Practice
    III. Best Practices for Young Children
    IV. Early Childhood Careers in the Twenty-First Century

Each chapter includes organizing objectives, margin notes that define key terms, biographical and other text boxes, salient quotations to build interest and encourage reflection, and chapter summaries. Every chapter is based on principles that define and support the thesis of the text. The principles are meant to motivate early childhood professionals to perform the following:

- To acknowledge a rich and informing history of child care and early education.
- To rely upon current knowledge of child growth, development, and learning when making decisions about their practices.
- To value the strengths and needs of children and to use this knowledge in making decisions about individual children.
- To view families and communities as integral parts of any early childhood program.
- To prepare environments especially suited for infants and young children.
- To provide a wide variety of experiences and activities for children.

- To reflect on and model appropriate interactions with young children.
- To recognize that learning occurs best in a community of learners and in a context that the teacher facilitates.
- To continue to expand their knowledge of children and families to further their own professional development and to broaden their advocacy efforts.

Additionally, the end of each chapter contains a set of issues upon which students are asked to reflect, suggested field experiences, recommendations for further reading, and selected helpful Web sites. The authors and Delmar Learning affirm that the Web site URLs referenced herein were accurate at the time of printing. However, due to the fluid nature of the Internet, we cannot guarantee their accuracy for the life of the edition. Extensive appendices include the following:

- A beginner's list of learning center materials
- Recommended adult to child ratios
- Code of Ethics of the National Association for the Education of Young Children
- Code of Ethics of the Division for Early Childhood of the Council for Exceptional Children
- Comprehensive roster of regional and national professional early childhood associations
- Child Development Associate credential competency goals and functional areas
- Division for Early Childhood of the Council for Exceptional Children's Parent Checklist for special education programs
- A strategy for developing a professional development portfolio

## SUPPLEMENTS

### Instructor's Manual

An Instructor's Manual is available that provides learning objectives, outlines, key concepts, key terms, extension activities, reflections, field experiences, and review questions for each chapter.

### Computerized Test Bank

An extensive computerized test bank containing 1,000 questions keyed to chapter content is available. The test bank includes essay, short answer, multiple choice, completion, matching, and true/false questions.

### Online Resources™

The Online Resources™ to Accompany *Teaching Young Children: An Introduction to the Early Childhood Profession, Second Edition* is your link to early childhood education on the Internet. The Online Resources™ contain many features to help focus your understanding of the early childhood profession:

- Case Studies present situations faced by early childhood educators and suggest responses to the situations, bringing concepts presented in the book to life.
- Discussion forums and reflections encourage you to think about how you will apply theories and knowledge learned in the book.
- Web Activities challenge you to use the Internet to conduct further research and expand your knowledge.

 The Online Resources™ icon appears at the end of each chapter to prompt you to go on-line and take advantage of the many features provided.

You can find the Online Resources™ at www.earlychilded.delmar.com

We hope this text encourages students to become early childhood professionals committed to serving the best interests of children and their families and to understand that professional development is a career-long process.

## ACKNOWLEDGMENTS

We continue to benefit from the responses to this text by students who read and use it. Their uniquely user perspectives guide the format and content of our revisions. We especially want to thank the peer reviewers whose critiques and suggestions were considered and often incorporated into the revisions. They are: Nancy Baptiste, Ed.D., New Mexico State University, Las Cruces, NM; Audrey Beard, Ed.D., Albany State University, Albany, GA; Linda Gamble, University of Maine at Farmington, Farmington, ME; Nina Mazloff, Becker College, Worcester, MA; and Patricia Weaver, Fayette Technical Community College, Fayetteville, NC. The editorial and production team at Delmar Learning were helpful in bringing this book to completion and to them we express profound appreciation. Special thanks are extended to Erin O'Connor, Ivy Ip, Pat Gillivan, and Joy Kocsis.

# ABOUT THE AUTHORS

**Margaret Brous Puckett, Ed.D.,** is a retired professor of education from Texas Wesleyan University in Fort Worth, Texas, where she served as chair of the departments of early childhood education, elementary education, and graduate studies in education. Following full-time teaching and administration, Dr. Puckett continues to teach and provide consulting services to universities, school districts, state agencies, and local boards and committees. She currently serves as the child care and education consultant to the Tarrant County Work Force Development Board and has chaired its child care oversight committee. She has taught courses in child development, early childhood education, elementary education, and child care administration at the University of North Texas, Texas Tech University, and Tarrant County College. She has taught young children ages two through eight years.

Dr. Puckett received her B.S. degree from the University of Texas at Austin, her M.S. in child development from Texas Woman's University, and an Ed.D. from the University of North Texas. Dr. Puckett is a past recipient of funding for faculty enrichment provided by the Sid W. Richardson Foundation and has visited and studied child care and education in Israel and England.

She is a past president of the Southern Early Childhood Association, the Texas Association for the Education of Young Children, and the Fort Worth Area Association for the Education of Young Children. She has served in numerous leadership roles at the local, state, regional, and national levels. She has received honors and awards from the University of North Texas (Outstanding Alumnus in Early Childhood Education Award) and from Texas Wesleyan University (Faculty Recognition Award for Excellence in teaching, research and professional outreach). The author of a number of books and articles, she was a contributing author to the expanded edition of *Developmentally Appropriate Practices in Programs Serving Children Birth Through Age Eight*, published by the National Association for the Education of Young Children. She coauthored with Janet K. Black, Ph.D., the books, *The Young Child: Development from*

*Prebirth through Age Eight* and *Authentic Assessment of the Young Child: Celebrating Development and Learning.*

**Deborah Diffily, Ph.D.,** is an assistant professor of Early Childhood Education at Southern Methodist University in Dallas, Texas. She received a Ph.D. from the University of North Texas. As a former prekindergarten, kindergarten, and first grade teacher in Fort Worth, Texas, Dr. Diffily has practical experience teaching and learning with young children. Using both theoretical background and practical experience, she makes state and national presentations, and also shares her knowledge through journal articles and books. Her most recent book, *Project-Based Learning with Young Children*, was coauthored with Charlotte Sassman. Dr. Diffily's primary areas of interest are supporting emergent literacy and scientific development, teaching young children through projects, and working with families.

**PART ONE**

# Foundations of Early Childhood Education

# CHAPTER 1

## Early Childhood Principles

*After reading this chapter, you should be able to:*
- Describe why the early childhood years are so important.
- Discuss the roles that adults play in the lives of young children.
- Identify principles that guide the practices of early childhood educators.
- Define *developmentally appropriate practice* and discuss its primary components.
- Discuss some of the myths related to developmentally appropriate practices.
- Identify components of a high-quality early childhood program.

**S**HARITA JONES rushes into the child care center where her nine-month old daughter, Sheneka, is cared for while she works. She is carrying Sheneka, a diaper bag, a box of disposable diapers, and her purse. Sharita is running behind schedule this morning and fears she will be late for work. She accidentally overslept this morning and has been rushing since the moment she woke up. Sheneka senses her mother's anxiety and has been fussy all morning, which only made the whole process of getting ready to leave the house more difficult. Sheneka continues to make whimpering noises as Sharita fumbles with the center door and then the door to the toddler room. As she steps inside the room, Ebony, Sheneka's caregiver, realizes Sharita's stress and meets her at the door. "It's okay," Ebony says as she takes the infant into her arms and puts the diaper bag and other items into Sheneka's cubby. "Sit down just a minute and say goodbye to Sheneka. You'll feel better if you do." Sharita smiles for the first time that morning and sits for a moment before leaving the center to go to work. Sharita is able to feel comfortable leaving her daughter in Ebony's care because she knows that Sheneka will receive the very special care that all young children deserve.

Not all mothers are able to find the high-quality child care that Sharita found for her daughter. She found a center that was accredited by the National Association for the Education of Young Children (NAEYC), a clear sign that high-quality care existed at that center. The caregivers at Sheneka's center are warm and caring people and knowledgeable early childhood educators. They recognize the importance of the first few years of life and accept their roles in facilitating the development and learning of young children.

## CRITICAL NATURE OF EARLY YEARS

The field of early childhood education defines itself as serving children from birth through age eight. These early years are the most important years in a person's life. Even a casual observer can see the vast changes that occur during these eight years, growth from a dependent infant to the sophisticated communicator and problem solver of an eight-year-old. Environments and experiences for these children are critically important, as they shape the child and who he or she will become.

Several decades of research show that high-quality experiences enhance children's physical/motor, social, emotional, and cognitive development. As important as this is, more recent research on the functions of the brain indicates that high-quality experiences not only affect a child's development, but also actually change the physical structure of the brain (Dana Alliance for Brain Initiatives, 1996). The implications of this research are great for parents, caregivers, and teachers of young children. The physical and psy-

---

*Roles of Early Childhood Educators*

Teachers of young children find themselves fulfilling multiple roles as they work to meet the needs of the children in their care. Some of these roles include:

Curriculum writer
Family educator
Psychologist
Play therapist
Conflict resolution mediator
Procurement officer
Nurse
Scholar
Researcher
Child advocate

---

chological environments adults create for children, the interactions adults have with children, and the experiences adults provide children have life-long implications (Schweinhart & Weikart, 1996; Frank Porter Graham Child Development Center, 1999; National Institute for Child Health and Human Development, 1998).

## IMPORTANT ROLES OF EARLY CHILDHOOD EDUCATORS

More families are depending on early childhood educators today in helping to care for their children than ever before. Almost eight million children are cared for by someone other than their parents (Children's Defense Fund, 2001). Because relationships with adults are such a critical factor in determining young children's development, early childhood educators accept the important responsibility of caring for and guiding the children in their care. The roles and responsibilities of early childhood educators are vast and varied. As described by the leading professional organization for early childhood educators, the National Association for the Education of Young Children (NAEYC), adults who work with young children:

- Respect, value, and accept children and treat them with dignity at all times.
- Make it a priority to know each child well.
- Create an intellectually engaging, responsive environment to promote each child's learning and development.

- Make plans to enable children to attain key curriculum goals across various disciplines.
- Foster children's collaboration with peers on interesting, important enterprises.
- Develop, refine, and use a wide repertoire of teaching strategies to enhance children's learning and development.
- Facilitate the development of responsibility and self-regulation in children (Bredekamp & Copple, 1997, pp. 17–19).

As early childhood educators fulfill these roles, they are mindful of a few basic principles that guide their decisions about young children. These principles—and discussion of issues that surround them—are the basis of this book.

## PRINCIPLES THAT GUIDE EARLY CHILDHOOD EDUCATORS

A few important principles guide the decisions early childhood educators make as they work with young children and their families. These principles include learning about early childhood history; learning about child growth, development, and learning theory; learning about individual children; learning from families and communities; preparing environments; making decisions about curriculum; interacting with children; and creating communities of learners. Summaries of these principles follow.

### Learning about Early Childhood Education History

Early childhood educators look to their history as a foundation for making decisions about their practices. The field has a rich history of both theory and practice. For those who work with young children, being knowledgeable about historical people and events is like "standing on the shoulders of giants." What we now know about how young children develop and learn is based on the work of many who have gone before us. Current beliefs about early childhood education are influenced, in part, by Friedrich Froebel's belief that young children learn through concrete materials, John Dewey's belief in the classroom as a model for democracy, in Erik Erikson's stages of psychosocial development, and Jean Piaget's and Lev Vygotsky's understandings of how children learn. Each of these theorists has made important contributions to the framework early childhood educators use to view children. The practices of those who worked with young children in past decades can still be seen in high-quality early childhood classrooms today in the unit blocks created by Caroline Pratt and in self-help skills encouraged by Maria Montessori. These individuals and many others provide a rich history of early childhood education. A detailed discussion of the roots of contemporary early childhood education can be found in chapter 2.

## Learning about Child Growth, Development, and Learning Theory

Early childhood educators know that all children proceed through predictable stages in all areas of development, although each child does this at a different rate. Adults who are knowledgeable about the theories of child growth, development, and learning use this knowledge to make educational decisions. When people who work with young children are aware of typical stages of development, they can make age-appropriate decisions for the children in their care. They are able to prepare appropriate environments and plan meaningful experiences for those children. Chapter 3 contains a summary of widely held expectations for different age groups and a discussion of how early childhood educators base their practices on this knowledge.

## Learning about Individual Children

While it is important to be aware of typical development and expected age-appropriate behaviors of children, it is also important to get to know every child in an early childhood program. Being aware of the differences in development and individual children's strengths and challenges allows early childhood educators to plan curriculum that will meet each child's developmental needs. Educators who expect the same behaviors and abilities from children who are the same age can actually harm children developmentally, especially children with special learning and developmental needs (Mallory, 1992). Educational decisions about curriculum, materials, and expectations need to be made for each child in an early childhood program. Early childhood educators can learn about children as they observe them carefully and document these observations. They make decisions about practices based on what they learn about individual children. Details about different methods of assessing individual children can be found in chapter 4.

## Learning about Families and Communities

Early childhood educators can learn much about individual children from their families and their communities. It is important that adults who work with young children also work with the families of these children. Close relationships between child, teacher, and family benefit all parties. Chapter 5 contains a discussion of the rationale for collaborating with families and specific suggestions for keeping families informed and for involving them in early childhood programs.

*Early childhood educators can learn about children as they observe them carefully and document these observations.*

## Preparing Environments

Young children learn from concrete, hands-on experiences. Early childhood educators create rich learning environments by choosing materials that interest the children in their programs and by offering these materials to the children in an organized manner. Learning centers are generally accepted as the best way to organize different learning materials so that they are easily accessible to children. Learning centers—their organization and the materials that can be offered in them—are discussed in chapter 6.

## Making Decisions about Curriculum

An appropriate curriculum for young children builds on what they already know. An early childhood educator uses multiple sources of information to create a curriculum for young children. An appropriate curriculum integrates all areas of development (physical/motor, social, emotional, cognitive), includes all disciplines (reading, writing, math, science, social studies), and takes into consideration the interests, skills, and abilities of the children in the program. Most important, the curriculum must be meaningful to the children in each individual early childhood program. Chapter 7 discusses these issues.

### Interacting with Children

The positive—or negative—interactions between teachers and children have profound effects on children. Children develop self-concepts from the ways they are treated by others. Often adults discipline young children according to unconscious ideas about children. Chapter 8 discusses theory and practice in planning for individual and group social and emotional well-being and in modeling and facilitating positive and supportive relationships. Suggestions are given for establishing developmentally appropriate limits and group rules as well as how to address inappropriate or challenging behaviors.

### Creating Communities of Learners

Relationships are an important context for learning. In high-quality early childhood programs, all children are valued for who they are and are therefore encouraged to develop respectful relationships with everyone else in the program. Adults and children grow to care about each other and to work together as a community. Details of how to create a community of learners are discussed in chapter 9.

Chapter 10 concludes the book by discussing career opportunities for early childhood educators as well as examining the challenges and opportunities for the field now and in the future.

## DEVELOPMENTALLY APPROPRIATE PRACTICES

All of these principles together guide early childhood educators as they work to implement **developmentally appropriate practices (DAP)**. Developmentally appropriate practices represent what we now know from research and practice is best for young children. DAP encompasses all facets of the early childhood program, beginning with the climate of the classroom and how individual children's needs are met, and extending to the more global aspects of a program such as its policies. It includes the physical environment, the daily schedule, and the learning experiences adults structure for the children.

Developmentally appropriate practices can perhaps be best understood when compared to practices that are inappropriate. For very young children like Sheneka, who was discussed in the opening vignette, appropriate and inappropriate practices, as defined by NAEYC, include those shown in Table 1–1.

By the time Sheneka is four years old, the caregivers at her center will be making decisions about a very different child. Appropriate practices for a preschool-aged child are very different than those practices appropriate for an infant (see Table 1–2).

**developmentally appropriate practices** pertains to age appropriateness: the predictable patterns of growth and development that occur in children; and individual appropriateness: the uniqueness of each child in individual rates and patterns of growth and development in physical/motor, cognitive, language, literacy, learning styles, psychosocial development, and family, linguistic, and cultural backgrounds.

*Early childhood educators create rich learning environments by choosing materials that interest the children in their programs and by offering these materials to the children in an organized manner.*

These examples serve only as an introduction to "best" practices for young children. For a more complete listing of developmentally appropriate and inappropriate practices for infants and toddlers, three- to five-year-olds, and six- to eight-year-olds, please refer to the 1997 NAEYC publication, *Developmentally appropriate practice in early childhood programs* (Bredekamp & Copple, 1997).

Early childhood programs vary greatly in the quality of care and education they provide and in how closely they align their practices with guidelines of developmentally appropriate practices. In fact, only 14% of child care centers and 10% of family child care homes are of sufficient quality to be considered a positive factor in children's development. However, this text does not focus on the inappropriate practices that exist in early childhood programs. Rather, it focuses on what the field of early childhood education indicates is best for young children and that is developmentally appropriate practice.

### Age Appropriateness and Individual Appropriateness

There are two primary components of developmentally appropriate practices: age appropriateness and individual appropriateness. Programs for young children must consider the predictable patterns of growth and

**TABLE 1–1**

*Developmentally Appropriate Practices Versus Inappropriate Practices for Very Young Children*

| Appropriate Practices | Inappropriate Practices |
|---|---|
| • The play areas are comfortable; they have pillows, foam-rubber mats, and soft carpeting where babies can lie on their stomachs or backs and be held and read to. A hammock, rocking chair (preferably a glider for safety), overstuffed chair, and big cushions are available for caregivers or parents and infants to relax in together. | • The play areas are sterile, designed for easy cleaning, but without the different textures, levels, and colors that infants need to stimulate their senses. There is not an area where an adult can sit comfortably with an infant in her arms and read or talk to the baby. |
| • Space is arranged so children can enjoy moments of quiet play by themselves, have ample space to roll over and move freely, and can crawl toward interesting objects. Areas for younger infants are separated from those of crawlers to promote the safe interactions of infants in similar stages of development. | • Space is cramped and unsafe for children who are learning how to move their bodies. |
| • Toys provided are responsive to the child's actions: a variety of grasping toys that require different types of manipulation; a varied selection of skill-development materials, including nesting and stacking materials, activity boxes, and containers to be filled and emptied, a variety of balls, bells, and rattles. | • Toys are battery powered or windup so the baby just watches. Toys lack a variety of texture, size, and shape. |

*Source:* From Bredekamp, S., & Copple, C. (Eds.). *Developmentally appropriate practice in early childhood programs* (rev. ed.; p. 75), by National Association for the Education of Young Children, 1997, Washington, DC: Author. Copyright 1997 by the National Association for the Education of Young Children. Reprinted with permission from the National Association for the Education of Young Children.

**TABLE 1–2**

*Developmentally Appropriate and Inappropriate Practices for Four-Year-Olds*

| Appropriate Practices | Inappropriate Practices |
| --- | --- |
| • Teachers plan and prepare a learning environment that fosters children's initiative, active exploration of materials, and sustained engagement with other children, adults, and activities. In choosing materials and equipment, teachers consider children's developmental levels and the social/cultural context—for instance, the geographic location of the program and the backgrounds of the children. | • The environment is disorderly and without structure or predictability; children wander aimlessly without purpose or direction. The environment and materials provide too little variety, interest, or choice for children (for instance, puzzles are too easy or have missing pieces). The noise level is stressful for children and adults, impeding conversation and learning. |
| • Teachers maintain a safe, healthy environment and careful supervision. They anticipate and avoid accidents or problems before these occur. Teachers guard children's safety, while also encouraging children to do what they are capable of doing for themselves. | • Teachers are frequently inattentive or careless about supervising children and monitoring the safety of the indoor and outdoor environments. Teachers do things for children that they could do themselves, because it is faster or costs less money. Children do not have access to playground equipment, woodworking tools, or cooking equipment. |
| • Teachers support children's age-appropriate risk taking within safe boundaries—for instance, supervising children wearing safety goggles as they use real tools for woodworking or children exploring a climb-on apparatus that is securely anchored, with adequate cushioning material in place. | • Learning materials are primarily workbooks, ditto sheets, flash cards, and other materials that focus on drill and practice rather than engaging children's problem-solving and other higher-order thinking skills. |

**TABLE 1–2 (Continued)**

*Developmentally Appropriate and Inappropriate Practices for Four-Year-Olds*

| Appropriate Practices | Inappropriate Practices |
|---|---|
| • Teachers plan a variety of concrete learning experiences with materials and people relevant to children's life experiences and that promote their interest, engagement in learning, and conceptual development. Materials include, but are not limited to, blocks and other construction materials, books and other language-arts materials, dramatic-play themes and props, art and modeling materials, sand and water with tools for measuring, and tools for simple science activities. | • The primary criterion for planning activities is that they be fun and entertaining to children, with no attempt to build higher-level abilities or connect the activity to intellectual or social goals. |

*Source:* From Bredekamp, S., & Copple, C. (Eds.). *Developmentally appropriate practice in early childhood programs* (rev. ed.; pp. 125–126), by National Association for the Education of Young Children, 1997, Washington, DC: Author. Copyright 1997 by the National Association for the Education of Young Children. Reprinted with permission from the National Association for the Education of Young Children.

development that are predominant for each age group and the typical interests for that age group. This represents age appropriateness. It is this component of developmentally appropriate practice that was considered when NAEYC defined developmentally appropriate and inappropriate practices (Bredekamp & Copple, 1997). But programs must also take into consideration each child's developmental level, interests, family, linguistic, and cultural backgrounds. This represents individual appropriateness. Both components must guide the practices of early childhood educators.

### Age Appropriateness

The age-appropriate component of developmentally appropriate practice is guided by principles of child growth and development. Early childhood educators are well aware of widely held expectations of different developmental areas for the age of the children with whom they are working. For example, behavioral expectations for typical development for an infant in language and communication include:

- Cries to signal pain or distress
- Smiles or vocalizes to initiate social contact
- Responds to human voices, gazes at faces
- Uses vocal and nonvocal communication to express interest and exert influence
- Babbles using all types of sounds, engages in private conversations when alone
- Combines babbles, understands names of familiar people and objects, laughs, listens to conversations

The age-appropriate expectations of four-year-olds in the area of language development and communication would look more like the following:

- Has a vocabulary from 4,000 to 6,000 words
- Speaks in five- to six-word sentences
- Sings simple songs
- Knows many rhymes and finger plays
- Uses verbal commands
- Expresses emotions through facial gestures and read others for body cues
- Controls volume of voice for periods of time if reminded
- Uses more advanced sentence structures
- Learns new vocabulary quickly if related to own experiences
- Retells a four- to five-step directive or the sequence in a story

These anticipated child behaviors in the area of language development merely demonstrate the vast differences in what should be expected from young children of different ages. Widely held expectations have been established for young children of all ages in all areas of development. Teachers, aware of these age-appropriate expectations, can more easily plan activities and experiences to support and enhance children's development.

When implementing age-appropriate practices, one important factor to consider is the ratio of children to adults caring for them. Younger children require more time and individual attention. The younger the child, the fewer children a caregiver should be primarily responsible for. Early childhood professional organizations publish guidelines on these ratios, suggesting that one adult should care for only four infants or fifteen four- and five-year-olds. Recommended adult-to-child ratios, as suggested by the NAEYC, can be found in appendix B.

Learning materials are another consideration of age appropriateness. Materials that are appropriate for four- and five-years-olds would not necessarily be appropriate for younger children. Small math manipulatives that are used in prekindergarten and kindergarten classes would not be appropriate for two- and three-year-olds who are still inclined to put things in their mouths. The possibility of swallowing these small objects would make them inappropriate for use with very young children. On the other hand, push toys that are very appropriate for toddlers are not appealing to older preschoolers. Early childhood educators know which materials are appropriate for each age group; however, within any group of children who are the same age, different abilities and interests of individual children require a variety of materials with varying levels of challenge.

## Individual Appropriateness

Developmentally appropriate practices must not be only age appropriate, but they must also be individually appropriate. Within each age group, a range of behaviors and abilities is expected. Kindergarten teachers at the beginning of the school year plan learning opportunities for typically developing five-year-olds. Teachers plan for what they know about five-year-olds, what they are usually interested in, and what activities they usually enjoy. That is, teachers plan age appropriately until they get to know each of their students. After getting to know a group of kindergarten students, some children may be demonstrating behavior of a three-year-old level in specific developmental areas whereas other children may be demonstrating behavior of a seven-year-old level in that same area. These differences could be related to maturation rates because different children simply develop and mature at different rates. Differences in children may also be related to previous experiences they have had in their homes or in other child care settings. As the teacher of a group of children gets to know each child individually, she begins to change the way she plans so that she meets the needs of individual children.

The physical environment, the activities offered to children, and the ways in which adults interact with young children should depend on the information the teacher obtains about each child. The teacher arranges learning centers that are appealing to all children in the classroom, those operating at the higher range of typical behaviors and those who are still progressing toward typical behaviors of that age group. Centers in a kindergarten classroom are set up so that they attract the interest of a child who is demonstrating behaviors on a three-year-old level as well as the child who is operating on a seven-year-old level. Activities for large and small groups are varied in an effort to provide successful experiences for all children in the class based on individual developmental levels. Teachers also adjust the way they interact with children so that they communicate at a level each child can understand.

## Cultural and Linguistic Appropriateness

While the definition of developmentally appropriate practices includes only the two subcategories of age and individual appropriateness, it is important to recognize the increasing diversity of children in early childhood programs. Professional early childhood teachers take special care to learn about the cultural and language backgrounds of each child in the program and are responsive to these important components that contribute to a child's development.

## Misunderstandings about DAP

The term *developmentally appropriate practices* (DAP) was first defined in a 1986 NAEYC position statement. An expanded definition was published a year later (Bredekamp, 1987) in what became known simply as "the green book." This explanation of developmentally appropriate practices was intended to help adults create programs that meet young children's needs, both in terms of age-appropriate curricula and individually appropriate activities. Now, more than a decade after the publication of NAEYC's DAP guidelines and the issuance of a revised edition (Bredekamp & Copple, 1977), developmentally appropriate practices are still not well understood by some people. The term *developmentally appropriate practices* has, in some cases, become a catch word that individuals use to describe almost anything associated with early childhood.

Some people believed that the 1987 DAP document was written as a set of strict guidelines for programs rather than as a framework for accepted practices. This and other misconceptions about DAP have been openly discussed over the past ten years. Many of these misconceptions were clarified in the 1997 DAP document, but some people continue to misconstrue developmentally appropriate practices. Just as it is helpful to review inappropriate practices in order to achieve a better understanding of appropriate practices, it is useful to consider misunderstandings of developmentally appropriate practices in order to understand what DAP is (Kostelnik, 1992).

One misconception about developmentally appropriate practices is that there is only one way to implement it. To the contrary, there is no single "right" way to implement DAP. Few educational practices are *always* appropriate or inappropriate. Elementary school practices that are developmentally appropriate for six-, seven-, and eight-year-olds are inappropriate for preschoolers. Common preschool practices that are developmentally appropriate for three- and four-year-olds are inappropriate for toddlers. Even appropriate practices for one group of toddlers might not be appropriate for another group of children the same age. When planning for children in their care, early childhood educators consider the particular children and decide what is both age appropriate for the group and individually appropriate for each child (Bredekamp & Rosegrant, 1992).

Another misconception about developmentally appropriate practices is that early childhood educators should abandon previous experiences and knowledge in order to implement DAP when in fact much of what they already do may be considered developmentally appropriate. The reality is that developmentally appropriate practices are built on Piagetian, Vygotskian, and Eriksonian developmental theories that have been used as

## BIOGRAPHY BOX  *Sue Bredekamp*

Sue Bredekamp, Ph.D., is the Director of Research at the Council for Early Childhood Professional Recognition and a consultant for the Head Start Bureau. She is the primary content developer and on-air faculty for *Heads Up! Reading*, a satellite distance learning course on early literacy. From 1984 to 1998, she served as Director of Professional Development of the National Association for the Education of Young Children. She coauthored *Learning to Read and Write: Developmentally Appropriate Practices for Young Children*, the 1998 joint position statement of the International Reading Association and NAEYC.

Her major contributions to the work of NAEYC were developing and directing a national, voluntary accreditation system for which she wrote three editions of *Accreditation Criteria and Procedures* and *Guide to Accreditation*. She is the primary author of NAEYC's highly influential and best-selling publication, *Developmentally Appropriate*

*Practice in Early Childhood Programs*, the 1987 and 1997 editions. She also researched and wrote NAEYC position statements on standardized testing and curriculum and assessment, and edited the two-volume, *Reaching Potentials: Appropriate Curriculum and Assessment for Young Children*.

Dr. Bredekamp is author of numerous articles related to standards for professional practice and professional development and has coordinated development of training videotapes as well as videoconferences. Dr. Bredekamp holds a Ph.D. in Early Childhood Education from the University of Maryland. Her professional experience includes teaching and directing child care and preschool programs for children ages two through six, training child care personnel at a community college, and serving on the faculty of the Human Development/Childhood Education program at Mount Vernon College in Washington, D.C. In 1998, she was a visiting lecturer at Macquarie University in Sydney, Australia, and in 1999 at Monash University near Melbourne.

Photo courtesy of Sue Bredekamp.

theoretical underpinnings in high-quality preschools and nursery school programs for decades. DAP is not a new concept. It is well rooted in historical research and good practices.

Still another prevalent myth is that developmentally appropriate classrooms are unstructured. In actuality there is often much more structure than in traditional academic programs for young children. In DAP classrooms, the structure is built slowly by the teacher by encouraging self-direction and self-control within the children. The activity level and frequent movement of children in developmentally appropriate classrooms evolves around a very defined structure. This structure is provided by the physical arrangement of the environment as well as specific behavioral guidelines established by the teacher and children working together. Developmentally appropriate classrooms are active ones. That is, these classrooms are child-centered. In a child-centered classroom, several children may be moving from one center to another, and several conversations may be going on at the same time. Some people may view this activity and noise level as chaotic, but on close observation, the underlying structure of children making their own plans and implementing them is evident.

Some people believe that in developmentally appropriate classrooms, teachers do not actually teach. Once again, this belief is far from the truth (Bredekamp, 1993). The role of the teacher in a developmentally appropriate classroom is different than the role of a traditional teacher. In more traditional classrooms, the teacher lectures and makes assignments. Most of the interaction between the teacher and the children is in large group situations. In a developmentally appropriate classroom, the teacher creates the environment and organizes a schedule to help children make good learning choices. During child-selected activities, the teacher moves through the classroom working with individuals or small groups of children. The role of the teacher in a DAP classroom is more of a facilitator of learning than that of an instructor. It is typically more challenging to facilitate young children's learning than it is to simply tell them facts. Teachers have to know their students better in order to arrange learning experiences that meet individual needs. It takes patience to help children learn self-control as opposed to making rules and enforcing them through adult control. Teachers in developmentally appropriate classrooms are "teaching" every moment in many different ways: the way the classroom is arranged, the behaviors they model, the questions they ask about children's involvement in different centers, and in direct instruction of specific skills and knowledge with small groups of children who are ready for that instruction.

Others claim that in developmentally appropriate classrooms teachers water down the curriculum and that children learn less. This assumption may come from the idea that what a teacher should do is stand in front of the whole class and "teach." In developmentally appropriate classrooms, early childhood educators concentrate less on instructing the whole group on specific concepts. Instead, they choose to teach in a variety of ways. Teachers ensure that learning takes place in a context that is meaningful to children. They work to provide concrete, hands-on experiences that help young children construct their own knowledge and make connections between home and school. In this type of learning environment young children learn and remember more than they do in traditional, academically oriented programs.

Along similar lines of faulty logic is the idea that academics have no place in developmentally appropriate classrooms. An example of this can be understood by examining the parallel myth that phonics has no place in classrooms. The truth about both myths lies in the fact that there is a place for both phonics and academics in early childhood classrooms, but they should not be overemphasized or taught in isolation. In the current understanding of how children learn best, specific skills are viewed as enablers that should be taught to individuals and small groups of children when children need those skills to accomplish something they are pursuing. Academics and skills definitely have a place in developmentally appropriate classrooms, but they are taught in the context of something meaningful to children instead of in isolation or simply because a teachers' edition or a curriculum scope and sequence indicates a particular skill is the next one to be taught.

Another myth is that developmentally appropriate practices can be defined according to dichotomous positions, that every practice is either appropriate or not. This position may have resulted from the way DAP was presented in the 1987 document. In it, practices are listed as appropriate or inappropriate, but as has been stated before, it is important for each early childhood educator to know individual children and to make decisions about developmentally appropriate practices based on what they know about individuals. Rarely is a practice always appropriate or always inappropriate.

Several people have claimed that developmentally appropriate programs are suitable only for certain kinds of children. This claim is usually made by those who believe that the DAP guidelines were based on experiences with middle-class Caucasian children, to the exclusion of other ethnic groups. By definition, developmentally appropriate practices are both age appropriate and *individually* appropriate. Practices must be appropriate for each ethnic group represented in a program to be truly individually appropriate.

Finally, many people have decided that developmentally appropriate practices are just another fad that will pass in time. Developmentally appropriate education is not simply a fad. Its roots are deeply embedded in developmental and educational theory, dating back to Comenius and Rousseau of the seventeenth and eighteenth centuries. DAP is based on the professional analysis of educators who have worked with young children, observing them and discerning how young children learn best. Developmentally appropriate practices and the way they are described will always be modified (Fowell & Lawton, 1993; Kessler, 1991; Mallory & New, 1994) as we learn more about young children and the ways they learn best, but DAP is not in jeopardy of going the route of "new math" or "open classrooms" as abandoned experiments in educational practice. Developmentally appropriate practices continue to be the framework for helping adults provide "what is best for young children."

## HIGH-QUALITY PROGRAMS FOR YOUNG CHILDREN

Although high-quality programs for young children may be found in many different settings and the services they offer vary, each program deemed to be "quality" has some fundamental characteristics in common. Programs for young children should be developmentally appropriate, meaning that the programs are age appropriate, individually appropriate, and culturally appropriate (Bredekamp & Copple, 1997). All programs should nurture children; provide safe, stimulating environments; and meet physical/motor, emotional, social, language and literacy, and cognitive needs. The way this is done depends on the age and developmental level of the children enrolled in the program.

### High-Quality Programs for Infants and Toddlers

Infants have special needs that must be met by adults. They are in a period of rapid physical and cognitive growth unlike any other period of their lives. Infants are totally dependent on adults for care. They need adults to respond to their cries quickly. They need to be diapered and fed when they express needs through crying and/or body movements. They need the adults who care for them to interact with them individually throughout the day. While toddlers, too, are beginning to demonstrate the need for independence as they explore their environment, they are also very dependent on adults. Toddlers have limited language, so they need the adults in their lives to be responsive to their cries and other cues of need and/or unhappiness. Toddlers need adults to support their growing independence by providing appropriate environments and interactions. Programs for the youngest children keep these developmental characteristics uppermost as they work with infants and toddlers.

*While toddlers are beginning to demonstrate the need for independence by exploring their environment, they are also very dependent on adults.*

Because infants and toddlers are so dependent on adults, the ratio between children and caregivers must be low enough to allow one-on-one interaction throughout the day. Adults in high-quality programs respond to infant and toddler needs immediately. Adults adjust to infant and toddler feeding and sleeping schedules. They hold and carry infants frequently. They closely observe toddlers so they can support those who are acquiring new skills. Adults provide a safe, clean environment and practice health and safety precautions in order to prevent accidents and limit the spread of contagious illnesses.

Adults create an aesthetically pleasing environment and ensure that a wide range of age-appropriate toys and equipment are available to children. For infants, toys should include mobiles, bells, busy boards, balls, vinyl-covered pillows to climb on, large beads that snap together, nesting bowls, small blocks, shape sorters, music boxes, squeeze toys that squeak, clutch balls, rattles, spoons, teethers, rubber dolls, low climbing structures, and books that are heavy cardboard with rounded edges (Moyer, 1995). For toddlers, many of the same toys and equipment would be made available, as well as push and riding toys. Children are always under the direct supervision of adults who are warm and responsive to them. They have training in child development and early education that is specific to the needs of infants and toddlers.

Ebony, the infant caregiver mentioned in the opening vignette, regularly attends local workshops and presentations and reads publications from the National Association for the Education of Young Children (NAEYC) and ZERO TO THREE. She does this so that she can learn more about child growth and development of infants. She wants to learn more about the needs of the infants with whom she works, and she particularly enjoys hearing presentations made by colleagues, those who actually work with infants on a daily basis. She gets ideas about arranging the room to better meet infants' needs, about materials that seem to attract the attention of and stimulate infants, and books that are good to use with the youngest children. The more information she learns, the better she is able to implement developmentally appropriate practices for the infants she cares for every day.

## High-Quality Programs for Preschoolers and Kindergartners

Preschool children and kindergartners—three-, four-, and five-year-olds—are developmentally very different from infants and toddlers. They are generally more cooperative than toddlers although they are consistently developing independence in more areas. They often want to dress and undress themselves, feed themselves, brush their own teeth, wash their own hands, and help pick up toys. They enjoy helping adults by setting the table, finding a fresh diaper, cleaning up messes, spraying window cleaner, and putting away groceries. They generally want to please adults. Children in this age group construct knowledge from their active exploration, experimentation, and play.

Keeping these developmental characteristics in mind, early childhood educators who work in high-quality programs provide stimulating environments for children to explore. They are warm and affectionate toward preschoolers. They support the children in their efforts to be independent, even though it would be faster and usually easier to do it for the children. They realize that they are helping children develop important habits and learn life skills. Adults realize that preschoolers are not able to participate in group experiences for long periods of time, so they keep group meetings short and provide multiple opportunities for children to play alone, in pairs, or in small groups, as they choose. Adults provide many experiences so that children can develop large motor skills through running, jumping, riding tricycles, and throwing and catching balls and bean bags. Adults support children's fine motor skill development by offering materials such as puzzles, pegboards, beads to string, blocks to stack, and art materials. They provide experiences so that children can explore their environment and learn through open-ended materials such as blocks, math manipulatives, and clay. Adults support children's language learning by listening to them and extending their abbreviated speech, by answering their questions and, in turn, asking questions of children. They provide many experiences with books, nursery rhymes, poems, finger plays, and action songs. Adults provide a safe environment for preschoolers and supervise them very carefully. They have training in child development and early education that is specific to preschoolers (Bredekamp & Copple, 1997).

Caregivers who care for three-, four-, and five-year-olds in the NAEYC accredited center with Ebony are just as eager to continue learning about the age groups with whom they work. They also attend workshops and conferences and read professional journals. This gathering of colleagues has formed a study group. Together they chose a book and agree to read one chapter every month. They meet for dinner once a month and talk about what they have read and how the information in that chapter might influence the daily decisions they make as they work with preschool-aged children and kindergartners.

## High-Quality Programs for Primary-Aged Children

Again, primary-aged children are developmentally very different from either of the two younger age groups of children. By the time children reach the ages of six, seven, or eight, they have acquired a wide range of abilities. Some are more capable than others in the areas of reading, writing, and mathematics. Others have strengths in the physical/motor domain. Still others have strengths in the areas of creativity or in working with peers. In high-quality programs, these differences are respected. Children are viewed as unique people who have different strengths and rates of growth and development. Early childhood educators are able to identify "where the children are" and help them move forward toward deeper understandings and higher levels of performance.

*Early childhood educators provide experience so that children can explore their environment and learn through open-ended materials such as blocks, math manipulatives, and clay.*

Primary-aged children are much more independent than other age groups of young children. They are capable of directing more of their own learning if the environment is arranged to promote this independence and teachers are careful to put into place procedures that the children understand. Early childhood educators ensure that curriculum is integrated for primary-aged children. Instructional strategies are flexible depending on the group of children and the curriculum being implemented. Active exploration and play are cornerstones of high-quality programs for primary-aged children, and the teachers who work with them are trained to work specifically with this age group.

As Sheneka grows older and leaves the child-care center her mother so carefully selected, Sharita hopes that the public school teachers assigned to her daughter are eager to stay current about issues related to early childhood development. Sharita herself is beginning to learn about developmentally appropriate practices, and she hopes Sheneka will have knowledgeable early childhood educators as teachers through the third grade.

## DIFFERENT TYPES OF EARLY CHILDHOOD PROGRAMS

While early childhood programs serve children from birth through age eight, these programs vary in the ages they work with and in their focus. Fewer children are spending their days being cared for by a parent than in previous generations. With more mothers working outside the home, early childhood educators are caring for a large percentage of America's young children. Most parents seek high-quality care for their young children and find this care in a variety of settings. For purposes of this discussion, early childhood programs have been grouped into four primary types. Children spend much of their time in family child care homes, child care centers, preschools, or elementary schools. These different types of programs meet the needs and philosophies of families in different ways.

### Family Child Care Homes

Many parents place their children in family child care homes. Of children under age five whose mothers are employed, 23.5 percent of them are cared for in family child care homes. This represents more than a million children (Children's Defense Fund, 2001). In this type of care, the child care provider cares for a small group of children, usually between two and eight children. Family child care home care is very individualized (Zigler, 1995). Because the setting for family child care is the provider's home, the environment is warm and more intimate than many child care settings. Many parents choose this type of care for this intimacy. Families also chooses this type of child care for other reasons. Family child care homes are typically less expensive than other settings, and providers are almost always more flexible in service hours and in caring for children who are mildly ill. Often families appreciate a multi-age setting for their child.

Family child care home providers assume a wide range of responsibilities. They have to balance caring for their own families with the responsibilities of caring for other people's children in their homes. They must meet the needs of all the children in their care all day long, with no one to give them breaks or share multiple responsibilities related to child care. Alone, they establish policies for their program, plan and implement curriculum, research and purchase toys and other learning materials, shop for food, prepare nutritious meals, maintain the business part of the program—all while meeting the needs of several young children who typically vary in age.

The quality of care varies from home to home, depending on how much the caregiver knows about child growth and development and early childhood education. Most of these in-home programs are not regulated; therefore, no early childhood training is required of the providers. But more often in recent years, family child care home providers are volunteering to be licensed or registered locally or by state agencies. They are also joining together as early childhood educators in professional organizations of their own.

Historically, parents have been unable to use financial subsidies for family child care home care, but that also is beginning to change. As more

*Child Care Arrangements of Children Under Age Five with Employed Mothers*

| | |
|---|---|
| Family Child Care Homes | 23.5% |
| Relatives | 21.4% |
| Parents | 22.0% |
| Child Care Centers | 25.1% |
| In-Home Care | 4.9% |
| Other | 3.1% |

Source: Children's Defense Fund, 2001.

providers are becoming licensed and as state and community programs reevaluate social policies regarding child care, some family child care homes are being approved for subsidized child care.

## Child Care Centers

More than 25 percent of parents who are employed and have children under five turn to child care centers for the care of their children during their working hours (Children's Defense Fund, 2001). Just as family child care homes vary, child care centers vary greatly in terms of where they are located, what services they provide, what quality of care they offer, and how they are funded and managed. Center-based programs are located in stand-alone buildings, community facilities such as YMCAs and YWCAs, recreational facilities, churches and synagogues, public housing complexes, and corporate buildings. Centers typically operate from 6:00 or 7:00 in the morning until 6:00 or 7:00 in the evening, although some provide care for children during late evening hours for parents who work during this time. A few centers, such as those located in some hospitals and corporations, even offer twenty-four-hour care. Centers typically care for children from infancy until they are five or six years old, although different child care centers serve different ages of children. Many do not provide infant care. Some provide before- and after-school care for elementary school children. Only a few provide sick-child care. Various centers provide a drop-in service. Individual child care centers set their own policies about the types of services they will provide to families and set their own fees.

Child care centers also vary greatly in terms of quality care they provide. High-quality care is not inexpensive. In many child care centers, quality has been sacrificed because of budgetary concerns. Unfortunately, high child-to-adult ratios, low salaries, the hiring of personnel with little or no early childhood training, coupled with the absence of appropriate programming for the children, are common in many programs. The reason these issues are so prevalent is the cost of addressing these problems.

However, many child care centers do provide high-quality care for children. They maintain appropriate child-to-caregiver ratios, require pre-service as well as ongoing training for caregivers, and provide age-appropriate and individually appropriate programming for children. The management and staff of many child care centers work very hard to provide the best of care for young children, surpassing state licensing standards and meeting the standards of the early childhood profession. NAEYC accreditation (Bredekamp, 1991) is one way that high-quality child care centers can demonstrate that they meet the standards of the profession.

Child care centers vary in their funding and management as well. Most are privately funded through fees paid by the parents, although some child care centers receive tuition fees that are supplemented by state and federal funds. The 1990 Child Care and Development Block Grant mandated expanding the availability of child care for low-income families. The Family Support Act of 1990 provided funding for center-based child care for families who were enrolled in work training programs. The 1996 Welfare Reform Act includes funding for subsidized child care, but decisions about how this

*NAEYC accreditation is an important sign that a child care center meets the standards of the profession.*

funding is used are made at local and state levels. Some center-based programs are fully funded through local, state, and federal funding. Many are privately funded, with some public fund subsidy. Some are totally privately funded and many are for-profit centers, set up as a service- oriented business.

## Preschools

Preschools typically provide care for children who are three to five years old and use the term "preschool" to indicate an educational emphasis to their programming. While some preschools offer full-day programming and are difficult to distinguish from child care centers, many offer limited hours and view themselves as enrichment programs.

Many programs are available to preschool children who are considered at-risk for school failure (Campbell & Taylor, 1996). Head Start, a federally funded program that began in the 1960s, is an example of this type of program. Additionally, in many states, three- and four-year-olds who are determined to be at-risk attend preschool programs that are located in the public schools.

## Elementary Schools

While some preschool children attend elementary schools for special programs, elementary schools typically serve kindergarten, first-, second-, and third-grade students. The traditional elementary school model of teacher-directed activities, desks in rows, and quiet students is characteristic of too many elementary schools today. Elementary school teachers who are trained in early childhood education recognize that all young children learn best through active exploration, movement, and play—even those who attend first, second, and third grades (Bredekamp & Copple, 1997). Early childhood practices should continue in elementary schools through the third grade.

All states offer kindergarten programs, but not all are mandatory. There is a combination of half-day and full-day kindergarten classes in many states, and today kindergarten programs vary greatly. Traditionally, kindergarten has been viewed as a transition year from home or child care settings into elementary schools. Some kindergarten programs continue the tradition of transition and focus on learning through play. These programs emphasize social-emotional development and help children learn to function in large groups. Other kindergarten programs are very structured and focus on formal academic skills.

While the field of early childhood defines itself as serving children from birth through age eight, not all elementary schools view the early grades as a distinctly different time in a child's life. All too often, the classroom organization and the focus of curriculum in many schools looks the same for young children as they do for older elementary school children. However, many elementary school teachers and principals have recognized the need to continue developmentally appropriate education through the third grade, and many primary grade classrooms are appropriate for those students.

These four types of early childhood programs—family child care homes, child care centers, preschools, and elementary schools—are just the beginning of programs available to young children. There are a number of programs for children of all ages: partial and full-day programs, custodial care and educational programs, intervention and enrichment programs. In each type of program, high-quality early care and education should have many characteristics in common, those characteristics of developmentally appropriate practices.

## CONTEMPORARY ISSUES IN EARLY CHILDHOOD EDUCATION

Professionals who work in the field of early childhood education accept developmentally appropriate practices as the unifying concept for all early childhood programs. They acknowledge the principles described earlier in this chapter. This does not mean, however, that people outside the field agree on what early childhood education is or should be.

To a great extent, contemporary issues in early childhood education are being raised by those outside the field. Currently, beliefs held by most early childhood educators are both being fortified and challenged by those outside the field. On one hand, recent brain research is reinforcing the importance of the early years and the teaching and learning practices recommended by early childhood educators. The findings of recent brain research reinforce many early childhood concepts. On the other hand, too many governmental policy makers and decision makers in educational settings are not using the growing body of knowledge about young children's learning to make decisions about practices that affect young children.

In recent years, research on brain growth and neurological development has reinforced much of what early childhood education has promoted for young children for decades. Early childhood educators have long believed that the nurturing care of adults plays a critically important role in the social and emotional development of young children.

Brain research has also expanded the field's understanding about the importance of the first years of life. Neuroscientists now believe that the experiences adults provide for young children go much further than simple support. Neuroscientists contend that infants' and toddlers' experiences physiologically shape the brain. Brain research shows that when infants are held and rocked, their brains release important hormones that promote growth. Many research studies demonstrate that when adults talk to, sing to, and read to infants, important connections between brain cells are formed, and that when a single connection is used over and over, it becomes permanent. On the other hand, if a connection is not used very often, it is not "cemented." In practical terms, a child who is rarely spoken

*Brain cell growth is promoted when adults talk, sing, and read to infants.*

to during his or her first few years will have thousands fewer connections related to language and may have difficulty mastering language skills as a toddler or preschooler. A child who is rarely played with may have trouble with issues of social development. Young children depend on the adults in their lives to provide the experiences necessary for wiring the brain for later learning (I Am Your Child Coalition, 2002).

Neuroscientists have also found dramatic changes in the level of energy used by children's brains between infancy and middle childhood. At birth, these levels of energy are relatively low. In the first few years of life, the level of energy used by the brain goes through a rapid rise followed by a gradual decline to adult levels between middle childhood and the end of adolescence. In other words, children's brains are working very hard during the early childhood years (ZERO TO THREE, 2002).

Educational experts have studied recent brain research and discussed the implications for classroom practice (Caine & Caine, 1994; Caine, Caine & Crowell, 1999; Jensen, 1998; Sylwester, 1995, 2000; Wolfe, 2001). According to these experts, classrooms must have a positive climate, both physically and emotionally. They reinforce the notion that classrooms where children feel threatened or stressed are places where children learn less than they would otherwise. These experts advocate routines and procedures that not only make a classroom run more smoothly, they establish explicit patterns that facilitate wiring of the brain. These educational experts contend that "the brain's capabilities are enhanced by positive social interactions" (Kaufeldt, 1999, p. 59) and that children actually learn more when they are a part of a community of learners (Sylwester, 2000). All of these concepts were part of common early childhood practice before they were promoted by experts because of brain research studies.

In 1999, the National Research Council established a Committee on Integrating the Science of Early Childhood Development to update scientific knowledge about development in children birth through age five and the importance of early experiences and to discuss the implications of this knowledge for policies and practices related to young children. This committee determined that despite the growing body of knowledge about early childhood, 24 million infants, toddlers, and preschoolers, and millions more school-aged young children are being affected by policies that are not based on this knowledge (Shonkoff & Phillips, 2000). Among the recommendations made by this committee were:

- To devote resources for supporting young children's emotional, regulatory, and social development
- To develop school readiness initiatives to reduce the disparities in skills of children with differing backgrounds
- To make new investments for addressing mental health needs of young children
- To improve the qualifications and increase compensation for caregivers
- To support collaboration of education, health, and human services groups on professional development for early childhood educators (Shonkoff & Phillips, 2000)

Among the issues affecting young children from outside early childhood education are: assessment of young children based on grade-level standards, a general trend toward more standardized testing, and more specifically, standardized testing being used as the sole determinant for educational decisions. Across the nation, states either have or are developing standards expected of students at each grade level (Lewis, 2002). Despite the fact that early childhood educators know that all children develop at their own rate, when these children reach public schools, they are expected to reach the same standards by the end of the school year (Kohn, 2001). More and more young children are being required to take standardized tests by state- and/or district-mandates (www.fairtest.org, 2002). This practice continues to grow despite the fact that early childhood educators know that standardized testing is rarely valid or reliable for children under the age of eight. Just as the administration of standardized testing is increasing, so is high-stakes testing where educational decisions are made based on single test scores (DeCesare, 2002). This occurs despite early childhood educators' strong belief that all educational decisions should be based on multiple sources of information about children (Bredekamp & Copple, 1997).

## Summary

The field of early childhood education is vast and complex. Deciding to become an early childhood educator is not a decision to be taken lightly. Young children need adults who are warm and caring, but children are also dependent on knowledgeable teachers to help support and enhance their development. Early childhood educators must learn about child growth and development theories, about the theory and practice of developmentally appropriate practices, and about the children and families with whom they work. Working in a high-quality program for young children requires dedicated, well-trained adults who are willing to continue learning about young children and how best to meet their needs.

With more young children than ever before spending large portions of their day in group care, the need for early childhood educators is continuing to increase. While there are many different types of early childhood programs, high-quality programs for young children have several common characteristics. They have low child-to-staff ratios to ensure sufficient time to interact with individual children. They nurture children; provide safe, stimulating environments; and meet children's developmental needs through implementation of developmentally appropriate practices. These characteristics—considered developmentally appropriate practices—are well grounded in theories and practices developed over a long period of time. The rich history of early childhood education is described in chapter 2.

## Reflections

**1.** Consider the reasons why you are thinking about becoming an early childhood educator.
**2.** How much do you already know about all the aspects of early childhood education so that you can meet the needs of young children? What are the areas you need to study more?
**3.** From the introduction to developmentally appropriate practices in this chapter, consider the early childhood settings you've observed. How developmentally appropriate do you think they are?
**4.** As you continue reading this text, compare its definition of high-quality early childhood programs to settings you've observed.

## Field Experiences

**1.** Interview two early childhood educators about appropriate and inappropriate practices as listed in earlier in this chapter. How do they implement appropriate practices?

**2.** Obtain a copy of *Developmentally Appropriate Practice in Early Childhood Programs* (1997), edited by Sue Bredekamp and Carol Copple, and read all sections of appropriate and inappropriate practices. Choose one age group (infants and toddlers, three- to five-year-olds, or six- to eight-year-olds), observe a class of this age group, and compare your observations to the lists of practices.

**3.** After reading the sections of appropriate and inappropriate practices listed in *Developmentally Appropriate Practice in Early Childhood Programs*, choose one practice for each age group. Interview several parents about this practice and document their answers. Back in class, share the answers you gathered in small groups and try to determine to what degree parents agree or disagree with practices promoted by the field of early childhood education.

## Case Study

### So What Is Early Childhood?

It was Thanksgiving Day, and an extended family gathered at one house to share the holiday. It was an active, busy morning, as the adults prepared the meal and tried to keep all the young children in the house busy and happy. Of the five adult siblings in this family, four of them have their own children under the age of five.

Before lunch, there were five different discussions—otherwise known as arguments—about caring for young children. The mother of the only infant in the group responded to her child each time he cried, sometimes stroking his back and speaking in a calm, soothing voice, but most of the time, picking him up and holding him. Those actions prompted discussion #1, whether an infant should be held every time he cries. That argument led to discussion #2, about whether infants should be fed on a schedule or fed on demand.

An argument between the two toddles over the same push toy led to adult discussion #3 about whether toddlers should be expected to share toys. When the mother gave in to her preschooler's demands to help prepare lunch, discussion #4 about when to say "no" to children began.

By the time lunch was actually served, all these discussions about whether or not children should "be in charge" of what they do, when they eat, and when they get held led to a larger issue, discussion #5, about the merits of child care and whether young children were better off being cared for by their own mother at home versus family child care versus for-profit child care.

### What to Do?

Each person who voiced an opinion was convinced that his or her beliefs about young children was the "right thing to do." Each parent knew that he or she was right. Even aunts, uncles, grandparents, and cousins expressed their opinions, convinced that they were right. If you were the only person at this family dinner who had studied child growth and development, what would you say about each of the "discussions" that emerged?

## Further Reading

Bredekamp, S., & Copple, C. (Eds.) (1997). *Developmentally appropriate practice in early childhood programs* (rev. ed.). Washington, DC: National Association for the Education of Young Children.

## Helpful Web Sites

### National Association for the Education of Young Children
www.naeyc.org
*NAEYC is the largest professional organization for early childhood educators. This Web site offers information ranging from best practices for working with young children to advocacy efforts for young children and their families.*

### Association for Children Education International
www.acei.org
*ACEI has a long history of providing professional development literature and research for educators from infancy through adolescents. This Web site provides information about the organization, its resources, and its focus on child development and education. This organization also provides age-related information on infants and toddlers, pre-K and kindergarten, elementary, middle school, and teacher education.*

### Southern Early Childhood Association
www.southernearlychildhood.org
*SECA is the largest regional early childhood association with affiliate organizations in fourteen states. This Web site provides information about the organization, its mission, and its focus on child development, child care, and early childhood education through the primary grades.*

### Division for Early Childhood (DEC) of the Council for Exceptional Children (CEC)
www.dec-sped.org
*This Web site provides information about DEC and its focus on children with special needs, birth through age eight, and their families. Its emphasis is on policies and practices that support families and enhance optimal development of children.*

Check the Online Resources™ for expert practitioners' responses to each case study.

For additional information on teaching young children, visit our Web site at **http://www.earlychilded.delmar.com**

"This is the wood-work box."

# CHAPTER 2

## Roots of Contemporary Early Childhood Education

*Early Childhood Principle* Professional early childhood educators acknowledge a rich and informing history of child care and early education.

Travels to centuries past engage our curiosities about how the early childhood profession came to be what it is today. Accounts of historical practices and relationships with children arouse a variety of emotions ranging from horror, to incredulity, to relief and even humor. Rising out of dubious societal treatment and expectations of children during historical periods of time are scholarly responses in the forms of philosophy and theory often translated into practices that have informed and enlightened, guided and endured throughout the centuries. The hopes and dreams of professional early childhood educators for best care and practices in early childhood find support in similar hopes and dreams of great minds of the past.

*After reading this chapter, you should be able to:*
- Identify early philosophers and their theories on child care and early education.
- Contrast early philosophy and practice with developmentally appropriate philosophy and practice.
- Recognize the different, yet intersecting, pathways through which child study, child care, nursery schools, kindergartens, and primary grades emerged.
- Discuss how contemporary practice has roots in history and philosophy.

## ROOTS OF DEVELOPMENTALLY APPROPRIATE PRACTICES

Early childhood practices in our schools and child care programs have a long and rich history that actually dates to ancient times. However, much of today's knowledge and practice in early childhood education can be traced to specific historical social and political contexts dating from the sixteenth century forward. Much of our early childhood education history has European roots. A review of history explains the dynamics of an increasingly informed field of study, present practices, and possible directions of future research. In an especially enlightening way, reviewing our past both affirms and guides our present.

Philosophy and practice in early childhood care and education is based on scientific discoveries and behavior studies about how children grow. Early care and education practices based on this knowledge emphasize hands-on, concrete materials and activities, oral language development, positive interaction between and among children and adults, and topics of study and activities based on real-life experiences. For some time the prevailing belief has been that learning occurs best through children's interactions with one another, with adults, and through their explorations and use of mind-engaging materials. The belief that children learn through play is evident through the provision of play-enhancing props and materials, outdoor play activities, and child choice from a wide selection of materials wisely chosen to enhance physical, cognitive, language, social, and emotional development. Most early childhood practices today are based on principles such as these.

Philosophers, educators, and human growth and development experts generally agree that for young children to have their best chances to succeed in the important tasks of growing up, early experiences must be whole-child oriented, nurturing, supportive, and positive. When adult expectations of children are reasonable, challenging, yet achievable, and when school curricula are developed with age and capabilities in mind, they are said to be developmentally appropriate. As we shall see, developmentally appropriate practices were encouraged by some of our earliest philosophers, researchers, and theorists. Only in recent history has the term become widely acknowledged.

When did this term become part of the nomenclature of the education profession? During the late 1970s and throughout the 1980s, as more and more states were implementing public school kindergartens, prekindergartens, and early childhood special education programs, increasing emphasis on early learning played out in policies, curricula, and classroom practices that differed markedly from generally accepted principles of early childhood care and education. Practices often exceeded what were thought to be reasonable expectations for young children. Educators, psychologists, pediatricians, and other professionals around the country became concerned. They argued that the trend toward more formal, subject- and skill-based academic instruction of young children placed undue emphasis on rote learning, memorization, whole-group instruction, and isolated skill/drill exercises. These practices came to be called "push-down" programs because younger children were being confronted with expectations and academic content better suited to older children. The kindergarten child might well be expected to learn and perform tasks typically taught in first grade, first-grade children were expected to learn and perform tasks typically taught in second grade, and so on.

This trend aroused concerns among parents and teachers about the readiness of individual children for these accelerated expectations. Testing, admission, placement, and retention practices emerged to identify children deemed "ready" or "too immature." Children were often "red-shirted" or held back to give them an extra year to grow before entering kindergarten or first grade. Kindergarten and preschool classes began to look more and more like traditional first-grade classes in room arrangement, materials, and instructional procedures, in spite of the fact that numerous studies were finding long-term deleterious effects of such practices on child development and learning (Elkind, 1986, 1987; Gredler, 1984; Meisels, 1987; Shepard & Smith, 1985, 1986, 1987, 1989).

The term *developmentally appropriate practice* emerged as a result of mounting concern relating to the question of how best to care for and educate young children. As professional early childhood associations and other education and civic organizations publicized and distributed their position statements expressing opposition to push-down curricula and proposing alternative strategies, it became evident that opposition was widespread (Goffin & Meyers, 1989). The National Association for the Education of Young Children, in response to these mounting concerns, sought nationwide input from professionals from which guidelines for early childhood care and education practices could be developed. The concept of developmentally appropriate practices was derived from this unprecedented and widespread professional consensus. It continues to represent best understanding and applications of valid information about how young children grow, develop, and learn. Today, the term *developmentally appropriate practice* gains further relevance as mounting scientific information proliferates about key timings or "windows of opportunity" in brain growth and neurological development.

The use of the term *developmentally appropriate practice* has not been without controversy. Many have misapplied this concept in classroom practice, generally assuming that rich and supported play is sufficient for the early years. Others adamantly maintain that developmentally appropriate practices are not sufficiently challenging or instructive. Both of these positions misinterpret the definition and the spirit of developmentally and individually focused practices, which stress a mating between age and individual characteristics and needs and the content and instructional procedures of the early childhood program.

As this chapter will illustrate, throughout the history of education there has been tension among proponents of early childhood education about how best to educate young children. Some have proposed predeveloped curricula with focused, more formal instructional strategies, while others have supported enriched classroom learning centers with emphasis on child choice and less formal opportunistic instructional strategies. This tension exists today as educators attempt to respond to calls for early reading proficiencies and school accountability.

Were the **child-centered practices** prevalent throughout history based simply on romantic notions about how infants and young children should experience life? Do **curriculum-centered approaches** that emphasize "back to the basics" skill and drill and **test-driven curricula** really serve the best interest of young children over the long term? Was or is there philosophy or research that encourages more formal, academic approaches to early childhood care and education? These questions beg for an exploration of the roots of today's early childhood practices. Let us begin by peeking into a seventeenth-century classroom.

## THE SEVENTEENTH AND EIGHTEENTH CENTURIES: PHILOSOPHY AND PRACTICE

It is Saturday, and the students are feeling a bit weary. Their school-week extends from Monday through Saturday and from 6:00 A.M. to 5:30 P.M. The week has been a grueling one for this group of five- to fourteen-year-old boys from well-to-do families. Their Greek and Latin lessons have become quite advanced and difficult. It seemed that all they ever do is memorize and recite lessons in grammar, logic, rhetoric, and arithmetic. They had also spent quite a bit of time this past week on lessons in religion. From time to time they study geometry and astronomy. Once a day their music and what little recess they are allowed provides welcome relief, especially after sitting on backless benches with feet dangling at long wooden tables that are uncomfortably tall. They had a particularly bad day yesterday. A classmate giggled and talked during the arithmetic recitations. From their book *The Schoole of Good Manners*, they had been admonished to "Sing not, hum not, and wriggle not." So this misbehavior caused all forty classmates to be punished by being marched in a circle and getting whipped as they passed by the schoolmaster who was not only a drill master, but an ominously strict disciplinarian (Adamson, 1905).

This vignette set in a seventeenth-century school illustrates very formal instruction and strict disciplinary procedures. Education was provided for young boys of wealthy families. Girls were expected to be taught at home

**child-centered programs** early childhood programs that consider the individual and developmental needs of each child and provide curricula, materials, schedules, enrichment opportunities, and guidance strategies commensurate with those needs and with sound principles of growth, development, and learning.

**curriculum-centered approaches** early childhood programs that ascribe primary importance to curriculum goals, including adherence to topic sequences, skill sequences, and time blocks for completion of segments of the curriculum.

**test-driven curricula** curricula that focus unduly on the content of achievement tests or other standardized test(s), severely restricting the range of content and experience essential to a well-balanced education.

and were excluded from formal education. Less fortunate children, from a very young age, sometimes as early as three years old, worked in the factories for very long and arduous hours. Discipline in these early schools was quite harsh; chastisement and whippings were common, for teachers were judged according to how well they conducted a disciplined class. Curricular emphases were derived from religions and prevailing moral beliefs. Teaching of moral rules was a major emphasis. Curriculum content and methodology were rigid with great emphasis on rote memory and recitations. The goals of these schools were to train boys to take their proper place among the aristocratic class. Long days and long weeks were characteristic, though school was held usually for only six months of the year.

## John Amos Comenius (1592–1670)

One of the great philosopher/theorists of the seventeenth century was John Comenius. As the previous vignette illustrates, the classrooms of Comenius's time were not particularly pleasant places for children. Children were expected to memorize, recall, and recite their lessons. Comenius opposed this model for teaching and proposed that:

- Children should understand that which they are required to learn.
- Children should study topics closely related to their experiences and intelligence.
- Instruction should begin with concrete stages; if real things are not available, the teacher should use models, pictures, diagrams, or other representations.
- The foundation of instruction lies in the child's sensory perception.

Comenius described this teaching philosophy in his book *The Great Didactic* (1896/1628–1632) in which he set forth many principles that remain basic today. Among his principles are the following:

1. All children should be educated, not just by a tutor, but in common schools organized according to ages.
2. School lessons should respond to the child's nature and be based on the child's interest and ability to learn them.
3. Foundations for all learning are built during the early years.
4. Teaching and the process of study should involve the scientific method of induction from specific facts to broad conclusions and concepts.
5. The most essential aims of education are self-knowledge, self-discipline, and character development.
6. Children learn best through firsthand experience with objects and social situations and through practical use of new knowledge.

**BIOGRAPHY BOX** *John Amos Comenius*

John Comenius (birth name: Jan Amos Komensky) (1592–1670) was born in Moravia to a poor family who belonged to the much persecuted Church of the Bohemian Brethren/ Protestant Unity of Czechoslovakia. Brethren of this sect established schools emphasizing faith in God, teaching moral conduct, and rejecting the Catholic Church. Both of his parents died when he was twelve, after which he lived with his aunt. He left home at age twenty-one to study at the universities of Herborn and Heidelberg where he wrote influential works on education and theology. Upon his return to Moravia, where he taught in the Latin School and was soon ordained as a priest, he married and started a family. Soon after, because of his religious affiliation and Protestant preaching, he was forced to leave home when the Thirty Year's War broke out in 1621. He lived in hiding for ten years and finally was forced to leave his homeland. He had to leave his wife and children behind where unfortunately they died of the plague soon after his departure and he never saw them again. He later married again, and again, religious and political opposition to his views forced him into exile. He fled to Poland where he began his pedagogical work for which he became famous. He wrote prolifically about his wish for universal education for all boys and girls, stressing the importance of the early years of children's development. In his book *School of Infancy* (1628), he wrote about the importance of the home in early education and stressed that the greatest service parents can render to their children is to encourage play. He was a much sought-after educator and adviser, and while engaged with the government of Sweden to develop new educational plans, he was again forced into exile and settled in Amsterdam, where he spent the final years of his career. He died there in 1670.

Photo © Bettmann/CORBIS.

7. Subject matter should be organized from the most familiar to the least familiar and from simple ideas to more complex ones.
8. Boys and girls should receive education, so that *all* children will develop into good citizens and virtuous, God-fearing human beings.

Many of the principles he believed in are the basis for modern education. He was one of the first to stress universal education for boys and girls, whether rich or poor. Comenius's philosophy, "nature awaits the favorable moment," demonstrated his belief that learning occurs according to natural laws of growth and development. In association with this belief, he encouraged parents to let their children play. He wrote the *School of Infancy* (1896/n.d.), one of the first early childhood books in which he claimed that children from birth to age six learned the basics of all knowledge. He was the first to mention the mother as a child's first teacher, when he referred to the "Mother School," where he proposed that children from birth to age six should be educated by their mothers, and a simple handbook or a book of pictures portraying "everything picturable" should be provided for them and their children. His book, *Orbis Sensualium Pictus* (*The World of Sensed Objects in Pictures*, 1654) was the first children's textbook.

## John Locke (1632–1704)

John Locke was another philosopher who emphasized the importance of the early years. In his book, *Some Thoughts about Education* (1693), he defined education as virtue, wisdom, breeding, and learning, with learning being the least important of the four. He stressed that learning should begin with simple experiences building to complex ideas in a spiraling manner.

In his "Essay Concerning Human Understanding" (1668), he proposed that the mind obtains knowledge from sensory experiences and is itself a passive recipient or "tabula rasa" (blank slate). The mind as a blank slate absorbs from sensory experiences simple concepts that later become associated or combined with other simple concepts to form complex understanding. Locke was a staunch defender of religious, educational, intellectual, and cultural liberty. His "liberty" concepts, however, did not necessarily apply to everyone. He declared that the education of women and the poor should come from studying the Bible and learning skills essential to their daily endeavors. He believed that sons of the wealthy were the most likely candidates for formal education.

The purpose of education in Locke's view was to develop in children all the powers of body and mind necessary for them to be healthy, virtuous, and successful in life. He believed that the young child needed strict discipline in order to learn "fixed habits" of "right thinking" and "good behavior" and to be able to adjust to hardships and disappointments. He did caution, however, that discipline of young children should not be too harsh as it could arouse resentment and animosity toward the tutor. Rather, discipline and punishment should be viewed as natural consequences of misbehavior. In this regard teachers were instructed to respect each child's temperaments and opinions.

## Jean Jacques Rousseau (1712–1778)

Rousseau was a philosopher whose writings focused on educational, religious, social, and political issues of his time. He is frequently cited as the father of early childhood education and the father of progressive education. In his writings, he encouraged a child-centered education that was practical and sensory. He felt that curriculum should have a direct relationship to the interests of children. Rousseau's beliefs about young children were shared in his book about an imaginary child, *Emile* (1762; trans. n.d.), who was reared with care by his mother and educated by a tutor. Using the fictitious Emile as an example, Rousseau emphasized the importance of a child's education beginning at birth.

Rousseau was born in Geneva, Switzerland, in 1712. His parents were French émigrés from Paris and Geneva. His mother died soon after he was born. His father, a watchmaker, was prone to violent temper and in a rage beat Rousseau's older brother so severely that he left home and never returned. He was, however, indulgent and affectionate toward Jean Jacques and invested a great amount of time in teaching him to read and discuss the works of the great writers and thinkers of the day. Nevertheless, his father was a poor role model displaying irresponsibility and indiscretions, impulsiveness, and a lack of self-discipline. In his mother's absence, Rousseau's emotionally disturbed aunt took care of him until he was eight years old. She was influential in inspiring in him a great love for music and composing. At age ten, Rousseau's father was convicted of violence against another person, and to escape imprisonment, he fled from home to another city. Rousseau then lived with an uncle who sent him away to a school in a village near

Geneva. After a number of unsuccessful apprenticeships and odd jobs, he was employed by a wealthy family to tutor their children. It was an unpleasant experience for him but awakened his interest in the challenges of teaching. As a young adult in Paris he met and engaged in a long-standing unmarried relationship with a maidservant. He claimed in his autobiography that she had borne him five children whom he placed in a home for foundlings.

In spite of his inauspicious life, Rousseau's scholarly and artistic works earned him a place among some of the greatest thinkers reformers, and philosophers in education, religion, and sociology. He favored tolerance of all faiths democracy, and the rights of individuals; he believed that children were born innately good and that growth and development follow the laws of nature. He was the first to propose that there are definable stages in growth and development: birth to five years, five to twelve years, twelve to fifteen years, fifteen to twenty years, and twenty and over. He prescribed appropriate interactions and learning experiences for each of the stages. In his book *Emile* (1762), he described his idealistic views of education. He died in Paris in 1778.

Rousseau was instrumental in dispelling the then-prevalent view of the child as a miniature adult. He believed that the child is endowed with innate goodness and that "Everything is good as it comes from the hand of the Creator; everything degenerates in the hands of man" (Rousseau, 1762; trans. n.d.). He stressed that stages of development are independent and should not be viewed as preparatory. His influence on schooling for all was evident in his declaration that education was the single most important business of the state, and national education is the privilege of free men.

### Johann Heinrich Pestalozzi (1746–1827)

Pestalozzi believed that early education was the best means to eradicate the evils of society. In his school at Neuhof, Switzerland, he taught children, usually about twenty boys and girls to a class, the art of gardening, weaving, cooking, sewing, reading, writing, arithmetic, and skills in group discussion. Though he fed and clothed the children who in his care prospered and progressed, his school failed in 1780 for lack of funds. He wrote about his pedagogical views in the *Evening Hours of a Hermit* (1780), and his novel *Leonard and Gertrude* (1781) brought him worldwide fame. He later wrote *Illustrations for My ABC Book* (1787) and *How Gertrude Teaches Her Children* (1801). These and many other writings articulated Pestalozzi's basic principles of learning. In them he postulated that learning should begin with sense perception, observation, and contacts with nature, firsthand and real experiences rather than through books or word of mouth. He believed that conversation and practical use are the natural ways of learning. Pestalozzi's guiding principles included the following:

- Education should be based on child psychology.
- Children develop physically, mentally, and morally through experience.
- Experiences must include sense impression, careful observations, clear understandings, and the application of that learning in the child's everyday activities.
- Learning progresses through induction from the simplest to the more complex, and from the concrete to the abstract, and from experience to judgments, conclusions, and rules.
- Teachers should consider and respect each child's interests, readiness for further learning, free self-expression, and emotional and social needs.
- Discipline, where required, must be just and instructive, not punishing.
- When children are interested and active, harsh discipline becomes unnecessary.

What can we find in the philosophies of Comenius, Rousseau, Locke, and Pestalozzi, that presaged what we now refer to as developmentally appropriate practices? Table 2–1 contrasts the views of childhood and subsequent early care and education practices proposed by these seventeenth- and eighteenth-century scholars. Perhaps you might extrapolate additional ones from this brief discussion.

## THE NINETEENTH CENTURY: THE FIRST KINDERGARTEN

Many schools for young and school-age children followed the tenets of Comenius, Locke, Rousseau, and Pestalozzi. The influence of these early philosophers is felt in the following description of an early nineteenth-century classroom designed particularly for young children.

**TABLE 2–1**

*Antecedents of Developmentally Appropriate Practices in Seventeenth-
and Eighteenth-Century Philosophy*

| From | To |
| --- | --- |
| Children working in factories as early as three years of age | Recognition of childhood as an important period |
| Formal education of well-to-do boys only | Education of both boys and girls |
| Curricula based predominantly on religious and moral beliefs of the period | Recognition of the importance of sensory perception to learning |
| Pedagogy dominated by rote memory and oral recitations | Curricula related to the experiences and intellectual capabilities of children |
| Very long school days and weeks for six months of the year | Use of real objects, models, pictures, and diagrams to support learning |
| Adult-size furnishings | Introduction of books with pictures |
| Rigid discipline with harsh punishment | Recognition of the mother as an important first teacher |
| | Recognition of the importance of play to the intellectual development of children |
| | Recognition of the need for learning to proceed from simplest to more complex |
| | Child-friendly education settings and child-size furnishings |
| | Increasing opposition to harsh discipline |

The "garden of children," a school for children before the age of six, provided a place for spontaneous play with the gentle guidance of a motherly teacher. The teacher is often heard quoting to their mothers the words of the school's founder. "Education should begin with the child's first breath." She would stress that education was not to impart knowledge, but to lead the child to observe and think. The opportunity to play with other young children was an indescribable joy for these little ones. There are physical exercises, rest times, attention to nutrition and clean clothing, and encouragement to exercise their minds. These young children especially enjoy the songs, poetry, stories, myths, legends, fables, and fairy tales that make up a large part of the day. The frequent nature walks and gardening are quite special. Through "gifts" and "occupations" the children are learning to explore the nature of objects and actions around them.

The gifts include a set of six wooden balls, each a different color, for the very youngest in the group; a box of three hard, wood objects—a sphere, cube, and cylinder, each two inches in diameter; and a large, wooden cube divided into eight small cubes of equal size representing a whole to which its parts can be related. The occupations consist of modeling in clay, paper folding and weaving, kindergarten sewing, bead threading, and painting. Children are gently guided toward morality through the songs, stories, and "mother plays" they hear and recite. It is clear that the teacher and the school's founder hold a profound love for humanity.

## Friedrich Wilhelm August Froebel (1782–1852)

The person who conceptualized this "garden of children" was Friedrich Froebel, who is considered the founder of the kindergarten. About his garden of children, Froebel said, "I do not call this by the name usually given to similar institutions, that is *Infant School*, because it is not to be a *school*, for the children in it will not be *schooled*, but freely developed" (Froebel, 1905, p. 33).

Froebel was a disciple of Pestalozzi, having spent two years studying with him. He adopted many of the features of Pestalozzi's education system, but attempted to improve upon it. He emphasized self-activity, which he believed to be the foundation for learning and designed teaching materials he called "gifts" (colored balls, wooden spheres, cubes, cylinders, oblongs, splints, metal rings, seeds, beans, and pebbles), all of which were to be explored and manipulated in various ways according to a specific sequence. He called the lesson instructions he developed "occupations." As did Comenius, Froebel stressed the importance of play and the use of concrete objects to enhance learning. He encouraged self-expression, physical activities, dramatization, drawing, and social development as essential elements in early education. He worked closely with mothers, providing gentle guidance and instruction on educating their babies and young children. He used songs and mother plays to teach both mother and child. His book *Mother Play and Nursery Songs with Finger Plays* (1878/1905) illustrates the author's romantic view of children as being one with nature. His instructions for mother plays enhance the young child's natural tendencies to learn through play. It is said that Froebel legitimized happiness in the classroom.

## BIOGRAPHY BOX *Friedrich Froebel*

Friedrich Wilhelm August Froebel, a renowned German educator, was born in Oberweissbach, Germany. His mother died before his first birthday, and his father, who was chief parish pastor of the local Lutheran church, was rarely at home to tend to the needs of his children. Froebel, therefore, was often left in the care of servants or one or more of his four older brothers.

When Froebel was four years old, his father remarried a woman who at first was a caring and nurturing stepmother, but upon the birth of her own son, became less and less attentive, and Froebel's care was again left to the servants and his older brothers. Left unsupervised much of the time and with little schooling to speak of, Froebel wandered the woods near his home and enjoyed the scenes and "lessons" of nature. He listened to the sounds of nature, observed the animals, collected and planted seeds, and watched plants grow into ferns, flowers, and other foliage. Though his father attempted to teach him to read, Froebel received no formal instruction until he was ten years old. At that time, an uncle sought to have Froebel live with him so that he could oversee his education. The uncle, a distinguished educator and religious leader, provided a loving and trusting home for Froebel, bringing to Froebel his first stable and secure environment. Of this education, Froebel wrote: "We repeated our tasks parrot-wise, speaking much and knowing nothing; for the teaching on the subject had not the very least connection with real life, nor had it any actuality for us, though at the same time we could rightly name our little specks and patches of color on the map" (as quoted in Bowen, 1906, p. 9). About his spelling and writing lessons, he wrote: "I do not remember with what subject the teaching of spelling was connected; I think it was not connected with any; it hung loosely in the air" (Froebel, n.d./1906, p. 11).

Bored with school, and not particularly successful, Froebel returned to his father's home at age fourteen. He became an apprentice to a forester which again brought him close to nature, and though he attended the University of Jena for a year, he found his studies there uninteresting. Finally, in 1816, Froebel opened his own school with only five pupils, some of whom were nieces and nephews. In his most well-known work, *The Education of Man* (1887), Froebel laid out his principles and methods of educating very young children (ages one to seven years). He postulated that educating very young children was the only way to develop their natural abilities and character. In 1837, he organized his school for very young children, and in 1840, he named it the "kindergarten," or "garden of children." His kindergarten was successful and became famous. However, due to financial difficulties, it did not survive long. After he was forced to close the kindergarten, he traveled throughout Germany, holding positions at universities, assisting in the establishment of institutes of learning, and lecturing widely on his education theories.

Sadly, Froebel's views became confused with the socialistic teachings of his nephew Karl Froebel, a Prussian revolutionary, and he was forbidden to organize kindergartens in Prussian states. It was believed that his kindergartens represented a form of socialism in which children would be taught atheism. This confusion remained until 1860, but it continued to haunt his efforts throughout the rest of his life. A very religious man, Froebel was deeply hurt by the accusations, and thereafter, threw himself into work in other parts of Germany.

While preparing to lecture to a national conference of teachers, Froebel, then 70, was deeply moved when the entire assembly rose to their feet as he approached the lectern. It was a triumphant moment for him, and his last. He died within months. Louise Levin, Froebel's widow to whom he had been married less than a year, continued his work for a time, and many educators from around the world traveled to Germany to be tutored by her. Among those who sought her tutelage was Elizabeth Peabody.

# THE NINETEENTH CENTURY: KINDERGARTENS IN THE UNITED STATES

Froebel had many followers, some of whom became near zealots in promoting his practices. Educators of young children traveled from around the world to observe and learn from him. His kindergarten theories and practices were brought to the United States during the early 1800s by followers who had either studied with him themselves or taught his theories and practices to others. Kindergartens spread rapidly throughout the United States during the 1800s.

## Elizabeth Peabody (1804–1894)

Perhaps one of Froebel's most enthusiastic and well-known followers was an American kindergarten teacher named Elizabeth Peabody, considered the founder of the American kindergarten, who conducted her own kindergarten in Boston for a time, organized with her colleagues in the Froebel Society, and wrote and lectured widely on the Froebelian philosophy. She had grown concerned about the direction that philosophy and practice were taking in the United States, so she traveled to Europe to visit and study with Froebel's widow and many of his European students to learn as much as she could about his theory and practice. Upon her return, she independently published the "Kindergarten Messenger" (1873–1877), a newsletter about Froebelian kindergartens and practices. Many of her lectures took place in the **normal school** classes for teacher training. Perhaps her best-known book is *Lectures in the Training Schools for Kindergartners* (1886). (*Kindergartner* is a term originally used to refer to kindergarten teachers.) She wrote many others.

Elizabeth Peabody's devotion to Froebel's philosophy is evident in her early writings. She wrote in her 1906 preface (page 7) to the English translation of Froebel's *Mother Play and Nursery Songs: Poetry, Music and Pictures for the Noble Culture of Child Life with Notes to Mothers* (1878):

> In his study into the divine meaning of the instinctive spontaneous plays of childhood, it was Froebel's purpose to elevate the mother's instinct into insight and thereby purify it from idiosyncratic infirmities; so that she might see, in the unconscious play of the child, the same laws working that make the archangel in his heavenly sphere; even as the same laws that whirl the planets in their vast orbits guide the stone flung from a child's hand.

Peabody eloquently (and romantically) revealed Froebel's poignant combination of mother-education with his concept of playful learning. Perhaps this could be considered an early example of parent education.

A number of notable men and women, enamored with Froebelian philosophy, carried the kindergarten movement forward. There were purists such as Susan Blow (1843–1916) who in collaboration with William T. Harris, the then superintendent of the St. Louis schools, opened in 1873 an

**normal schools** the first teacher-training institutions, many of which became teacher colleges and later departments of education in colleges and universities.

*Elizabeth Peabody*
Photo © Bettmann/CORBIS.

experimental kindergarten in a public school in St. Louis where Froebel's kindergarten philosophy could be demonstrated. This is believed to have been the first public school kindergarten. Susan Blow insisted that kindergarten methodology follow the Froebelian model without modification or experimentation. She was convinced of the importance of play to the educative process, yet she used Froebel's "gifts" and "occupations" in a strict and sequential manner. She became a noted kindergarten teacher educator, or "kindergartner" as they were called then, at Teachers College, Columbia University.

However, in other parts of the country, pure Froebelian philosophy was giving way to more progressive approaches. Anna E. Bryan (1858–1901), though having been formally trained in Froebelian method, began to find it too restrictive and wanted to explore other approaches. Having taught kindergarten in Chicago and having studied child development with G. Stanley Hall, Bryan returned to her home state of Kentucky where she established the Louisville Kindergarten and Training School with a program that emphasized child development and a respect for individual differences among children and cultures, and promoted creativity and spontaneity in classroom activities. Bryan's philosophy and practice and that of many of her like-minded colleagues (Alice Temple, John Dewey, G. Stanley Hall, and others) created a stir among the kindergartners. Considerable debate waged among them at annual meetings of the kindergarten department of the National Education Association.*

One of Anna Bryan's better known students was Patty Smith Hill, who became a teacher in Bryan's school upon completion of her training and was to eventually direct the school when Bryan returned again to Chicago to study with John Dewey and to assist him in creating a kindergarten in his laboratory school at the University of Chicago.

Patty Smith Hill, (1868–1946) an innovative thinker, much as her mentor had been, soon became nationally known for her progressive methods, and visitors from around the country came to the Louisville Training School to learn about them. After studying with G. Stanley Hall, Hill began to move even further away from the strict Froebelian philosophy. She sought to find "some happy means between the extremes of absolutely free play and painful dictation" (Osborn, 1991). Hill designed large building blocks and other manipulatives that have been standard equipment in preschool classes over the years. She was the author of "Happy Birthday," the rights to which belong to the Association for Childhood Education International, an organization that grew out of a committee she chaired for the International Kindergarten Union. Hill would eventually chair the kindergarten department at Teachers College, Columbia University. Historians believe that Hill's speeches and publications during the great kindergarten debate set the tone for the philosophy that continues to influence kindergarten education today (Osborn, 1991). Also interested in the nursery school movement, Hill was a key player in the organization of the National Association for Nursery Education, the forerunner of the NAEYC.

## THE TWENTIETH CENTURY: PROGRESSIVE EDUCATION MOVEMENT

As the kindergarten movement was gaining momentum in the United States during the late 1800s and the early to mid-1900s, another movement was emerging. The **progressive education movement** grew out of new philosophies about the purpose of schooling for children of all ages. Prominent among the progressive education philosophers was John Dewey.

**progressive education movement** a period during the late 1800s to the 1950s in which resistance to rigid, teacher-dominated practices of the past were challenged by more student-centered and democratic philosophies.

*For a lively discussion of this divisive period in kindergarten history, the reader is referred to Evelyn Weber (1969), *The Kindergarten: Its Encounter with Educational Thought in America.* New York: Teachers College, Columbia University.

John Dewey (1859–1952), whom you will learn more about in chapter 7, established a laboratory school at the University of Chicago where he could test the tenets of progressive education. In 1916, Dewey wrote *Democracy and Education* (1966/1916), which has been acclaimed as one of the great educational works of all time (Meyer, 1951, 1975). In his book, Dewey asserted that education is the chief vehicle for the improvement of society, and he emphasized that the school is an essential institution for the development of social interactions and skills and for the demonstration of democratic practices. He viewed the classroom as a miniature society. He asserted that schooling was not preparation for life, but life itself.

The progressive education movement had many proponents. The Progressive Education Association was formed in 1918–1919 to further the cause. Many public and private schools were organized around progressive education philosophy. Progressive educators wanted to eliminate the traditional rigor and stiffness of schooling for children and to break down hard-and-fast grade and subject-matter boundaries. Broad units of study and project methods were incorporated into the curriculum.

One such school, the Fairhope School of Organic Education, was organized at Fairhope, Alabama, by a teacher who had years of experience in traditional elementary and secondary schools and had normal school teacher training. The mother of a six-year-old, Marietta Johnson sought more flexible methods of instruction that were sensitive to the needs of the individual learner. She noted in her lectures that "The child is not a little adult. The mother who takes such pride in her child's reading at an early age; who is so happy over the thought that the child can sew; who boasts of her child's reliability and responsibility, is misguided." She further urged that, "Children should not *try* to grow mentally any more than they should *try* to be heavier or taller. Learning at this age should be through wholesome experiences. There should be less teaching of facts and more time for assimilation" (Johnson, 1929, cited in Meyer, 1951, 1975).

Many innovative practices grew out of the progressive education movement. Note that many of these practices appear with contemporary descriptions of developmentally appropriate practices. Schooling practice promoted by the progressives included:

**realia** Real items used in classrooms to provide concrete, firsthand concept development and knowledge (such as sea shells, magnets, and indoor gardens).

Curricula based on child interests
Recognition of individual differences
Attention to the physical and emotional needs of children
Employment of motivating strategies to bring children into learning events
Whole-child perspectives
Varied concrete materials, **realia**, and firsthand experiences
Child-initiated activities
Learning together through dialogues and group problem solving
Teachers as facilitators of learning

Group projects and field trips
Comfortable child-friendly classroom settings and furnishings

While the progressive education movement was going forward, the **child study** and the **nursery school movements** taking place in Europe and the United States were gaining momentum. The time period for the child study and the nursery school movements dates from the early 1900s through the 1960s. The first nursery schools were established in response to the appalling health conditions of young children of poverty, to their neglect, and in some cases to the employment of very young children to work. What were these early nursery schools like?

## The Beginnings of the Nursery School

"Come on," urges the gentleman on the street as he summons passersby to join him. "Come an' 'ave a look at the little ones!" His excitement reveals that these children whose ages ranged from one to seven years were seldom noticed as they wandered the alleyways and muddy streets, susceptible to disease, unclean, and often neglected. Now they are clean and safe, their health and education overseen by the nurse/teacher. Situated near their tenements, the open-air nursery school is a fenced parcel of land with an especially designed shelter for classrooms, toilets, sleeping areas, and dining room. The shelter is airy and sunlit through screen walls, large windows, and sliding doors. The garden is surrounded by tenement housing where a thousand windows overlook the space coveted for its fresh air and the sunlight it provides. In the windows faces are watching the activity as though it were an outdoor theater. As with the excited gentleman, the neighbors are curious, amazed, and amused at the serenity of these nurtured little ones, frolicking happily and heartily among one another in a setting designed for them. In the garden, fruit trees have been planted, a stone wall has been built to encourage the growth of gooseberry bushes. There are grassy areas and enchanting pathways. It is complete with a greenhouse constructed by the older children, terraces to break the wind, herb gardens planted as much for their scent as for use in food preparation. There is a kitchen garden in which vegetables are grown, wood planks for walking and climbing, sand pits, steps for climbing and jumping, a "rubbish heap" of stones, cans, pots, and pans with which to play, shallows in the concrete to collect water for boats and floating things. There are flower gardens and a tool shed. The nurse-teacher values this playground because it encourages very young children to run "in order to feel their life in every limb." Such a place for very young children has never been seen before. Early morning baths, nutritious meals, and nap times are scheduled into a healthy day in the nursery school. Each day each child is observed for head circumference, chest width, length of limbs, condition of skin, and state of muscles. Singing, dancing, marching, and other motor activities both delight the

**child study movement** a period during the early 1900s in which the focus of interest in children moved from how to teach certain topics or skills to how children grow, develop, and learn.

**nursery school movement** a period during the early 1900s in which early childhood programs for infants, toddlers, and three- and four-year-olds were being developed. Most early nursery schools were associated with university child-study departments.

*In short, the Nursery-School, if it is a real place of nurture, and not merely a place where babies are "minded" till they are five, will affect our whole educational system very powerfully and very rapidly. It will quickly raise the possible level of culture and attainment in all schools, beginning with the junior schools. It will prove that this welter of disease and misery in which we live, and which makes the doctor's service loom bigger than the teacher's can be swept away. It will make the heavy walls, the terrible gates, the hard playground, the sunless and huge classroom look monstrous, as they are. It will give teachers a chance.*

*The arrival of thousands of beautiful and strong children will bring down the gates. Through the awful and grim corridors the light of joy as well as youth will pass. The bastilles will fall at last by the touch of a little hand.*

*-Margaret McMillan*

children and enhance development. Clay sculpting, coloring, pasting, learning numbers, shapes, and the alphabet are also part of the curriculum. The motto voiced by Rachel McMillan, founder, is "Educate each child as if he were your own" (adapted from McMillan, 1921).

Among the first to conceptualize a new school for very young children were the McMillan sisters, Rachel and Margaret, whose open-air nursery school established in Deptford, England, in 1909 brought widespread attention to the needs of very young children, particularly children living in the unhealthy conditions of the ghettos and on the streets. Margaret McMillan trained specialists in nursery education and later introduced nursery school teacher training at Teachers College, Columbia University. This gave strength to the child study and the nursery school movements.

Margaret McMillan is credited with coining the term "nursery school," and after the untimely death of her sister Rachel, Margaret carried on their dream of providing a healthy climate and growth-enhancing school for infants and toddlers. She particularly wanted to distinguish a type of education for children who ranged in age from three months to five years, from the more common government-sponsored "day nurseries" that, in her opinion, were generally poor-quality, drab places often run by "unenlightened women" (McMillan, 1921). The word "school" denoted for the McMillans that there would be something more than custodial care. She was certain that the kind of care and education she could provide for these children would assure greater success in school. Note the passion in her quotation.

As a response to the poor health conditions of impoverished city children, the open-air plan was designed to provide sunshine and fresh air for improving the children's well-being and reducing the recurrence of illnesses. Routines were established with child health in mind. Daily morning "health inspections" excluded children who were ill in order to prevent the spread of disease. Daily baths, freshly laundered smocks (or uniforms), emphasis on hand washing and other hygienic habits, substantial outdoor play, and regular warm meals were the order of the day. The McMillans' child-health emphasis, child-centered curricula, and institutes for nursery school teacher training were acclaimed in both England and the United States and initiated the nursery school movement.

## The Nursery School and Child Study Movements

As the nursery school movement found its way to the United States, a growing scientific interest in child growth and development was concurrently emerging around the world. This interest would spark what is now known as the child study movement. Prior to the child study movement, children were described through observations and baby biographies (usually recorded by their parents'), which often proved to be subjective and inaccurate. At the turn of the century, a "new psychology" emerged in

*Froebel encouraged self-activity as the foundation of learning.*
Photo © 2002 Froebel Foundation USA.

which children were studied in a more controlled scientific manner. The child study movement was a natural outgrowth of this new psychology, and colleges and universities around the world established "laboratory nursery schools" to gather information on how children grow and learn at different ages. These laboratory nursery schools provided settings for early childhood education, child development research, and teacher training, and perpetuated the proliferation of nursery schools around the world.

The nursery school movement was characterized by the juxtaposition of what scientists were discovering about human growth, development, and learning, and what early childhood educators practiced. It embraced new "scientific" knowledge about child development and was characterized by emphases on several themes:

- The early years lay the basis for later development.
- Children during their early years require special attention, freedom, affection, and guidance.
- To grow and develop properly, children must have opportunities to play.
- Where such opportunities are not available, preschool experiences are especially important (Lazerson, 1972).

During the period from 1920s to the 1940s, most of the early nursery schools were located in or near colleges and universities. As more was understood about how children grow, develop, and learn, turn-of-the-century early childhood educators adapted their practices to adjust to the unique characteristics of young children while still maintaining the traditional focus on health, good habits, and moral development. Figuring prominently among the pioneers of the child study movement was the founder of child psychology, G. Stanley Hall.

### Granville Stanley Hall (1844–1924)

By the turn of the century, G. Stanley Hall had established himself as a leader in child study after publishing *The Content of Children's Minds on Entering School* (1883) and establishing a center for applied psychology at Johns Hopkins University. He originated the first English-language, psychology periodical when he published the *American Journal of Psychology*. He was instrumental in founding the American Psychological Association, and it was at Clark University (which he founded and served as first president) that he established a department of child study that influenced the expansion of the child study movement.

Hall taught that there were wide differences between the infant's mind and the adult's. He was disturbed by the failure of kindergarten to adequately address the health of young children. He found Froebel's romanticism impractical and out of pace with new information about child development. Further, he felt that Froebel's "gifts and occupations" were too sedentary and failed to recognize the child's limited small muscle coordination. His studies were finding that development proceeded from fundamental (or large muscle coordination) to "accessory" muscles (or small muscle coordination), and the most important way to promote this growth and development was through free play with large materials. He believed that each stage of development needed to be lived through completely if children were to grow and develop normally. Because in the young child reasoning was inadequate, he felt that the emotional life of the young child was more fundamental than the intellectual. He believed that teaching methodologies should be based on the nature of childhood at its different stages of development. He opposed formal, structured practices with young children.

G. Stanley Hall is perhaps the originator of parent education as we know it today, for he was instrumental in convening a large meeting in 1897 that established an organization known as the National Congress of Mothers, which later became known as the Parent-Teacher Association. His research and writings contributed to the fields of child development, child and adolescent psychology, and psychoanalysis.

Hall gave scientific validity to the study of young children in their natural surroundings and encouraged other scientists to study children by observing them within natural contexts and keeping anecdotal records of their observations. He taught child study and trained teachers. During the child study movement, massive amounts of data were collected from teachers, parents, and laboratory school researchers. The child study movement became so important that the National Education Association in 1893 established a Department of Child Study. The child study movement focused attention on *childhood* and its uniqueness as a special stage in human development. One of Hall's most famous students was Arnold Gesell.

## Arnold Gesell (1880–1961)

An outstanding contributor to both the child study and the nursery school movement was Arnold Gesell. He established a Clinic of Child Development at Yale University where he conducted much of his research on the "ages and stages" of early growth and development. Gesell and his colleagues at Yale University established norms for motor skills, adaptive behaviors, language, and personal-social behavior. Gesell became internationally acclaimed for his systematic descriptions of the way in which human behavior develops. Considered the first **developmentalist,** he demonstrated through his studies that while each child is a unique individual, growth and development occur according to a patterned, predictable process that is similar for all humans. He argued that children should begin school on the basis of their behavioral characteristics rather than their chronological age. Hence, the term "readiness" became part of the vernacular. This term, as you shall see in chapter 3, led in the 1980s to controversy over preschool and kindergarten admission and retention policies. Arnold Gesell and his research will be discussed more fully in the next chapter.

**developmentalist**
a professional who bases his assumptions about children on principles of human growth and development.

## Maria Montessori (1870–1952)

The directress spent a large amount of time carefully preparing and structuring the classroom environment and sequencing the arrangement of her **didactic** materials that the group of three- to seven-year-old children will use. The pupils are seated comfortably in furnishings that are child size, carefully measured to accommodate the heights of young children. They are enjoying working with objects and puzzles that are easy to grasp and manipulate. This small mixed-age group of boys and girls are working both independently and with partners to master the unusual and beautifully designed materials that must be used as directed and explored in a sequence that proceeds from simplest to more complex. As each self-correcting puzzle or manipulative is mastered, the pupil may progress with assistance to the next level of difficulty. In this group of children thought to be mentally deficient, motor-sensory capabilities are encouraged and deemed essential to learning, as are practical life activities such as folding clothes, tying

**didactic instruction**
instruction that presents information to children in a structured, drill and practice format, teaching discrete skills in small units or steps.

shoes, and pouring from a pitcher. There is no allowance for creative use of the materials or art media. There is also little encouragement of pretend play.

Maria Montessori, the first woman physician in Italy, developed her method for teaching young children out of her experiences in working with children thought to be mentally deficient, as well as impoverished children living in the slums of Rome. Based on her knowledge of human anatomy and development, she believed that young children should develop "all aspects of themselves" through sensory experiences. She believed that mental deficiencies were a matter of education rather than medicine. As a keen observer of child work and choice, Montessori developed teaching materials and apparatuses that met what she perceived to be the developmental needs of children. She believed that the child's use of such materials would enhance sensory-motor skills and be more effective than simple recall and recitations (Montessori, 1973). She believed that a well-prepared environment could teach as effectively as direct instruction. Montessori referred to the period from birth through age three as the period of the "unconscious, absorbent mind," a period when children are taking in the sights and sounds of their surroundings. She referred to the period from three to seven years as the period of the "absorbent mind" when children begin to mentally make sense of their surroundings.

To demonstrate her beliefs and findings, she opened Casa dei Bambini (Children's House) in a tenement district in Rome in 1907. She had many followers, some of whom brought her methods to the United States where at first they were novel and well received. As word of her unique methods spread, scholars such as G. Stanley Hall, Arnold Gesell, Jane Addams, and Helen Keller's teacher, Anne Sullivan Macy, visited her Casa dei Bambini. However, her work was criticized by John Dewey and other progressive education proponents who thought that her emphasis on independent use of materials was counter to the progressive philosophy that stressed cooperative problem solving and group projects.

The Montessori method as a pedagogical approach remained outside the mainstream in the United States, though, ironically, during the 1950s it became viewed as a desirable program for children of affluent families. It was not until President Lyndon Johnson's War on Poverty awakened the nation's consciousness to the poor that the Montessori method became widely used. Montessori concepts flourished during the 1960s and 1970s and today are found in public as well as private schools around the country.

The NAEYC grew out of the nursery school and child study movement. The National Association of Nursery Education (NANE) was established in 1926 by a selected group of progressive education, child study, and nursery school leaders. From its inception, NANE's members emphasized whole-child concepts and family development. The organization began publishing the *NANE Bulletin* in 1945, which later was named the *Journal*

**BIOGRAPHY BOX** *Maria Montessori*

Maria Montessori was born in Chiaravelle, a small town in Italy near the Adriatic Sea. Her father, a military man and later a civil servant, was descended from a noble Bolognese family. Her mother was the niece of a famous Italian philosopher-scientist. When she was five years old, her family moved to Rome so that Maria could have a better education. In school she exhibited an interest and special abilities in mathematics and chose to study engineering at a boy's school although her parents were not in favor of her doing so. She later discovered that she had a special interest in biology, which later led to her career in medicine. In spite of her parents opposition, she pursued studies in medicine. Being the first woman in Italy to apply for admission to medical school, it is reported that she had to appeal to Pope Leo XIII to help her get admitted (Kramer, 1976). In 1896 she became the first woman in Italy to earn a medical degree. In her work at the University of Rome Psychiatric Clinic, she visited and observed children with retardation, most of whom lived in asylums where only custodial care was common. She became curious about the learning of these children and concluded that their natural inclinations to learn were not being encouraged. She entered the University of Rome, where she studied psychology and pedagogical anthropology. Through her work with mentally challenged children and later with impoverished children in the slums of Rome, she discovered methods that increased her students' abilities sufficient to be admitted to public schools. Montessori believed that schools could not only serve well these children, but also that school reforms were needed for "normal" children as well. She opened her own school, "Casa dei Bambini," or Children's House, in 1907 in San Lortenzo, Italy, and further developed her methodology. She spent her later years traveling and lecturing about her methods and philosophy.

Photo courtesy American Montessori Society, 281 Park Ave. South, 6th Floor, New York, NY 10011.

*of Nursery Education*; still later, in 1964 the name changed to the one we recognize today, *Young Children*. The organization changed its name to the National Association for the Education of Young Children in 1966 and has its headquarters in Washington, D.C.

## THE BEGINNINGS OF CHILD CARE IN THE UNITED STATES

In 1854, the Nursery and Child's Hospital in New York opened a nursery in which former patients could leave their babies for daytime care. This is cited as the first day nursery in the United States (Zietz, 1969). Day nurseries (or day care centers) emerged rapidly during the Industrial Revolution of the 1800s and again during World Wars I and II and the Great Depression of 1929—times when great numbers of women joined the work force. While many of the traditional nursery schools for the most part offered half-day programs and "extended day" care for working mothers, day nurseries emerged as the primary source of such care. Unlike most traditional nursery schools, day nurseries were open sometimes twelve or more hours a day six days a week particularly during the war years, and some provided nighttime care. Later these programs based their hours on more typical eight-hour work day schedules.

Until the child study movement, child caregivers were usually women who had been denied an education and were not thought to need more than their loving instincts in order to care for infants and young children. The child study movement brought emphasis to the uniqueness and vulnerability of young children. Hence, training for caregivers was offered in many settings and through various auspices: normal schools, teacher training institutes, universities, community agencies, federally and state funded special projects, and private consultants. This training has remained a critical element in high-quality care and education of young children and is required by law in many situations.

The name most often associated with the origins of day nurseries is Robert Owen (1771–1858), an industrialist, philanthropist, and social reformer. Robert Owen was concerned for children of all ages who were being subjected to unreasonable labor. He is generally credited with establishing the first infant schools, first in Scotland in the early 1800s, and later when he moved to the United States. Children entered his infant school as soon as they could walk and continued through age twelve. In the New Harmony, Indiana, cooperative community, which he formed during the 1820s, he forbid children from working until they could at least read. Children under twelve were limited to six hours of work per day, while children over twelve worked twelve to fourteen hours a day. The common practice then was for children as young as five years to work up to fourteen hours daily without lunch nor provision for their education (Cahan, 1989; Osborn, 1991). Owen defined the scope of his infant schools in a way that suggested the concept of child care as we know it today:

> For this purpose the Institution has been devised to afford the means of receiving your children at an early age, as soon almost as they can walk. By this means many of you mothers of families will be enabled to earn a better maintenance or support for your children; you will have less care and anxiety about them; while the children will be prevented from acquiring any bad habits and gradually prepared to learn the best (cited in Steinfels, 1973, p. 35).

As with Table 2–1, we can again connect scholarship and philosophy of earlier times to the present emphasis on developmentally appropriate practices. Table 2–2 lists examples of philosophy and practices during the ninteenth and twentieth centuries that antecede contemporary early childhood education.

**TABLE 2–2**

*Antecedents of Developmentally Appropriate Practice in the Nineteenth- and Twentieth-Century Progressive Education, Child Study, and Nursery School Movements*

| From | To |
|---|---|
| Emphasis on rigid schedules for sleep, meals, physical exercise | Recognition of varying individual needs for food, rest, and exercise |
| Recognition of mothers as intuitively good first teachers | Increasing emphasis on spontaneous play |
| Education as preparation for participation in the aristocracy | Recognition of the child's needs to observe and discover as part of the learning process |
| Rigid, assignment of specific subject matter to specific grades | Educating mothers (and eventually both parents) on how to enhance learning in their children |
| Formal, structured instruction | Education as a means for the improvement of society |
| | Broad units of study and project methods that overlay and integrate subject and recognize different capability levels in each grade |
| | Increasing emphasis on the early childhood years as foundational and as an important influence on later school performance and personal success |
| | Hands-on learning with real objects and real-life activities derived from the child's immediate experiences and planned events, such as field trips and special resource visitors. |
| | Increasing emphasis on whole child development |
| | Recognition of the need for early childhood educators to have specialized training |

## THE UNITED STATES GOVERNMENT AND YOUNG CHILDREN

The U.S. government has played an important role in child welfare and education issues since the first White House Conference on Children and Youth was assembled by President Theodore Roosevelt in 1909. The U.S. Children's Bureau was an outgrowth of this first conference, as were many laws, and it subsidized programs for child care during periods of war and economic depression. Significant among these programs were the Works Progress Administration (WPA) nursery schools established during the Great Depression of 1929 through which federal funds were made available for day care (in 1933) to provide employment for unemployed nurses, teachers, nutritionists, clerical workers, cooks, and janitors in day nurseries serving low-income families. WPA nursery schools were funded by the government until 1942.

The prototype for comprehensive government-sponsored early childhood programs could well have been an industry-sponsored child care program developed by the Kaiser ship-building company in Oregon, with funds from the U.S. Maritime Commission, under the leadership of one of the nation's most renowned early childhood educators, James L. Hymes, Jr. The Kaiser Child Service Centers (of which there were two) provided state-of-the-art buildings and services to children and families virtually unheard of in child care programs at the time: arranging for dental appointments for children; arranging for the purchase of food for individual families; and providing a trained social worker, a nursing staff, and a chief nutritionist. The centers were open twenty-four hours a day for 364 days a year. It was of the highest quality and employed trained and skilled caregivers whose professional development was enhanced during their employment in the centers. Unfortunately, this program existed for only twenty-two months, from 1943 to 1945.

The most significant and expensive government-sponsored early childhood education program in world history was the Head Start program launched in 1965. The Follow Through program launched in 1967 was also part of this commitment. These projects were designed to provide **compensatory education programs** for "disadvantaged children." There were sociopolitical influences driving this initiative that grew out of President Lyndon Johnson's "War on Poverty" (a campaign promise), such as growing concerns about our allegedly "falling behind" educational system and increasing unemployment among the poor. However, among educators there was simultaneously growing acknowledgment of the importance of the early years in child development that was supported by emerging research.

**compensatory education programs** early childhood programs designed to compensate for potential disadvantages of growing and living in poverty.

### The First Large-Scale Preschool Program: Head Start

Two particular publications influenced social and political policy relating to children and were influential in the conceptualization of Projects

## BIOGRAPHY BOX *James L. Hymes, Jr.*

During the early 1900s, Dr. James Hymes was one of only a few men in the early childhood profession. He was a tremendous influence in the child development and early education fields. He received his M.A. and Ed.D. from Teachers College, Columbia University, in child development and parent education. During the Great Depression, he worked with the federal Works Progress Administration project in establishing and supervising WPA nurseries throughout the state of New York. During World War II, Dr. Hymes established and directed one of the nation's first corporate-sponsored child care centers, the Child Care Service Centers of the Kaiser Ship Building Corporation in Portland, Oregon. He served as professor of child development and early education at State University of New York at New Paltz, Peabody College, and the University of Maryland. Dr. Hymes served as president of NAEYC and, as vice-president of ACEI, was one of the founders of the Southern Association for Children Under Six (SACUS, which is now known as the Southern Early Childhood Association, SECA). He was invited to present the keynote address at its first regional conference. His topic is as timely today as it was then. "What Is Good Education for Young Children?" He helped to conceptualize and launch Project Head Start. His writings over the years have been prolific and include such titles as *A Pound of Prevention; How Teachers Can Meet the Emotional Needs of Young Children* (1947); *Being a Good Parent,* (1946); *Teacher Listen: The Children Speak* (1949); *Three to Six: Your Child Starts to School* (1950); *A Child Development Point of View* (1955); and *Teaching the Child under Six* (1968). During the 1970s while he continued to publish books, articles, and chapters in other works, he developed an audiotape series of speeches titled *Tape of the Month in Early Childhood* that was used for in-service training during a period in history when there was wide expansion of early childhood programs throughout the nation. He also wrote and narrated *Early Childhood Education; The Year in Review* (another audiotape series) and published a series of pamphlets by the same title each year until 1991. James Hymes is often referred to as the "Father of Early Childhood Education" and is among the field's most revered experts. His career spanned many decades, and he continued to be a spokesperson on behalf of high-quality programs for young children until his death in March 1998.

**Head Start and Follow Through.** The research of J. McVicker Hunt reported in his *Intelligence and Experience* (1961) that intelligence was not a fixed characteristic, as previously thought, but was dependent on the *experiences* children have during the early years. He challenged the notion of an Intelligence Quotient (or IQ score) and proposed that such scores could be increased or mitigated against by factors in an individual's early experiences. A complementary thesis was forwarded by Benjamin Bloom in his book *Stability and Change in Human Characteristics* (1964). Bloom provided additional insight by asserting that the first five years of a child's life are the optimal time for promoting cognitive development. Together, these two publications turned attention to the young child's early environments, interactions with others, and cognitive experiences.

*The problem for the management of child development is to find out how to govern the encounters that children have with their environments to foster both an optimally rapid rate of intellectual development and a satisfying life.*
*-J. McViker Hunt*

Responding to this research and similar findings among other scholars and practitioners, Congress mandated in 1964 the federal agency through which Projects Head Start and Follow Through would be conceptualized and launched. The agency was named the Office of Economic Opportunity (OEO).

### Project Head Start (1965 to Present)

Conceived by a group of child development and early childhood education experts, including some of the finest minds in the field—Urie Bronfenbrenner, Edward Zigler, James Hymes, Keith Osborn, and others—Head Start was (and is) a massive effort to extend comprehensive services such as education, health screening, immunizations, nutrition, and parent education to disadvantaged young children and their families (Greenberg, 1990). Since its inception, unprecedented federal funds and widespread professional energy and support have been devoted to this ambitious undertaking. The expansion of Head Start programs throughout the nation are evident today in the investment the federal government has made in the program, increasing from $404 million in 1974 to more than $6 billion in 2001. Today enrollment across the fifty states approaches 1 million children. The Head Start program has served 19,397,000 preschool age children since its beginning in 1965. In 1994, Congress established the Early Head Start program for low-income families with infants and toddlers. The Head Start program is administered by the Head Start Bureau, the Administration on Children, Youth and Families (ACFY), Administration for Children and Families (ACF), Department of Health and Human Services (DHHS) (Head Start Bureau, 2001).

### Project Follow Through

A federally funded primary-grade (grades 1 through 3) program, Project Follow Through, established in 1967, was conceptualized as a "sequel" to the successful Head Start program. It was designed, as its name implies, to "follow through" into the primary grades with children who had been enrolled in Head Start and similar preschool programs for disadvantaged children. This project provided many of the same services available through Head Start, as well as resource specialists, teaching aides, and non-teaching professionals (e.g., speech therapists and school psychologists) to assist either in the classroom or with individual students. Innovative primary-grade instructional practices were demonstrated and studied.

While slow to be integrated into existing public school instructional practices, Follow Through nevertheless provided new insights for instruction in the primary grades that were based on child development principles and new learning theories. These child-centered primary-grade classrooms addressed academic work (reading, writing, math, science, and social studies) through child-centered curricula. This approach included the use of

**BIOGRAPHY BOX** *Edward Zigler*

Edward F. Zigler, Sterling Professor of Psychology at Yale University, earned his Ph.D. from the University of Texas at Austin. He is director of the Bush Center in Child Development and Social Policy and a noted author and editor of numerous scholarly publications. His research, writings, and presentation in child development, psychopathology, and mental retardation have had enormous influence in public policy forums and the early childhood care and education professions. He may be best known and acclaimed for his role in planning and guiding the Head Start Project over the years. His commitment to Project Head Start inspired President Jimmy Carter to name him chair of its fifteenth anniversary celebration in 1980. Dr. Zigler was the first director of the U.S. Office of Child Development (now the Administration on Children, Youth, and Families) and has served as chief of the U.S. Children's Bureau.

Photo courtesy of Michael Marsland, Yale University Office of Public Affairs.

concrete materials, oral and written language activities, project work that required group planning and problem solving, committee responsibilities, meaningful field trips, creative and physical/motor development activities, and social development through interactions with one another. Parent participation was required. Classes were small and volunteers and parents assisted on a daily basis.

From the outset of these two programs, the government funded a series of longitudinal research projects to study various aspects of Head Start and Follow Through. These research projects took place in many cities around the country in universities and local and state agencies. **Longitudinal studies** followed children through these different experimental models for a number of years to determine long-term effects on various aspects of child growth, development, and learning. Other studies centered on the program models themselves and the effects of each model's unique characteristics.

**longitudinal studies** research that collects information about the same subjects at different ages over an extended period of time, sometimes spanning several years or even decades.

### Head Start and Follow Through Studies

The first of a series of reports on Head Start children came from the Consortium for Longitudinal Studies in which investigators around the country reported similar findings about the effects of early compensatory care and education (Lazar & Darlington, 1982). In the summer of 1983, other researchers began to report outcomes similar to those in the Consortium studies. Together, these studies found that

- Children in well-designed Head Start programs made immediate gains in basic cognitive competence, school readiness, and achievement.

- Head Start children generally outperformed other low-income children into elementary school but continued to score below norms on most standardized tests.
- Head Start children usually perform better than non-Head Start children on indicators of school success (less likely to be retained in grade; fewer inappropriate placements in special education classes, and reduced drop-out rates).
- Head Start children sometimes maintain superiority on achievement test scores into later school years.
- Head Start improves language development especially for bilingual children and children with special needs.
- Those who appear to benefit the most from Head Start are the most needy children from families whose mothers had a tenth-grade education or less, children of single-parent families, and children with low IQ scores at the beginning of the program.

Some recent studies have focused on children who are not poor but from more advantaged circumstances. There is recent research evidence that low-risk children whose families were both economically and educationally advantaged also benefit from high-quality preschool experiences. Larsen and Robinson (1989) determined that third-grade children who attended a developmentally appropriate preschool (in this study, a university-based program) scored significantly higher on the spelling and language portions of school achievement tests than did their counterparts who had not had the preschool experience. In addition, 90 percent of these third-grade children participated in extracurricular activities such as music lessons and sports compared with only 68 percent of the children who did not attend preschool. Boys in particular seemed to achieve long-term benefits. This program, like the Head Start programs, had a strong parent-education and participation component. Continued data collection in this longitudinal study may in the future provide evidence of benefits when these children reach adolescence and adulthood.

## The School Reform Movement and Early Childhood Education in the 1980s

The school reform movement dominated the 1980s. During the school reform movement, philosophy and practice became more politicized than ever before in education history. Federal and state governments appointed task force groups to study school performance and recommend changes and legislation.

The school reform movement was inspired by the findings of two unsettling reports on the outcomes of schooling in America. (Many such reports soon followed.) The National Commission on Excellence in Education, a federal study group, called for improved academic preparation of all school children in its publication *A Nation at Risk* (1983). Chief among their concerns were insufficient instruction and low performance standards in computer science, mathematics, general science, English, and the social sciences. The Commission recommended assigning more homework and increasing the hours of instruction at all grade levels.

The other publication at the outset of the school reform movement was a book by John Goodlad, a professor of Education at the University of California at Los Angeles, published in 1983, *A Place Called School*. This book was based on a study that spanned several years of systematically collected data in more than 1,000 elementary, junior high, and senior high school classrooms. While Goodlad assessed all grade levels, of particular interest was his focus on early childhood and primary-grade education.

Goodlad praised the positive aspects of Head Start, nursery schools, and other early childhood programs with parent-involvement components. He criticized elementary practices on several fronts:

- A lack of classroom learning centers
- Teacher-dominated instruction
- Classrooms that lacked warmth and child appeal (e.g. plants, displays of children's work, appealing educational displays, rugs, pillows, and psychosocial warmth)
- Emphasis on competition over cooperation and positive social interaction
- Ability grouping and tracking

Goodlad recommended that

- Students begin school at age four.
- Schools stagger school entry by admitting four-year-olds on their fourth birthday to maximize each child's opportunity for individualized instruction from the beginning.
- Schools implement multi-age classrooms that could range from age four to seven years.
- Same classes remain with the same teacher for more than one year.
- Curriculum based on age-related capabilities rather than grade levels.
- Educators pay greater attention to self-confidence building and social competence in children.
- Schools remove pressures for early childhood teachers to focus on academics such as reading, spelling, and writing in order to integrate this learning through block building, music, creative activities, stories, and other concrete literacy development strategies.
- Curriculum and educators guide reading, writing, and mathematics learning in a naturally progressive manner from rich experiences to spoken language, to symbol recognition and use, to connecting symbols with objects or events, to using abstract printed symbols to convey meaning.

- Schools improve teacher education to bring about more child-centered approaches.
- A new view of education be developed that extends beyond the school doors and becomes a lifelong process.

In a subsequent report, *First Lessons* (1986), authored by William Bennett, then U.S. Secretary of Education, a need for policy makers to focus more on early education and elementary schools was emphasized. Bennett's report called for greater emphases on literacy development, hands-on science, acquisition of computer skills, and increased attention to health and physical education. He also proposed more instructional time during each school day and a lengthened school year. Today, though not as popular as in their beginning, year-round schools exist in many school districts. Bennett maintained that the single best way to improve schooling for children would be to increase parent involvement. Note that parent involvement was a key component in the success of the Head Start programs of the 1960s and 1970s. Parent involvement strategies are required today for all early childhood programs receiving federal funds.

These proposals had an impact on early childhood education. Many states enacted laws that mandated provision for state-funded kindergarten programs. Some states mandated compulsory attendance in kindergarten. Others established prekindergartens in public schools for certain populations, usually four-year-olds whose family incomes fell below the poverty level, non-English-speaking children, and children believed to be at-risk. Under federal mandate, inclusion practices spread. Mandatory curriculum components such as "essential elements," "learning objectives," and "mastery levels of learning" were established. Some states legislated full funding for kindergarten programs with accompanying attendance requirements. Class sizes were reduced for early childhood classrooms from as many as thirty (sometimes more) children per class to fifteen to twenty-two children. Some school districts improved adult-to-child ratios by providing aides to assist in the classrooms. However, the provision of aides to teachers is a practice that has not become as widespread as professionals in the field would prefer.

## Programs for Children with Special Needs

Both public and private programs are now subject to federal legislation and guidelines regarding equal access and reasonable accommodations for individuals with disabilities. The Individuals with Disabilities Education Act (IDEA), passed in Congress in 1991, and the Americans with Disabilities Act (ADA), passed in 1992, both mandate that individuals with disabling conditions are entitled to equal rights in (1) public accommodations such as child care centers, family child care homes, preschools, and public

*Technological advances provide many opportunities to broaden and expand children's learning and curriculum.*

schools; (2) state and local services; and (3) employment. These laws furthered the practice of including children with special needs in regular classrooms and provided funds to public schools for programs and services for children from ages three to twenty-one. The practice of inclusion assists all children in becoming aware of and sensitive to human diversity, requiring educators to consider the unique strengths in each learner.

## THE TWENTY-FIRST CENTURY: REACHING FOR FULLEST POTENTIALS

The school reform movement helped and hurt the cause of developmentally appropriate practices. For the first time in history the nation was truly confronted with the importance of the early and elementary school years in human growth and development and to a better-educated citizenry in the long run. Yet, concern over low standards and declining test scores put pressure on early childhood teachers to have prekindergarten, kindergarten, and primary-grade children "ready" for the next grade. This resulted in the push-down curricula discussed at the beginning of the chapter. Reacting to school reform pressures, many schools removed the "fluff" activities of recess, rest times, music, and sociodramatic play. In the extreme, some went so far as to create classroom environments that mimicked upper-grade classrooms with seating arrangements at tables or desks. In these extreme classrooms, learning centers were transformed into folder games and a few hands-on activities the students could engage in upon completion of their seatwork, which again mimicked upper-grade paper/pencil, workbook tasks.

If professionals in early childhood education were disheartened over this adverse turn of events, it was not to last long. With new brain-imaging technologies, the biological and neurological scientists of the 1990s were returning our focus to child study. Publication of research findings on brain growth and neurological development affirmed what developmentalists have professed for decades (yes, even centuries). Premises such as the crucial importance of earliest learning and psychosocial development, the concept of critical periods in which certain learning must occur, the importance of rich talk and effective communication, and the critical role of sensory and motor activity to neurological development are again being stressed as extremely important. This affirming and renewed focus on human growth and development holds promise for bringing early childhood education practices into harmony with the child development knowledge base (Brazelton & Greenspan, 2000, Sylwester 1995, 2001). The topic of brain growth and neurological development will be covered more fully in chapter 3.

**high stakes testing** tests for which life-influencing decisions are made based on the student's score (e.g., retention, promotion, graduation, admission to special programs).

The 1990s was a period in which educators focused on helping children reach their fullest potential. The successes and sometimes fallacies of school reform proposals resulted in more discerning decisions about what and how young children should be taught. The standards movement during this decade drew front-page attention as state legislatures began to require the development of academic goals with subject- and grade-level standards. The standards are aligned with assessment strategies, often **high stakes tests** to determine if the standards are being met. Thus, schools, teachers, and students are held accountable. School districts, individual schools, teachers, and students are rated according to progress toward attainment of the standards as revealed by student test scores.

While educators and parents can be guided by well-framed goals and standards, when companion assessments are narrowly focused, curricula often become constricted and narrow as well. The standards movement, then, is a mixed blessing, which has engendered no small amount of debate. The standards movement has both helped (providing guidelines and grade-level expectations) and hindered (narrowed the curriculum and subjected young children to testing of dubious accuracy) the education of young children (Kohn, 2001a, 2001b; Pellegrino, Chudowsky, & Glaser, 2001).

If the school reform movement brought some developmentally *in*appropriate practices, into early childhood education, it also ironically highlighted the importance of high-quality care and early childhood programs, including the critical nature of teacher preparation.

This is illustrated by the fact that Congress in 1998 mandated a requirement that 50 percent of each Head Start program's teachers must have an associate's degree in early childhood education by the year 2003. At the state level, scholarship and loan forgiveness programs are being formulated to encourage advanced education in early childhood education, and teacher training programs are collaborating across institutions from high school to two-year and four-year colleges to create a continuum of educational and professional development opportunities for aspiring early childhood professionals.

As we make our way into the twenty-first century, tensions arise again among scholars and policy makers as emphasis on early literacy, yearly testing of younger children, subject and grade level standards, and a definition of school readiness are debated. Professional early childhood educators continue to seek strategies for caring for and teaching young children that respect each child's uniqueness and sets forth age and individually appropriate expectations. The 1997 publication of the revised edition of NAEYC's *Developmentally Appropriate Practice in Early Childhood Programs* reaffirms the profession's commitment to age and individually appropriate practice and acknowledges its deep roots in the philosophies and scholarship that have evolved throughout the history of early childhood education.

## Summary

From crudely built, hard, backless benches and "hickory sticks," to flower-sprinkled gardens for children, to prepared environments with child-size furnishings and equipment, to modern-day classrooms with learning centers and futuristic technologies, the history of early childhood education has followed a long and often bumpy path. Over the years, philosophical points of view have converged, diverged, and clashed in spirited interaction. Yet, educators have applied to their daily teaching practices the theories and ideas of early scholars and philosophers whose points of view have often proven to be as valid today as they were in years past. Most have converged into a loosely woven tapestry of agreement as professionals affirm a common belief in the essential connection between child development and education practices.

In this chapter we have covered significant historical periods in which philosophy and pedagogy were tested, challenged, and modified. These challenges were often an outgrowth of changing ideologies and enlarging knowledge bases. Views as diverse as they often are today emanated from philosophies emerging from religious, civic, philanthropic, medical, psychological, and pedagogic contexts.

Throughout our discussions we have related historical events and theories to contemporary thought and practice in child care and education. Selected theorists and their theories have been described along with some biographical sketches. Other theories and theorists will be introduced throughout this text in chapters that draw upon and relate to their scholarship and research. Individuals whose leadership and advocacy have made a significant contribution to our understandings and policies are also introduced. It has been quite a journey, traveling different pathways to modern-day practices through the evolution of child care and early education from some of the earliest recorded histories.

## Reflections

1. Reflect upon your own childhood. How were children perceived? What types of clothing, toys, and experiences characterized your childhood? How did parents and teachers teach and discipline you? What did your early classrooms look like? Feel like? What changes do you notice in today's practices? Relate any of your early education experiences to any of the philosophies or theories described in this chapter.

2. With which of the early philosophers' positions would you likely identify? How might your understanding of the philosopher(s)' points of view influence the manner in which you might relate to children of your own or of others?

3. Select a theme that seems to reappear throughout the various philosophical positions. Chronologically follow that theme to present-day practice. How is that theme played out in classrooms in which you observe and work?

## Field Experiences

1. Visit a library. Locate and read the works of some of the early scholars mentioned in this chapter. Or you may choose to visit a museum, art gallery, school district archives, historians in the community, or other possible sources of historic information about children, child care, and education. Examine historical pictures and paintings depicting children during

the 1600s to 1700s and then through the 1800s to 1900s. How are young children portrayed? What childhood contexts do the pictures reveal? What types of clothing, playthings, activities, or pedagogies are revealed in these pictures? How have they changed from one era to another? How have they remained similar?

## Case Study

### Philosophical Challenges

Miss Baker is a kindergarten teacher in a large public school district. She has become increasingly aware of the fact that some educators and policy makers within her school district believe that the concept of developmentally appropriate practices is an inadequate one and fails to meet the high standards being imposed on local districts by state mandates. Some of her colleagues insist DAP is a fad that like other education fads will soon pass into obscurity. How might Miss Baker draw upon history to support the philosophy and practices associated with DAP?

### Committee Assignment

Miss Baker has been assigned to a committee to collect historical information about the elementary schools in her district. The school district is seeking to enhance its archives, having neglected its history for many years. The district is particularly interested in obtaining information about the earliest grades in elementary school—kindergarten through third grade. There are twelve elementary schools in the district. Other members of the committee are kindergarten and primary grade teachers.

### What to Do?

Where should Miss Baker begin? How might she tap her knowledge of early childhood history to outline the types of items and information that can inform and enrich the archival collections? How might the archival collections once assembled and cataloged be used by other teachers to inform and guide their current practices?

## Further Reading

Adelman, C. (2000). Over two years, what did Froebel say to Pestalozzi? *History of Education, 29*(2), 103–115.

Cahan, E. D. (1989). *Past caring: A history of U.S. preschool care and education for the poor, 1820–1965.* New York: School of Public Health, Columbia University, National Center for Children in Poverty.

Hewes, D. W. (2001). *W.N. Hailmann: Defender of Froebel.* Grand Rapids, MI: Froebel Foundation USA.

Hill, P. S. (2001). *Kindergarten: A reprint from the American Educator Encyclopedia.* Olney, MD: Association for Childhood Education International. (Original work published 1844).

Hymes, J. L. (1991). *Early childhood education: Twenty years in review: A look at 1971–1990.* Washington, DC: National Association for the Education of Young Children.

Moore, M. R. (Fall 2002). An American's journey to kindergarten's birthplace. *Childhood Education, 79*(1), 15–20.

Safford, P. L. (1996). *A history of childhood and disability.* New York: Teachers College, Columbia University.

Snyder, A. (1972). *Dauntless women in childhood education, 1856–1931.* Wheaton, MD: Association for Childhood Education International.

Wolfe, J. (2000). *Learning from the past: Historical voices in early childhood education.* Mayerthorpe, Alberta, Canada: Piney Branch Press.

Wortham, S. C. (2002). *Childhood: 1892–2002.* Wheaton, MD: Association for Childhood Education International.

## Helpful Web Sites

### Association for Childhood Education, International (ACEI)
http://www.udel.edu.bateman/acei
*This professional educators' association grew out of the debates surrounding kindergarten during the early 1920s. It is today one of the major professional associations for early childhood and elementary teachers. ACEI publishes a number of books on the topic of history and philosophy in education. The association publishes the journals* Childhood Education: Infancy through Early Adolescence *and the* Journal of Research in Childhood Education.

### Froebel Web site
www.uiwtx.edu/~moore/index.html
*The Web site provides a journey to the roots of kindergarten to see first-hand the artifacts remaining of Friedrich Froebel, Father of Kindergarten. One can learn of other firsts that Froebel fathered while visiting virtually the landscapes that influenced his life, his vision, and his work.*

Check the Online Resources™ for expert practitioners' responses to each case study.

For additional information on teaching young children, visit our Web site at **http://www.earlychilded.delmar.com**

## PART TWO

# Information That Informs Practice

# CHAPTER 3

## Basing Practices on Knowledge of Child Growth and Development

*Early Childhood Principle* Professional early childhood educators rely on current knowledge of child growth, development, and learning to make decisions about their practices.

Integral to the concept of developmentally appropriate practices is knowledge of child growth, development, and learning. The study of child growth and development encompasses research from many disciplines: education, medicine, neuroscience, sociology, psychology, anthropology, and others. From these allied fields, scholars gain information about biological and neurological events that presage growth, development, and learning and environmental influences that affect early sensory experiences and human interactions.

In recent years emphasis on the contexts in which children grow and develop has led professional early childhood educators to give serious consideration to the social, cultural, and economic aspects of children's lives (Bronfenbrenner, 1989; Mallory & New, 1994; Shonkoff & Phillips, 2000; Small, 2001). Early childhood professionals have been challenged to consider these influences more fully in the political contexts in which families and children live. Considering a multiplicity of factors influencing human growth and development, professional early childhood educators strive to help each child succeed and become healthy, self-assured, and cognitively, socially and morally competent human beings.

*After reading this chapter, you should be able to:*
- Discuss important growth, development, and learning occurring during early childhood in each of the major developmental domains.
- Discuss the importance of early neurological development and brain growth in children.

- Identify "windows of opportunity" where early childhood experiences at home and in early childhood programs have their greatest potential impact.
- Suggest developmentally appropriate early childhood experiences that enhance growth and development in each of the developmental domains.
- Discuss the importance of understanding the cultural, social, and political contexts in which young children grow and develop.

**M**S. SANCHEZ is in her first year of teaching and has had only three weeks with her class of prekindergarten children. She remembers her child growth and development courses in college and wants to consider child growth and development principles in her planning. She understands that individuality reflects each child's genetic makeup, race, culture, family life, and family values. She also knows that children have individual temperaments, interests, motivations, needs, and strengths.

To acquaint herself with the individual characteristics of each child, Ms. Sanchez will begin by initiating an observation and portfolio strategy. She will start with only four or five children, observing and keeping preliminary notes that she will place along with samples of their work and other information in a folder she has created for each child. She will observe small groups of students from day to day until she has obtained first impressions of each child's growth, development, interests, and needs. She will use these observations to plan the curriculum for the first weeks of school.

As the year progresses, she will become more adept at observing "on-the-run" and will assemble additional assessment information from checklists, anecdotal reports, and both teacher- and child-selected examples of each child's work. Ms. Sanchez may also include photographs of block constructions, clay sculptures, and children at work in learning centers (after obtaining permission from the parents to take photographs of their children). She may also place in the student portfolio audio recordings of children's language development as they converse, tell stories, and share books and poetry with one another. Notes from her collaborative meetings with children's families will also provide suggestions for planning.

Initial observations may take two or more weeks, and, of course, assessment of child progress will be a continuing process throughout the year. Here is a sample of the notes and portfolio contents she has begun and from which she will begin her initial curriculum planning:

# SHERRY

Though somewhat awkward, enjoys physical activity, particularly climbing, running, dancing, and movement activities. Voice: loud indoors and out. Social interactions are frequently aggressive and hurtful (verbally and physically) to others. Limited language and social skills. Enjoys singing; mispronounces many words, does not articulate well. Generally follows instructions after they have been repeated. Mother suspects a hearing problem.

*Sherry's portfolio contents:* large-motor and fine-motor checklists; photograph of balance beam attempt; dictated letter to "Mom" about what she likes at school; audio tape of pretend book reading; Mother's note of concern about her hearing and ability to pay attention. Mother expressed eagerness for Sherry to do well in school.

# Jason

Loves to sing, remembers words to new songs; enjoys group singing. Quite verbal, enjoys others, laughs readily, keen sense of humor. Fascinated by song books, piano, and other musical instruments. Takes song books to the reading corner to read. Difficulty with book-handling skills. Rough and rowdy in outdoor play. Plays with abandon. Tends to lead; enjoys talking and telling stories to the class. Is a sought-after playmate.

*Jason's portfolio contents:* First-day photograph sharing his favorite song with the group; crayon drawing of his family with dictated "story," large- and fine-motor checklists; audio tape of singing "The Little White Duck," notes from curb conference with father. Father expressed no pressing concern, just wants him to have a good time and to "mind the teacher."

# Tamika

Shy in new situations, easily frustrated, cries often. Has one best friend (Kelly); not easily consoled when Kelly plays with others. Pouts and plays alone when Kelly is not available. Enjoys books and pictures, math activities, and drawing pictures. She wants to have extended conversations with the teacher, and during these times her vocabulary and voice inflections seem quite adult-like. Though she is often emotional and cries readily, Tamika follows directions well, stays with a task until completion, and is generally compliant.

*Tamika's portfolio contents:* Large- and fine-motor checklists; dictated letter to "Mommy and Daddy" about "What I like at school"; audio tape of story-sharing with Kelly. Notes from parent conference. They wonder if her interest in math is unusual for her age, and if they should get some workbooks and coach her at home. They are concerned about her attachment to Kelly, and wonder if she will make other friends.

# Brian

Physically awkward, frequent falls and bumps. Frequently complains of hunger. Tired and irritable at the beginning of the week. Difficulty attending and following directions. Anger flares easily; easily frustrated; easily embarrassed, and can be verbally abusive with classmates, particularly if laughed at or teased. Sometimes uses expletives. Enjoys science experiments, though needs close supervision in use of science materials. Wants to run and "be wild" on the playground; frequent accidents. In spite of difficulties, wants to please, is eager to make friends, and can be very affectionate.

*Brian's portfolio contents:* Large- and fine-motor checklists; photographs of bean-classification activity and working in the science center classifying rocks; dictated story about recent playground soccer game; anecdotal record of confrontations with playmates and emotional outbursts. Need to schedule parent conference soon.

# Mario

Prefers to work independently. Particularly enjoys the writing center; experiments with various writing tools and papers; draws marks resembling letters and numerals and some letters of his name, though not in sequence. Friendly, well liked by others, sought-after playmate, though he often chooses to retreat from group activity. Limited English, but very observant and imitative; appears to be acquiring English quite readily. Parents are concerned about his language development, since he was almost three before he began talking.

*Mario's portfolio contents:* large- and fine-motor checklists; audio tape of story reading from his dictated story; copy of the dictated story; photograph of animal clay sculptures. Parent conference held before the first day of school. Their main concern is his apparent inability to communicate in English.

## CONSIDERING CHILD GROWTH AND DEVELOPMENT

*The human brain is the best organized, most functional three pounds of matter in the known universe. It's responsible for Beethoven's Ninth Symphony, computers, the Sistine Chapel, automobiles, the Second World War, Hamlet, apple pie, and a whole lot more.*

*–Robert Sylwester*

With these preliminary observations and portfolio contents, Ms. Sanchez can chart directions from which her curriculum might flow and take shape. She has initial, albeit limited, information from which to set goals for each child, both short-term goals (e.g., using appropriate voice level in the classroom) and long term goals (learning how to deal with anger). She will continue to revise and modify these goals as she observes further and learns more about each child and as children grow and change throughout the year. As she continuously observes, she will seek ways to match what she knows about child development to curriculum goals and daily activities. In so doing, she is creating a child-centered classroom that meets the criteria for developmental appropriateness.

What should teachers observe in children? The best way to become acquainted with the developmental characteristics of individual children is to read about and observe growth and development in the following domains:

- Neurological and sensory development
- Physical growth and motor development
- Emotional and social development
- Cognitive, language, and literacy development
- Moral or character development

It is always best to take a whole-child view when observing child growth and development, taking into consideration each child's uniqueness and needs in each of these developmental domains (Puckett & Black, 2000). Young children have needs in many areas of their lives. Too often children in school are observed and tested for cognitive abilities and gains with little regard for the interrelationship and integrated nature of all of the other developmental domains. All developmental domains; brain growth and neurological development; physical growth and motor coordinations; and emotional, social, moral, cognitive, language, and literacy development occur in tandem with one another and are interdependent. None is of greater importance than the others. The following describes these domains. (For in-depth study of child growth and development, see the Further Reading section of this chapter.)

## Neurological and Sensory Development

The brain is an overwhelmingly complex organ. With the formation of the **neural tube** during the first weeks of prenatal development, neurological cells are forming at a startling rate of an estimated 250,000 a minute; and at birth, the brain's 100 billion or more **neurons** and **glial cells** have formed more than 50 trillion connections, or **synapses**. This growth is so rapid that by the end of the first year, the infant's brain is two-thirds its adult size, and by the end of the second year it will be about four-fifths of its adult size. Neurons have spun off **axons** and **dendrites** that transmit information throughout the body.

One scientist likened this brain to a massive telephone system, where the trunk runs between large communication hubs and ancillary lines run throughout the system. Carla Shatz, professor of neurobiology at the University of California–Berkley, used this metaphor in her presentation at the 1997 White House Conference on Early Childhood and Learning (Shatz, April 17, 1997). Shatz, continuing this metaphor, compared an individual's genetic blueprint for brain development to the trunk line between various telephone systems. For this system to work, a massive wiring process must take place in which the neurons that have been developing rapidly during prenatal development grow axons (or "long distance" lines) to transmit messages to other locations in the brain. The axons, in turn, send branches that will loosely connect with many other locations. At this point, chemical and electrical activity in the brain results in either permanent connections or unconnected sites as the brain selects what it needs and

**neural tube** the vertebral canal from which the brain and spinal cord arise.

**neuron** a nerve cell and its connections; the basic functional unit of the nervous system.

**glial cells** supportive cells found in the nervous system that play a role in myelinating axons and guiding the regrowth of damaged axons.

**synapses** the point of electrical or chemical interaction and contact between two neurons or between a neuron and a muscle fiber.

**axon** long and slender, axons are the major communication link between neurons, sending messages that will be received by dendrites.

**dendrites** bushlike, branching extensions of nerve cell that *receive* neurological messages.

discards those connections that are not nurtured. According to Shatz, the brain continuously runs these "test patterns."

While much of this dramatic development is taking place prenatally, after the infant is born critical connections continue to form. A second neurological growth spurt occurs as axons, which send signals, and dendrites, which receive them, burst forth in enormous numbers during the first months and years. Environmental sensory stimuli cause the brain to develop its own unique circuitry and determine which connections will last and which will **atrophy**.While all of this is taking place, fatty tissue called **myelin** begins to cover the nerve cells. Myelin promotes efficient transmission of messages along the neurons and facilitates synapses. Its growth coincides with the development of vision and auditory systems, large- and small-motor development, language, emotions and feelings, and information processing. Figure 3–1 illustrates this spectacular neurological communication system.

How do we know about all of this activity in the human brain? Modern-day brain imaging technology, computerized scanners, and sophisticated techniques for measuring electrical impulses and chemical composition and changes in the brain have made it possible for scientists to study it with finite precision. Scientists can actually observe on television monitors color representations of the brain doing what it does. Through these images, electrical and chemical changes in the brain can be observed and recorded. In newborns and infants, scientists can see the brain forming microscopic connections that will be responsible for feelings, learning, problem solving, memory, and other capabilities. Through such imaging, scientists can observe the brain responding to various stimuli, such as the pleasant sound of a human voice.

From contemporary study of brain growth and neurological development, we have gained a greater appreciation for the miracle of learning, and the art and science of teaching. These studies have affirmed what early childhood educators have asserted for decades: *the early years are critical ones for the growth, development, and integrity of the human organism.* Earliest experiences have life-long implications. As is often said, "Good beginnings never end."

What implication does this knowledge have for parenting and teaching infants and young children? Not dissimilar from the theories of some of the early philosophers, such as Rousseau, Froebel, Montessori, and contemporary ones as well (see following section on Erikson), these new studies suggests that there are sensitive periods, or **windows of opportunity,** in which environmental stimuli may have their most powerful impact. Challenged now is the old notion that one's intelligence is innate and for the most part unalterable. It is interesting to note that researchers in the 1960s believed that earliest experiences were important when they studied the impact of experience on the IQ scores of disadvantaged children during the inception of Head Start programs and found that such scores could be favorably

**atrophy** to waste or wither away.

**myelin** fatty tissue that partially covers some axons. Myelin serves to increase the speed with which impulses travel along nerve fibers.

**windows of opportunity** critical periods during which essential experiences have their greatest impact.

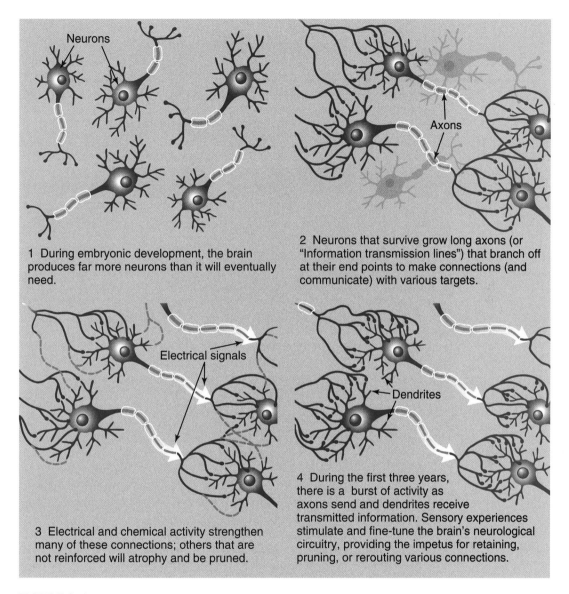

1 During embryonic development, the brain produces far more neurons than it will eventually need.

2 Neurons that survive grow long axons (or "Information transmission lines") that branch off at their end points to make connections (and communicate) with various targets.

3 Electrical and chemical activity strengthen many of these connections; others that are not reinforced will atrophy and be pruned.

4 During the first three years, there is a burst of activity as axons send and dendrites receive transmitted information. Sensory experiences stimulate and fine-tune the brain's neurological circuitry, providing the impetus for retaining, pruning, or rerouting various connections.

**FIGURE 3–1**

*Early Neurological Development*

altered by experiences associated with well-designed, high-quality early childhood care and education programs.

Experience (all the sensory input the child receives) affects neurological development by strengthening the synapses. Neurological connections that are not strengthened through experience, or are not used over a period of

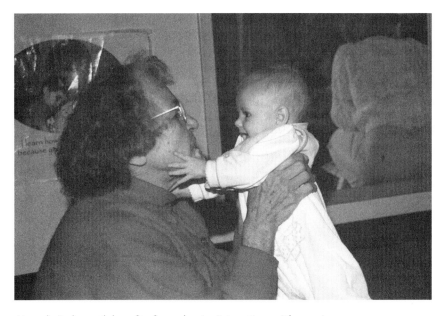

*Neurological growth benefits from pleasing interactions with caregivers.*

time, wither away or are pruned. Windows of opportunity for strengthening synapses in almost all developmental domains have been identified. This identification of windows of opportunity provides important information for early childhood educators and parents from which they determine appropriate experiences for children during various periods of brain growth.

From birth onward, healthy prenatal development, health-promoting care, and appropriately stimulating experiences are critical to neurological development. Neurological development and brain growth appear to occur most profoundly within the first three to four years for some developmental achievements, and up to seven to ten years for others. From then on a sculpting process shapes the brain's neurological development, pruning away excess and unused neurons (Restak, 2001). As some have said, it is a "use it or lose it" situation. Table 3–1 lists these windows of opportunity.

This new knowledge about the importance of the early months and years of a child's life does not suggest a need for elaborate play equipment or a need to purchase the most current commercial "educational" toy. Actually, the most significant contributions to early neurological development are the simplest ones to provide. Infants need simple meaningful interactions to promote brain growth and neurological development: cooing, talking, naming people, objects and actions; singing and listening to music; cuddling, rocking, strolling, and varying the infant's visual fields; providing toys of

**TABLE 3–1**

*Developmental Windows of Opportunity*

| | |
|---|---|
| Social Attachment | Birth to 2 years |
| Control of Emotions and Ability to Cope with Stress | Birth to 3 years |
| Vision | Birth to 2 years |
| Motor Development | Birth to 4 or 5 years |
| Vocabulary | Birth to 3 years |
| Second Language | Birth to 10 years |
| Math and Logic | 1 to 4.5 or 5 years |
| Language | Birth to 10 years |
| Music | 3 to 10 years |

various textures, colors, and shapes; selecting safe household items to explore and manipulate; playing *with* infants and young children as they explore their own capabilities and their surroundings; and providing visual and auditory cues to arouse interest and curiosity, and many other similar growth-enhancing interactions. Infants, toddlers, and young children need safe places to explore and discover. They need adults to talk about their routines and discoveries with them.

As children get older, they benefit from many of the same experiences as those listed previously as well as increasing opportunities to play with other children. Adults can support neurological development by continuing to converse and provide children with a rich language environment; providing props that encourage pretend play; exposing children to music of all types, dance and rhythm, chanting, and poetry; reading and sharing story and picture books; role-playing stories and events; planning together daily schedules and other events or activities, and organizing those plans with needed materials or supplies; engaging in simple science experiments, posing "what if" questions and simple hypotheses; and engaging in problem-solving discussions around the child's personal experiences.

Adults play an important role in the brain's wiring for feelings and sense of well-being when they play games *with* children. Moreover, adults who help children gain the most from children's television programs by sharing and talking about these programs, encourage children to distinguish between real and unreal events, as well as acceptable and unacceptable behaviors. Other activities can include providing raw materials (paper, glue, crayons, paints, clay, and so on) to stimulate creativity and construction; engaging in extended conversations; taking walking or riding excursions about the neighborhood, town, or community; allowing children to help with daily tasks such as feeding and caring for pets, watering plants, managing and caring for personal belongings, and learning a variety of self-help skills. As you can see, this list of interactions with children can become quite long; yet none involves outlays of money or are stressful for parents and teachers to do. They do entail focused attention, time, verbal and social interactions, and emotional empathy and support. Their value is immeasurable; the need for them is critical. As these suggestions are made, a cautionary note must be mentioned, however.

One need not go overboard in attempting to help infants and young children in this early development. Infants and children must have time to explore and discover using their own existing sensory, motor, and cognitive abilities. Attempting to force skills and learning with intensive instruction and intrusive interactions can cause the child to use immature or inappropriate neural networks and thus distort the natural growth process. Adults must be aware that there is a range in the amount of stimulation the infant and young child can comfortably tolerate. As with all learning, it takes time to practice, use, and internalize new capabilities, and children need this time before they progress to additional learning. Adults need to be sensitive to the child's cues of fatigue and resistance, and watch for signs of overload. Pushing children can do as much damage as limiting their interactions (Healy, 1990, 1994; Herschkowitz & Herschkowitz, 2002).

## Physical Growth and Motor Development

**maturationist theory**
theory suggesting that the origins of growth and development unfold from within the human organism.

Historically, studies of physical growth and motor development have been based on **maturationist theories** that suggest an unfolding of characteristics and capabilities within the human being that leads progressively to more and more mature forms. Maturationist theories propose that all development unfolds according to a genetically preprogrammed plan or blueprint for growth. They believe that this blueprint dictates fixed patterns of growth and development that are only slightly influenced by environment. Today's scientific emphases on neurological development, human sensory mechanisms, and environmental influences provides a more complete understanding of human growth and motor development.

Nevertheless, there are maturationist principles on which developmentalists continue to rely. One of the major principles of maturationist theory is that growth and development proceed from the head downward and from the central axis of the body outward. This principle is demonstrated in the predictable sequences often assigned to specific types of development. For instance, according to maturationists, the emerging development leading to the ability to catch a large ball follows a predictable pattern beginning at birth and proceeding toward an expected age of competence, around age five or six:

Innate reflexive activity
Motor development in the head and neck region
Motor development in upper arms and chest region
Motor development and coordination in the trunk region
Motor development in the legs and feet
Motor development and coordination in the lower arms, hands, and
    fingers
Eye-hand coordination
Development of grasping and pincer abilities
Reaching and retrieving movements
Eye-foot coordination
Eye- and moving-object coordination
Stopping a rolled ball
Catching a thrown ball

This type of pattern holds true for most children. The issue with progressions such as these is that they often are applied too rigorously, particularly when age of appearance is attached to each new development. Such application can lead to inaccurate assessments of growth and development often resulting in a "deficit model" in which developmental problems are assumed if a child's development does not follow a particular age or sequence. A deficit model is focused on identifying deficiencies in children and prescribing special treatments as deemed needed. While it is appropriate to identify developmental issues early, deficit approaches to understanding child growth and development often lead to labels that can be inaccurate and damaging.

A child who still has difficulty catching a ball at age six or seven may be mislabeled as having a perceptual-motor problem, when actually all that is needed is more experience with large-motor activities. Children who are not able to "stay within the lines" when drawing or writing are often considered "slow," and in need of practice, when indeed all they may need are more large- and small-motor activities that foster motor coordinations. Additional opportunities to engage in large motor activity are more likely to achieve results than the largely ineffective task of practicing writing one's name ten or twenty times on guideline paper. Similarly, a spirited and active child inaccurately labeled "hyperactive" may never be free of that label and might spend unnecessary time in special classes.

To avoid these mistakes, it is best to consider multiple influences on human growth and development and the inevitability of wide variations among children. Variations among children can be attributed to socioeconomic factors, ethnic and culture uniqueness, accessibility to health care and prenatal supervision, enrichment and learning opportunities, parenting styles and expectations, learning styles, developmental challenges, or debilitating conditions. Diversity in any of these categories need not suggest deficiency.

Profound or persistent departures from the norm, however, signals a need for further assessment.

A well known maturationist theorist was Yale University scholar Arnold Gesell. During the 1920s through 1940s, the studies of Gesell and his colleagues identified observable sequences of growth and development, leading ultimately to maturation (Gesell, 1925, 1930; 1940; Gesell & Armatruda, 1941; Gesell & Ilg, 1949). These studies at the Yale University Child Study Clinic led to the establishment of **norms** for various types of development. Gesell and his colleagues delineated norms for motor skills (similar to the previous sequence), adaptive behaviors, language, and personal-social behavior.

**norms** the average age of the emergence of certain behaviors or average scores on tests that are based on large representative samples of a population.

Norms provided parents, teachers, and pediatricians with a set of developmental milestones by which "normal" growth and development and individual "readiness" for new experiences were gauged. These milestones led to later formulations of tests to determine readiness for kindergarten and first grade (Ames, Gillespie, Haines, & Ilg, 1979). The Gesell School Readiness Test has been administered widely across the nation in kindergartens and first grades and was both popular and controversial during the 1970s and 1980s. Concern over the uses and abuses of readiness and achievement tests with young children is expressed widely in contemporary child development and early childhood education literature. (Anderson, 1998; Kohn, 2000; Meisels, 2000; Southern Early Childhood Association, 1999). We discuss this issue further in chapter 4.

Gesell's child study focused attention on biological influences in child growth and development and provided some general principles of development that continue to guide thoughtful developmental assessment of children. His work provided the first scientific attempt to illustrate the role of heredity in human growth and development, and provided a framework for characterizing "ascending levels of maturity in terms of typical behavior patterns" (Gesell, 1940). Gesell asserted that the earliest periods of development are always the period of most rapid, most intense, and most fundamental growth, a belief that holds today.

### Growth and Development Trends

Growth is quite rapid in the early months and years. Brain growth is externally evident in head circumference measures often employed by pediatricians during regular physical examinations during the child's first three years. Small-for-age head circumference at age two may suggest developmental delay. Rapid growth is also demonstrated through early weight and length/height measures. By the age of five to six months of age, healthy infants have usually doubled their birth weight and increased birth length by six to seven inches. By age one, birth weight may have tripled, and ten to twelve inches may have been added to birth length. During the second year, the growth rate decelerates though it still keeps a steady pace. By age four and five, children are gaining about four to five pounds each year and

---

**BIOGRAPHY BOX** *Arnold Gesell (1880-1961)*

Arnold Gesell was born in Wisconsin, where he received most of his education. His first degree was in teaching, and later in 1906, he earned his Ph.D. in psychology at Clark University in Massachusetts. In 1911, Gesell took a position as assistant professor of education at Yale University and earned an additional doctorate in medicine. He established a Clinic of Child Development in the Yale School of Medicine in which he taught and conducted research for the next thirty-seven years.

After his retirement from Yale University, several of his coworkers set up a private institution near Yale in New Haven, Connecticut, which became known as the Gesell Institute of Child Development. Through his retirement years, Gesell served as a consultant to the Institute. Gesell's contributions were significant to the field of child study and were widely disseminated during the child study movement. His research was later criticized for its limited population of upper-middle-class children enrolled in the Yale University laboratory school during the late 1920s to the 1940s.

Photo © Bettmann/CORBIS.

---

two to three-and-one-half inches a year until around age six. Between ages six to eight (or nine), there is a slight decline in rate of growth as height increases about two to three inches each year. Weight gain at this age averages around four to five pounds a year until around age ten or eleven. Height and weight variations among children are related to genetic makeup, health, nutrition, activity levels, and metabolic rates.

While these gains are observable and easily measured, other growth changes less observable are occurring. Body proportions and locus of balance change over time, making it progressively possible to perform more and more mature large- and small-motor coordinations. Infant facial features begin to disappear and facial proportions change as deciduous teeth erupt. More mature facial features are influenced by the eruption of permanent teeth between the ages of six and ten years. Fatty tissue is replaced by muscle tissue as locomotion takes over, and ossification of bones and skeletal changes alter body appearance, strength, and endurance. Control of bladder and bowel emerge during the second and third years, though young children may not gain complete control until age six, seven, or eight years.

## Promoting Child Health in Early Childhood Programs

During the period of rapid growth, it is especially important to pay close attention to the overall health of each child. Particular attention is given to the integrity of the child's sensory system. Vision and hearing need to be assessed soon after enrollment. Most early childhood programs provide this early screening. On a daily basis adults observe children for signs of fatigue, restlessness, hunger, distractability, symptoms of illness, and poor large-

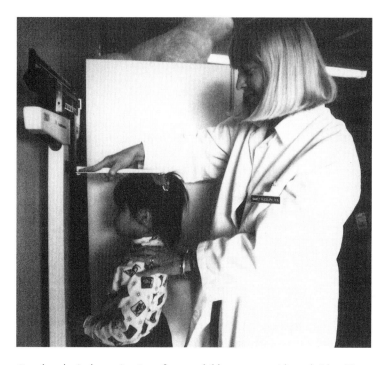

*Regular physical examination of young children can provide early identification of developmental delay.*

and small-motor coordination. There may be a need to enlist appropriate health care support personnel to address individual nutritional needs, dental health, personal hygiene, and immunization status. Early identification of health needs prevents more serious physical and health problems later and curtails the spread of communicable illnesses. Monitoring the health status and needs of children is an important responsibility of early childhood educators.

Ms. Sanchez's preliminary observations suggest that Sherry may have a hearing impairment, since it is common for children with hearing impairments to speak louder than necessary and to frequently mispronounce words. While these are certainly not sufficient symptoms to assert that a hearing impairment exists, they do suggest the need for further observation and perhaps a physician's diagnosis. Ms. Sanchez will want to observe Sherry in many different contexts, watching for signs of hearing difficulties.

Freddie's frequent falls and bumps could suggest visual impairment, large- and small-motor coordination difficulties, poor nutrition, lack of sufficient sleep, or more serious neurological problems. He also might benefit from a pediatrician's assessment. Ms. Sanchez will observe him further, watching for signs of visual impairment or possible difficulties in **perceptual-motor development**. Focused observation in a variety of contexts helps teachers to determine if further assessment is needed. They are then better able to plan activities and daily routines around individual physiological needs. In some cases, problems such as Freddie's may represent simply a matter of age and a need for further growth-enhancing experiences. His tall-for-age stature should not be construed as indicative of greater maturity, but rather as a growth rate and pattern that is uniquely his.

Further, it is critical that early childhood educators observe carefully for other indications of special needs, particularly with infants, toddlers, and very young children. Recognizing the relationship between early experiences and later outcomes, educators working with families and other appropriate resource professionals seek to identify and intervene when children exhibit symptoms or behaviors suggestive of developmental challenges or disabilities.

The Division for Early Childhood (DEC) of the Council for Exceptional Children (CEC) has published a code of ethics for working with children with special needs (appendix D) and recommended practices in early childhood intervention and special education (Sandall, McLean, & Smith, 2000). These recommendations address partnering with parents, developmentally appropriate and comprehensive assessments, group size and composition, classroom space and materials accommodations to promote children's safety, active engagement in learning, and participation and membership within the group. Further the recommended practices include expectations for adult interactions, inclusion and guidance strategies, teacher training and professional development, use of assistive technologies and equipment, and policies that reflect both the letter and spirit of legislation regarding individuals with disabilities. The goal of DEC and of quality early childhood education regardless of setting is to assure that all children regardless of ableness receive early assessment and timely intervention, and have opportunities to benefit from inclusive, child friendly, nurturing, and supportive learning environments. A parent checklist derived from these recommendations is exampled in appendix G.

### Importance of Motor Development and Movement in Early Childhood

Movement skills progress from reflexive activity in later prenatal stages and early infancy to rudimentary movements (reaching, grasping, crawling) during the first two years, to fundamental movements (walking, running, kicking, jumping, climbing) that emerge during the years from age two to seven years, to specific skill-related movements associated with and leading to specific abilities (sports, dance, gymnastics). Ms. Sanchez began with a simple checklist of fundamental large and small muscle coordination activities. Her goals include improving fundamental movement skills and physical and motor fitness.

**perceptual-motor development** refers to the coordination of perceptions (sensory learning) and motor abilities.

*Behaviors Suggestive of Hearing Impairments*
Frequent ear infections
Drainage from one or both ears
Complaints of ear pain or itching
Frequent requests for repeated statements
Inappropriate responses to questions, directions, or requests
Failure to respond when spoken to in a normal voice
Poor articulation
Difficulty with certain speech sounds
Monotone speech

*Behaviors Suggestive of Visual Impairment*
Red or swollen eyelids
Squinting
Tearing or drainage from one or both eyes
Excessive blinking or grimacing
Eyes that do not track or align properly
Persistent rubbing of the eyes
Frequent bumping into objects and people
Holding face very close to books or table work
Unintentionally intruding on others' "personal space"

Physical fitness refers to muscular strength, muscular endurance, flexibility, and circulatory-respiratory endurance. Motor fitness refers to speed, coordination, agility, power, and balance (Gallahue & Ozum, 1995). To address these developmental needs, Ms. Sanchez will provide many opportunities for children to use their emerging abilities spontaneously during both indoor and outdoor play. She may also plan such activities as the following:

• Simple exercises to increase balance and stability

This might include simple activities of bending, stretching, reaching, lifting, rolling, jumping forward then backward on two feet (and later on one foot), jumping in place on two feet then one, balancing on one, then the other foot, walking a balance beam, and responding to various types of music.

• Opportunities to enhance fundamental movements

This can include walking within a defined space on toes, on heels, in very small steps, in "giant" steps, or using side steps or glides; walking with

*Young children need varied opportunities to develop motor coordination, strength, and endurance.*

arms stretched high in the air, with arms swinging vigorously, or on "all fours" imitating the walk of different animals; hopping, leaping, running with abandon within safe boundaries; walking up and down steps with one foot then alternating feet; jumping high, forward, backward, or from low heights and a specified distance; moving in left and right directions; positioning one's body in front of, beside behind, on, or under a specified object; climbing and sliding on safe and well-constructed playground equipment; participating in simple cooperative games that involve large-motor skills; and swaying or dancing to a variety of rhythms.

- Early specific skills development

To enhance this development, Ms. Sanchez may include specialized movements such as skipping, marching, and galloping; following directional instructions involving left/right, up/down, forward/backward, high/low, soft/loud, and so on; sliding; tossing bean bags and balls at a target; rolling a ball to a target; catching or kicking a rolling ball; hand bouncing a ball (or dribbling); striking a ball with a bat or racket; jumping a short rope or a long swinging rope; traversing a simple obstacle course; simple folk dancing and responding to music using props such as scarves, streamers and hoops.

- Physical and motor fitness

  Ms. Sanchez will gradually lengthen the duration, endurance requirements, and complexity of children's large-motor abilities, through activities such as simple aerobic exercises, dance routines, and sports-related activities, which may include running around the track or other specified distance, carrying bean bags or other objects of increasing weight, or playing games that require quick stops and starts, stooping and reaching, and quick directional decisions. These activities increase endurance, strength, flexibility, speed, and agility.

- Small-motor coordinations

  Significant small-motor developments include eye–hand coordination, prehension (coordination of fingers and thumb to permit the grasping of small objects), and dexterity (ability to make quick, precise movements of the hands and fingers). Dexterity is dependent upon right- or left-handedness, which emerges slowly from infancy but does not become dominant until around the ages of six or seven. To support this development, Ms. Sanchez will provide an array of manipulative activities and materials requiring various fine-motor skills, such as stacking, dumping, fastening, zipping, buttoning, stringing, lacing, turning, twisting, spreading, pouring, sorting, placing, connecting, tearing, cutting, drawing, pasting, constructing, writing, and many more. Throughout the year, a variety of manipulative materials and activities will be incorporated into the different learning centers. There will be play dough; large beads and strings; pegboards and puzzles (with and without knobs); button and lacing boards; assorted containers and lids; large nuts and bolts; a hammer, nails, and soft wood; geoboards; vessels used to pour water; hole punchers, large tweezers, and clothespins; keys and locks; and many more.

- Perceptual-motor abilities

  Perception is a process by which we organize and synthesize information gathered through the various sense organs. Motor activity enhances perceptual development by varying the sensory stimuli and broadening the base of sensory information. In turn, perceptions enhance motor development in such concepts as body awareness, direction, space, depth, speed, size, weight, and others. In addition to benefits to health and physical development, young children rely on a wide variety of large- and small-motor activities to gain information about the world around them.

  Finally, children who have healthy bodies and are increasingly developing better large- and small-motor coordination generally exhibit higher levels of self-esteem and self-confidence. A sense of competence in movement and management of their bodies motivates children to try new motor activities. Physical activity is often cathartic, relieving stress and providing a constructive outlet for emotions. Social interactions and skills

*Eye–hand coordinatiuon and dexterity are enhanced through exploration of manipulative materials.*

are practiced as children engage in cooperative games and spontaneous movement activities. Overall health and well-being depends on activities that enhance physical and motor fitness.

## Emotional Development

The emotional development of young children is a very complex process. The study of emotional development addresses temperament, feelings, reactions, self-concept, and self-esteem. Emotions and feelings play a role in everything we experience in work, play, learning, and human interactions. Emotions are universal and evolutionary in that they help humans survive, adapt, and learn (Hyson, 1994, 2002). Individuals from all cultures recognize expressions of emotion—happiness, anger, grief, fear, humor, and others. As with older children and adults, young children's emotions are evident in their facial expressions, gestures, posture, other body language, vocalizations, language, communicative style, and the manner in which they use and create with toys and learning materials.

Emotional development is a slow process, and learning to control emotions begins when infants find what psychologists refer to as "self-comforting behaviors." Self-comforting behaviors include thumbsucking, humming and other vocalizations, holding a special toy or blanket, rocking, or listening to surrounding sounds. Gradually, children learn to self-regulate their emotions. During the preschool years emotions are expressed intensely, outbursts are usually short-lived, and verbal expressions are quite frank, such as "I don't like this present." Children continue to learn how and when to express emotions as they observe role models and receive tutelage within their individual cultures. Different cultures have different expectations about how and in what context certain emotions can be expressed.

Supportive adults help, young children to name, understand, and manage their emotions. The role of adults in supporting children's emotional development and well-being is important because emotions enhance or impede all learning, and play a primary role in the development of a positive sense of self and social and moral competence.

As Ms. Sanchez observes her students, she will be cognizant of the types of situations that arouse both positive and negative emotions in children. She will observe individual children for emotionality and signs of stress. She will pay particular attention to the frequency, duration, and intensity of emotions in individual children. Because she believes that just as safety and protection from physical harm is essential, a psychologically safe classroom environment for children is also necessary. Therefore, she will attempt to create a classroom in which children can express feelings and emotions without fear of embarrassment, rejection, or punishment, while learning to modulate and control emotions through guidance that teaches healthy outlets. She will encourage interactions between children and adults and classmates that are guided toward positive, self-affirming ends.

*Attachment*

Attachment is defined as a strong emotional relationship between two individuals, characterized by mutual affection and a desire to maintain proximity. Attachments grow out of early bonds between parent(s) or primary caregivers and infants during the early weeks and months of postnatal life. A psychiatrist and pioneer in the study of attachment, John Bowlby (1969/1982, 1973, 1980) studied children raised in institutions and focused on their inability to form lasting relationships. He also studied children who, after experiencing strong infant-mother attachments, were separated from their mothers for long periods of time and found that they also became resistant to close human ties.

In his studies of institutionalized children, Bowlby found that while the infants and children were safe, fed well, clothed, bathed, and provided other healthy routines, their caregivers seldom responded to the infants in an affectionate, nurturing, emotionally, or socially interactive way. They failed to respond promptly to infants' cries, return their smiles, and acknowledge their coos and babbles or carry them about. Bowlby established that even though their physical needs were met, infants in these settings failed or were severely impaired in their ability to relate to their caregivers. Other studies of attachment have stressed the need for children to form sturdy attachments during their early months or years and that failure to do so may have deleterious effects on later healthy personality development and social interaction skills (Ainsworth, 1973; Bretherton & Walters, 1985; Zeanah, 2000).

The extent to which infants and toddlers willingly leave the "safe base" of an attachment person's lap to explore the environment depends on the trust and self-confidence they derive from the attachment relationship (Isabella, 1993). When children have formed strong attachments, exploratory behaviors are more forthcoming.

Infants and toddlers also develop strong attachments to non-parental caregivers when the caregivers are sensitive and responsive to their emotional and social cues. These attachments, as well, have long-term implications for successful relationships as children get older. Sometimes strong attachments develop between children. Remember Tamika's unhappiness when Kelly would play with others?

When Tamika was born, her mother took a two-month maternity leave from her work. When she returned to work, Tamika was placed in a family child care program, in which Mrs. Shaw cared for a group of two very young infants (Kelly, twelve weeks old, and Tamika, eight weeks old) and two toddlers (sixteen months and two years of age). Kelly had been enrolled in Mrs. Shaw's program for about a month when Tamika entered. Being very close in age, the two infants shared most of their daily experiences in the same setting and with the same caregiver. They were often awake at the same times during the day, sat in their baby seats or high-chairs side by side, rolled about on a big quilt spread on the floor, and exchanged stares and clumsy attempts to reach and touch one another. Their naps were in cribs in the same room, and their playtimes were marked by first vocal and reaching interactions, then crawling one behind the other as they explored their surroundings. As they grew to be toddlers, walking and beginning to talk, their social interactions became more intense as they toddled about in the play areas struggling and squabbling with one another over toys, intruding on each other's space and their claims to Mrs. Shaw's attention. In spite of their unskilled social interactions, they began to exhibit distress on separation from one another at departure times. When they could talk, they whined and begged their parents to let them go home with one another. They were bored and lonely when the other was absent.

Just before Kelly was three years old, her family was transferred out of state, and Tamika continued to attend Mrs. Shaw's family child care home. Tamika's mother reported an increase in crying, tantrums, and difficulty going to bed at night. As she tried to understand Kelly's absence, Tamika assured herself verbally that Kelly would be back "tomorrow."

As is typical of children this age, she had enormous difficulty under-standing concepts of "far away" and "some day." Gradually, Tamika adjusted to Kelly's absence, though she spoke of her often during pretend play and moments of longing for her.

A year later, Kelly's family was transferred back to Tamika's town. Their families by surprise one Sunday encountered each other when they brought Kelly and Tamika to Sunday school. The two, then almost four years old, embraced and hugged, laughed and jumped up and down for several moments, each surprised and thrilled to see the other. They played gleefully together during Sunday school, and when departure time arrived, cried with intense emotion upon separation. The promise from both parents that they would see each other frequently was of little com-fort. They wanted to be together *now*. As they enter prekindergarten, their attachment behaviors will remain quite strong, though each will gradually learn to take those venturing steps briefly away from the secure base of their mutual attachment and into other relationships. Both par-ents and teachers will want to be sensitive to this special relationship while assisting both Tamika and Kelly in forging new friendships, learn-ing as they go that, for as long as they want it to, their special bond can continue.

### Temperament

Individual temperaments can be divided into three major types: *easy, diffi-cult*, and *slow-to-warm-up* (Chess & Thomas, 1987). These temperaments have a set of characteristics that determine the manner in which an indi-vidual child responds to others. *Easy* children, for instance, are usually easy-going and even-tempered, can tolerate change, and are playful and eas-ily comforted when upset. They eat and sleep with regularity, and overall, display positive moods. *Difficult* children, on the other hand, have diffi-culty with eating and sleeping routines, tend to be irritable, appear to derive less pleasure from play activities, have difficulty adjusting to changes in routines or caregivers, cry more often, and express greater intensity of emo-tions. *Slow-to-warm-up* children display relatively mild positive and nega-tive reactions, resist new situations and people, are often moody and less adaptable, and may resist displays of affection such as cuddling or holding hands. There is some indication that temperament types are genetically determined (Chess & Thomas, 1987).

Temperament influences human relationships at all ages. Professional early childhood caregivers and educators are sensitive to individual tem-perament characteristics. They recognize that temperament influences the manner in which children relate to others. Early childhood professionals know that child behaviors and adult behaviors reciprocally affect each other. They strive to find in themselves what Chess and Thomas refer to as "goodness of fit" in which the personalities of the adult and child can be in accord. This may mean, for example, altering first inclinations to respond and thinking carefully about the needs of the individual child. Often, acting on first inclinations results in negative feedback or inappropriate guidance. For example, inappropriate responses might include insisting that a slow-to-warm-up child join an activity such as role playing or speaking in front of the group on the assumption that such experience will encourage the child, when indeed, such a practice can only exacerbate the child's reticence. Inappropriate responses also include falling into patterns of over-responding and overcorrecting the behaviors of a difficult child or perhaps failing to provide sufficient interactions and support for the easy child. (Someone once admonished, "It is easy to *impose* on a content and compliant child.")

### Self-Concept and Self-Esteem

Self-concept is the summary definition a person devises of oneself; it represents an awareness of self as a separate and unique individual. Self-concepts emerge during infancy and follow a series of steps during early childhood leading to positive or negative self-regard:

1. *Self-awareness* begins in infancy and is marked by the infant's growing awareness that she is distinctly separate and apart from others and objects she may be grasping. Later, during the toddler period, the child's attempts to be independent are ambivalent at best, struggling between emerging and conflicting needs for dependence and independence. Adults are challenged to find a balance between encouraging independence and allowing continued dependence, such as allowing toddlers to make choices where possible (not whether to wear a sweater on a cool day, but "which sweater shall you wear—the red one or the blue one?"). Appropriate toilet-learning experiences (encouraging and affirming, rather than rushed, anxious, and punishing) promote healthy self and body awareness, as well as confidence in managing personal needs.

2. *Self-recognition* is the ability to hold a mental image of oneself. This ability emerges around eighteen months to two years of age. It is marked by the ability to recognize one's reflection in a mirror or one's picture in a photograph.

3. *Self-definition* emerges as children use language to describe themselves: "I am big." and "I can do it!" and "Watch me run fast." Responding affirmatively to children's attempts to describe themselves conveys acceptance and respect and encourages the development of a positive self-image.

4. *Self-esteem* is derived from the self-evaluations children develop from their interactions with others. These self-evaluations include children's notions about their own physical attributes, gender, race, family, friends and cognitive and social abilities. The child's own

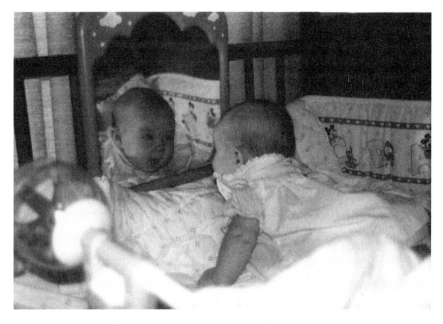

*Recognition of oneself in a mirror signals emerging self-awareness.*

authentic accomplishments are also an integral part of self-esteem. When children feel loved, valued, respected, and competent, they develop positive self-regard.

Self-evaluations continue to occur as children experience a variety of interactions in many contexts beyond the home. Self-concepts and self-esteem are modified (positively or negatively) as children experience successes or failures in these interactions. When successes are more prevalent than failures, self-esteem and a sense of competence and confidence become well established. Well-established self-esteem is not as readily shaken in the face of challenges or setbacks. On the other hand, children who have experienced too many failures, reprimands, or embarrassments develop very fragile and vulnerable self-evaluations. The role of the caregiver and teacher is clear. Provide positive, authentic, self-affirming feedback to young children. Match expectations and tasks to individual capabilities and facilitate success.

## Social Development

Social development begins at birth and emerges from the interactions that infants and young children experience in their homes and later in a variety of out-of-home contexts. Social development is an emerging process through which children learn about self and others and about making and maintaining friends. Social development is influenced by a number of socializing agents and affiliations: home and family, extended family members, faith-based organizations, child-care and education settings, playmates and peers, neighbors, and the media. Children themselves play a role in their own socialization. Individual attachment behaviors, temperament, and sometimes health and disability issues influence the types of interactions children initiate and the friendships they pursue.

Just as there are stages in learning about the self, there are, as well, stages in learning about others, their emotions intentions, and points of view. (Hoffman, 1988). Young children tend to have egocentric perspectives, assuming that others perceive events and situations the same as they do. With guidance that teaches, children can gradually become aware of the perspectives of others, learning that there can be many different points of view.

### Social Conventional Knowledge

Another aspect of social development is the acquisition of social conventional knowledge. Social conventional knowledge includes learning about the conventions (or the do's and don'ts) of one's culture, including its language, inflections, expressions, and its code of conduct and manners. Social conventions are learned from others; they are taught rather than mentally constructed, as with the acquisition of physical or logical-mathematical knowledge (Piaget, 1952). Children learn social conventions through repetition, reminders, and observation and imitation of others (Waite-Stupiansky, 1997).

While social conventional learning is essential, unless children also acquire deeper levels of understanding regarding the reasons for social rules, their respect for them will be superficial at best. Their social conventional behaviors will rely on continual reminders, rewards, and punishments, rather than on internalized understanding of the importance of the rules (Waite-Stupiansky, 1997). Children who understand reasons for rules interact with others in ways that are referred to as prosocial.

### Prosocial Development

An important aspect of social development is the ability to interact with others in a prosocial manner. Prosocial behaviors include **empathy** (ability to recognize the feelings of others and to vicariously experience those feelings) and **altruism** (intent to help another without expectation of reward). These abilities are dependent on level of cognition, egocentrism and perspective-taking ability, temperament and individual personality, as well as learned social interaction skills. Studies have shown that when children observe and experience adults interacting in kind and prosocial ways, they are more inclined to use prosocial strategies in their own interactions with others. This is particularly true when the role model is someone with whom the child has a warm relationship (Kontos & Wilcox-Herzog, 1997).

**empathy** ability to vicariously experience the feelings of others.

**altruism** helpfulness without the expectation of recognition or reward.

## Moral Development

Widely accepted theories of moral development are those of Jean Piaget (1932/1965) and Lawrence Kohlberg (1984). In Piaget's theory of moral development, children below the age of six are said to be in a **premoral** stage of development due to their limited understanding of rules and the reasons for them. Their play behaviors may impose rules from time to time, but these rules are momentary and usually arbitrary and unilateral, not carrying over to another activity. In fact, rules change frequently as children play together. Reasons for rules are not yet of great importance to them.

**premoral** earliest stage of moral development in which the child is unaware of moral rules or values.

When children enter the stage of **moral realism**, they become more rule bound and believe that rules are established by some all-knowing authority figure and are therefore unalterable. Children during this stage also believe that others perceive the rules as they do. Behavior is judged to be right or wrong on the basis of the consequences associated with it.

**moral realism** morality that focuses on rules and consequences with little regard or understanding of intentions.

During this stage of morality children are unable to take into consideration the intentions of others and often perceive unintentional acts as personal affronts. Lacking a reasoned sense of justice, young children perceive any deed that is punished as wrong, regardless of the appropriateness or fairness of the punishment. Often during this stage, children associate their own misdeeds with some later misfortune; for instance, the departure of a parent during separation or divorce is often perceived by the child as a result of some recent event in which he or she was reprimanded or punished by the parent.

Kohlberg's description of the premoral stage is quite similar to that of Piaget's. Kohlberg refers to this level of morality as *obedience oriented*; he believed that at this stage the child does not yet have a conscience. Moral behaviors in children are oriented toward avoiding punishment through blind deference to a more superior power. In Kohlberg's theory the premoral stage is also characterized by a second stage, that of *naive instrumental hedonism* in which children view behaviors that are right to be those that satisfy their own needs and occasionally the needs of others. Kohlberg's third stage of moral development, which he referred to as *morality of conventional role conformity*, is one in which children are learning social conventions and want to please others. At this level, understanding of intentions emerges. Kohlberg's fourth stage of moral development, *authority-maintaining morality*, is one in which the child's behaviors are oriented toward maintenance of the social order. Showing respect for authority and doing one's duty become important motivations for behavior. Kohlberg's last stages of moral development involve *postconventional moral thinking*, which includes the ability to consider intentions and mitigating circumstances in resolving moral dilemmas through a morality that is based on personal convictions and a conscience.

As we shall see in chapter 8 where we discuss the important goals of guidance, moral development has origins in intellectual development, social cognition, early socialization, and feedback resulting from prosocial behaviors. Recent theories of moral development are concerned with the manner in which young children construct moral meaning from their experiences (DeVries & Zan, 1994, 1995; Sylwester, 2000a, 2000b) and develop skills in taking the perspectives of others (Kohn, 1996).

## Psychosocial Theory and the Development of a Healthy Personality

Erik Erikson, a noted psychoanalyst, set forth a *psychosocial theory* in which he proposed that personality development follows a genetically preprogrammed sequence (Figure 3–2). Erikson placed considerable emphasis on the role of family, culture, and society in the development of an individual's personality. He recognized that the social environment in which children grow, develop, and learn can influence appreciably the outcomes of personality development. Erikson's theory outlines a series of eight psychosocial oppositional crises marking critical periods of development in which one must be resolved in favorable ratio to the other. Erikson proposed that these critical steps constitute turning points in human personality development in which progress or regression occurs and integration of favorable resolutions of the crises into one's personality lead to human strength. Figure 3–2 illustrates Erikson's theory. The first four of these stages are described in chapter 8 as we determine the types of interactions and guidance that support healthy personality development and social and moral competence.

Integrity vs. Despair

Generativity vs. Self-Absorption

Intimacy and Solidarity vs. Isolation

Identity and Repudiation vs. Identity Diffusion

Industry vs. Inferiority

Initiative vs. Guilt

Autonomy vs. Shame and Doubt

Trust vs. Mistrust

**FIGURE 3–2**
*Erickson's Stages of Healthy Personality Development*

**BIOGRAPHY BOX** *Erik Erikson*

Erik Erikson was born to Danish parents in Frankfurt, Germany, in 1902. His father died while he was still an infant, and his mother's second husband adopted him.

In Vienna, Erik Erikson's training prior to becoming interested in psychoanalysis was in fine arts. During the late 1920s, he was an aspiring artist, often earning extra money by private portrait painting. He first entered teaching in a small American school in Vienna where he studied under Anna Freud at the Vienna Psychoanalytic Institute. He was also influenced by his acquaintance, Anna's father, Sigmund Freud. Interestingly, Erikson received a Montessori teaching certificate, making him one of very few men to be so credentialed. He married an American artist and occupational therapist. In

1933, Erikson was invited to lecture in Boston, which he did for two years, prior to accepting a position as a Research Fellow in Psychology in the department of neuropsychiatry at the Harvard Medical School. After a few years, he accepted a position at the Institute of Human Relations and the Yale School of Medicine. He also held positions at the San Francisco Psychoanalytic Institute, the University of California, and the Menninger Foundation in Topeka, Kansas. His book, *Childhood and Society* (1950), described his psychosocial theory of development, which proposed that while maturation influences the onset of different stages of development, it is the demands of society that exert very powerful personality-shaping forces. He presented his now well-known theory at the Mid-Century White House Conference on Children in 1950. He died in 1994.

Erikson's theory has important implications for early childhood education. It suggests that earliest experiences and interactions with those most important to the infant and child play a critical role in the psychological health and well-being of the older child, adolescent, and adult. The extent to which trust, autonomy, initiative, industry, and so on are allowed to flourish during their predictable time periods determines the extent to which there will be positive outcomes in psychosocial development over the years.

### Cognitive, Language, and Literacy Development

Cognitive development refers to that aspect of growth and development that deals with perception, attention, thinking, memory, problem solving, creativity, and language. It influences and is influenced by other areas of human growth and development—neurological, physical/motor, emotional, social, moral, language, and literacy. From infancy forward, cognitive abilities change and are influenced by (1) increasingly more complex interactions between an individual and the environment, (2) greater language facility, and (3) acquisition of knowledge through literate behaviors.

*Jean Piaget (1896–1980)*

The most familiar theory of cognitive development is that of Swiss psychologist Jean Piaget (1936/1952). Piaget described cognitive development as occurring when individuals interact with people and objects in their environment, and through these interactions construct mental **schemata** (or schemes). Schemata and other cognitive structures are created through two intellectual processes, organization and adaptation. Piaget believed that children are continually mentally organizing schemata into higher-order mental structures and adapting or adjusting them to the demands of the environment. Adaptation occurs through two mental processes—**assimilation** and **accommodation**. Through assimilation, the child attempts to make sense of new information on the basis of existing schema. For example, when infants are weaned from breast-feeding to bottle-feeding, their schema for taking in food (breast-feeding) must assimilate a new experience relating to taking in food from a bottle, which then imposes a need for adaptation in order to achieve success in bottle-feeding. When a new experience is particularly unusual, the learner must modify existing schema in such a way that they are compatible with the new input. For example, an infant is exposed for the first time to a large stuffed animal. She may attempt to grasp it with one hand, a schema that exists from

**schemata mental** structures or categories of perceptions and experiences.

**assimilation** process of incorporating new motor or conceptual learning into existing schemata.

**accommodation** process by which ways of thinking (schemata) are modified to conform to new information.

---

**BIOGRAPHY BOX** *Jean Piaget*

Jean Piaget was born in Neuchatel, Switzerland. He was a very bright child who published his first work at age ten. It was a one-page paper on the albino sparrow. He wrote and published numerous works throughout his schooling, which mostly realted to his interest in biology. In graduate studies at the University of Neuchatel, he studied the behavior of mollusks and wrote his dissertation on that topic. He was particularly interested in the interactions of the mollusks and other organisms with their environments. A prolific reader, he read in the fields of philosophy, religion, sociology, biology, and psychology. He combined his interest in biology with psychology and became interested in the relationship of biology to learning. He studied his own three children, observing their behavior and keeping copious notes. He conducted experiments with them and developed interview techniques to ascertain their intellectual capabilities throughout their growing years. Piaget trained and worked with Alfred Binet in France and helped establish norms for Binet's intelligence testing. In doing this work, he became intrigued, not with the number of correct answers which was his task to tally, but with the types of errors children made on the test. This aroused his curiosity about the development of intelligence and suggested to him that there must be a sequential pattern to cognitive development. Though his studies and works were prolific at the turn of the century, his theory was not recognized in the United States until the 1950s. Piaget died in 1980.

previous experience with rattle toys. This one-hand grasp does not work with the larger toy, so the child must alter the schema to accommodate grasping using both hands. Piaget demonstrated that through these processes, young children *construct* knowledge. Piaget outlined a series of sequential stages of cognitive development (Table 3–2).

In the first stage of Piaget's sequence, infants are said to be in the *sensori-motor* period, which extends from birth to the onset of gestures and language at around the age of two. Cognitive development is an outgrowth of early reflex behaviors, a neurologically controlled phenomenon. In just a few months, these reflex behaviors develop into more sophisticated sensory and motor activity. Inadvertent consequences of early responses to sensory stim-

## TABLE 3–2

*Piaget's Stages of Cognitive Devlopment*

| Stages/Ages | Characterictics | Role of Adults |
| --- | --- | --- |
| Birth to 2 years Sensorimotor period | Responds to reflex activity, becoming gradually more coordinated; intentionally repeated behaviors and actions; development of a sense of object permanence; development of mental schemas; imitative behaviors. | Respond to and enhance the infant's sensory experiences of touch, taste, sight, sound, and smell; provide sensory-rich toys and experiences; provide safe and sanitary toys and objects to hold and manipulate; talk to infant. |
| 2 to 7 years Period of pre-operational thought | Egocentric, perception-bound thinking; emerging language system; rich imagination; performs simple mental operations, but has difficulty explaining them. | Provide toys and props to support imaginative and sociodramatic play; provide raw materials such as crayons, paper, glue; engage in a variety of musical experiences; listening, singing, dancing, responding in a variety of ways; allow for experimentation. |
| 7 to 11 years Concrete operational thinking | Can solve concrete problems with physical objects; thought is reversible; thinking is based on prior experience; ability to mentally conserve emerges; beginnings of simple logic. | Provide opportunity to pursue areas of interest; help obtain materials, particularly in special interest or talent areas; share interests in school and other activities and accomplishments. |
| 11 years to adulthood Formal operational thinking | Formulates and tests hypotheses, can think abstractly; uses deductive reasoning; employs more logic. | Challenge with hypothetical problems to solve; discuss ethical issues; encourage and support personal responsibility. |

uli and uncoordinated movements lead the infant to repeat them in search of the same outcome. For instance, five-month-old Christa was kicking playfully in her crib. Inadvertently, she noticed that the yellow birds on the mobile over her were moving and shaking. Lying quite still, her eyes fixated on the birds until they no longer wiggled. When she moved again, she noticed that the birds on the mobile also moved. Thereafter, she kicked purposefully to make the birds wiggle. In this process, Christa established a mental scheme (a moving object) that she assimilated into her existing scheme (kicking) and then accommodated to this new information by purposefully kicking to make the birds move. This mental process allows the child to organize and think about her actions and experiences. Another major cognitive development during infancy, according to Piaget, is that of **object permanence**, in which the child comes to know that objects or people exist though they may not be visible or detected through other senses. When a toy is hidden under a blanket, it is searched for by the infant. Prior to object permanence, infants do not seek the missing toy.

Children between the ages of two and seven are in the **preoperational** period of cognitive development. This period is characterized by the acquisition of representational skills: mental imagery, language, and drawing. The child can use words, concepts, mental images, signs, and symbolism to construct and convey meaning. An example of early symbolism is demonstrated in pretend play and miming actions. The use of a block to symbolize a truck during pretend play is an example of symbolic behavior. Language development is particularly rapid during this period.

Piaget described the child's thinking processes during the preoperational stage as *egocentric*. The child has difficulty understanding other points of view or another perspective. Also, at this stage, the child's logic is limited because he cannot think backwards or mentally reverse the steps of a task from the end to the beginning. For instance, a child may be shown two rows of five coins each. The coins are spaced the same distance apart on each row. Then the child observes as the coins are spread wider apart on one of the rows. When asked which row has more coins, the preoperational child will point to the longer of the two rows. The child's inability to reverse to the beginning of the activity where the rows were the same in length prevents her from understanding that both rows have the same number of coins. Piaget called the ability to think backward **reversibility**, a mental operation that does not emerge until the next stage.

Children between the ages of seven and eleven move into the period of **concrete operations**. At this point children can take other points of view; they realize that objects can be changed or transformed (as with the rows of coins) and still conserve their original size, quantity, length, mass, volume, weight, or other attribute, and they recognize that such changes can be reversed. Piaget referred to this cognitive ability as **conservation**.

During the concrete operations stage, children are able to **classify** or group objects into defining or descriptive categories, at first relying on a

**object permanence** the realization that objects and people exist even though they cannot be seen or heard.

**preoperational thought** the stage of cognitive development between ages two and seven in which the child has mental structures for sensorimotor actions but cannot engage in operational or logical thinking.

**reversibility** ability to reverse thinking and to return to an original or beginning point.

**concrete operations** ability to think logically only when problems that are posed can be visualized or considered in concrete terms.

**conservation** the concept that physical attributes (mass, weight, shape, configuration) stay the same even when the appearance changes.

**classification** ability to focus on one or more attributes of objects and group them according to various categories (color, shape, texture, etc.).

single characteristic, such as color (all objects that are red), then using additional characteristics, such as shape and color (all red triangles). More advanced classification skills include the ability to create or recognize classes that fit into each other—for instance, a dog and a cat each represent a different class, but both fit into a class known as animals. Later, they may learn classes of animals, such as farm, jungle, pets, and so on.

Another cognitive skill emerging during the period of concrete operations is that of **seriation**, or the ability to arrange objects, colors, and weights in orderly fashion—smallest to largest, lightest to darkest, heaviest to lightest, and so on. With the ability to seriate, children are able to develop concepts of before, after, and between (also greater than and less than) and understand simple graphs, such as a birthday graph on which classmates' birthdays are charted for most and least in each month.

**seriation** ability to arrange objects or events in sequential order according to selected attributes (large to small, first to last, and so on).

Piaget's theory of cognitive development has had an enormous impact on thought and practice in philosophy, psychology, and education for almost half a century. He taught that young children do not think like older children and adults. He taught that by observing carefully and paying attention to the ways children think and solve problems, adults gain a greater understanding of the child's understanding. He taught that from this vantage point, educators are better able to provide learning environments and instruction that match children's emerging cognitive abilities. From Piaget, educators learn that children can be trusted to learn many things on their own when adults provide appropriately challenging opportunities, materials, and interactions. Educators now recognize that learners construct their understandings from meaningful interactions with objects and people.

• Cognitive abilities of children with sensory and motor impairments

In recent years scholars have challenged various aspects of Piaget's theory. Of particular interest are recent studies of children who are visually, auditorally, or motorically impaired. By comparing the cognitive abilities of these children to Piaget's stages of cognitive development, neo-Piagetians have argued that in spite of such difficulties, cognitive development proceeds nonetheless (Bebko, Burke, Craven, & Sarlo, 1992). These studies suggest that often infants form concepts earlier than Piaget proposed. It is believed that children with visual, auditory, and motor disabilities construct meaning from their perceptual experiences and the mental imagery that they are able to form, rather than through their sensory capabilities, as Piaget's theories assert.

• Language as integral to cognitive development

The work of Russian psychologist Lev Vygotsky (1934/1986) focused on children's ability to acquire concepts. While Piaget portrayed young children as developing concepts mostly through their own actions, Vygotsky believed that cognitive development was much more dependent

## BIOGRAPHY BOX *Lev Vygotsky (1896-1934)*

Born to a Russian Jewish middle-class family, Vygotsky was one of eight children. As a child, he was thought to be precocious, and indeed, in his short life of thirty-seven years he became a highly respected scholar and prolific writer in the fields of psychology and education. Because universities in Russia allowed only 3 percent of their populations to be Jewish, enrollees were selected by lottery (not merit). Fortunately, Vygotsky was allowed to pursue a college education at Moscow University. He lived and worked for most of his career as a psychologist, theorist, and researcher at Moscow's Psychological Institute. Having suffered from tuberculosis for many years, in 1931, Vygotsky became quite ill. Sensing that he had not long to live, he worked frantically over the next three years to complete projects and to write as much as he could. It is reported that Vygotsky even dictated from his death bed the last chapter of one of his most important works, *Thought and Language* (1934) which was published shortly after his death (Berk & Winsler, 1995).

Photo courtesy of the Archives of History of American Psychology, University of Akron, Akron, Ohio 44325-4302.

on important people in the child's life. He stressed that a child's culture determines what and how the child learns; the culture guides and supports learning along culturally unique pathways. He also proposed that adults and older children serve as teachers and tutors, and as such, provide assistance that he referred to as **scaffolding**. Through interactions with others, children observe and become familiar with objects and their labels. Vygotsky demonstrated that children who are provided words and labels form concepts more readily than children who were not provided words and labels.

Vygotsky gave major importance to language. He believed that thought and language eventually converge into meaning, particularly in those cultures where verbal interactions are important. He proposed that dialogue with others is transformed by the child into **inner speech** (or private speech), which leads to thinking. One often sees young children mouthing as though talking to themselves. Vygotsky considered this an external indication of inner speech that is directing the child's thought. Children and adults rely on inner speech to help them think. Language allows one to communicate more precisely to formulate and express ideas, and to ask questions.

**scaffolding** a changing quality of assistance provided by a skilled partner (peer or adult) in which help is adjusted to less and less as the learner gains competence and autonomy.

**inner speech (or private speech)** silent, inner verbal thought; speech to oneself that directs behavior and assists understanding.

• Brain-based learning and teaching

Brain-based learning has been advocated by scholars Renate and Geoffrey Caine (1994, 1997). In their theory, these scholars distinguish between the types of knowledge and skills learners needed during the Industrial Age and those that are now needed in a more complex and global information age. They argue that rapid change in society and around the globe render traditional approaches to teaching and learning insufficient.

Instead of viewing learners as "absorbers" of information, the scholars describe learners as dynamically interacting with information. Teachers are described not as deliverers of knowledge, but as facilitators and knowledgeable guides who invite interest and engage students in the process of learning. These scholars acknowledge the brain's unlimited capacity to memorize meaningless information often required in traditional ways of teaching, but they also assert that the brain has a need to place memories and experience into meaningful wholes. Hence, they argue that learning is most successful when it is embedded in rich and meaningful contexts. They see the need to fit skills and content to the learner, rather than the traditional approach of fitting the learner to preselected curricula.

**downshifting** a psychophysiological response to education expectations that the learner deems meaningless or threatening, resulting in less sophisticated use of the brain.

Through their research, Caine and Caine have promoted the concept of downshifting. **Downshifting** is a psychophysiological response to threat associated with learner fatigue and perceived helplessness. Downshifted learners do not use effectively their capacities for creative thought and higher-order thinking, and under stress revert to previously learned behaviors and a sense of helplessness. Downshifting mitigates against creativity, problem solving, exploring options, and thinking about outcomes. The authors suggest that the brain can become "hard wired" to this less competent way of thinking and learning, a prospect that could diminish interest and success and lead to disinterest in school. Caine and Caine's concept of downshifting has implications for early childhood educators as they plan developmentally appropriate experiences for young children. Children need not be presented with tasks meant for older children or isolated bits and pieces of information presented out of meaningful contexts from which children can form associations and meaning. Developmentally inappropriate expectations can cause feelings of helplessness, then downshifting, which is consequently followed by less effort and diminished enthusiasm for learning.

- Contextualized learning

**ecological systems theory** a theory emphasizing the concept that a variety of social and cultural systems influence the development of the child.

Another perspective on learning is that of contextualized learning. Early childhood professionals know that young children learn in all types of contexts and through an infinite number of interactions with others. Since cognitive development is viewed as an ongoing interactive process between the individual and the environment, contextualistic theories provide comprehensive perspectives on social, cultural, and political influences on growth, development, and learning. Bronfenbrenner's **ecological systems theory** (described in chapter 9) delineates the cultural and social contexts that influence and are influenced by the child (Bronfenbrenner, 1979, 1986, 1989). Bronfenbrenner asserts that cognitive development continually changes as does the contexts in which it occurs. As children move from the inner circle of the family to ever-widening circles that include neighbors, peer groups, schools, and faith-based organizations, and as families rely on and participate in services, support systems, community agencies, and the workplace, a complex array of social and political influences begin to have an influence on child development outcomes. Cognitive development, then, is seen as having multiple influences. Bronfenbrenner also points out that from this multiplicity of influences, child growth and development proceeds in varied directions and in all developmental domains simultaneously.

- Individual intellectual strengths

Traditional ways of identifying children with intellectual strengths (or more popularly referred to as "gifted" children) have relied on Intelligence Quotient (IQ) tests and achievement tests. The use of these tests has historically been based on a limited view of what it is that constitutes human intelligence. Traditional beliefs have held that intelligence exists in every individual, but to greater or lesser extent depending on genetically predetermined characteristics, and that intelligence can be measured by standardized tests.

As you will learn in chapter 4, such assumptions are no longer tenable, and though still widely used, standardized IQ tests have fallen from grace in recent years as experts have learned more about human brain development, the complexity and uniqueness of each child's life context(s), and the importance of appropriate experiences during specific developmental windows of opportunity (Bronfenbrenner, 1986; Shonkoff & Phillips, 2000).

A significant challenge to the IQ concept is found in the scholarship of Howard Gardner (1983, 1993, 1998, 1999). Gardner's theory of *multiple intelligences* proposes that individuals learn and perform through a number of intelligences that reach well beyond the types of information measured by traditional IQ tests. By defining intelligence as ". . . the ability to solve problems or to fashion products that are valued in one or more cultural or community settings" (1993, p. 7), Gardner has sought to illustrate that individuals have different human skills, cognitive strengths, and learning styles. Each of us develops through a biopsychological process combined with cultural influences, a unique intelligences profile. Initially, Gardner and his research colleagues explored and identified seven intelligences that could be found in lesser or greater degrees in individual intelligences profiles. Each type of intelligence could be described with its own defining characteristics:

- Linguistic
- Musical
- Logico-Mathematical
- Spatial
- Bodily-Kinesthetic
- Interpersonal
- Intrapersonal

Gardner's continuing explorations into this topic have led to elaborations and revisions to his MI theory and has suggested other intelligences: naturalist, spiritual, and existential (Gardner, 1999). Of these three, Gardner proposes that individuals who had a proclivity toward the natural order of animal and plant life and the ecology that influences that life (the naturalists) could not readily be classified in terms of any of the other types of intelligences he previously defined.

Perhaps it is helpful to describe how these types of intelligences are characterized and how they are expressed in the behaviors and accomplishments of individuals. These descriptions suggest to educators a need for deeper, more broadly based curricula than is common, and divergent teaching strategies to tap the strengths of all students. Further, as you explore these brief descriptions, it should arouse curiosity about how to best assess the accomplishments and potential of each child.

*Linguistic intelligence* is the ability to use written and spoken words effectively. Linguistically talented children listen intently to the words of others and mimic unusual words, forming unique phrases and sentences. This is demonstrated by thirty-month-old Mavis's use of a word mimicked from adults but used in proper context. Having been reprimanded for some misdeed, Mavis said angrily to her mother, "You are not being 'dispectful.'" Two-year-old Jacob, after having bitten another child, replied, "My angry is up," and six-year-old Andy requested a book on the Greek alphabet in the school library. Others play games with words and expressions and derive enjoyment from their own creations, which may include acts of rhyming sentences or creating streams of words, attempting tongue twisters and, in older children, using puns and riddles. Linguistically talented children may also spin tall tales and play out unusually elaborate sociodramatic scenarios in which verbal creativity is noticeable. These children are creative and expressive writers and usually have good memory for names and places. They ask lots of questions and enjoy extended conversations. Poets, orators, politicians, commentators, authors, and literary critics are said to have linguistic intelligence.

*Musical intelligence* is characterized by an unusual ability to respond to rhythm, pitch, melody, and qualities of tone. Gardner proposes that during infancy, normal children sing as well as babble, emitting sounds, prosodic patterns, and tones, and imitate patterns and tones sung by others with "better than random accuracy" (Gardner, 1983, p. 108). At about age two, children begin to spontaneously invent songs and to produce small sections of familiar songs such as "EI-EI-O . . . he ruled the others with his quack, quack, quack." Another example of this type of behavior is demonstrated by Mavis the day after attending a baseball game with her father. She was heard singing repetitively her recollection of the song "Take Me Out to the Ball Game." Her version was an exact replication of the melody but with one exception. She began with both the second word and the second note, with more than due accent on "me", as in "*Me* out to the ball game . . . *Me* out to the ball game . . . *Me* out to the ball game." Children with musical proclivities enjoy singing; they pick up on words and melodies readily; they often hum or chant to themselves; and they are sensitive to environmental sounds. Remember Jason at the beginning of this chapter? Could it be that he is exhibiting musical intelligence? Refer back to the window of opportunity for the development of musical abilities. What implications can be drawn for Jason? Song writers, composers, music producers, choral and orchestra conductors, band leaders, choreographers, and the like exhibit this type of intelligence.

*Logico-mathematical intelligence* is the ability to sort and classify, reason, form logical patterns and relationships, develop hypotheses, infer, calculate, and use numbers effectively. Scientists, mathematicians, logicians, and computer programmers exhibit this type of intelligence. Children who exhibit logico-mathematical intelligence ask many questions about how things work; enjoy activities involving counting, grouping, and classifying; have a good sense of cause and effect; enjoy "what if" and "if/then" queries; and enjoy hearing "logical nonsense." For example, Andy, at age six, visited a college campus and was told that there was an elevator in one of the buildings that people could walk *through*. Overtly skeptical, yet curious, he asked to see the elevator. The professor escorted Andy to the building housing the elevator, located it, punched the button for it, and when it arrived a door opened exposing another door on the opposite side opening simultaneously to the outside of the building. The professor led Andy *through* the elevator, and they exited outdoors. Andy, still skeptical but wide eyed, expressed amazement as he exited the two-door elevator. He laughed an incredulous and gleeful laugh and then asked to walk back *through* the elevator. Andy enjoyed having his prior assumptions challenged.

*Spatial intelligence* is the ability to accurately perceive the visual-spatial world. With this intelligence, children are sensitive to line, color, shape, and form and can visualize spatial configurations and ideas. Interior designers, architects, anthropologists, and track and field athletes are examples of individuals who demonstrate spatial intelligence. Children demonstrate this type of intelligence through a keen sense of direction and often attempt to supply directions. Though the child's mental image may be accurate (or fairly so), the directions themselves may not be all that clear, as in "It is over there by that great big tree out there across the street from that park; you know, where we had that picnic that day not too far from my Grandmother's house; I can show you there." Children with spatial intelligence particularly enjoy block building and art. At age five, Dominic produced unusually detailed depictions of comic book characters that included meticulously detailed, proportional, and colorful features. With deep involvement and concentration, he drew and colored his pictures until they were just right. Then, an amazing activity would follow. He would turn the drawing over to the blank back side of the paper and proceed to create the backside of the character just drawn on the front of his paper with the same meticulous detail and identical color scheme. Later, with scissors, he cut out his characters that then had both a colorful, detailed front and back side. Children with spatial intelligence are as intrigued by pictures in storybooks as they are with the print.

*Bodily-kinesthetic intelligence* is characterized by refined large- and fine-motor coordinations, balance, agility, strength, speed, dexterity, and portrayal of ideas and feelings through whole body expression. Swimmers, tennis players, dancers, mimes, instrumentalists, surgeons, and mechanics are examples of this type of intelligence. Children with strengths in this area enjoy moving interpretively to music, accepting the challenge of the balance beam playing roles, leading finger plays, skipping and marching, following-the-leader activities, and attempting obstacle courses. These children are inclined to fidget, rock, tap fingers, clap hands and are generally a bit more "wiggly" than others.

*Intrapersonal intelligence* is demonstrated through keen self-awareness that includes the ability to adapt thinking and behavior on the basis of an accurate picture of oneself, including one's strengths, limitations, moods, motivations, temperaments, desires, and intentions. Children with this faculty have a strong sense of self-esteem and self-discipline. These individuals are very much in tune with their own feelings and can accurately verbalize them. Children demonstrate intrapersonal intelligence when they display autonomy and conviction. They usually have a good sense of their strengths and weaknesses and match aspirations to capabilities. Playing alone, enjoying hobbies, and studying independently are also characteristic. These children are typically introspective. Religious leaders, school counselors, child psychologists, and psychotherapists exhibit this type of intelligence.

*Interpersonal intelligence* is the ability to take the perspectives of others and perceive others' moods, intentions, motivations, and feelings.

*Refined large and small motor coordinations are characteristics of bodily-kinesthetic intelligence.*

This type of intelligence includes sensitivity and effective responses to facial expressions, tone of voice, and body language. Children with interpersonal intelligence enjoy socializing with other children, have close friends, are usually sought out as playmates, have exceptional abilities to work out conflicts with others, and are receptive to guidance in social interactions. They are willing helpers and seek to assist classmates having difficulties. Counselors, ministers, teachers, and persons in positions of leadership often demonstrate interpersonal intelligence.

*Naturalistic intelligence* is the ability to recognize important distinctions in the natural world among plants and animals, which typically include differentiating between ecological, geographic, topological, and anthropological characteristics; natural phenomena and changes over time that affect the life and growth of plants and animals; and enhance or impede the capacities of the human organism. Anthropologists, biologists, botanists, and various persons in farming and hunting cultures exhibit this type of intelligence.

With the identification of these intelligences, Gardner recommends that teachers become "student-curriculum brokers" who design learning experiences that relate to individual children and their interests, needs, and special capabilities (Shores, 1995). By observing children in naturalistic contexts, noting carefully each child's natural behaviors and interests in the classroom, on the playground, at lunchtime, and in other contexts, adults are better able to determine individual intellectual strengths. Assessments derived from focused, naturalistic observations provide far more usable information for planning for individual children than do the scores from IQ or achievement tests. Through naturalistic observations and authentic forms of assessment (described in chapter 4), early childhood professionals find that children exhibit strengths in one or more of the eight types of intelligences and that the different intelligences often influence and support the others.

## Language Development

Children acquire language at an amazing rate. It is thought that young children learn and remember an average of nine words a day from the onset of speech until age six, so that by the time a child is age six or seven years he or she has acquired a vocabulary of approximately 14,000(!) words (Clark, 1983; Templin, 1957). Young children are able to use this ever-increasing vocabulary to form meaningful communications. When asked, "Where is your daddy?" three-year-old Mavis answers, "My daddy . . . my daddy . . . well . . . he's at the college." Mavis demonstrates not only that she understands the social give-and-take of conversation but also that she can form coherent and meaningful sentences and participate in meaningful and satisfying dialogue with other persons.

From early infancy, language is learned through social interactions with others and through many opportunities to hear and experiment with sounds and words. In addition, young children form their own grammars based on the sense they are able to derive from the spoken word. For instance, should Mavis have said, "My daddy goed to the college," which could just as well have been her answer, she would be demonstrating that she is constructing an understanding of past tense.

Infants begin acquiring language during their first few months, long before they can say their first words. There is some indication that infants are particularly responsive to **child-directed speech.** This is often referred to as "motherese" and "fatherese" speech, which is characterized by unique intonations and rhythms as parents talk with their very young children. Motherese generally involves asking questions such as "What is that you see?" or "Do you see your teddy bear?" or "Where are your toes?" Later, it becomes "Where did you put your shoes?" and "Do you remember Sally? You played with her at Jared's birthday party?" and even "What do you think we can do about that?"

Fatherese has not been studied to the extent that motherese has, but it is typically more playful, incorporating more commands and eliciting more sophisticated language from the young child (Genishi & Dyson, 1984; Lamb, 1977; Masur & Gleason, 1980). Studies have found that children who experience motherese and fatherese in which questions are frequently posed, nonverbal and verbal responses are acknowledged and accepted, and interactions convey that child's utterances are meaningful develop language more rapidly than others (Rutter, Thorp, & Golding 2000; White, 1985). This has implications for caregivers and teachers of infants, toddlers, and young children, who can employ the same interactive strategies to encourage language development.

The language of young children is generally characterized by these patterns of emergence:

Crying
Gurgling and cooing
Laughing aloud
Experimental vocalizations
Social vocalizations
Chuckles
Babbling
Echolalia ("ma-ma-ma-ma-ma")
Vocables (sounds that approximate words but are the child's own creations)
Expressive jabbers (sounds like an actual conversation but has no discernible words)
Repeats spoken words when coaxed
Imbeds discernible words in strings of expressive jabber.
Holophrases, or one-word sentences ("milk" can mean "I want some milk." "Where is my milk?")
Telegraphic speech or two-word sentences ("Mommy juice" can mean "Mommy, I want juice," "Mommy, I spilled the juice," or "This is Mommy's juice.")
Overgeneralized speech ("Boots" may be the name of the family dog but is also the word the child uses for the neighbor's cat and other animals.)
Undergeneralized speech (Mother's name is Sarah; therefore, Aunt Sarah cannot be Sarah; she must have another name.)

**child-directed speech (motherese and fatherese)** a special form of speech used when talking to children that has special characteristics such as short sentences and higher and more variable intonation than speech used to communicate with adults.

Conversational turn taking

Creative words (words used to meet the need for a word not yet learned or for which the child has no frame of reference. The cashier at the local fast food fried chicken restaurant is role played as the "chicken lady" during sociodramatic play, the next day.)

Verbalized curiosity about words ("What does that mean?" and "What did you say?")

Curiosity about print (pointing to printed words and asking, "What does that say?" or "What did I write?" after drawing pseudo-letters or attempting to copy letters)

Adults can encourage language development by interacting in positive ways and by modeling appropriate language through these interactions. Such modeling is spoken conversationally as with Bunh and Samantha: Sixteen-month-old Bunh says to his caregiver, "Me go!" to which the caregiver responds, "You want to go outside, too?" She takes his hand and leads him outdoors with the rest of the group, asking "Can you help me open the door?" Three-year-old Samantha says to her mother, "I gotted my shoes on the wrong feet." Her mother, bending down to help, says, "Yes, you've got your shoes on the wrong feet. Would you like for me to help you change them? It's kind of hard to remember which shoe goes on which foot."

Conversations such as these provide models from which children can construct a grammar system, extend both their understood (receptive) and spoken (expressive) vocabularies, and become motivated to interact verbally with others. Because language occurs in a social context, conversation and meaningful talk directed *to* the child is essential. Language develops best when children are treated as conversational partners and genuinely included in talk.

### Language Diversity among Children

One large metropolitan school district has identified sixty-four different languages among its enrollees. How many different languages or dialects are spoken in the schools closest to you? Whether children should be taught in their native language or immersed in English is a controversial subject among educators and school policy makers. For early childhood educators, there is sufficient empirical evidence to support the development and enrichment of the home language, if not first, then concurrently with the mainstream language (NAEYC, 1996; Perez & Torres-Guzman, 1996; Wright, Taylor, & MacArthur, 2000).

When confronted with contexts in which the dominant language differs from their own, such as when young children are learning a home language that is different from mainstream English or a dialect that is unique to their own cultural backgrounds, the child is faced with the added task of learning two languages concurrently. These children are dependent on the learning environments both at home and at school to support their language development in both languages. Developing proficiency in one's first language is a prerequisite to proficiency in a second language. A substantial amount of research supports the importance of learning the first language well and for children to use their first language to think, solve problems, and discuss ideas (Hakuta, 1986; Krashen, 1996). Children who have not developed proficiency in their home language may have difficulty with vocabulary skills, auditory memory, discrimination skills, simple problem solving tasks, and the ability to follow sequenced directions (NAEYC, 1996). Language difficulties such as these often can result in the linguistically and culturally diverse child being over-referred to special education and classified as learning disabled and perceived as "'developmentally delayed'" (NAEYC, 1996, p. 8). Linguistically different children follow similar patterns as depicted earlier in this chapter; however, as the development of two languages proceeds, we might observe from time to time one language forging ahead of the other (Hakuta, 1986; Huerta-Marcias, 1983).

Teachers who value diversity are also sensitive to the difficulties children experience when theirs is not the mainstream language. Remembering that children must gain proficiency in the native language before they can become proficient in another, we must then provide early childhood experiences that enhance their first language. When curricula and communications support the emergence of first language, more subtle outcomes occur. Rather than perceiving themselves as inept learners and their families as inferior because they do not speak the language that the classroom promotes, children develop more positive self-concepts and an eagerness to learn. Such programs convey that their individual cultures, families, and languages are respected and appreciated.

## Literacy Development

The notion that literacy has its origins in infancy is a relatively new one. In the past, learning to read was thought to occur through formal instruction traditionally begun in the first grade. But, today experts have demonstrated that there is a continuum of literacy development that begins during the infant sensorimotor period.

### Infancy

From the beginning, parents and caregivers can share books with infants. Cradling infants in their arms, adults can "read" the pictures of baby books to them. In addition to holding infants and sharing picture books with them, as soon as infants can hold their heads up (at around three months), baby books can be placed within their visual field in the crib. Most infants can see objects within a distance of ten to twelve inches, so standing open books in a corner of the crib or on the floor in front of the infant provides another visual stimulus and evokes interest. Infant books should contain large clear pictures of one simple object, preferably a familiar object, such as a teddy bear or other stuffed toy, ball, rattle, baby bottle, human face, and so on. Most bookstores today have an array of infant books from which to choose. The easiest to stand in this manner are "board books" which are constructed of thick heavy cardboard.

During infancy, singing, reciting rhymes and chants, and naming objects in pictures introduce infants and young children to the language of books. Eventually very young children learn that the print tells the story along with the pictures, and still later during their preschool years children will come to understand that print alone can convey a message. When infants begin to grasp and put things in their mouths, cloth or vinyl books make better choices than cardboard or paper books. In child care settings, these are particularly nice to have because they can be washed, thus preventing the spread of contagious diseases.

Holding infants and toddlers in your lap while paging through their books and pointing to and naming objects in pictures is a very satisfying activity for them. Eventually, toward the end of the first year, infants can open books and attempt to turn the pages, demonstrating their knowledge that each page has something else to see, point to, and be named. While crawlers generally enjoy playing on and with newspapers and magazines, it is best not to make these available as the chemicals in the print can be harmful to them.

### Toddlers

Toddlers who have become familiar with books and have had them read to them often form attachments to a favorite book. They carry it about and fetch it at reading times in anticipation, of having it read to them. Sometimes the book is a "friend" that is taken to bed after it has been read. Favorite books become sources of comfort that are packed in diaper bags for travel to child care, the baby-sitter's, or visits to grandparents.

As children begin to talk, they enjoy naming the objects in the pictures and "retelling" the story once again while pages are turned. This ritual can occur over and over again in one sitting. When books have been read to them with expression and colorful intonations, beginning talkers may imitate these inflections and intonations in their own "interpretations" of the pictures and stories.

Because language is emerging rapidly from age two on, young children enjoy books with repetitions, songs, and chants. If children have been hearing such things as nursery rhymes, chants, and songs since birth, the words are familiar, and while they may not be articulated well, their attempts to talk or sing along with the reader indicates their familiarity and enjoyment. Some have called these attempts to talk along with the reader "book babble" (Schickedanz, 1999).

Toward the end of the second year, children begin to enjoy theme books that have little story and no plot, such as Tana Hoban's *Red, Blue, Yellow Shoe* (1986). This board book has a photograph of an object, a dot of that color, and the color word printed in the color it names. Such books help children build vocabulary and specific concepts, in this case color. Later, in another context, providing paper and nontoxic crayons or finger paints of the same colors provides an extension activity that reinforces the concepts illustrated in the book.

Young children demonstrate their awareness of environmental print when they recognize familiar signs and logos. As children begin to talk, it is quite common for them to call out some words seen in environmental print. The words they recognize are typically words that are associated with previous experiences: brand names of their favorite foods and chain restaurants, STOP signs, restroom logos, and many others.

## Ages Three to Five Years

From ages three to five, children enjoy short and simple story books, as well as theme books, picture stories with no text, and predictable books in which the same refrain or similar event recurs throughout the book. Counting books and alphabet books become interesting to young children as well. Again, extending book experiences through activities that relate to them enhances vocabulary, content understanding, and focused attention when stories are read again. Sets of counters, such as small cube blocks, plastic teddy bear counters, or other small objects that cannot be swallowed are a nice accompaniment to counting books. For older preschoolers, a grocery bag of objects that begin with the letters represented in the alphabet book to sort and locate as each letter is described makes the letters more meaningful and contextualized. Puppets that represent characters in stories that are read enhance participation and spontaneous read-along attempts. When children enjoy their book and story experiences, it is not unusual to see them reading to their dolls or to each other, pretending to be a teacher reading to the class, or requesting favorite stories to be read over and over again.

Beginning readers enjoy reading aloud to others, though they still very much enjoy and need others to continue reading to them. Because reading is often a tedious and tiring task for beginning readers, it is helpful to take turns with them. The child reads until he wants to stop, then the adult reads for a while until the child signals to have another turn. Sometimes alternating sentences or pages prevents reading fatigue and enhances enjoyment of the shared story. It is best to allow beginning readers to read without corrections unless the meaning is severely altered. When meaning is altered, one can simply ask, "Did that make sense?" "Do you want to try again?" But it is best to avoid criticizing or interrupting with corrections of the child's early attempts to read.

### Primary-Grade Children

Primary-grade children become increasingly able to retell the stories that are read to them. Retelling the stories increases the child's awareness that print makes sense. For this reason, reading material provided for beginning readers must indeed make sense. High-quality literature and classic, familiar children's books and stories are essential both at home and in early childhood programs. High-quality literature places familiar and not-so-familiar words in meaningful contexts making them more easily recognized and remembered. Being exposed to high-quality literature builds enjoyment of learning and assists children in comprehending the printed word, which in turn, motivates children to read for information and pleasure.

By the time children reach primary-grade ages, they have had considerable experience with print, both incidental and focused. While there are wide variations among children in the types and quality of literacy experiences they have had, most children by ages six and seven have well-developed receptive and expressive vocabularies and language abilities, and understand that print conveys meaning. Most can recite the alphabet and recognize the letters of the alphabet, and they are beginning to distinguish between upper and lowercase letters. They can write their names, recognize a number of words in print, use phonemic spelling in their own writings, and have begun to make letter-sound associations.

During the primary grades children are introduced more formally to the skill-based aspects of learning to read: the alphabetic principle (the understanding that written spellings represent the sounds of spoken words), phonemic awareness (the ability to detect individual sounds within spoken words), letter-sound correspondence, blending sounds, listening skills and comprehension, spelling (using both phonemic, or "invented" spelling, strategies and conventional spelling), punctuation, and capitalization. By the end of the primary grades, children have become fairly fluent readers and, if the process in learning to read has not discouraged them, will seek opportunities to read for both information and pleasure. They should by now, be able to use different strategies for deriving meaning from text, decode unfamiliar words using phonemic strategies, and use writing for many purposes such as writing reports, making lists, communicating with classmates, and creating stories and poetry.

### Learning to Write

Becoming literate is more than just learning to read. Learning to write is an integral part of the process of learning to read. Today, few professional early childhood educators talk about learning to read only, but also of *emerging literacy*, which encompasses the concept of becoming both readers and writers.

Early scribbles often represent attempts to write. From the time a child can hold a crayon or pencil, there is a developmental progression toward mature forms of writing. In the beginning scribbling may represent explo-

**1. July 30**

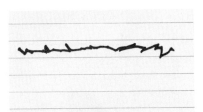

**3. November 25**

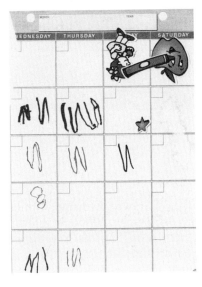

**2. September 17**

**4. January 12**

**5. March 30**

**FIGURE 3–3**
*Learning to write one's name is a process that begins with random scribbling and gradu-*
*ally advances to copying letters and attempting to write one's name.*

ration with new media—crayon and paper. Random scribbling later is
accompanied by naming of the scribbles, then moves toward making marks
that look like letters (or pseudo-letters), to stringing these marks together
into what resembles a message, to copying letters and attempting to write
one's name (Figure 3–3), to writing words, then sentences, and stories.

**FIGURE 3–4**
*Children sometimes merge writing and drawing.*

Beginning writers are often confused about whether they are drawing or writing. For example, one child may announce "I drawed my name," while another may say, "I writing a picture" (Fields & Spangler, 2000). Scribbling that represents writing differs somewhat from scribbling that represents drawing. Scribble-writing usually differs from scribble-drawing in that it is linear, either horizontal or vertical depending on the child's culture. For example, Chinese children tend to create vertical strings of scribbles while American children often create horizontal ones. Children imitate the writing behaviors of those around them. Children often dictate labels or a "story" to go with their drawings, and sometimes they merge writing and drawing as in Figure 3–4.

As young children observe others using writing for meaningful purposes, they too begin to write for what is to them meaningful messages. Tamika wrote "I lk u" on the easel and exclaimed, "Look what I writed!" She has written a meaningful message. Using her emerging letter and sound awareness, she has created readable words. This type of word making is referred to as *invented* or *developmental* spelling. Tamika's teacher acknowledges and respects Tamika's emerging spelling and writing. She does not, at this point, attempt to correct her spelling because she recognizes this as an important phase of early literacy development. In respecting these early attempts at writing, the teacher establishes an environment in which children are free to construct knowledge of letters, words, and grammar in both spoken and written contexts.

*It youngsters had their baby talk and incomplete and ungrammatical sentences corrected every time they spoke, they probably wouldn't talk very often or make much progress in speech.*

*–Marjorie Fields & Katherine Spangler*

Tamika's teacher recognizes that Tamika is connecting letters with their sounds, an important development in becoming a skilled reader. Sounds in the contexts of her own writings and conversations, along with sounds in stories, poems, chants, and finger plays in a print-rich environment, provide Tamika with essential print- and sound-rich experiences to move toward conventional spelling and more skilled reading.

## Summary

With emphasis on whole-child perspectives, we have attempted to provide important theories and information about how children grow, develop, and learn. Attention has been given to each of the developmental domains; neurological development and brain growth; physical and motor development; and emotional, social, moral, cognitive, language, and literacy development. Implications for child care and early education have been interwoven. The objectives of this chapter are based on the authors' beliefs that child growth and development knowledge is basic to the ability to provide developmentally appropriate experiences for young children. This knowledge helps early childhood educators to focus on individual strengths and needs of children in order to plan appropriate experiences for them. Assessment of children to determine these strengths and needs is the subject of chapter 4.

## Reflections

**1.** Emerging scientific knowledge about early neurological development and brain growth holds great promise for guiding parenting and education practices. How might early childhood educators use this information to the best advantage for children? Is it possible for this information to lead to inappropriate practices? What are the ethical implications for learning about and applying new knowledge about how children grow, develop, and learn?
**2.** As a parent, what types of information about your child and your family would you wish a professional early childhood educator to know? What types of developmental information do you believe the teacher needs to know to tap the strengths and interests of your child?
**3.** From your readings and classroom observations, is it your belief that current practices reflect whole-child perspectives? Is it possible to teach with just one or two developmental domains in mind? Explain.

## Field Experiences

**1.** Visit an early childhood education program of high quality (preferably one that is accredited through NAEYC or other professionally recognized accrediting organization) in which infants and toddlers are enrolled. Observe and record the growth and developmental characteristics of infants and toddlers in each of the developmental domains. Discuss your observations in class.

**2.** Visit an early childhood education program of high quality in which children of ages five, six, seven, and eight are enrolled. Compare your observations of their growth and development characteristics to your observations of infants and toddlers. How do their needs differ? Why is it important to have an understanding of child growth and development in order to work with young children?

**3.** Select a young child (infant to age eight) to observe during this course, at least once a week. Plan age and individually appropriate activities to share with the child. Begin a portfolio of observation notes and samples of the child's art; dictations; conversations; writing work; and photographs of block buildings, experiments, and discoveries; and demonstrations of large- or small-motor abilities. Assemble notes and artifacts into developmental domain folders (physical/motor, social/emotional, cognitive/language/literacy). After several weeks (or near the end of the semester) write a developmental description of the child based on the observations you have been able to make and a description of the assembled portfolio contents.

## Case Studies

### I Am Bored and Tired

Lupe, a first-grade student, is taller than most of her classmates. Yet, a comparison of her height and weight with national growth charts indicates that she is significantly underweight for age and height. Her teacher, Ms. Carson also observes that Lupe's food choices at lunch are limited to mostly carbohydrates and sweets—potatoes, rice, breads, chips, desserts, and chocolate milk.

While Lupe has spurts of energy during the day, she is often listless and inattentive. At afternoon recess she complains of being hungry. Ms. Carson has also observed that Lupe exhibits little self-confidence, even fear in using playground equipment such as climbing structures, slides, and swings. When hungry and tired she is irritable and sometimes rather accident prone. Her playmates have a difficult time getting her to play with them, and when she does, her interest lasts briefly and then she retreats to more solitary, less active play.

In the classroom, she enjoys crayons and drawing and working puzzles, and she prefers picture books to more difficult readers. She finds writing activities tedious and frustrating and pays little attention during reading activities. Ms. Carson provides guideline paper to encourage her to write with greater skill and a print model of the upper and lower case alphabet to use when writing. In spite of these supports, Lupe has considerable difficulty with the task and rubs a hole in her paper with the eraser trying to correct her "mistakes."

### What to Do?

What principles of development are illustrated in this vignette?

As you reflect on Lupe's situation, how would you prioritize her health, social, emotional, and academic needs? Be specific.

What types of activities, curriculum projects, or other strategies might Ms. Carson provide to encourage Lupe's interest and effort in school activities and to address her general well-being?

What responsibilities for Lupe's health and well-being does her classroom teacher have?

### Am I Going to Fail?

Joshua is seven years old. His father is a university professor and his mother is a human resources director for a large insurance company. Both parents work long, sometimes odd hours, travel some in their work, and often bring work home with them to pursue during the evening hours. They are loving parents who want the best for their only son. Joshua's care during infancy and until age three was provided by a college-age live-in nanny.

During his first three years, his nanny was dependable and conscientious, though she did make every effort to find time for her college night course assignments and requirements. Joshua's routines (rest, meal times, play periods, and accompanying adults on errands) could best be characterized as irregular and unpredictable. Frequently, his parents insisted that his dinner and/or bedtime be held until they could be home to spend some time with him.

His nanny was caring, playful, and entertaining, but seldom provided meaningful or enriching experiences for him. His parents indulged Joshua with every new toy, fashionable clothes, elaborate and large birthday parties, special vacation trips once a year, and as he got older, two-week camp experiences. Now age seven, he is involved in extracurricular soccer, children's choir, and violin lessons.

The second-grade school year is drawing to a close and Joshua, who has struggled all year, is unable to meet second-grade expectations in just about all subject areas. Joshua appears to daydream a lot and to distract other students by wanting to talk with them at inappropriate times. He is easily frustrated with demanding or challenging tasks and devises ways to escape them (restroom break, coughing spell, lost books or papers, and so on). His parents have been advised that his academic progress is a serous concern. His reading fluency and comprehension is far below expectation for age and grade, as is his mathematics understanding and use. He shows little interest in school work and claims an intense dislike for school.

Joshua's parents feel they have provided for Joshua an enriching childhood that should have afforded him a background of experiences prerequisite to success in school. They are confused, disappointed, anxious, and a bit antagonistic toward the schooling process.

### What to Do?

What prerequisites do you feel young children need in order to benefit from experiences and expectations of the earliest grades?

What does Joshua now need in order to gain his footing with the academic expectations of formal schooling?

If you could rewrite the scenario for Joshua's early years, without being judgmental, how would you write it?

## Further Reading

American Academy of Pediatrics. (1999). *Guide to your child's nutrition.* Elk Grove Village, IL: Author.

American Academy of Pediatrics. (1997). *Injury prevention and control for children and youth.* Elk Grove Village, IL: Author.

American Public Health Association and American Academy of Pediatrics. (2002). *Caring for our children: National health and safety performance standards: Guidelines for out-of-home child care programs.* Washington, DC: Author.

Bergen, D., & Coscia, J. (2002). *Brain research and childhood education: Implications for educators.* Olney, MD: Association for Childhood Education International.

Berk, L. E. & Winsler, A., (1995) . *Scaffolding children's learning: Vygotsky and early childhood education.* Washington, DC: National Association for the Education of Young Children.

Brown, W. H., & Conroy, M. A. (Eds.). (1997). *Including and supporting preschool children with developmental delays in early childhood classrooms.* Little Rock, AR: Southern Early Childhood Association.

Gardner, H. (1999). *Intelligence reframed.* New York: Basic Books.

Katz, L. B., & McClellan, D. E. (1997). *Fostering Children's social competence: The teacher's role.* Washington, DC: National Association for the Education of Young Children.

Martin, P. (1996). *I already know how to read: A child's view of literacy.* Portsmouth, NH: Heinemann.

Neuman, S. B., Copple, C., & Bredekamp, S. (2000). *Learning to read and write: Developmentally appropriate practices for young children.* Washington, DC: National Association for the Education of Young Children.

Puckett, M. B., & Black, J. K. (2001). *The young child: Development from prebirth through age eight* (3rd ed.). Columbus, OH: Merill/Prentice Hall.

Shores, R. (1997). *Rethinking the brain: A summary of research.* New York: Work and Family Institute.

## Helpful Web Sites

### Child Health Alert

www.childheathalert.com

*This Web site provides current information about development and issues affecting child health and safety. Brief synopses of professional health related journal articles are provided.*

## ZERO TO THREE
www.zerotothree.org
*The Zero to Three National Center for Infants, Toddlers, and Families is a national nonprofit organization devoted to promoting the healthy social, emotional, and intellectual development of infants and toddlers. The organization provides a bimonthly bulletin; information about research, programs, and trends; and resources for individuals in the early childhood profession. Some materials are provided in Spanish.*

### Frank Porter Graham Child Development Center
www.fgp.unc.edu/
*This Web site connects to the University of North Carolina multidisciplinary center for the study of young children and families. It provides information about child development and health, contemporary research, activities to employ with young children, and information about risk factors, developmental problems, and early intervention.*

Check the Online Resources™ for expert practitioners' responses to each case study.

For additional information on teaching young children, visit our Web site at **http://www.earlychilded.delmar.com**

# CHAPTER 4

## *Basing Quality Practices on Assessment*

*Early Childhood Principle* Professional early childhood educators value strengths and needs of children and use this knowledge in making decisions about individual children.

Teachers in high-quality early childhood programs do not make educational decisions based on what publishing companies say is appropriate for children of a particular age. They do not follow a scope and sequence developed for a grade level. They do not read to children from teachers guides.

Teachers in high-quality programs use what they know about child development and from each of the disciplines to plan curriculum, but equally important in this decision making is what they learn about the individual children in their care. They observe children very carefully and talk with children extensively in order to get to know as much about the children as possible. They use multiple methods to document what they learn about children and use this information to make decisions about how to arrange the classroom, what activities and experiences to offer children, how to guide children, and how to create a community of learners.

*After reading this chapter, you should be able to:*
- Discuss the purposes of assessment, evaluation, and testing.
- List the criteria for good assessment for young children.
- Discuss the role of observation/kidwatching in assessing young children.
- List and describe methods of documenting teacher observations.
- Describe how portfolios can be constructed.
- Discuss how teacher observations can be used to plan appropriate experiences for children.

**F**olders and papers are spread across tables and all around the floor of a third-grade classroom. Children are talking with each other, asking those sitting near them for advice about which of their papers is best. Other children are pulling papers from manila folders filled with work they had previously chosen as good work and placing that work in a red portfolio folder. Still other children are writing reasons they selected a particular piece of work and what they think it shows they have learned. During this concentrated activity, different children can be overheard to say:

- So, do you think this literature response really shows that I am a good reader?
- I'm putting in my reading log. I couldn't believe how many books I read this year until I counted all the books in reading logs. I read a whole lot this year.
- I think what I am going to do is pick this story about my grandma. I wrote it at the beginning of the year, and then I decided to revise it last month. The second one is really a whole lot better. My lead character is stronger. I put dialogue in this one, and Johndra helped me edit and type it so other people can read it better. Plus I think I'll write in my rationale that I learned how to use spell check when I typed this story. Yeah, these two stories really show that I've grown a lot as a writer this year.
- To show myself as a mathematician, I am picking the survey my group did for the carnival. We talked to a bunch of people and asked them what booths they wanted at the carnival this year, and we spent days organizing the data. This does show that I can gather data and make sense of it and use graphs. That's a good math piece.

These comments may sound sophisticated for third-graders, but these students have been involved in the assessment process since they were in kindergarten. They have been looking at their work, choosing work to revise, selecting their best work, and explaining what that work shows about them as a learner. During this working session, children are putting together year-end portfolios. They are examining reading, writing, math, science, social studies, and project work that they had previously selected as "good work." Now, at the end of the year, they are choosing their very best piece from these working folders. They are analyzing each piece selected for their portfolio and writing a rationale explaining why they chose that work and what they think it shows about their learning. Both the work and the rationale will be placed in the year-end portfolio that they will present to their families at a portfolio conference.

# PURPOSE OF ASSESSMENT, EVALUATION, AND TESTING

Simply put, **assessment** is the process of developing an accurate depiction of what a child knows and how he goes about the process of learning. The students in the third-grade class discussed previously had been learning how to develop accurate portrayals of themselves as learners for several years. Obviously younger children are not cognitively capable of this kind of assessment. For children younger than second- or third-grade or for those who have not had extensive experiences in developing portfolios, assessment is the primary responsibility of the early childhood educator. For these children the most important form of assessment is teacher observation and documentation of what a child does and how he does it. Teachers use this information to develop an understanding about a child's individual capabilities, interests, and ways of learning. Unlike testing, which attempts to measure a student's knowledge or skills in a specific area, assessment attempts to put together a rich description of the whole child (Herman, Aschbacher, & Winters, 1992).

**assessment** evaluation of children's progress.

Assessment has many different purposes. These are the three primary reasons for assessing the learning of children: (1) to inform instruction, (2) to inform families about the progress of children, and (3) to determine the quality of the educational program (Hills, 1992). Assessment no longer occurs at the end of teaching a particular skill or related set of facts. The teach-then-test form of evaluating students has given way to a more integrated form of teaching. Assessment is an integral part of teaching (Bredekamp & Rosegrant, 1992, 1995; Puckett & Black, 2000). As the teacher works with children, she is constantly observing what the child does and how he does it, then documenting these observations. From analyzing these observations, the teacher knows how to structure future learning experiences for the children in her care. She is better able to communicate with families because she knows each child intimately. Finally, she can evaluate the educational program she is providing children. High-quality assessment of children is very valuable.

*The ultimate reason for observing and recording is not just to learn what children are like, but to help them grow and develop.*

*–Janice Beaty*

## The Nature of Assessment

Today, assessment of what children are learning is much more **qualitative** than in previous generations. Number or letter grades are considered, at best, snapshots of children's capabilities. Observation of children at work or play and documentation of these observations are considered more valid assessments because they provide a richer picture of each child. However, for the documentation of observations to be truly reliable, observers must remain objective and record only what they see.

In public schools, many early childhood educators are required to use number or letter grades to report their students' achievement. Grades can

**qualitative assessment** evaluation of children's progress that is reported descriptively, quite often in the form of a narrative report, as opposed to quantitative assessment, which is number or letter grades and is reported in the form of a report card.

be derived from children's authentic work, but the reporting of such grades gives families only a very general idea of how their child is actually doing in the class. Most high-quality early childhood educators who are required to distribute report cards supplement this information with other methods of revealing the progress that children are making. Often they have individual family conferences to share the child's work and to share their own observations of the child.

**kidwatching** careful observation of children for assessment purposes.

Observation as discussed in this chapter is much more than just watching. Yetta Goodman coined the term **kidwatching** (Goodman, 1978) to describe an informal but informed method of observing children. Through kidwatching, adults can learn many important things about children's development. They learn children's likes and dislikes, how they like to be comforted when they are distressed, how they seek out other children to play with, or how they enter into play themes already underway. They notice if the children can count to ten, walk down stairs using alternating feet, pour juice into a glass, or how they use scissors. They listen for children speaking in sentences or playing with rhyming words. They observe how children draw pictures and how they use language in their dramatic play. They watch children pretend to be reading picture books or trying to write notes to their friends. Although this is a limited list of behaviors that a teacher of two- to six-year-olds might want to observe, it is an example of behaviors that cross all the developmental areas: social/emotional, physical, language/literacy, cognitive, and aesthetic. Through kidwatching, teachers become aware of each student's growth in all of the developmental areas and therefore are able to support individual development. Based on knowledge of child development, they can also offer special help when developmental needs are identified.

*Planned observations in all developmental domains are essential if the teacher is to engage in relevant and helpful collaborations with individual students.*
*-Margaret Puckett and Janet Black*

Assessment is not only more qualitative today, it is also continuous. Rather than relying on periodic testing, today's assessment is ongoing. Teachers observe children on a daily basis and document their observations regularly. Multiple observations of children in different settings help teachers develop realistic understandings of their students.

Current assessment also occurs in more natural settings. Rather than pulling children away from their daily activities to evaluate specific knowledge and skills, teachers look for times when children use what they have learned or exhibit skills as they work. Assessment occurs in the context of what the children are already doing. Teachers observe during large group meetings, as they work with children in small groups, and as children work with others in different learning centers.

Assessment as children go about normal classroom activities often yields more accurate information about young children than in testing situations. For example, in most kindergarten classrooms, knowledge of letters and the sounds associated with them is generally considered important. In more traditional classrooms, children are called away from their peers and shown

*Teachers learn important information about children as they observe their work and play activities.*

flash cards of capital and lowercase letters and asked to identify both letter name and the sound associated with that letter. The results of that one
testing situation is reported to parents on report cards. Today in kindergarten classrooms where the teacher is using current assessment methods,
the teacher would be assessing that same knowledge very differently. The
teacher listens carefully to the children's comments during shared story
times or other group discussions, observes them writing in the writing center or home center, observes signs they make to use in the block or science
center, and eavesdrops on conversations as children are gathering their possessions and getting ready to go home for the day. In each of these classroom
situations, children may comment on letter names or otherwise indicate
their emerging knowledge about the alphabet and how it is used to communicate. The teacher would document references that her students made
about letters and letter sounds and would share this information with families. In the traditional classroom, these comments would go undocumented.

*Criteria for Effective Assessment of Young Children*

**Assessment** should consider the whole child, covering all developmental domains.

**Assessment** should be continuous, over time and in multiple settings.

**Assessment** should be documented by several people in the life of a child, using a variety of methods.

**Assessment** should be valid, providing information related to the goals and objectives of the early childhood program.

**Assessment** should be used to determine a child's progress, share with families, and evaluate the program.

The only knowledge that would count for the report to parents would be the responses given to the flash cards.

In a testing situation, a child might not always respond with all the knowledge he or she has. For example, Laura, a kindergarten student, was shown an index card marked with the letter "I." She responded, "I don't know," and the teacher marked the letter identification checklist she was using to record the child's answers "No" for the letter "I." Laura may not have been able to identify that letter, or she may have forgotten the letter at the moment, or she may have felt awkward being separated from her friends for this quizzing session. Later that same day, Laura was overheard in the home center saying to one of her friends who was writing a grocery list for a pretend shopping trip, "If you can't write ice cream, just write an 'I' and I'll know what to buy." In the traditional classroom where the teacher did not routinely listen to children's conversations and document them, Laura's obvious knowledge of that letter would probably have been missed, and the report the parents received would have been limited to the testing information. In a classroom where the teacher was using current assessment methods, she would have noted Laura's comment about the letter "I" and that home center event would have been one part of the teacher's developing understanding of Laura's knowledge of the alphabet. It is important to note that Laura's teacher was assessing her knowledge and skills during the natural classroom events. She learned quite a bit about what Laura knew about letters and the sounds associated with them from carefully observing her at play. Teachers learn important information about children as they observe their play.

## What Can Be Learned from Assessment?

An important early childhood principle is that early childhood educators accept children where they are and help move them forward. Assessment helps establish where children are. Vygotsky (1978) believed that true

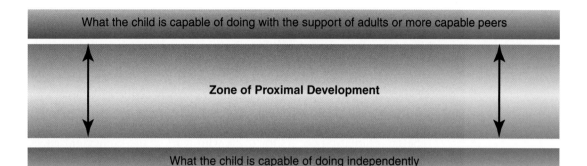

**FIGURE 4–1**
*Zone of Proximal Development. The area between these two lines is the zone of proximal development. Alone, a child in kindergarten might be able to write D3B to represent "The Three Bears." With the support of a teacher saying each word slowly and reminding him that a space should be left after each word, he might be able to write THE THRE BRS. This zone of proximal development exists for every child in each developmental area.*

teaching occurs in each child's **zone of proximal development** (Figure 4–1). Working with a child within this zone means the teacher must know a child well. When a teacher does know a child's individual capability, she can plan learning experiences so that activities are challenging but achievable. The child will accomplish things he or she cannot do independently, but is able to do with the help and support of another person (Berk & Winsler, 1995). This zone of proximal development is different for every child in each developmental domain, but can be determined through repeated, documented observations. Continuing assessment helps the teacher determine when the zone of proximal development changes for a child.

**zone of proximal development** the distance between what a learner can accomplish independently and what he or she can accomplish with the help of a more skilled classmate or an adult.

## OBSERVATION OF YOUNG CHILDREN

The single most effective way to assess where young children are and to determine the progress they have made over a period of time is through the observations of a qualified early childhood educator. Carefully observing young children offers a wealth of information about them. However, to remember important information gained through observations, the observer needs to record his/her observations in some manner.

*What a child can do in cooperation today, he can do alone tomorrow.*
*–Lev Vygotsky*

### Documentation of Observations
Adults believe that they have the ability to remember all the important events that occur with the children in their care, but the simple truth is that

*Observing is probably the oldest, most frequently used and most rewarding method of assessing children, their growth, development, and learning.*
        *—Carol Seefeldt*

so much can occur in any given day that it is impossible to remember without a little assistance. Parents enjoy recalling events such as the time their child took her first steps. Even though they try remembering all the details that surrounded this important moment, they cannot visualize it all. With the help of a photograph or notes in a baby book, they are able to reconstruct a clearer picture of the circumstances which might have otherwise been forgotten. With the reminder of the photo or notes, this important moment in their child's life is captured forever.

The same situation occurs for those who work with young children. A teacher simply cannot rely on memory to recall the multitude of things that occur in class on a daily basis. Special comments the children make as they are reading stories, the varied ways children manipulate learning materials in centers, and the things they say to one another are occurrences worthy of remembering. To work effectively with young children, in addition to knowing them well and carefully observing their actions, early childhood teachers document what is seen, heard, said, and done in their classrooms.

There are many ways of documenting what occurs in a center or classroom. Anecdotal records, checklists, rating scales, interviews, photographs, tapes, samples of student work, and notes about progress are some of the methods that can be used by adults to record children's behaviors.

### Anecdotal Records

Anecdotal records are one method that documents adult observations of children's behaviors. These records can be either formal or informal. Some experts believe that anecdotal records should be formal (Wortham, 1990). Formal anecdotal records are written accounts of a child's behavior, documented in the context of a particular event and written in very objective language. Each formal anecdotal record includes the name of the observer, location of the incident, child(ren) involved, type of development observed, date, and time. This contextual information is followed by a description of the observed behavior, carefully written to avoid any subjectivity on the part of the adult recording the event. Any notes or comments about the event or behaviors observed are written in a separate column of the anecdotal record. It is important to note that the less time that occurs between observing the event and writing the anecdotal record, the more detailed and accurate the anecdotal record will be (Puckett & Black, 2000).

Collected over time, formal anecdotal records can be a rich source of information about children. Samuel Meisels (1993) suggests that at least one anecdotal record should be written every week for each child. This suggestion takes into account the time-consuming nature of this type of documentation for busy early childhood educators. At least ten minutes is usually required to hand write a formal anecdotal record. Typing them from brief notes does reduce the time to some degree, but a minimum of two hours would be needed to produce one anecdotal record for each child in a class of twenty children.

*Formal Anecdotal Record*

Child's Name    Stephanie                     Date    September 8

Age    5                                      Date    9:15–9:25 A.M.

Location    Home Center                       Observer    D. Diffily

Type of Development: Literacy

**Incident:**

Stephanie chose to "read" books in the home center today as she was playing with Mackie, Whitney, and Will. She spent several minutes sitting at the center table leafing through Eric Carle's *The Grouchy Ladybug* and Tana Hoban's *Of Colors and Things*. Then she moved down to sit on the floor beside the doll crib, put a doll in her lap, and began pretend reading to the doll.

**Notes/Comments:**

This is the first time she has chosen to interact with books on her own, although she participates in small group reading and DEAR ("Drop Everything And Read") times when I ask her to. Maybe she sees herself as a reader.

Given the richness of the information to be gained from anecdotal records, perhaps more informal anecdotal records would be more practical. Informal anecdotal records are more like quickly jotted down notes from the teacher to herself. Abbreviations for children names, center names, and other classroom activities can be used to decrease the time spent recording the observed behavior. These notes can be written on a variety of paper: adhesive notepads, blank computer labels, or simple notebook paper (with a separate page for each child clipped to a clipboard or filed in a three-ring binder behind a divider for each child).

Teachers can jot down what a child chooses to do first during center times, topics the child writes about, and books the child reads during independent reading. They can jot down comments children make as they work alone or conversations they have with other children who are working near them. These informal anecdotal records are just as valuable as more formal records for documenting observations, but are not appropriate for audiences beyond the teacher and the child's family. Because of the abbreviations, they may be unreadable to other people, and because of the subjective language, they may not provide the type of information that others should read.

Both types of anecdotal records can be used to record teacher observations. The more informal, less time-consuming ones can be used to capture daily events and the more formal ones can be written to document milestone behaviors. Center choices or self-selected books can be documented with informal records. The first time a child tries invented spelling on her own, the first time two children who normally do not work together choose a joint project, or a time when a child risks climbing on a piece of climbing equipment might be documented with the more formal anecdotal records.

### Checklists

Checklists are usually a list of behaviors in a particular developmental area. Simple marks on the checklist indicate whether a child exhibited a behavior during a single observational period. These marks are usually a "y" or "✓" for yes, the behavior was observed or "n" or "-" for no, the behavior was not observed. Checklists are usually easy for adults to use. They help focus observation on a few related behaviors and can be marked quickly.

A checklist completed one time may help early childhood educators identify certain behaviors that need to be encouraged for a particular child. For example, a teacher may observe that one child cannot pour liquid into a glass without spilling. Noticing this behavior because of her focused observation on fine-motor development, the teacher may decide to add more pouring containers in the water center or add small pitchers and a set of plastic glasses in the home center (Beaty, 2001). When the same checklist is completed two or three different times over the course of one year, it can provide the teacher and families the opportunity to see growth graphically in particular developmental areas.

While checklists can provide some valuable information, they also have limitations that should be considered. Because the teacher is either checking "yes" or "no," no information is recorded about how well the child accomplished a task. If a teacher is observing large-motor development on the playground, she may check "yes," Jamie can climb up and down climbing equipment with ease. However, there may be extenuating circumstances that should be considered related to this observation of Jamie. She may be a reluctant climber, but on this day of observation, several of her friends were surrounding the climbing equipment encouraging her to climb higher and higher. On other days, Jamie did not attempt to climb at all. The information about her usual reluctance and her willingness to climb with the encouragement of peers should be noted along with the "yes" check to capture more fully the accuracy of this observation. Some published checklists are organized with designated space for additional notes such as this (Beaty, 2001).

When an early childhood educator first begins to use checklists to document observations of children, it is usually easier to use checklists developed by others, such as those offered by Janice Beaty (2001). After working with these checklists for some time, many early childhood educators develop checklists of their own. Self-developed checklists can more closely reflect the behaviors the teacher values most.

For example, teachers can create blank grids to record specific behaviors they notice. In one prekindergarten class toward the end of the year, after hearing the teacher read *Strega Nona* by Tomie de Paola (1975), the

*Checklist for Small Motor Skills for Kindergarten*

Name _____                              Observer _____

Dates _____

Place a ✓ beside skills the child demonstrates on a regular basis and an X beside skills not observed.

| **Skill** | **Evidence** | **Date** |
|---|---|---|
| __ Works puzzles of several pieces | | |
| __ Pours liquid from pitcher | | |
| __ Zips zippers | | |
| __ Buttons buttons | | |
| __ Ties shoes | | |
| __ Strings beads | | |
| __ Places pegs in pegboard | | |
| __ Snaps linking cubes | | |
| __ Connects interlocking building blocks | | |
| __ Uses scissors with accuracy | | |
| __ Controls a variety of writing tools | | |

students took different kinds of pasta and colored stringing buttons from the math center into the home center. They transformed the living room and kitchen of the home center into a restaurant. Within a few minutes, they were giving away pasta in platters and bowls, like Big Anthony had, and were sorting and selling the colored buttons as pizzas. During lunch, the teacher took a blank grid and entered these behaviors at the top of the page: sorting by color, sorting by attribute, one-to-one correspondence, oral counting, and writing numerals. Each was a behavior observed during the morning center time by those children playing in their converted restaurant. That afternoon, the teacher was easily able to document the students who demonstrated each of these five math-related behaviors.

Another teacher in a kindergarten class reorganized the home center in his classroom to try to elicit more literacy behaviors from students. He put logos on the wall from food he knew the children ate: popular cereals, soups, breads, lunch meats, and vegetables. He placed grocery circulars and pads of paper labeled "Grocery List" on the table and put canned food in the pantry. Stationery, envelopes, and a class-made book of children's addresses were on one shelf. A telephone book was near the play telephone. The students began incorporating these props into their dramatic play. Once again, the teacher used the grid to document the behaviors he expected. Down the left side of the grid, he wrote children's names and across the top of the grid, he wrote this: reading familiar books to the "babies" or to other children, reading logos, knowing that print is written from left to right (as children copied from the grocery circulars on to the grocery list pads), using functional print (such as looking up a phone number in the telephone book to "order" pizza). With the personalized grid he completed, he was ready to quickly check off the literacy-related behaviors that he observed.

Other forms of checklists can be created by teachers. Maria, a teacher of three-year-olds, created a simple checklist of her centers down the side of the page and the days of the week across the top. For one week at the beginning of the year, she meticulously noted every center change each child made. She repeated the same checklist procedure in January and then again in May. By comparing these three checklists, she had information about which centers each child was choosing and how many changes they made each day. Checklists can usually be completed fairly quickly and can provide valuable information to the teacher about children's behaviors.

### Rating Scales

Rating scales are similar to checklists in that they usually list related behaviors. Instead of marking that the teacher does or does not observe certain behaviors, a rating scale allows the adult to indicate how often a child exhibits particular behaviors. For example, on an emergent literacy rating scale, items might include "chooses literature for own enjoyment," "pretend reads," and "knows what a title is."

Rating scales tend to rank the frequency of behavior on a five-point scale, such as 1–never, 2–seldom, 3–occasionally, 4–frequently, 5–always. In many cases, rating scales are more practical than checklists for many types

---

*Literacy Rating Scale for Three- through Six-Year-Olds*

Name _____     Date _____

| | Always | | Sometimes | | Never |
|---|---|---|---|---|---|
| Chooses books for enjoyment | 5 | 4 | 3 | 2 | 1 |
| Asks that books be read again | 5 | 4 | 3 | 2 | 1 |
| Can retell familiar stories | 5 | 4 | 3 | 2 | 1 |
| Recognizes name in print | 5 | 4 | 3 | 2 | 1 |
| Reads logos | 5 | 4 | 3 | 2 | 1 |
| Knows what part of page is read | 5 | 4 | 3 | 2 | 1 |
| Knows what an author is | 5 | 4 | 3 | 2 | 1 |
| Knows what an illustrator is | 5 | 4 | 3 | 2 | 1 |
| Draws for enjoyment | 5 | 4 | 3 | 2 | 1 |
| Draws to show something learned | 5 | 4 | 3 | 2 | 1 |
| Writes to communicate | 5 | 4 | 3 | 2 | 1 |
| Enjoys receiving notes | 5 | 4 | 3 | 2 | 1 |

of behaviors. If a teacher wants to document social/emotional behaviors such as sharing materials, taking turns, or working cooperatively, it makes more sense to document how frequently a child exhibits these behaviors than merely noting a "yes" or "no" reaction. However, rating scales need to be completed after several observations have been made of the behaviors listed on the scale. A rating scale completed at the beginning of a year and again toward the end of the year provides comparative data that is more meaningful than one isolated scale.

Like checklists, rating scales rarely provide information that substantiates the rating; therefore, these scales can be subjective. That is, some adults may allow factors other than careful observation of behaviors to influence how they rate some children. Some teachers may rate a child on an emotional basis rather than an objective one. This possibility should be considered when using rating scales to document observations, and great care should be taken to maintain objectivity.

## Interviews

Interviews with children can provide great insight into how they perceive their world. Interviews can be informal or formal. An informal interview may be something as simple as a teacher kneeling down in the block center and saying to the children working there, "Can you tell me about your block structure?" or a teacher asking children in the reading center what they think about the book they are reading. Quick notes reflecting the children's responses can provide interesting information about how children think and how they view their work.

One spring afternoon, a prekindergarten teacher watched three children build several tall towers from hollow blocks and lay unit blocks around the towers that appeared to be roads. They each made several trips to the math center, gathering pattern blocks and linking cubes. Each time they returned to their block structure and dropped the math manipulatives into the hollow blocks. Finished with this stage of construction, one child drove a pretend car to one of the towers and the other two children kicked down the towers, scattering blocks and cubes all over the floor. Curious about this type of play, the teacher made a point to observe what the children would do next. They recreated the same block structure again, meticulously collecting all the math materials and dropping them down into the hollow blocks. Again, the same child drove the car to a tower and the others kicked down the towers. The teacher walked over to where the children were beginning to rebuild the towers and asked, "Would you tell me about your buildings?" The driver of the car responded, "It's office buildings in Oklahoma City. A car bombs it and all the children die." It had been months since the tragic bombing of the federal building in Oklahoma City. The teacher had not heard any mention of the incident before this day. The child's answer to this simple interview question provided very important information about children in her classroom, how they were feeling about a specific incident, and how they chose to deal with their anger and confusion, though the teacher thought that the issue of the Oklahoma City bombing had been dealt with at the time of the event. At the time, she had encouraged children to draw and dictate stories about how they felt about the bombing. The class had talked about the bombing at several class meetings, and the teacher had informed families of those conversations so they could continue them at home to reassure children that they were safe. Obviously, from the block play, the children still needed some of these activities, and she planned experiences for them to express these continuing feelings. Her observation and informal interview directly informed the decisions she made about classroom experiences and activities she would offer children. Even simple interview questions can give teachers information they would not otherwise have about children.

In formal interviews, adults decide in advance what questions will be asked of the children. A formal interview can help teachers learn more about children or give insight into a child's thought process and documents his or her expression of the answers. Questions like those in the following section help kindergarten teachers understand a child's perceptions of literacy in her home.

Like other forms of assessment, some formal interviews can provide valuable comparative information when the same interview is repeated several months apart. Children's answers to the same questions asked in intervals (e.g., September, January, and May) indicate improvements in language development, growth in cognitive development, and changes in thinking. The interview in the following section shows tremendous growth in a first-grade student's understanding of mathematics over a nine-month period of time.

---

*Sample Interview about Literacy at Home*

| Questions | Kindergarten Child's Answers |
|---|---|
| Do you have books at your house? | Yes. |
| Who reads to you at home? | My mom and my dad and my sister. |
| What is your favorite book? | It's this dinosaur book. |
| Can you tell me the story? | It's pretty long and it has chapters. The whole book is that fat (indicating four inches with fingers). |
| Do you have magazines at your house? | Yes, thousands. |
| Who reads them? | Almost the whole family, like my dad and my mom and my sister looks at them. |
| What are the names of the magazines? | I don't know the names. |

*Formal Math Interviews with a First-Grade Student*

| August 30 | May 11 |
|---|---|

**What do you think math is?**

Math is counting and pattern blocks.

**What do you think math is?**

I think it is good because you can learn stuff and then you can get better grades. I don't get grades now, but I will get grades someday. Math is something you can learn and do. You could do math games and you can do math sentences and you could do all sorts of things like somebody says a math problem to you and you have to answer it and you have to think a lot to get the answer. You think and concentrate and concentrate about what the math sentences is and what you already know or you could use a math strategy like a chicken laid a egg and he had five eggs but two of them got eaten, how many would there be? You would see first how many eggs there were, then when the animal ate one and one more you would think how many less there would be. The answer would be three.

**How do you feel about math?**

I like math.

**How do you feel about math?**

I feel good because it is fun and I like it. How I feel about it is I like it, so I like to do it and when I do it, I think that it is kind of fun and I like word problems we do in our math like logical reasoning and drawing pictures and all the other strategies.

**What have you done in math that makes you feel successful?**

I do good patterns and I can count and that is successful.

**What have you done in math that makes you feel successful?**

I concentrate doing the math and I concentrate finding out the answer and what the answer is and then I think, then I raise my hand to see if I got it right because it might not be right but sometimes it is and that makes me feel good. I feel successful when I play math games or use math strategies because I like it. When I like math, then I feel good.

Another form of interviewing can be used to show parents—and even the children themselves—what students have learned during one unit of study. Sometimes it is difficult for families to understand how much learning occurs in a play-oriented, integrated curriculum. One way to help parents see the content that children are learning is to share with them what children say they know about a topic before and after unit of study. Teachers can take dictation from children prior to starting a unit of study to establish what the child knows before the unit begins. After the unit is complete, they can take dictation again, using the same prompt, "Tell me all you know about _____." While this is not a totally accurate measure of everything a child might know about a topic, comparing the two different dictations gives teachers and parents a good idea of what content children are learning. The following box provides an example of this open-ended interview technique.

### Notes about Children's Work

Children's work can provide valuable information about them. Collecting a representative sample of each child's work over a period of time can be a compelling way of showing progress in drawing, painting, and writing. A child's work shows developmental growth in ways that teacher notes cannot. Teachers need to collect all kinds of work: tempera, watercolor, and

---

*Before- and After-Unit Study Dictation from First-Grade Student*

| **Before** | **After** |
|---|---|
| **All I Know about Space, August 2** | **All I Know about Space, August 31** |
| I know that planets are full of rocks. I know that there is not such things as aliens. When you go out in space, you have to wear a certain kind of suit. The sun is not a planet. It is a star. | Shooting stars are not really shooting stars. They are rocks. When they are in outer space, they are called meteors. And Pluto could be a moon. There could be more than nine planets. Jupiter has a red spot. The red spot is a big storm. You can fit two Earths in it. Saturn is the longest plant. Jupiter is the biggest planet. The moon orbits around the earth. The earth orbits around the sun. The moon has lots of craters. The first man to land on the moon put his suit in the Museum. Astronauts have these bitty telescopes that they look through and it can take pictures. Astronauts use Specially Sealed suits so nothing will come out. |

*(continued)*

*Before- and After-Unit Study Dictation from First-Grade Student (continued)*

**After**

And astronauts always need food. So their food won't float up they hook it to the ground. They always need a cord if they are going to fix something. Astronauts always need to have a safety kit in case anyone gets hurt. If they get too sick and the medical kit can't do it, they have to get to a doctor fast. They have phones in space ships. And space-men always need to breathe. Nothing helps them to breathe except the pack on their back. It only helps them breathe for seven hours. Jupiter is a gas planet. Saturn is too. Astronauts always need something to buckle them to the ground, so they will not float. Whenever they land on the moon, they wear heavy shoes. It will keep them on the ground because it is so heavy. The sun is the hottest thing in the solar system. If you are outside, and you see a star moving, it might be a meteor. You cannot see a black hole. If there [sic] are 50,000 feet away, the black hole can still suck you up. Inside the sun, it is 27 and 2000 degrees. The sun is made of many gases and fire and hot lava. The black hole is not really black. It is really squeezed up together. Shooting stars, you can barely see when it's early. If you look very late, you will have to be a good watcher, 'cause shooting stars go very fast. In the night, it looks like the sun is going down. The moon really covers the sun. The sun doesn't move a bit. The sun could be smaller than a black hole. Saturn's clouds are yellow and it is very hot. When you fly a space ship, you have to have three kinds of tanks. Two small ones are hooked on the tank and one is hooked on the space ship.

mixed media paintings, stories, letters, lists, signs a child creates, and ways the child uses numbers.

The work of young children usually provides more information if the circumstances surrounding the production of a piece of art work or a written story accompanies the child's work. The processes a child used to create something may be just as important to understanding the child as the actual product. Adults who observe children as they work should consider jotting down notes about where the child was working, the names of other children who were working in the same general area of the room, and the conversations that occurred as the work proceeded.

In one prekindergarten classroom, Ismael became upset when he learned through his teacher's reading of a book about turtles that reptiles lay their eggs and leave the nest. He could not believe that reptiles did not take care of their babies. Later in the art center, Ismael painted yellow oval after yellow oval, repeating, "There goes a turtle egg, there goes a turtle egg." Then he picked up several brushes in each hand and swept the brushes over all the eggs he had painted, commenting, "Now cover them up so they'll be safe." The actual painting Ismael produced was little more than a brown blob. Without a note from the teacher attached to this painting, no one else looking at Ismael's painting would understand its significance. That morning Ismael was using the process of easel painting to work through his feelings and reinforcing concepts he learned.

In this case, adult notes attached to a child's work explained the importance of the work itself. That pre-K teacher might have remembered the story of Ismael's reaction to reptiles when the piece of artwork was shared with his family or she could have forgotten the story entirely. Without documentation of the teacher's observation, Ismael's painting was just a random combination of mixed colors. With notes that took five minutes to jot down, Ismael's painting became an important piece of work showing the way he dealt with a specific problem he encountered.

To create these collections of children's work, the teacher needs to keep several pieces of children's work. Some teachers have problems with children wanting to take their work home instead of allowing the teacher to keep it. This problem can be somewhat alleviated in the way the teacher presents the idea of keeping student work in the classroom. By valuing the children's work verbally, displaying it in the classroom, or having a place of honor for storing "special" work, students may begin to feel more comfortable leaving their work in the caring, responsible hands of their teacher. In other cases, especially with drawings or writing, the teacher may be able to photocopy the work. The original can be filed and the photocopy taken home.

### Photographs

Photographs can be used to document all areas of development. Keeping a camera loaded with film or having a digital camera in the classroom allows documentation of special moments. Photographs can be used to capture specific activities such as how a child uses math manipulatives or how they choose the books to read during self-selected reading times. They can document how a child maneuvers on a piece of climbing equipment, how he or she tries to comfort an upset friend, or the way he or she expresses himself or herself at the easel. Photographs can also show developmental progress over time. For example, the complexity of a child's block structures throughout the year is not easily documented through written description but can be easily portrayed with a series of photographs. The evolution of a child's four-block house in September into cities that cover the entire block center by April is important progress to note and can be documented with applicable photographs as well as written description.

Unlike other methods of documentation, photographs have multiple uses. They document specific events in the classroom. These can also be used to share information with families and visitors about the activities and the learning that takes place in the class. For example, photographs of children's block structures could be placed in a blank book and kept in

*Photos can be taken to document the creation of masterpieces.*

the block center. New photographs could be added to the book throughout the year. Stories about each block structure dictated by the children would add another aspect of literacy to the classroom as children create new stories and return to the old stories again. Similar photo books can be created for the other centers. In the dramatic play center, photographs would document children's play themes over time. In the art area, snapshots would document creative "masterpieces" as they were being developed. A collection of photographs taken during one particular activity such as a cooking activity can be posted in or outside the room. Accompanied by the teacher's written explanation of the learning that occurred during that activity, these photos can help families and visitors understand the learning processes that were embedded in the activity.

### Audio Tapes

Audio tapes can be used for assessing several different types of learning. They can record interviews with children, story retellings, and conversations between children during work at centers. Just as in other methods of documenting children's development, audio tapes are most effective if children are taped regularly over a period of time. Early childhood educators and the families of children can listen to the audio tapes and learn more about the development of a particular child or a group of children. One way to make audio-taped information more accessible is to transcribe the recorded information. The transcript would then be available for further notation and study for the teacher. The transcripts can also be shared with families.

**story grammar** understanding of beginning, middle, and ending of stories, characters, plot, and problem.

The two retellings shown on pages 150–151 demonstrate in a rather dramatic way how transcribed story retellings can show growth in a kindergarten student's understanding of **story grammar** as well as her ability to remember plot and dialogue from familiar storybooks. Every child will not demonstrate this much growth in the retelling stories over a three-month period, but the comparison of one retelling to the same retelling several months later will indicate the amount of progress the child has made in a given area.

### Videotapes

Videotapes can be used to document children's behaviors in a variety of activities. Of course, videotaping depends on the availability of a video camera and/or someone to operate the equipment. With young children, it is advisable that an additional adult be present on videotaping days, so that children's needs can still be met while someone operates the camera. There is an alternative if no volunteer can be found. A video camera can be set up on a tripod and left to run continuously focused on a particular center; however, sometimes the result is that the classroom noise overwhelms the specific conversations going on in that center.

Videotapes can be shared with families so that they can more easily envision what their child may be doing during the day. Comparison videos can be a very good tool in helping parents see the progress their children are making. A video of center time taken early in the year, compared to one taken toward the end of the year, can indicate longer attention spans, increased complexity of the student's work, and more cooperation and problem solving initiated by the students themselves. Comparative videos of a younger child can demonstrate increased large-motor skills and more sophisticated oral language. Comparative videos of an older student making an oral presentation to the class can show increased organizational skills, more attention to audience, and a greater command of the topic they chose. Videos can demonstrate growth in ways other methods of documentation cannot.

## Portfolios

Portfolios are being used for assessment quite often in early childhood classes today. High-quality early childhood programs have always included multiple ways of assessing children's progress and have shared children's drawing and writing and photographs of children at work with their families. Portfolios are just an extension of what many early childhood educators have always done (Hanson & Gilkerson, 1999). Portfolios are, in essence, collections of children's work samples and documented teacher observations. Portfolios can be a collection of some or all of the assessment methods discussed previously (Diffily & Fleege, 1993a). Portfolios can include anecdotal records, checklists, rating scales, interviews, notes about children's work, photographs, audio and videotapes, but do not have to include all of these methods of documenting children's progress. However, it is important that children's portfolios be collected systematically. The same criteria that guide good assessment should guide the construction of the portfolios of young children.

*The trick is being sure that our assessment is authentic and trustworthy and that it communicates clearly to other people.*

*–Linda Lamme*

Before beginning to develop portfolios, teachers should think about five fundamental issues: what it will look like, what will go in it, how and when contents are selected, how the portfolio is evaluated, and how portfolios can be presented to families and perhaps passed on to other teachers (Vavrus, 1990). Answers to these issues will vary from teacher to teacher depending on their assessment needs. Portfolios offer the flexibility to feature the strengths of individual children and the progress made during a year. This flexibility is particularly beneficial for children whose progress is different from typically developing children.

However, it takes time to think through all the issues related to portfolios and to maintain them (Diffily & Fleege, 1993b). Reading about how others have constructed portfolios is a good idea.

Portfolios can be stored in a variety of containers. Some teachers organize their entries by using a series of file folders labeled by developmental area and placed in hanging files. Other teachers use pizza boxes or large

*Comparative Retellings*

**KC Retelling of *Strega Nona* by Tomie de Paola**
**September 17**

"Bubble bubble pasta pot, boil me some pasta nice and hot . . . to fill me up . . . Bubble bubble pasta pot, to . . . make me some pasta to fill me up, bubble bubble pasta pot . . . Now I'm going to do the end verses. Simmer down my pot of clay until I'm hungry another day."

**KC Retelling of *Strega Nona* by Tomie de Paola**
**December 17**

"This is the story about Strega Nona and the pasta pot. The story is by Tomie de Paola. Strega Nona was old. She helped people if they had warts. She made a magic potion and she made the warts go away and she could make headaches better. She was getting old and she needed someone to help her in her little house, so she put the sign up in the town square and Big Anthony, that didn't listen to anybody, came to see Strega Nona. Strega Nona said, 'You must sweep the house and weed the garden and milk the goat. For that I will give you a place to sleep and good food to eat, but you must not touch the pasta pot. It is very valuable.' 'Oh, boy,' said Big Anthony. Big Anthony worked every day and he got food and a nice place to sleep. One day when he was working in the garden, he heard Strega Nona singing over the pasta pot. She was singing, 'Bubble, bubble, pasta pot. Boil me some pasta nice and hot. I am hungry and it's time to sup. Make enough pasta to fill me up.' And the pot bubbled and boiled until it was full. Then Strega Nona sang, 'Enough, enough my pasta pot. I have my pasta nice and hot, so simmer down my pot of clay until I'm hungry another day.' But too bad for Big Anthony. He did not see Strega Nona blow the three kisses to the magic pasta pot. Strega Nona called Big Anthony in for dinner. When he was getting water from the water fountain, he told everyone in the town square about the magic pasta pot. They all laughed at him. He was mad and that wasn't a good thing to be. He said, 'I'll show them.' The day came before Big Anthony even knew. Strega Nona said to Big Anthony, 'I'm going to see my friend, Strega Amelia. You must sweep the garden and milk the goat and you must not touch the pasta pot.' 'Yes,' said Big Anthony, but inside he was thinking, 'My chance has come.' As soon as Strega Nona was out of sight, he went into the house, grabbed the pasta pot off the shelf and started singing, 'Bubble, bubble, pasta pot. Boil me some pasta nice and hot. I am hungry and it's time to sup. Make enough pasta to fill me up.' So the pot bubbled and boiled and he quickly ran outside, jumped on the fountain, and yelled, 'Pasta at Strega Nona's house.' They all laughed, but Big Anthony yelled, 'Get forks, spoons, bowls, and platters. Come to Strega Nona's house for pasta.' But they went home and got their forks, spoons, platters, and bowls and they got pasta. And they ate both seconds and thirds. After a while they were done. So Big Anthony went inside and said, 'Enough, enough my pasta pot. I have my pasta nice and hot, so simmer

*(continued)*

*Comparative Retellings (continued)*

down my pot of clay until I'm hungry another day.' But he didn't blow the three kisses. So one of the sisters of the convent said, 'Big Anthony, look, the pasta is coming out.' So Big Anthony ran back inside and said the words, but the pasta kept boiling, so he picked it up off the floor, but it still wouldn't stop and he got the lid off and said one it, but the pasta lifted the lid and Big Anthony too and more pasta came out and went out the door of the little house and if someone wouldn't get poor Big Anthony, he would be covered up by the pasta. Everyone ran ahead of the pasta trying to get ahead of it so they wouldn't be covered up. The priest said, 'Get doors, chairs, anything so we can make a barricade.' And they tried but nothing helped. Strega Nona didn't have to look twice to know what happened. So Strega Nona said, 'Enough, enough my pasta pot. I have my pasta nice and hot, so simmer down my pot of clay until I'm hungry another day,' and then she blew three kisses to the pasta pot and the pasta came to a lult [sic] and all the people thanked Strega Nona and then they turned on Big Anthony. All the people said, 'You must string him.' But Strega Nona said, 'Wait. The punishment must fit the crime' and took a fork from a lady standing nearby and she said, 'Big Anthony wanted pasta from my magic pasta pot, then you eat it. So eat it.' So Big Anthony started to eat and he ate and he ate and he ate, ate, ate, until it was finally all gone. So she got to sleep in her little bed that night. And poor Big Anthony, how upset he was for no drink. The end."

sheets of construction paper folded in half and stapled. Some simply use large grocery bags to keep children's entries separate. The manner of storing portfolio entries depends on the teacher's preference and the ability of the children to access their portfolio. Whatever the manner of organization, the most important factor to remember about portfolio assessment is that the contents should be evidence of children's progress over time through a variety of assessment methods.

Portfolios should be constructed by both the teacher and the student. Each makes decisions about what is placed in the portfolio. The teacher may choose to include a checklist, comparative rating scales, comparative story retellings, a book created by the child, and several formal anecdotal records. The teacher can also select specific pieces of a child's work to showcase the growth of the child over several months. She should explain to the child why she chose those pieces and what she thinks they show about the child. Modeling the process of reviewing several options, making a portfolio selection, and giving reasons for choosing the piece is an important factor in helping the child develop the ability to make these decisions himself (Puckett & Black, 2000).

Students should also select work to include in the portfolio. Often teachers encourage children to select their best work to put in portfolios.

*Students can be asked to select their best work, their favorite work, or a piece that means the most to them for their portfolios.*

At other times, students may be asked to use different criteria for choosing a particular piece of work. They could be asked to choose favorite work, most meaningful work, or the most difficult or challenging work they have completed in a given period of time.

After making a selection for the portfolio, children are asked to dictate or write rationales for why they selected certain pieces to include in their portfolios. They are also asked to identify what they think they learned doing that particular piece of work.

Younger children, or students who have not had many experiences in this process, tend to give rather simplistic reasons for selecting a piece of work. They tend to choose work based on personal preferences: "I picked this story 'cause it is about a dog and I like dogs" or "I like this book because it has stamps and stamps are really neat to me actually. I picked it because it had stamps in it and I liked it." Children also tend to choose work based on their egocentric perceptions about what makes work good: "I picked this cause it's got all the colors," or "I liked this one because I worked hard on it and because the name is neat."

As children observe an adult modeling the rationale process of making portfolio selections and have many personal experiences doing this, they become more sophisticated in the process. They will begin making more realistic selections and offering more reasoned rationales. The rationales mentioned above were all dictated by one kindergarten student. As a first-grader, here are some possible rationales: "I picked this book because it is about rain forests. I wanted to learn about rain forests and this helped me. I did a lot of work. I read a lot of books and I wrote a lot about rain forests and I drew a lot of pictures and the pictures and the words are about the same thing. David and I worked together and we learned a lot of stuff about rain forests by making this book," or "This is my script for the videotape for Stephanie's class. I picked it because I like it and I worked hard on it and I put periods and spaces between words. And I writed neatly so other people could read it and did not mess up. I learned how to do scripts and I learned how to do a videotape and I learned to make lots of words." Children learn to choose work that demonstrates their ability to progress and get better through many experiences. They learn to explain these choices through their observations of the modeling of the teacher and through many opportunities to try to explain their reasons (Diffily, 1992).

Selecting work to be placed in a portfolio and giving reasons for choosing a particular piece of work helps children learn to value their own work and serves as an important tool in developing self-directed learners (Paulson, Paulson, & Meyer, 1991).

Portfolios should be evaluated in terms of how well they depict the whole child and how well they demonstrate the progress a child has made in a given period of time. Portfolios should be presented to families at a time when they can spend sufficient time examining the contents, listening to their child discuss what he thinks about different pieces, asking questions, listening to the teacher's interpretation of the child's work, and talking about what they learned about their child.

The portfolio for a two-year-old will look very different from that of a seven- or eight-year-old. The younger the child, the more the portfolio selections will be documented observations of the teacher. This documentation may take the form of checklists, rating scales, audio tapes, or any of the other methods of documentation discussed earlier in this chapter. Two- and three-year-olds will probably not be able to select from their drawings and paintings pieces of work that demonstrate developmental growth. They will choose pictures they like. This behavior is typical of four- and five-year-olds, too. However, with plenty of opportunities to choose their best work and think about why they selected particular pieces, six- and seven-years-old children will be making most of their own portfolio selections, complemented by a few pieces of documented teacher observations. By the time children are seven and eight years old, most of the portfolio contents will be their own work samples accompanied by their own rationales.

The children in the opening vignette had been working in a portfolio environment since they were in kindergarten. As third-graders, they were

**BIOGRAPHY BOX**  *Samuel J. Meisels*

Dr. Samuel Meisels is president of The Erikson Institute: A Graduate School in Child Development. He has served on the faculty of the University of Michigan where he was a professor of education and a research scientist and is now an emeritus professor. He has held positions as a Visiting Senior Fellow at the Centre for International Child Health at University College, London; faculty member of the Child Study Department at Tufts University and Director of its Eliot-Pearson Children's School, and senior advisor in Early Childhood Development for the Developmental Evaluation Clinic of Boston's Children's Hospital. He holds a doctorate from the Harvard Graduate School of Education and was a teacher of preschool and kindergarten–first grade for several years.

Dr. Meisels is the nation's leading authority on the assessment of young children, having published numerous articles, books, and monographs on the topic. He is coauthor of the *Work Sampling System: The Early Screening Inventory* and *The*

*Handbook of Early Childhood Intervention.* He is currently president of the Board of Directors of ZERO TO THREE: The National Center for Infants, Toddlers, and Families and is an advisor to the Head Start Bureau. He has served as a senior investigator for the National Early Childhood Longitudinal Study-Kindergarten Cohort, sponsored by the National Center for Education Statistics and the Center for the Improvement of Early Reading Achievement (CIERA).

Dr. Meisels's research focuses on the development of alternative assessment strategies in infancy, early childhood, and the elementary years; the impact of standardized tests on young children; developmental screening in early childhood; and developmental consequences of high-risk birth. Currently, he is working on two major projects. One is a study of the conditions under which poor children perform well in kindergartens. The other is the development of a performance assessment for children from birth to three year olds and their families, designed for use in Early Head Start, early intervention, and community programs for infants and families.

quite sophisticated in their ability to look at their work, make portfolio content decisions, and write rationales for those decisions. They were able to work with only occasional teacher support because they had had experiences over a four-year period related to creating portfolios. They had listened to group discussions about what constituted good writing, good math work, good reading responses, and so on. They observed their teacher verbalize her thinking about several pieces of their work and discuss her reasons for selecting specific pieces. They had many opportunities to examine their own work and try to articulate why one piece was better than another. They had worked in pairs and in small groups to identify characteristics of good work and had talked about good work with each other and with their teacher. All these experiences brought this group of students to the place where they could construct portfolios on their own.

Regardless of the age of the child or who takes primary responsibility for selecting the contents, portfolios are a systematic, dated collection of student work and teacher observations. They provide a rich description of students, their performance and their progress over a period of time.

Because of this rich description, portfolios are particularly powerful in helping families understand their child's progress (Diffily, 1992; Diffily & Fleege, 1993b).

### Student Self-Assessment

Third-graders constructing their own portfolios and sharing them with their families is a sophisticated form of self-assessment. However, they need many experiences to develop the capability to do that. Experts are encouraging early childhood educators to involve all their students in self-assessment activities (Bredekamp & Rosegrant, 1995; Potter, 1999). For younger children, around two or three years old, self-assessment might be as simple as the teacher asking them to recall their work at a center or what they think about a particular activity. Older students are capable of much more. Children who are four, five, or six years old may be asked to describe how they are good listeners when others are talking. They can be asked to evaluate their participation in a group activity, how cooperative they are, and what they might change in future group work. They can be asked to analyze their own work, discuss what makes it good, and identify what they think they need to work on next. In the following section, a first-grade example of this type of self-assessment is shown. Children who are six, seven, or eight years old and have become fluent writers may be asked to keep learning logs. These can be blank books in which they note at the end of each day or week those things they learned or want to know more about. Children can also work in pairs to write self-assessments and help each other remember things the other can do well.

It is important to consider the age and maturity of each child when asking children to assess themselves. Young children are, by nature, egocentric, which means they see the world through their own perspective. They tend to believe their work is always their "best." They overstate what they have learned (Diffily, 1992). This characteristic can have a definite influence on their self-assessment. For example, in one three-year-old class, the teacher established a weekly routine of the children dictating learning cards. Every Friday each student dictated an ending to the sentence, "This week I learned . . ." Because of the egocentric nature of the students, what was dictated was not always accurate from an adult perspective. On September 15, one boy in the class dictated, "This week I learned to be quiet." In reality, he had not learned to be quiet that week. What he had learned was that using a quiet voice was a behavior expected of him at school.

Transcribing one sentence per child does not require a major investment of time and can indicate a great deal about the child's understanding of his or her own learning. Early in the year, the students in a kindergarten class tended to dictate very global statements like "This week I learned to read." Toward the end of the year, they were dictating much more specific statements, like "This week I learned that Mercer Mayer puts a spider and a grasshopper in all his illustrations." Collected over a long period of time, these learning cards can demonstrate how children develop through the use

*Children who are fluent writers may be asked to keep a learning log of things they have learned or want to know more about.*

of this type of self-assessment. Teachers can use what they learn about students to design appropriate learning experiences for them.

## STANDARDIZED ASSESSMENT

The assessments described previously are often described as informal assessment to differentiate the observation-based assessment from the more formal evaluation of standardized assessment. Standardized assessment often begins in the pediatrician's office when the doctor compares an infant's height and weight to charts of standardized heights and weights of children of the same age. At other times, a young child may be evaluated with different types of standardized tests to measure specific behaviors. These standardized tests tend to be developmental screenings, readiness tests, or achievement tests. It is very important that any test given to young children be carefully selected and used only for the purpose for which it was designed (NAEYC, 1988).

*Self-Assessment of Writing*

| | |
|---|---|
| **What I am good at:** | I am good at putting periods at the end of my sentences. I am good at putting colors in my drawings. I am good at drawing illustrations. I am good at writing different stories. Some books I do are just picture books, but some books I write are long stories with lots of words. I believe that is what I am good at. |
| **What I need to work on now:** | I need to work on putting quotation marks and commas. |

## Developmental Screenings

Developmental screenings are used to identify children who may be in need of special educational services—above what the classroom teacher may be able to provide. Recently, the American Academy of Pediatrics Committee on Children with Disabilities published a statement on developmental surveillance and screening. "In doing so, they have appropriately called attention to the need for continuous developmental surveillance using procedures that are simple, valid, standardized, and reliable, as well as culturally sensitive and appropriate to the population. This recommendation could be applied as well to the surveillance of growth, which is an essential aspect of health maintenance" (Frankenburg, 2002, p. 144). This type of testing attempts to determine a child's ability to acquire skills rather than testing the skills he or she has already learned. These tests should be used only after extensive teacher observation and discussions with the child's family. The results of this type of testing should be used to guide educational decisions. A child should never be placed in a special education program or removed from his or her classroom based on a single test score. High-stakes educational decisions, such as placement in special programs, should be made on the basis of multiple sources of information. The results of a developmental screening might be one piece of information, but teacher and family observations should also be weighed in making such decisions.

## Readiness Tests

Readiness tests are typically administered to children entering public school kindergarten or first grade who are considered to be at-risk for success in school. These tests attempt to measure knowledge and skills that the child has already gained. The results of readiness testing should be used, in combination with other forms of assessment, to help teachers plan appropriate educational experiences for children. A single readiness test score should never be used to decide whether or not a child should enter a particular grade level or be retained in a grade.

## Achievement Tests

Achievement tests are supposed to measure what children have learned from instruction. These tests tend to be administered in groups, in entire classes of children, frequently beginning as early as kindergarten. Achievement tests are typically multiple-choice tests that prompt a child to select the one "right" answer from a group of four alternatives. Achievement tests focus on discrete skills such as letter/sound association to test word attack skills, identification of main idea to test reading comprehension, and computation to test math ability. Some educators believe that scores from achievement tests are useful in planning curriculum (Popham, 2001). Other educators disagree (American Education Research Association 2000; Ohanian, 2002) claiming that achievement test scores are often used to label children as above-, below-, or on-grade-level.

## Cautions about Standardized Testing

At its best, standardized testing captures a child's ability on a particular day to answer a set of very narrow questions. By the very nature of standardized testing, most questions must be constructed so that single "right" answers exist. These close-ended questions do not probe a children's thinking and do not take into account variations in children's experiences and development when determining whether answers are "right" or "wrong." Test scores are derived from the number of "right" answers given by each child without considering the numerous factors that might affect the child's ability to produce the "right" answers on the day of testing. These factors include, but are not limited to, what background experiences the child has had, how the child feels that day, whether the child is hungry or sick or is living with stressful experiences outside of school, and how the child has developed cognitively or emotionally to this point. The American Educational Research Association's position statement about standardized testing stresses that any standardized tests for children include: protection against high-stakes decisions based on single tests, adequate resources and opportunities to learn, validation for each intended use, alignment between the test and the curriculum, and appropriate attention to students with disabilities (2000).

From a wide range of child development theorists, educators know that young children develop at different rates. These differences in cognitive and emotional development definitely affect their ability to take tests. Some may lack the auditory memory to follow directions required of them in testing situations. Many have short attention spans for activities that they do not choose. Some are easily distracted. Most cannot use abstract symbols required by standardized tests (Puckett & Black, 2000). These are all developmental issues that can dramatically affect the test scores of individual children. If a young child cannot concentrate long enough to focus on all questions or cannot understand the abstract nature of test questions, how can the test score be an adequate reflection of that child's intellectual ability or academic achievement?

Researchers who study standardized tests have come to the conclusion that many test questions have a bias against minority and low-income children (Medina & Neill, 1990). One question on a standardized test used to determine kindergarten children's need for special educational services asks five-year-old to tell the tester how many wheels are on a wheelbarrow. How many inner-city kindergarteners have even seen a wheelbarrow? How can test scores be valid when children are being asked questions about concepts outside their life experiences?

Similarly, educators have found that individuals have different ways of knowing and problem solving (Gardner, 1983). These differences do not indicate more intelligence or stronger academic abilities, but standardized tests do not recognize any other thinking than that used to determine the "correct" answer. One first-grade student chose answer B for this multiple choice question:

**1. How many hours are in a day?**  A. 24 B. 12 C. 8 D. 4.

From an adult perspective, the answer to this question is clearly A for 24 hours. When asked about her answer, the six-year-old responded, "The answer has to be 12 hours cause there are 12 hours in the day and 12 hours in the night." It is obvious that this child understood the concept being addressed by the question. She simply looked at the question from a different, though not wrong, perspective. Yet, her answer was scored as incorrect. Is testing that restricts a child's thinking a valid way to assess what he or she knows?

Testing of young children should always be done judiciously. Only when the potential benefit from the test results—identification of a particular challenge or access to needed services to support what an early childhood program is able to provide—should standardized tests be administered to children under the age of nine. For most children, the careful observations of an early childhood educator, documentation of those observations, and collection of children's work samples are adequate assessment methods.

## TRANSLATING OBSERVATIONS INTO DEVELOPMENTALLY APPROPRIATE PRACTICES

Careful observations of children—even those that are well documented— must be understood by the teacher in light of child development principles. Teachers need to be aware of this body of knowledge so that they can view each child and his or her development as unique, yet following general patterns of progression (Puckett & Black, 2000). Knowledge about child development helps teachers understand age-appropriate activities for children.

## Using Observations to Plan Group Experiences

Group experiences in early childhood classrooms can include the teacher— or a child—reading aloud to the whole group, shared action songs and other music experiences, nursery rhyme and poetry recitation, creative drama, very short teacher-directed lessons, and group meetings to talk about the day's opportunities or to review the day's activities. The length of these group experiences and their nature must be determined by what the teacher knows about the students in that particular group. For toddlers, group experiences are very short and always of high interest. Older children have the ability to sit in group times for longer periods of time, but the teacher should decide how long these sessions are based on observations of the children. Children's interests should guide the teacher in her selection of the books that are read aloud, the songs that are introduced to the group, and the types of drama experiences that are offered to children.

## Using Observations to Plan Individual Experiences

*Teachers must understand the normal stages of personal and social development before they can completely assess and evaluate young children.*

*-Cathy Grace & Elizabeth Shores*

Assessment as discussed in this chapter offers opportunities to learn much information about a child, what he knows and how he interacts with materials and with other people, how he processes information, connections he makes between new knowledge and what he already knows. This kind of in-depth knowledge about a child, combined with knowledge about child development principles, enables teachers to determine individually appropriate learning experiences for each child (Hannaford, 1995; Shepard, 1994).

When teachers use kidwatching techniques to really get to know their students, they are better equipped to plan learning experiences that are meaningful to that specific group of children. They may know from child development principles that most infants attempt walking between nine and twelve months; however, some children may begin walking as early as seven months or as late as fifteen months. Room arrangements may have to be changed for children who walk early or later. Teachers may know from child development that three-year-olds typically have attention spans of four to five minutes for a large group read-aloud. However, one group of three-year-olds who have had lots of experiences with shared reading may have attention spans two or three times that of typical children this age. Story times for these children can be extended to ten or fifteen minutes based on observations. Child development principles teach that children learn to play games with rules around the age of seven, but some children develop this skill earlier so teachers provide materials to support these emerging skills.

## Using Observations to Plan Changes in the Environment

Through kidwatching, teachers can identify strengths in the children and design learning centers to build on those strengths. When a child is accomplished at a skill, he or she does not need repeated experiences practicing that skill. A child who can use scissors effectively does not need to keep cutting scrap paper for collage. Teachers need to help children move forward, to more knowledge or more sophisticated skills. If a teacher observes a child who is particularly interested in guinea pigs, he or she might provide books such as *Guinea Pigs Don't Read Books* (Bare, 1985) or *Taking Care of Your Guinea Pig: A Young Pet Owner's Guide* (Piers, 1993) in the science center. If the teacher discovers that several children are choosing to reread the same book, they might find other books by the same author and place them in a prominent location in the reading center. If the teacher notices children who are making extensive plans for a project in a small group meeting, she may suggest that they write a list of the things they want to accomplish. Discovering what children are already doing and expanding on that is one way that teachers can use observations to offer developmentally appropriate environments and activities.

Teachers can also use observation to identify areas that need strengthening. From observations, teachers plan center and small group activities that will enhance these areas. When teachers are aware of behaviors that are typical of certain age groups, they will know to provide additional experiences for children who are not demonstrating those behaviors. If during repeated observations of a four-year-old child, a teacher finds that a child does not use language for creating and sustaining the plot of dramatic play, the teacher could offer opportunities for the child to read wordless picture books or use hand puppets. Both experiences offer practice in expressing action and dialogue in words. If a five-year-old has difficulty picking up small objects with ease, the teacher could make stringing beads, geoboards, and pegboards available to the child (Beaty, 2001). If a seven-year-old is having difficulty with two-digit place value, he can be shown this concept with linking cubes and place-value charts and encouraged to play double- and triple-dice addition games. Specific learning experiences should be offered to some children who would benefit from them.

At other times, observations let teachers know where on a learning continuum a child is. While there are no rigid hierarchies of skills and knowledge that children must master, there are some developmental continuums. Emergent writing is one example of a developmental continuum teachers should be familiar with. Young children typically scribble as their first approximation of writing. Then they usually begin to draw pictures, invent their own letters, and write strings of random letters. After these types of emergent writing, children typically begin to use invented spelling, writing the letters whose sounds they hear in the words they want to write. All these forms of emergent writing typically occur before children begin to use conventional spelling. Being aware of how children typically proceed through the continuum of emergent writing behaviors allows teachers to support children properly through this continuum.

## REVISITING SELF-SELECTION OF PORTFOLIO ENTRIES

As children in the third grade are selecting their best work to include in their portfolios, in a nearby kindergarten classroom, five-year-olds are also working on their portfolios. Instead of the sophisticated rationales the eight- and nine-year-olds give for their selection, the younger children are choosing their best work for more egocentric reasons. They select pieces of writing by whether they have lots of words or lots of colors on them. They also choose their best work by the topic of the piece of writing. For example, if a story is about a dog and they like dogs, they may select this piece even though it is not an example of their best writing.

The kindergarten teacher is not disappointed by these responses. She accepts the children's reasons for choosing their best work as they state them, knowing from the principles of child growth and development that their egocentricism contributes to their selection and reasons for them. She knows from observing individual children during the year that each child is making progress in this process and can demonstrate this progress to families by sharing work selections and reasons for the selections given by the children throughout the year.

### Summary

Ongoing teacher observation of children as they work in early childhood classrooms can provide valuable information about individual children and the peer group. These observations should be documented so that they can be remembered and thus be helpful for the teacher to form detailed descriptions of each child. Continuing observations, interpreted through child development principles, help teachers plan age appropriate and individually appropriate environments and learning experiences.

Many different forms for documenting observations are discussed in this chapter. Trying to implement them all would be very intimidating—and would almost certainly lead to frustration and/or failure. When beginning an assessment program based on teacher observation, it is wise to select one or two forms of documentation and incorporate these into the daily routine of the early childhood classroom. As completing each form of documentation becomes a habit, another method can be added. As teachers come to understand how much they can learn about children and how much more they have to share with families about the child, they will value observation and documentation as an important tool for assessment.

Teachers also realize how much they can learn about children from the children's family. In chapter 5, several methods of communicating and developing relationships with families will be discussed.

## Reflections

**1.** Compare your thoughts about assessment of young children before you read this chapter with the assessment methods you now know to be appropriate. How has your thinking changed?

**2.** Think about the methods of documenting teacher observations discussed in this chapter. Which ones do you think you will try to implement the first year you teach young children? Why do these methods appeal to you? What benefit do you expect to gain as the teacher? How will this type of knowledge about students help you be a better teacher?

**3.** Consider a child you have observed for a period of time. Did anything you observed bring to mind experiences that should be provided for that child? If you were the teacher, how might you incorporate those experiences into the classroom?

## Field Experiences

**1.** Visit a kindergarten or first-grade classroom where portfolios are used to assess student progress. With the teacher's permission, carefully review one portfolio and write a "rich" description of the child portrayed by that portfolio. Look for authentic children's work—artwork, writing, dictation—as opposed to worksheets. Look for the teacher's anecdotal records and determine if these are written in objective language. Look for other methods of documented teacher observations (e.g., checklists and rating scales). Most importantly, look for multiple measures collected over time.

**2.** Choose an early childhood classroom for any age group and observe for at least two hours. Observe a few children, maybe just four or five, and write informal, anecdotal records. Exchange them with another student in your class and see what they can tell you about your observations.

## Case Studies

### What Do I Do with All This Documentation?

From the workshops I've attended and the articles I've read, I believe teachers of young children should document their observations. So much goes on during any given school day that it is impossible to remember everything.

So I plan all kinds of documentation. I have checklists for physical development, large and fine motor. I have rating scales for social skills, literacy behaviors, and math skills. I audio-tape children's reading once a month and audio-tape retellings or interviews every other week. I take photographs all the time and I'm constantly asking children if I can keep some of their work for their portfolios. So here I am with all this information about my students, but it is all over the room. The checklists are on clipboards, so I can just grab them and mark the different skills when I see children show that they are using certain skills. The photographs are all together. I always put photographs in the same desk drawer when I get them processed. I keep meaning to write something on the back of those pictures and put them in student files, but so far, I haven't found the time. And, children's work samples—I've got this huge stack of drawings and writings, some of them dated, some of them not dated, just a big stack of papers. I'll admit, I'm not the most organized person I know. But, here I am. Conferences start next week and I want to share some of this information, but I don't know where to start.

### What to Do?

This teacher is well intentioned. She has collected quite a bit of information about her students, but had no plan for organizing the documentation she worked on. How useful is information that is gathered but not organized? What can she reasonably do before parent/teacher conferences the next week? What can she do to get more organized?

### Is This a Report Card?

A committee of early childhood teachers from all over the school district worked together last summer and created new report cards for all prekindergartens, kindergartens, and first grades. I was so happy to see the results of their work. The committee convinced the administration that number and letter grades were not appropriate for young children and that these didn't really tell parents what their child was learning. Instead of having to come up with number grades for my first-grade students as I have done for the past four years, now the report card lists skills and behaviors expected of first graders. Teachers mark one of four different levels of understanding and using each skill.

The report card made all kinds of sense to me. The skills and behaviors listed on the report card guided the observation of my students. I used those skills as a way to organize student work in portfolios. It just seemed that what I was teaching, how I was assessing their progress, and how I was reporting to parents all fit together.

I really expected parents to appreciate the new format of the report card. It gave them a lot more information about their child. Boy, was I wrong. The night that the first report card was sent home, I got phone call after phone call. We had told parents about the new report card in that first of school meeting, but there weren't many questions until they got that new report card. I listened to parents' complaints, explained the reasons for the new format of the report card, and tried to get them to see how much more they knew about their child's learning based on this information than they ever would learn by looking at a letter grade. I think I was on the telephone most of the evening.

**What to Do?**

With so many parents upset about the format of the new report card, what would be the best course of action for this teacher? Should she lay low and see if this situation calms down on its own? Should she wait for her principal or district administrators to handle parent concerns? Should she be proactive and provide information to the families in her class? If she goes on the offensive with information, what should she send home?

## Further Reading

Beaty, J. J. (2001). *Observing development of the young child* (6th ed.). New York: Merrill

Kohn, A. (1999). *The schools our children deserve: Moving beyond traditional classrooms and "tougher standards"* Boston: Houghton Mifflin.

Levine, M. (2002). *A mind at a time.* New York: Simon & Schuster.

Ohanian, S. (2002). *What happened to recess and why are our children struggling in kindergarten?* New York: McGraw-Hill.

Puckett, M. B., & Black, J. K. (2000). *Authentic assessment of the young child: Celebrating development and learning.* 2nd ed. New York: Merrill.

## Helpful Web Sites

### Students Against Testing

www.nomoretests.com

*As its URL suggests, this Web site argues against standardized testing. It offers information about standardized tests: articles, Q & A, research, quotes, a discussion board, and links. In addition to facts, this Web site may provoke a smile or two in its listing of 101 things to do besides standardized testing and its test entitled "The Best Standardized Test Ever."*

Check the Online Resources™ for expert practitioners' responses to each case study.

For additional information on teaching young children, visit our Web site at **http://www.earlychilded.delmar.com**

# CHAPTER 5

## Basing Quality Practices on Knowledge Shared with Families

*Early Childhood Principle* Professional early childhood educators view all families and communities as integral parts of early childhood programs.

An extensive body of research documents the fact that children benefit in many different ways—academically, socially, and emotionally—when their families are involved in their education. It is equally true that families and teachers benefit from close relationships between them. In high-quality early childhood programs, teachers take the lead in developing relationships with families so that true partnerships exist between home and early childhood classrooms. To reach different family members, teachers use a wide variety of communication methods to share what is happening in the classroom and why they believe in the teaching strategies they use. Teachers also schedule several different types of shared time—family meetings, family field trips, special event nights, family conferences—so family members become more comfortable with the teacher and more familiar with the families of other children.

### After reading this chapter, you should be able to:
- Identify the components of Bronfenbrenner's ecological system and describe how the systems affect young children.
- Discuss what early childhood educators can learn about a child from his or her family.
- Identify some of the family configurations that currently exist and describe how early childhood educators might work with those families.
- Describe the forms of written communication teachers might use.
- Describe additional methods of communicating, other than writing, that teachers and families can use.
- Define advocacy and describe why advocacy is important to young children and their families.

It is a busy first-grade classroom. Children are working in several learning centers. Two girls are sitting on the floor in the science center holding class pets. Four children are working in the block center constructing a zoo based on their experiences during a recent class field trip. Six children are seated at the writing center table, each working on different stages of bookmaking. Two boys had climbed into the loft that served as a reading center for the class and are reading *One Fish, Two Fish, Red Fish, Blue Fish* (Seuss, 1960) to each other. One boy is sorting through audio tapes, trying to decide whether the class should listen to the Chieftains or to a tape of Bach sonatas. Another child is writing words on the chalkboard. These activities are typical for these students. They are making their own plans and carrying them out.

But there is something unusual about the activities in this classroom. It is 6:20 P.M. The school day had ended almost three hours earlier. Families had come back to school and were actively involved in the children's activity choices. There are some mothers and fathers, some brothers and sisters, and even a few aunts, uncles, and grandparents. Some of the adults are chatting with each other though most of them are either petting the guinea pig, building a block zoo, writing a story, taking turns reading, or writing words on the chalkboard, involved in the same activities as the children. At 6:30 the adults excuse themselves from the activities and go to an adjacent room. The children continue their work, supervised by a college student, and the adults begin their monthly family meeting.

At first, the teacher, Pam Thomas, gives every adult a place-value mat and a reclosable bag filled with linking cubes. She leads them through a math activity of adding two-digit numbers with regrouping. Parents have the same experience their children did earlier that day. To represent the number 13, they connect ten linking cubes, place those in the tens place, and put three individual linking cubes in the ones place on the mat. To represent the addend 19, they repeat the process, putting a group of ten in the tens place and nine individual cubes in the ones place. They count the individual cubes in the ones place and check for a group of ten. They connect these cubes and move the set of ten into the tens place, then arrive at the answer 32 by seeing the three sets of ten and the two individual cubes. The parents repeat this process with another addition problem and talk about how using manipulatives helps children understand the concept of regrouping better than the repetitious paper-and-pencil computation that they had in first grade.

Thirty minutes into the meeting, the tone of the meeting changes from the teacher informing parents about curriculum issues to the group discussing other issues that affect the class. They talk about field trip possibilities and eventually choose two trips for the following month. They decide that the trip to the art museum should occur during school hours when the museum would be less crowded, but that the wildflower identification and search for monarch butterfly caterpillars should be a Saturday family field trip so that siblings can benefit from that experience too.

Next the families review a proposal the class had written about establishing a cooking club. Pam explains how the proposal came to be, and a few parents comment about how impressed they are that six-year-olds can express what they want in the form of a proposal. As they read through the proposal, several parents smile at some of the invented spelling the children use. Some family members tell stories about cooking with their own children, then one mother asks Pam what she thinks about the idea. Having anticipated this question, Pam shares a handout about the learning that can occur during cooking experiences. In only a few minutes, parents agree to "approve" the proposal and start a sign-up sheet for days they will supply ingredients. As some parents work on the cooking club details, other parents look at their calendars and set a date for the next family meeting. The families who have attended this meeting feel comfortable with the teacher and with each other. They have been meeting together once a month since the first week of the school year.

These meetings have several different purposes. During family meetings, Pam shares important information about why she uses particular teaching methods. She involves families in some of the same activities that she offers to children so that they better understand the learning strategies she teaches. She tells stories about the life of the class to personalize the learning occurring in the classroom, and families tell stories about their children outside the classroom. Together the teacher and the families make important decisions about the first-graders' activities. Families have opportunities to express concerns and get questions answered. All of the people who attend the meetings have the chance to get to know one another better. This kind of relationship between the teacher and the family members allows all the adults to make this a good year for the children in Pam's class.

## FAMILY SYSTEMS THEORY

In a sense Pam is incorporating a variation of family systems theory in working with families of the students she is teaching. **Family systems theory** proposes that every member of a family influences other family members. Something that happens to one family member affects other members of the family. This influence is evident when a parent loses his or her job. All family members are affected by this event. But a family is just as influenced if something occurs to one of the children. If one child has learned to fear a bully at school, the whole family is affected by this child's fear. No one family member can be understood without understanding family dynamics. Thus, counselors who use the family systems approach involve all

**family systems theory** the belief and counseling practice that presumes that all family members' lives affect all others in the family.

members of a family in counseling sessions, not just the individual who seeks counseling.

Early childhood educators generally agree with this theory and understand the important interrelatedness of child and family (McWilliam & Maxwell, 1999; Swick & Broadway, 1997). This conviction explains the strong belief in early childhood about working with young children *and* their families. Early childhood educators believe it is not enough to work with the children; they are convinced that they must help family members understand what is age appropriate for their child, how the class operates, and what they can do at home to support the child's learning. The more teachers and families work together, the more the child will benefit (Berger, 1999; Gestwicki, 2000; Griffith, 1996). Children whose families work closely with the school are typically more successful in both short-term and long-term intellectual development and have enhanced social and emotional development.

Families generally welcome support from teachers in the early childhood years as they face the challenges of rearing young children (Diffily, 2001b; Swick & Broadway, 1997). Families generally want what's best for their children, but sometimes lack the knowledge about child growth and development to help them make learning decisions that are age appropriate for their children. Teachers can offer this knowledge. Then family-teacher discussions about issues such as child development, learning environments, and the support of young children's learning can grow into true partnerships. Research shows that families who become involved in parent-education programs gain a sensitivity to their child's emotional, social, and intellectual development and needs.

But as important as teachers and families are to the lives of young children, children are influenced by more than just the people with whom they spend most of their time. Urie Bronfenbrenner (1979, 1986) presented an ecological systems theory that demonstrated that children were affected by large numbers of people, organizations, and institutions. Bronfenbrenner contended that children are a part of society at large and are affected by their neighborhoods, communities, states, countries, and even the global society.

Bronfenbrenner proposed four layers of systems that influence children (Figure 5–1). In the center of the circles of influences is the child. All four systems surround the child and affect, and are affected by, him or her either directly or indirectly. In the first system, the **microsystem**, the child is influenced by those closest to him or her. The next system, the **mesosystem**, consists of interrelationships in the home, the school or child care center, the church, and the neighborhood. The third system, the **exosystem**, consists of formal and informal groups of people. The informal groups of people in the exosystem are the friends of parents, neighbors, and the extended family. The formal groups include people who work with parents and people who make decisions that affect children such as school boards, local and state

**microsystem** relationships and experiences from the child's immediate environment.

**mesosystem** interrelationships and experiences among home, school, and the neighborhood.

**exosystem** settings in which the child does not actively participate but still affect him or her, such as parents' workplace, local government, and local corporations.

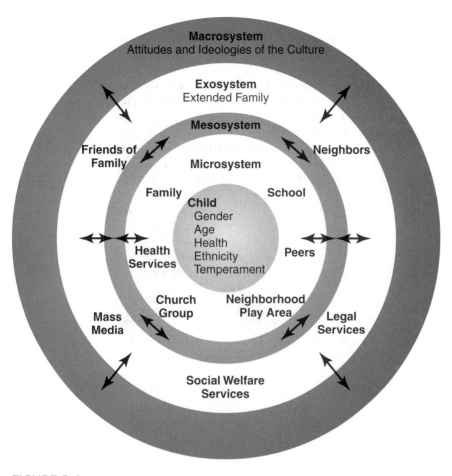

**FIGURE 5–1**
*Ecological Systems Theory*

governing bodies, mass media, and local corporations. The fourth system is
the **macrosystem,** which includes global societal attitudes, values, customs,
and laws.

    In the microsystem, the child is influenced by parents, siblings, and peo-
ple who are active in the child's life on a regular basis. At this level of influence, the child directly interacts with these people. In the home, the child has
close relationships with parents and siblings. At school, the child interacts
with the teacher and peers. At church, the child interacts with a few adults
and the peers in his classes. In the neighborhood, the child may be involved
with a few peers and their parents. The child learns values and attitudes and
early concepts from these people in his or her immediate environment.

    The mesosystem is characterized by a slightly expanded sphere of influ-
ence. The mesosystem consists of the interactions and interrelationships

**macrosystem** domi-
nant beliefs of society.

among those people with whom the child is directly involved. This includes the parents' relationships at school, in the neighborhood, and at church. The child is affected by the quality of these relationships. For example, in the relationship between the home and the school, the child will definitely benefit if the home and school hold similar values and work together. However, if the parents and teachers hold opposing views about how children learn best and do not work together to resolve these conflicts, the child may be negatively affected.

The exosystem in Bronfenbrenner's system consists of a number of groups of people and organizations that affect the child directly, but with whom the child is not involved. The child does not typically participate in activities at the parents' workplace, but company policies regarding sick leave and early release time for school involvement do directly affect the child. The child is not involved with the people who serve on the local school board or the state legislature, but these people make decisions that determine how many children can be enrolled in public school or childcare classrooms. Children are not involved in relationships with the media, but are definitely affected by decisions made by mass media about television programming, commercials, and news broadcasts.

Because the macrosystem consists of the dominant beliefs and ideologies of society, the child is directly and indirectly affected by these values. Societal tolerance of divorce may directly affect the child. The work ethic of a community directly affects children. The economic realities of today's welfare reform directly affect many children.

Bronfenbrenner's ecological systems theory helps early childhood educators realize just how many influences affect young children. A teacher should be aware of these influences and work to help create the best situation for children possible. Working with parents and helping them understand how they and their relationships affect the child, the teacher may be able to work to change some of the influences in the microsystem and mesosystem. The teacher may be able to change some of the influences in the exosystem by serving as an advocate for children with corporate boards, school boards, state legislatures, and other bodies that make decisions that affect children.

A teacher may become involved in many aspects of these areas of influence. This role of advocacy will be discussed later in the chapter. But teachers must first meet immediate responsibilities of the children they care for and the families of those children.

## RESPECTING AND LEARNING FROM FAMILIES

Pam, the teacher in the opening vignette, had learned an important lesson early in her teaching career about working with the families of the children she taught. She learned in college courses that families were an integral part of her work with young children. As she began teaching, she realized just how true this was. She found that she needed to communicate with families and that she needed to make time to listen to what they had to teach her about their children. The more families understood her classroom curriculum and goals, the more they could support their child's development. The more she knew about life circumstances, interests, and educational goals of the families, the better she understood her students.

Pam tried to be sensitive to the differences in families. Realizing that the adults who cared for her students at home might or might not be the parents of her students, she did not refer to the group as "parents." Some of these adults were grandparents. Some were aunts and uncles. Some were legal guardians with no biological relationship. She did not address weekly letters "to parents." Instead, she began her letters "to families" so as to include everyone. She consciously used the terms "family-teacher conference" and "family meetings" instead of "parent-teacher conference" and "parent meetings." This was a small change for Pam, but an important one for many of the adults associated with her students.

She respected parental responsibilities and the diversity of values held by families. She believed virtually all adults want what is best for children, but she also knew that not everyone agreed on what types of experiences were best for young children. Pam had taken a few child development classes in college, had worked with young children for several years, and regularly read professional journals and books. She believed that children learn best by active involvement and exploration, but she realized that many adults did not recognize this kind of learning, having only their own educational experiences on which to rely. For some of the families she worked with, first grade meant desks, reading groups with basal readers, spelling tests, and math worksheets. Because these experiences were familiar to them, they looked for desks and worksheets. Pam recognized it was her responsibility to share what she knew about six- and seven-year-olds and what research showed about how they learned best. She realized that she needed to explain why she arranged her classroom in centers and why she encouraged children to make so many of their own decisions during the school day. Pam had a lot of information to share with families about young children and how they learn.

However, Pam acknowledged that families had a lot of information to share with her too. The adults who cared for her students knew those children in ways that she could never know them. Many parts of her students' lives were hidden to her. She had not seen their first steps or listened as they said their first words. She never woke them up in the mornings or fed them breakfast. She never saw them at family gatherings or went on vacations with them. She knew that she had much to learn from families and valued them as an active part of her classroom.

Even before Pam met her students, she began to lay the foundation for good relationships with the families of her students with a letter sent to their homes similar to the letter in the following section. This type of letter serves several purposes. It gives families a glimpse into the classroom setting before they ever step into it. It lets families know a little bit about the teacher's basic educational philosophy. By sharing information about herself, she is showing herself as a person. Then by asking them to share information about their family with her, she is showing herself as someone who is interested in them and their children.

Not every family will respond to a letter like this, but many will. The teacher will gain valuable background information about children and their families from the return letters. Many families welcome the opportunity to tell a new teacher about their child and write long, enlightening letters. Some families will write brief notes. Even when families choose not to write a letter about their child, the teacher has begun to establish a warm, open attitude toward families. By showing her willingness to share information about herself and her life and asking about children's families, the teacher sets the stage for accepting families and working with them in a partnership.

## Variety of Family Configurations

Families of the twenty-first century are more diverse than ever before. Children live in a variety of family configurations. Today, some families:

- are headed by single mothers or fathers.
- have two parents who juggle dual careers, even commuter marriages.
- blend two separate families.
- rear children in two different homes because of joint custody court orders.
- expand their family by adopting children.
- have gay or lesbian parents.
- care for children within a foster care agreement.
- face particular challenges such as poverty, homelessness, violence and neglect, or parenting at very young ages.

The two-parent family with a stay-at-home mother represents a small percentage of today's families. While all families have some similar needs, different configurations of families have different lifestyles and need different kinds of support from teachers. Early childhood educators recognize their responsibility to try to understand the challenges that families face, to get to know individual families in their programs, and to reach out and work with all families (Grossman, 1999). To work effectively with all families, teachers become familiar with home languages, interactional styles, and values of different families (Rimm-Kaufman & Pianta, 1999; Voltz & Morrow, 1999). The following three sections discuss just a few of the ways teachers adjust their practices to meet the needs of families.

*Introductory Letter to Families*

July 12

Dear Families,

Very soon we will begin developing new relationships. School starts in less than two weeks and I like to get to know families as soon as possible. Letters are one way to begin getting to know each other. I thought I would share some things about me and my family, and I hope you will respond with some thoughts about your child and your family.

Until eight years ago, I worked in the field of development and fund-raising. Although my undergraduate degree was in education, I chose to work in the business world. After my son was born, I started taking graduate classes in early childhood at Texas Wesleyan University. At the time, I wanted information that would help me be a better mother, but quickly, I was hooked. After taking two or three classes, I decided that I wanted to work with young children. Early childhood is a critical time in a person's life. Life-long attitudes are formed in the early years, so I believe my work with young children is important. I love it.

I believe that young children learn best when they are active and when they make many decisions about their learning. You'll notice when you first walk into the classroom that it is organized by centers. Most of our day will be spent working in these centers. You may also notice that my classroom seems a little bare at the moment. That is by design. I want the children to feel a real sense of ownership of the room. Centers are established, but we will be creating bulletin boards, classroom labels, and adding learning materials to centers together.

My son, Michael, will be a third-grader this year. I talk about Michael in class quite a bit, so you may be hearing about him during the year. Michael is very science oriented. For the past year, he has been collecting rocks and fossils and is better at identifying fossils than I am.

I am married to Jim Diffily. He and I met fifteen years ago when we both worked at the Museum of Science and History. He still works there as the Director of Collections and Exhibits, but he is best known as "Mr. Diffily" who gives the live animal lectures to preschool classes at the museum.

As a family, we do things together, usually on the weekends—movies, fossil hunting, museum exhibits, and plays. Every night Jim and I both read to Michael and we try to play board games a couple of times a week. There are always lots of projects going on at my house. I am doing lots of writing at the moment and Michael and Jim are rebuilding a VW Beetle, making Adirondack chairs, and working on excavating a dinosaur about an hour south of our house.

Maybe this note will give you a little insight into me and my family. I would like to know more about your family. I know that my teaching must begin with making your child feel at home in our school and our classroom—and in helping families come together in a learning community. Would you

*(continued)*

*Introductory Letter to Families (continued)*

take a quiet moment to write whatever you think would help me get to know your child and your family? You may want to think about these questions. What is your child like? What are the things you know about your child that would be important for me to know? What are your family's interests and your child's interests? Thanks for taking time to write. I know that sharing information will help us all.

I am sure you have lots of questions. Let's plan on our first family meeting for Tuesday night, August 2, from 6:30 to 8:30 P.M. I'll hire a babysitter if you want to bring your children. We'll let the children have our classroom and the adults can meet nearby. These meetings are always informal with only a short teacher-led agenda. After that I'll answer any questions you have and we will make some plans together for this first nine weeks. Until that time, please know that you are always welcome in the classroom and if you ever have a question, you can write a note on the notebook paper in the folder (I'll try to answer it the same day) or you can call me at home.

I am looking forward to this year and the opportunities we will all create for the students in our classroom.

Sincerely,

Deborah Diffily

## Working Families and Single Parents

Economic conditions today often require that both parents work. Balancing the responsibilities of work and family life can be very stressful. These stresses are even more prominent for single-parent families in which one parent must assume all these responsibilities alone. The early childhood educator should consider the concerns of these families in communication and family involvement. Communication should be regular so that families know when they can anticipate hearing from teachers. Meetings should be scheduled well in advance so that families can arrange their schedules so they can attend. Family-teacher conferences should be offered at different times of the day, during early morning hours before school, around the lunch hour, during the evening, or on weekends. Teachers who offer such flexibility in scheduling meetings will have more participation from families. Meeting face to face is probably the best way for teachers and family members to talk. When this is not possible, telephone calls can add to methods of two-way communication between home and school. Even brief phone calls can keep parents up-to-date on their child's experiences. Teachers could survey families so they would know when telephone calls would be most welcome and make a call or two every day.

*Because of divorce and remarriage, many children today live with single parents and stepparents.*

## Blended Families and Children with Two Homes

Because of divorce and remarriage, many children today live with a parent and a stepparent. Some even live with two families because of joint custody and move between homes. Early childhood educators should be sensitive to all parties in these situations. Teachers should make sure they know about legal agreements regarding visitation, childcare, and other arrangements. All adults involved in the life of the child—parents and stepparents—should be involved in the life of the class. Teachers should take special care to use correct last names of family members and pronounce those names correctly. They should be invited to conferences and class or school meetings and receive all written communication from the class and the school. Even when these adults do not live in the area, arrangements can be made with noncustodial parents so they can receive written communication by mail.

## Families Facing Particular Challenges

Families who face the challenges of poverty, homelessness, violence, and neglect, or parenting when they are very young may need additional support to cope with these difficult situations. The teacher can serve as a source

*Be sure home correspondence, assignments, classroom assignments, and school events allow for the variety of family structures represented within your classroom. A child may want to bring a grandparent to Open House or create a Mother's Day card for an aunt, a stepmother, or the teacher down the hall*
*—Candy Carlile*

of information about community programs and agencies that can assist families. Families in these situations may feel uncomfortable in school or center settings and may need special encouragement to become involved in the life of the school. The teacher must reach out to these families and establish the foundation for working together for the benefit of children. Other families face different types of challenges. These families include, but are not restricted to, adoptive families, interracial families, immigrant families, and lesbian and gay families. These families also need the support and understanding of early childhood educators.

## COLLABORATING WITH FAMILIES

Collaboration is built on mutual benefit. Each party comes into a collaboration with something to offer that benefits the other. This is especially true for those who care for young children—families and early childhood educators alike. Both have important information to share. No one knows an individual child like that child's family, and early childhood educators know child development and research about young children not familiar to most families. Working in collaboration they can learn from each other and create the best possible situations for young children.

*Finding ways to get to know parents in advance of conferences is very helpful and eases the strain that most of us feel when talking to strangers about important matters.*
*-Susan McAllister Swap*

Young children need as much continuity between the different parts of their lives as possible. People at school need to understand children's lives at home and people at home need to understand their lives at school (Rosenthal & Sawyers, 1996). Information from home and school needs to be mutually shared. Earlier in this chapter, it was suggested that an introductory letter be sent from the teacher to all families before the school year began or before the child started attending classes. Written communication is good, but personal conversations are better.

## SHARING EARLY CHILDHOOD INFORMATION

Information about early childhood is specialized information. Why the room is organized by centers, what children learn through play, why the children are encouraged to solve their own problems—these are just some of the topics that could be shared with families. The early childhood educator needs to share why she operates her classroom the way she does, as well as regularly letting families know about activities that occur in the classroom. The teacher should use several different ways of communicating with families (Diffily & Morrison, 1996).

### Letters and Newsletters

The type of written communication from school to homes, which started with the "Introductory Letter to Families," should continue on a regular basis. A teacher should share specific information about the "happenings" of the class with families and continue to explain the "whys" of the early childhood program. As new materials are added to centers, the teacher should explain what children can be learning by working with these materials. As new books are read to the class or new poems and finger plays are learned, these should be shared with families. As new units of study are started, families should be told. One website for educators suggests that family letters or newsletters can also include:

- Announcements of upcoming events
- Invitations to class activities or open houses
- Reminders
- Lists of items parents could collect or save for class projects
- Thank you notes to families who help out
- Descriptions of study units and suggestions of ways parents can supplement units at home
- Library schedule
- Reprints of articles
- Explanations of grading policies, standardized testing, and other means for assessing and evaluating performance
- Explanations of behavior standards and consequences for misbehavior
- Highlights of community resources such as a museum exhibit, play, concert, or television show
- Children's writing and artwork
- News about classroom pets, trips, and celebrations (http://teacher.scholastic.com/professional/futureteachers/otherways.htm)

Some teachers prefer to write a weekly letter, such as the one in the next section, to keep families aware of what is happening in the classroom. It is a good idea to send the letter home the same day each week, so that families learn to look for the letter on that particular day. The same principle is true for newsletters. These should be sent home the same time each month so that families know when to expect them.

## Folders of Written Information

Many teachers buy a pocket folder for each child. They slip letters and other written information into the folder so that individual notes are less likely to be lost. In addition to letters about the class, other information can also be included in this folder: copies of articles from parenting magazines; suggested activities for families and children to share; notices of children's concerts, library or bookstore story times, new exhibits at museums or zoos; recipes from class-cooking experiences; brochures distributed by professional organizations; lists of books; copies of poems,

*In addition to letters about the class, other information such as photographs of children can also be included in a folder.*

finger plays, songs, and children's dictations; and work samples and photographs of children.

Some early childhood educators also add blank notebook paper to this folder so that the written communication can become two-way communication between home and school. Both family members and the teacher can use this paper for quick notes to each other. Families who are reluctant to interrupt the teacher to ask questions might write them on this paper. Then the teacher can answer parent questions during a break or as the children rest. If the folders are exchanged between school and home every day, parents' questions can be answered promptly. The teacher can also use this simple procedure for sharing something interesting a child has done or said during the day. A short personal note or two each week reinforces to the families how much the teacher cares and how much she does observe about individual children. Something as simple as blank notebook paper stapled together turns a folder into a system of written interaction between home and school.

*First Week Letter to Families*

July 29

Dear Families,

This is the first of many "Friday" letters you'll get from me. I like to send these letters home the same day every week, so you will know when to expect them. I will always try to write a note about what we've done during the week. From time to time, I'll send home articles for you to read, recipes to try, activities to consider, and samples of class work. I will keep most of the children's work for them to consider for their portfolios, so don't be surprised if few pieces of your child's work are in folders at the end of the week. You are always welcome to come to the class and look through children's writing, math, and project folders.

Thanks again to all the families who wrote letters to me about their children. I absolutely loved reading them. If you haven't had a chance to write your letter, please do.

This week has been a little hectic trying to get schedules in place and our class organized. We spent most of the week getting to know each other and setting up centers in our room. We read lots of books (mostly by Eric Carle), sang songs, talked about how we treat our school and each other. We painted and played with play dough. Everyone worked in most of the nine centers in the classroom.

We learned to "read" *The Very Hungry Caterpillar* and recorded it as a whole group for our listening center. All the children dictated their own version of this story and these dictations are posted in the hallway near our classroom. Each child also dictated a sentence or two in answer to the prompt: Tell the class something about your family. These are on their lockers. If you have a chance, you should stop by and read these dictations with your child. It is important that he or she understands that anything you say can be written down and that anything written down can be read back.

I've spent a lot of time convincing the students that they can read and write. Every day I write in front of the children, sometimes as a large group or a small group, sometimes in dictation from individual children. We always "read" back what is written. Every day, the children write stories, in whatever stage of writing they wish to use. As the year progresses, each student will move through several stages of writing. Every day we read books, signs, and logos. These activities are all part of emergent literacy that we'll talk more about at our family meeting next week.

I've had several questions about discipline in the classroom. If you are interested in my philosophy about working with young children, you may want to borrow a copy of *Positive Discipline*. That book pretty much summarizes how I think adults can work with young children to develop self-discipline. The biggest problem we've had this week is children talking in very, very loud voices. That doesn't sound like a big problem, but it can be with twenty-one loud voices and one quiet voice trying to dictate to me. This

*(continued)*

*First Week Letter to Families (continued)*

is the way I deal with loud voices: first, I remind the child to use a normal voice in the classroom. If it occurs again, I ask the child to find another center where he or she can work quietly. The third time, I choose a quiet center for the child. This is my general plan for behavior we have agreed is inappropriate for the classroom.

When two children are having a problem, I ask them to talk to each other instead of telling me the problem. At this point in the year, I usually have to help children with words to use with each other. Usually helping children talk through their problems and verbalize what they want—or don't want—from each other is enough to settle kindergarten problems.

You are welcome in the classroom to observe at anytime, but if you want to come work with the children, please let me know a day in advance so I can plan for those things you prefer to do with children.

Thanks for reading through all this. Remember, if you have questions, just call me.

## Surveys

Another method of encouraging two-way communication is through surveys or questionnaires. Teachers can create a simple questionnaire about a specific topic as a fast way to gather information from families. It can be sent home and returned to school in the children's folder. Topics can range from information about the child, the home environment, children's previous experiences in group settings, children's reactions to activities sent home, issues families want to discuss at the next family meeting, to services parents want the school to initiate.

## Parents' Lending Library

Many early childhood educators collect parenting books or early childhood books that parents might find interesting. They offer these books for family checkout and mention them in weekly letters or in family meetings. Not all families will take advantage of these books, but many will when the teacher recommends them and makes checking them out easy to do. Of particular interest are books such as *The Preschool Years: Family Strategies that Work—From Experts and Parents* (1991) written by Ellen Galinsky and Jane David. Galinsky and David offer advice on a wide variety of parenting issues.

## Checklists

The younger the child, the more often families would like to receive information about their children. The mother of an infant or toddler may not

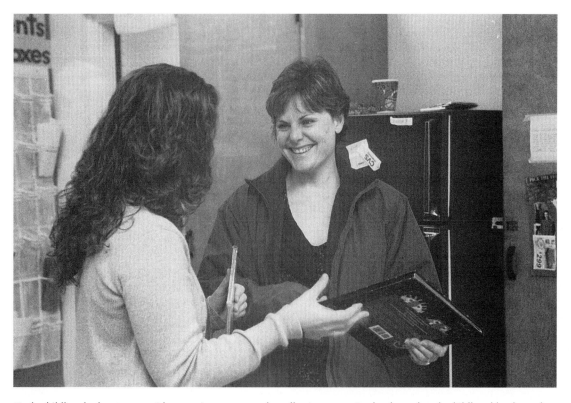

*Early childhood educators provide a service to parents by collecting parenting books and early childhood books and lending them to parents.*

want to wait until the end of the week to read a letter about her child's experiences at the child care center. Many child care providers create a checklist of typical infant or toddler behaviors and complete it as the day progresses. These checklists are sent home every day. A checklist for infants might include times of eating, napping, diaper changes, and play. A checklist for toddlers would include the same items as the infant checklist with an expanded section about the activities the toddler chose during play times. Child-to-teacher ratios for infants and toddlers are typically small enough that teachers can fill in times for items on a preprinted checklist without too much trouble. Families of the youngest children appreciate knowing what kind of day their child has had.

## Families' Reactions to Written Communication

Many families welcome this type of written information. It keeps them informed and gives them a regular way to feel connected to the class. One

*Suggested Books for a Parents' Lending Library*

Calkins, L. M., & Bellino, L. (1998). *Raising lifelong learners: A parents' guide.* Cambridge, MA: Perseus Press.

Cullinan, B. E. (2000). *Read to me: Raising kids who love to read.* New York: Scholastic.

Dyer, W. W. (2001). *What do you really want for your children?* New York: Avon Books.

Galinsky, E., & David, J. (1991). *The preschool years: Family strategies that work—From experts and parents.* New York: Ballantine.

Glenn, H. S., & Nelsen, J. (2000). *Raising self-reliant children in a self-indulgent world* (2nd ed.). Rocklin, CA: Prima Publishing.

Nelsen, J., Duffy, R., & Erwin, C. (1998). *Positive discipline for preschoolers: For their early years—Raising children who are responsible, respectful, and resourceful.* Rocklin, CA: Prima Publishing.

Rich, D. (1998). *Megaskills: Building children's achievement for the information age.* New York: Mariner Books.

Stipek, D., & Seal, K. (2001). *Motivated minds: Raising children to love learning.* Berkeley, CA: Owl Press.

Trelease, J. (2001). *The read-aloud handbook* (5th ed.). New York: Penguin.

family in a classroom where the teacher sent home family folders every Friday established a family tradition when their child was in kindergarten. Every Friday night they went out to eat and shared the contents of the folder together. They read the teacher's letter aloud, examined all the work samples, and talked about the work of the class together. This was a good match between teacher and family. The teacher took the time to compose informative letters and gather other written information that parents might find useful and the family valued this information.

Sometimes written information must be modified for families so they can benefit from it. Some families speak English as a second language and do not read English well. Letters and newsletters need to be translated into the language they read. Many times a teacher can find another parent in the school or center who would be willing to translate family letters. Local community resources can be located to translate. If finding someone willing to write out translations is not possible on a weekly basis, there are other options. A translator might be willing to record the translated information. In this case, the audio tape can be duplicated and sent home.

Still all parents do not benefit from written information. Some families may choose not to read the information sent home. In this case, there is little the teacher can do except offer similar information in other ways. Some of these methods are discussed in the following section. Some families cannot read the written information sent home. These families may be functionally illiterate and need to receive most information orally. Teachers are aware of reasons families do not benefit from written information as they come to know individual families. They explore other ways of sharing early childhood information and find the ways that are most effective in reaching the families with whom they work.

## Other Methods to Communicate with Families

Just as early childhood educators realize that children have different ways of learning the same information, teachers can offer general information about young children and specific information about their class in many different ways. A teacher can use home visits, family visits to the classroom, family members volunteering in the classroom, family meetings, family field trips, special events nights, formal family-teacher conferences, telephone calls, and informal conversations to share this information (Berger, 1999).

*Without meaningful, understandable communication, families with a language or reading barrier are less likely to feel a part of their child's education.*
*-Robert Rockwell, Lynda Andre, & Mary Hawley.*

### Home Visits

Home visits allow the teacher to observe the child and his or her family in familiar surroundings. While the primary purpose for home visits is to give the teacher an opportunity to interact with one child before having to interact with all the children in her care, these visits also allow the teacher and the family members to have personal conversations and begin to get to know each other.

Watson (1991) suggests that home visits can serve many different purposes:

- To get parents involved with their child's learning
- To use parents' skills and knowledge, family interests, and resources to teach children
- To teach parents developmentally appropriate ways to reach specific objectives
- To get families involved with the program, the school, and the community
- To determine and address needs of children and their families
- To provide information about community resources
- To provide guidance for families in getting the help they need
- To broaden the experiences of children
- To increase the self-esteem of children and parents

No single home visit can meet all these purposes, but virtually any time teachers take the time to go to the home of a family, they are demonstrating that they do care about the child and the family. Home visits can certainly help forge the beginnings of a relationship between the teacher and a family, a partnership, a collaboration. A collaboration requires that both parties make commitments to the relationship. Families need to share information about their child and support the learning experiences that are presented at school. Teachers need to share with families their knowledge about early childhood and what goes on in the classroom. In this sharing of information, true collaboration for the sake of the children emerges (Rosenthal & Sawyers, 1996).

### Family Visits to the Classroom

Families should feel comfortable visiting the classroom at any time. This kind of open-door policy allows family members to drop by as their schedule permits. They can learn a lot about their child and the way the classroom operates during even brief visits. Teachers should make this policy clear at the beginning of the year and remind families about it from time to time.

The school or center can make families feel more comfortable as visitors by posting signs in the languages represented in the school's population. Inviting, interesting, aesthetically pleasing bulletin boards about the school make good impressions. Displaying photographs of children and children's work, enlisting parent volunteers to greet families at the entrance of the school early in the school year, arranging for volunteer translators for families who do not speak English, and creating parent centers where parents can meet and talk among themselves at different times during the day are highly effective pursuits.

The teacher can make adults feel more comfortable visiting the classroom by providing a couple of adult-sized chairs, posting a bulletin board with information especially for families, offering a small library of parenting books and magazines for lending to families, displaying children's work for their review, or offering specific times, such as the end of the day, when parents are encouraged to join their children for a shared reading time. As families spend more time in the class, they learn more about it.

### Family Members Volunteering in the Classroom

As family members spend more time in the class, they may feel comfortable enough to begin helping facilitate the children's learning. Not all parents will be able to volunteer in the classroom, but the teacher should not assume that working parents cannot help. Many parents who work can arrange their schedules to go into work late one day a month or take an extra-long lunch hour if they feel that time spent in their child's class is important to the child and to the teacher. Early in the year, the teacher can offer specific volunteer opportunities (see following section) and ask family members to respond to this list. However, more parents are likely to volunteer if the teacher asks them to come to the class for a specific activity. For example, if the teacher calls Tommy's father and relates the story Tommy told about his father playing the trumpet after hearing the book *Ben's Trumpet* (Isadora, 1989), then asks him if he might be able to bring his

*Teachers can communicate with parents by creating a bulletin board for families.*

trumpet to class and play it for the children, the father is much more likely to respond to this specific request than a general call for volunteers. Or the teacher might ask a parent to volunteer to cut apples for the class's apple-sauce cooking activity. The more the teacher knows about family members, the more specific he or she can get when recruiting family volunteers.

*Early childhood educators family members to visit or volunteer in the classroom.*

Family members can volunteer to do things that benefit the class without actually being in the classroom. Teachers should let families know about things they can do at home if they cannot come to the class during the day. Parents could type newsletters, transcribe children's storytelling from audio tape, cut out construction paper shapes for a math activity, collect items for a construction project, or meet any number of specific needs.

### Family Meetings

One of the most effective ways of sharing information with families is a family meeting (Diffily, 2001a) such as the one described in the opening vignette of this chapter. In family meetings, the people closest to the children—the teacher and the parents—share information, tell stories, and make decisions together. Classroom issues can be explained. Questions can be answered immediately. Misperceptions can be cleared up. The shared time helps strengthen relationships.

*Volunteer Opportunities*
- *Read* to a small group of children.
- *Play* math games with two or three children.
- *Sponsor* a one-hour club on Friday mornings for four to six children.
- *Assist* with cooking experiences.
- *Shop* for groceries for cooking experiences.
- *Help* set up art experiences.
- *Drive* for field trips.
- *Play* musical instruments for the class.
- *Check out* books from the public library.
- *Take* dictation from individual children.
- *Transcribe* audio tapes.
- *Matte* children's paintings.
- *Bind* children's books.
- *Supervise* woodworking projects.
- *Anything else* you can think of.

Family meetings should be organized so that the teacher has sufficient time to share specific information about early childhood issues and learning occurring in the class. But families also need some unstructured time so they can ask questions they have, share stories about their children, and discuss parenting issues.

Family meetings can be less intimidating to parents than other kinds of meetings simply because several families of the same class are attending. This kind of meeting is not the one-on-one conference-type meeting where parents hear about their own child, and it is not the general all-school meeting where parents might not know anyone else in attendance. Families who can't read or write—or who do not read the written information sent home—can learn more about the class from the teacher's explanations and the interactions between parents. Those who speak other languages can have translators to help them understand the information being shared. Parents who are reluctant to ask questions about the classroom often find that other parents ask the questions they were thinking about. Even those parents who are reluctant to get involved in typical school events might come to family meetings, especially if they received a phone call from another parent specifically inviting them to a meeting.

## Family Field Trips

Another way teachers can share information about early childhood issues is through family field trips. Teachers can share information informally about how children learn—even in very casual settings. Because some family

*Family Meeting Notice*

Don't forget our family meeting next Thursday. We'll start at 6:30 P.M. and there will be a sitter for the children. If you can come a few minutes early, you can share some center time with your child or talk with me individually. I'll start the meeting discussing math games the children are learning in class and what they are learning as they play these games. I'll teach you the "rules" so you'll know how to play at home. We need to discuss the schedule for taking class pets home on weekends and plan our next family field trip—to the nature center perhaps? I will also ask you to sign up for a time to come in to the class for shared reading. Bring your calendars—and any questions you have. I'll see you Thursday night.

*Family Field Trip*

Saturday, September 23

9:00 A.M.–11:00 A.M.

Beaver Pond

This note is for your refrigerator so you won't forget our next family field trip. This beaver pond is on a small stream that is almost dry at this point of the summer. You won't have to worry about deep water, but you will have to worry about mud, so come dressed in old clothes. I will bring a taxidermied beaver and skulls from the Museum of Science and History. We will talk about beaver life and the similarities between the beaver and our pet rat, gerbil, and guinea pig (all members of the rodent family). We will make some notes in our science observation logs and sketch any animal tracks we find, as well as sketching the beaver lodge itself. I doubt we find beavers during this time of the day, but we'll look for signs of beavers (tracks, sliding marks in the mud, and chewed pieces of wood). I hope you and your family can join us. I will send home a map of the location of the beaver pond in next week's folder.

members have difficulty taking time away from their jobs to spend time in the classroom, evening or weekend field trips allow most families to spend time with the teacher and with other families related to the class. It is best if these field trips can be no-cost trips so that no family is excluded because of financial reasons. Nature-related field trips are usually easy to plan. Every community offers different opportunities and ideas: Go to a beaver dam, pond, river, or lake; venture out for rock or fossil hunting and identify leaves, wildflowers, and birds.

## Special Events Nights

Teachers can also organize special events nights as a means to share information about young children and the classroom. With three or four weeks' advance notice, most families can arrange their schedules so they can gather at school to celebrate their children's accomplishments and to learn more about the way the class works. There are many different "events" around which special nights can be arranged: poetry recitation, math games, sharing child-published books, previewing a children-created video, and many others.

Event nights provide an opportunity for a teacher to talk with families who do not benefit from written communication. Before the event begins, the teacher can spend a few minutes talking about what the children have done to prepare for the evening and the learning embedded in their work. She can also talk with individual family members before and after the event. She can use this time to share information about a specific child or summarize the information about the class that has been shared in recent letters.

## Family Conferences

Family meetings and event nights are good ways to reach groups of adults. But families also need time to talk about their child individually and in private (Rosenthal & Sawyers, 1996). Early childhood educators provide this time through regularly scheduled conferences, as well as specially scheduled conferences to discuss specific issues. In these conferences, discussions need to be two-way communication. Teachers plan enough time so they can share representative samples of the child's work and discuss their observations of the child. They also plan approximately equal time to discuss questions, concerns, and ideas of the family members. The meeting place for the conference should provide privacy and be arranged to be as inviting as possible. Something as simple as providing adult-sized chairs can be very important to many family members. There should be no distractions for the participants. Child care should be provided whenever possible.

Teachers should always begin a conference by describing positive aspects about the child. This can be facilitated by sharing some of the child's work samples, such as drawings, paintings, writing, or dictation, and some photographs of the child at work in the classroom. The teacher should not avoid discussing problem areas, but should use language that expresses concern not condemnation. The teacher should offer several opportunities for parents to ask questions about their child or to express concerns they have. The teacher should be prepared to suggest specific activities or strategies that the family can use at home to support their child's development. Concluding the conference is just as important as how it begins (Stephens & Wolf, 1989). Teachers should end conferences on a positive note.

### Phone Calls

Most families have telephones or access to one. Early childhood educators can use the telephone to communicate with families. All too often phone calls from the teacher are related to a problem—a child who has become sick during the day or a report about inappropriate behavior. The telephone can—and should be—used just as often to report good news. During the day, the teacher can use part of the lunch time or other breaks to call a parent and briefly describe an event where the child tried something new, said something humorous, or was particularly kind to another child. Sometimes the teacher can just leave a message. Parents who have home answering machines would certainly welcome a positive message from the teacher when they return from work. Evening phone calls could be made to families who do not read English to share information from the weekly letters or to tell parents about objects children have been asked to bring to school. Telephone calls do not need to be long, but they can be used in a variety of ways to share information with families.

*Early childhood educators can use the telephone to communicate with families.*

*Informal Conversations*

After class routines have been well established and children do not need the teacher's immediate attention to find meaningful activities, the teacher can use drop-off and pick-up times as an opportunity to chat with parents. These times can be used to share stories about their child or to explain information to family members, especially those who do not read English. Families should understand that the teacher's primary responsibility in the classroom is working with the children. Long conversations should occur at other times, but brief conversations before, during, or immediately after the school day are an effective way for the teacher and families to share information.

## Establishing Mutual Goals for Children

Children benefit the most from early childhood programs whose goals for children are congruent with the goals that parents have for their children (Murphy, 1997; Swick, 1997). When the goals of school and those of the family are divergent, this reduces both parties' attempts at helping children become successful learners (Swick, 1997). Teachers and families should collaborate to establish mutual goals for children. Then they should work together to help the child reach those goals.

Early childhood educators usually have age-appropriate goals already in place for children in their care. As they get to know individual children, they begin developing individually appropriate goals for each child. Public school teachers typically have grade-level goals and expectations for students already established for them by district and/or state administrators. While these goals are usually appropriate for young children, they do not include families in the goal-setting process.

Families and teachers need to work together for the benefit of children (Coleman, 1997). Because each party has different information about a child, both parties need to share what they each know about the child and set goals based on that information. Family members see their children in different settings than the teacher and may have goals for their children based on these observations. The teacher has knowledge about child development and developmentally appropriate practices and may have goals for children based on this knowledge. Both parties need time to share their information about a child. They need to talk about what they want for that child and describe the reasons for the goals they are suggesting. Only through the sharing of information can mutual goals for children be established.

Mr. and Mrs. Angeles, Carlos's parents, met with their son's kindergarten teacher early in the school year to set goals for him for the year. They were very concerned about two issues. Carlos was not able to hold a pencil correctly and he could not spell very many words correctly. The goals they wanted to set for Carlos were for him to develop good handwriting and good spelling skills. Mrs. Conrad, the teacher, explained that good handwriting was a result of well-coordinated large-motor skills and strong fine-motor skills. She discussed how large- and fine-motor skills develop and showed Mr. and Mrs. Angeles the materials she had placed in each center to enhance these skills. She also shared with the family some writing samples of kindergarten children and talked about how early childhood educators view writing as developing through stages. She explained that research showed that children who used developmental spelling became better writers and more conventional spellers. She walked Mr. and Mrs. Angeles through the centers again and showed them how writing was incorporated into all the centers. She described how she supported children as they wrote in class. After talking for more than an hour, the parents and teacher agreed on two major goals for Carlos during his kindergarten year. The first goal would be for him to experience a wide variety of activities that would strengthen his fine-motor skills. The second goal would be for him to write for a variety of reasons using the letters representing the sounds that he heard in words. When the parents left the goal-setting conference, they believed Mrs. Conrad had listened to their concerns. Mrs. Conrad believed the parents had listened to what she knew about how young children learn and had set more realistic goals for a five-year-old child based on information she shared with them. Both parties felt good about the goals they had set for Carlos and believed that they had established a good working relationship.

Mr. and Mrs. Angeles were considering traditional academic skills for their child. The teacher valued different educational goals that were based on child development principles and current knowledge about emergent literacy. This difference could have caused a real conflict between the teacher and the family, but the teacher carefully listened to what the parents had to say and tried to show how she would help the child achieve what they valued, just in a slightly different way than they were describing.

## Working through Conflicts between Teachers and Families

Not every conflict between a teacher and a family is settled as easily as the one between Mr. and Mrs. Angeles and their son's teacher. Families sometimes do become angry over real, or even perceived, situations at school. It is important that early childhood educators give families an opportunity to talk about the situation that upset them. The teacher needs to listen carefully and respectfully as the parents speak. It is often a good idea to avoid responding until parents have said everything they have to say. The teacher should then paraphrase what the parents have said and ask a few follow-up questions. This shows that the teacher has been listening to the parents' concerns. It is beneficial to remember that both parties want what is best for children and, based on that commonality, work toward a solution to the problem. Occasionally, an immediate agreement is not possible, in which case another time to talk should be scheduled so that both the teacher and the parents have some time to think about potential solutions. However, when relationships have been developed before the problem arose, it is easier to come to a mutually acceptable agreement.

## Challenges to Family Involvement

Conflicts between teachers and families may affect a family's willingness to get involved with their child's class. There are many other reasons that affect a family's decision about family involvement. Different families face different barriers that must be overcome before they will consider active involvement at school. Many adults are simply uncomfortable in school settings. Others are fearful of being judged by their child's teacher. Still others would like to be involved in their child's education, but they are unable to work out the logistics of getting to the school. Often, the time the teacher sets for family involvement activities is inconvenient. School activities conflict with work responsibilities. Many families do not have a car and cannot work out public transportation from their homes to the school. Other families face the issue of child care. Making arrangements for younger siblings can be difficult, and taking toddlers or preschoolers to school may be awkward. Sometimes it seems impossible to work through all these barriers. However, when teachers extend multiple invitations to families and help families work out logistics issues, most families who understood how much their children will benefit by their involvement will become involved.

## Advocating for and with Families

As teachers and families join together to make school and home experiences better for children, they are working in Bronfenbrenner's micro- and mesosystems. As these relationships grow, they may find themselves beginning to think about trying to make changes in the exosystem. They may write letters or make telephone calls to legislators about pending bills that affect child care regulations. They may approach the school board and ask for additional support for early childhood classrooms. They may lobby their congressional representatives and senators and ask them to vote for family-friendly legislation.

Working with policy makers to create a better environment for children is referred to as **advocacy**. Because young children are affected by so many influences, early childhood educators also accept advocacy for children and their families as one of their responsibilities. As advocates, early childhood educators work to help other people understand the needs of young children. Policy makers at the local, state, and national levels need input from early childhood professionals to help them realize how the policies they make affect young children and their families.

**advocacy** the work to educate decision makers about policies that are best for children and their families.

*Our caring cannot be restricted to our classrooms or offices if we truly want to improve the lives of children.*

*-Stacie Goffin & Joan Lombardi*

As Robinson and Stark (2002) note:

Advocacy takes place at many different levels—from families who approach their child's teacher or program director to ask for an arts program, to teachers who approach the school board to request additional funding for books to help their students meet rigorous academic standards, to groups of business leaders who form coalitions with early childhood caregivers, to professional associations who create opportunities for policy makers about a particular problem that young children face. At all these levels of advocacy, caring adults take a stand on behalf of children. (p. 4)

Whether it is with families or policy makers taking steps toward making the lives of young children and their families better, early childhood educators are typically involved in advocacy efforts.

The active nature of advocacy means that early childhood educators have to keep current on issues that affect young children. They make sure they know the facts related to the issue and then they take action. They write letters, make telephone calls, and schedule appointments to share their professional expertise and to make their beliefs about young children known to people in policy-making positions. They contact other people and ask them to support these issues, too. Essentially advocacy in early childhood means speaking out for the needs of young children and their families.

## REVISITING THE FAMILY MEETING

The monthly family meetings continued between Pam and the families of the students she taught. Over the course of the year, they had talked about the ways that young children learned to read and how adults could support that learning and how to encourage first-graders to write at home as much as they did at school. They read children's literature together and even dramatized some of the stories so they could see more clearly what children learned from creating their own plays from familiar stories. They worked through math problem-solving scenarios that the children were working on. Pam was particularly amused the night she proposed this problem: There are twenty-two children in this class. If half of the students were absent one day, how many people would be in the classroom? Almost every adult answered "eleven" without delay. Only one mother answered, "twelve," because there would be eleven children and one teacher. Earlier that day, twenty of the twenty-two first graders had answered "twelve," giving the same rationale, but then the students had spent the whole week examining the same type of problem. Through these shared experiences—and other methods of communicating through letters, reading the same magazine articles, participating in interactive homework, and going on family field trips—the families felt closer to Pam and she to them. Through these developing relationships, the children benefited as much as anyone.

## Summary

To be most effective in their work with young children, early childhood educators recognize the need to work with the children's families. They assume primary responsibility for developing real relationships with families by extending themselves in personal ways. They share their knowledge about young children and what is happening in the class by writing letters or newsletters. They also schedule different types of meetings so they can talk with families in person and involve families in the life of the class. They provide different types of opportunities for families to share what they know about their children and to ask questions they have. They also recognize the importance of advocacy for young children and their families with people in policy-making positions and involve families in advocacy work. In the next chapter, the importance of creating environments for young children will be discussed and described.

## Reflections

1. Think about a family you know. If this was a family of one of your students, how might you approach them to begin to develop a teacher-family relationship, respond to their concerns about early childhood issues, and encourage their classroom involvement?

2. Discuss what type of family might be the most challenging to involve in the life of an early childhood classroom and why you believe this. What are some of the things you might do to get to know them better and encourage their involvement?

3. Discuss how the communication with families would vary if you were the caregiver for infants or a public school teacher of third grade.

## Field Experiences

1. Interview two early childhood educators about their interactions with families. Discuss the methods they have found successful in involving parents. Ask about methods they have tried and found unsuccessful.

2. Interview the family of a young child who attends an early childhood center program or who is enrolled in prekindergarten through third grade. Ask about the opportunities that are available for their involvement in the child's class and ask about how they wish they could be involved.

3. Locate a teacher who holds regular family meetings and ask if you can attend one of the meetings as a visitor. Note the interactions between teacher and parents, as well as the interactions among families.

4. Collect samples of teacher-to-family written communication. Compare and contrast the letters or newsletters for how much information is shared about classroom activities, about why particular activities were offered to the children and what they might have learned while doing them, and how families might extend this learning at home.

**5.** Interview a teacher who has had a conflict with a family/parent. Find out what the conflict was and how it was resolved. If possible, get the family's side of the conflict and its resolution.

## Case Studies

### The Father vs. the Kindergarten Teacher

The first week of kindergarten had gone well. Two weeks before school, Cassandra mailed a letter to each family and a postcard to each student. In both, she welcomed them to the school and let them know a little about what to expect from kindergarten.

Parents seemed generally supportive. Cassandra held a family meeting the first week of school on Thursday evening. At least one person from almost every family came to the meeting and seemed generally supportive. No one voiced concerns. All comments about the first few days of school were positive.

The students seemed to be settling into the routines she was teaching. Considering they were all five-year-olds, there had been no real problems that first week.

Cassandra had no misgivings when she found a phone message in her box that second Monday from a parent. Bob called the school requesting an appointment after school as soon as possible. Cassandra returned the call during her lunch break and agreed to wait at school until 5:30 that evening so they could talk about what Bob referred to as "a few issues."

Bob arrived on time. He was friendly. He made several positive observations about the classroom and told a couple stories about his daughter and how much she loved kindergarten. Then he pulled a legal pad out of his briefcase and began to draw. At the left bottom of a page, he drew a circle and wrote a K inside the circle. At the right top of the page, he drew another circle and wrote "MIT" inside it. To the side, he wrote "SAT 1550." Finally, he connected the circles with a straight line. "This is my goal for my daughter," he began, "I want to know how far up this line you plan to get her this year."

### What to Do?

It is obvious at this point that the father and the kindergarten teacher view young children differently. They see the primary goals of education dissimilarly. They will have almost diametrically opposing goals for the girl's kindergarten year. How should Cassandra respond to Bob's initial question? How might she address his fundamental concern about his daughter being "the best"? What could she do over the coming weeks to help Bob learn about developmentally appropriate practices and the ways that children learn best?

**"I'm Here Because He's Not Learning Anything in Your Class."**

It was Monday morning about 8:40 A.M., and Bradley was still not in class. That was not surprising. Bradley was often late to school. Mrs. Duarte had started the morning read-aloud when Bradley and his mother came into the class. Mrs. Shipp stood by the door while Bradley put his things in his cubby and joined the class. She continued standing by the door until the story was over, and children were getting their Reading Response journals and finding a private place in the room to write their response to this morning's story. At that point, Mrs. Shipp walked over to Mrs. Duarte and whispered, "I'm going to spend the day in class. I don't think Bradley is learning anything in your class, so I want to see what it is that you do in here." Without waiting for a response, Mrs. Shipp walked to the back of the room, sat down, and began writing on a tablet of paper she brought with her.

**What to Do?**

It is obvious that Mrs. Shipp is angry. It is fairly obvious that she does not want to talk. What should Mrs. Duarte do at that moment? How should she handle the anger she feels the moment Mrs. Shipp makes her accusation and then makes it so clear that she does not want to talk? Mrs. Shipp does indeed stay the entire school day. What should Mrs. Duarte do the whole day? Should she consider changing her plans for the day? How often should she approach Mrs. Shipp, and what should she say?

**Further Reading**

Ballenger, C. (1999). *Teaching other people's children: Literacy and learning in a bilingual classroom.* New York: Teachers College Press.

Berger, E. H. (1999). *Parents as partners in education: The school and home working together.* New York: Merrill/Prentice Hall.

Hannigan, I. (1998). *Off to school: A parent's eye view of the kindergarten year.* Washington, DC: National Association for the Education of Young Children.

Hewitt, D. (1997). *So this is normal too? Teachers and parents working out developmental issues in young children.* St. Paul, MN: Redleaf Press.

Honig, A. S. (2002). *Secure relationships: Nurturing infant-toddler attachment in early care settings.* Washington, DC: National Association for the Education of Young Children.

**Helpful Web Sites**

**National PTA**

www.pta.org

*The national PTA assumes a leadership position in child advocacy. Of all the child advocacy organizations in the United States, the national Parent-*

*Teacher Association is the largest. The PTA encourages membership and involvement from not only parents and teachers, but students and other citizens active in schools or community.*

**National Coalition for Parent Involvement in Education**

www.ncpie.org

*NCPIE was founded in 1980, at the initiative of what was then the National School Volunteer Program (now National Association for Partners in Education), funded by the Ford Foundation and Union Carbide. Participating organizations include parent organizations and advocacy groups as well as national education organizations representing teachers and administrators. NCPIE's mission statement is to advocate for the involvement of parents and families in their children's education and to foster relationships between home, school, and community to enhance the education of all our nation's young people.*

**Hand in Hand**

www.handinhand.org

*Hand in Hand was a national campaign sponsored by the Mattel Foundation and coordinated by the Institute for Educational Leadership to build and strengthen partnerships to improve the education of all children. Although the campaign ended in 1999, the information developed for the campaign is still posted on this Web site and is still relevant for teachers and parents seeking effective ways to work together.*

Check the Online Resources™ for expert practitioners' responses to each case study.

For additional information on teaching young children, visit our Web site at **http://www.earlychilded.delmar.com**

## PART THREE

# Best Practices for Young Children

## CHAPTER 6

## *Preparing the Early Childhood Environment*

*Early Childhood Principle* Professional early childhood educators prepare environments especially for young children.

In many ways, how rooms are arranged and the materials that are organized in them determine the learning that will occur in that classroom. Young children learn from manipulating and interacting with a variety of materials, so early childhood educators carefully gather and arrange materials that will enhance children's development in all domains. In high-quality early childhood classrooms, the room is typically arranged in learning centers and those centers are filled with a range of materials that interest the specific children who are in that classroom. Teachers carefully observe how the children interact with materials and exchange or add to the materials in each learning center as children's interests change or as they determine that new materials are needed to meet children's developmental needs.

*After reading this chapter, you should be able to:*
- Describe how the early childhood educator establishes an appropriate physiological and psychological environment for young children.
- Discuss some important concepts that children learn as they play.
- Describe factors to consider when arranging an early childhood classroom.
- List commonly used learning centers and materials that might be placed in those centers.
- Describe how the environment would be arranged for infants and toddlers.
- Describe how the classroom could be arranged in elementary schools.
- Describe how the environment can be designed to accommodate children with special needs.
- Explain how teachers can organize and facilitate children's center choices.

- Describe how teachers can use children's interests to create curriculum.
- Discuss how the outdoor play environment can be used as a second learning environment.
- Describe community resources that can enrich children's learning experiences.

Cheryl Sassman, a kindergarten teacher in a large, urban, public school, is not scheduled to return to work for another week. She works in a district that pays for only one teacher preparation day, but she knows she needs more than a day to arrange the classroom and set up learning centers. So she comes to the school earlier than other teachers. She needs time to reflect about how young children learn best and how she will create a classroom to support that type of learning. Without knowing much about the students she will teach this year, she thinks about age-appropriateness for five-year-olds as she looks around the classroom on this first day back at work. She wonders where each center should be placed and how she can soften the institutional look of the classroom. Cheryl finds the folder where she files journal articles about room arrangement and rereads several of those articles. Then she sketches the classroom trying several different arrangements of centers.

The next morning Cheryl meets a friend, Joy, for breakfast. Afterward they go to Cheryl's school together. Joy is also a kindergarten teacher. Although they teach in different school districts, they often spend time together discussing issues related to their classes. That morning they spend the first hour or so just talking about the advantages and disadvantages of Cheryl's room arrangement sketches.

Then they discuss some factors they need to consider so that all children will find the classroom comfortable and inviting. Cheryl's class is an **inclusion** class and she has been told that one of her students uses a wheelchair for mobility and another child is visually impaired. As they plan the centers, they anticipate the children's traffic patterns and provide sufficient space for a child's wheelchair to maneuver in and around the centers. Cheryl and Joy will also make sure that the pathways are clear and uncluttered for the child who has challenges with his vision. They will be certain that materials are at a height on shelves that can be reached by the child in the wheelchair. Materials on or near the floor would not be accessible to that child. They will arrange furniture so that there is space at each table and work space for a wheelchair so that child will not be isolated from other children. They will also ensure that the environment contains sufficient contrasts to attract the attention of the visually impaired child. After Cheryl and Joy agree on the major elements of the room and the ways they can arrange the room to meet the needs of Cheryl's two students with special needs they begin moving furniture around the room.

First they create an area for the block center in one corner of the room. They use low shelving and a large piece of indoor/outdoor carpet to define that area. Next they arrange the dramatic play furniture in another corner to create a home center. Then they create the beginnings of a science center by placing two low tables, two bookshelves, and some empty aquariums near the classroom's only window. The placement of two easels, a low table, and art cart on the tile area of the room frame the art center. They arrange furniture for the reading, writing, and listening centers so that these centers are close to each other. Then they move the water table so that it is near the block center. They move a long rectangle table and some shelving between the listening and block centers for the math center. Scanning the classroom, Cheryl and Joy both begin to feel like the classroom is taking shape. They start reviewing centers, discussing each one and making notes about what materials Cheryl will introduce the first week of school. Cheryl creates another list of the things she wants to bring in to the classroom from home: pillows, curtains, and carpet squares she found at garage sales over the summer break; center signs she made and laminated; and the new books she bought for the math and block centers. She also starts a list of posters, photographs, books, stuffed animals, and plants that she wants to add to the room to make it more aesthetically pleasing. The rest of the week Cheryl works alone in the room. She continues reading about centers, talking to other teachers about her room arrangement, and reflecting on each item she adds to the room. She concentrates on one center at a time, reconsidering what she has read about that center and what she remembers about learning materials that five-year-olds find particularly appealing. For the first week of school, she will offer only a few material choices in each center until she gets to know the children and some classroom routines are established. Cheryl considers the extra time she spent in the classroom this week as well spent because she knows how important the physical environment is to a successful early childhood classroom.

**inclusion** the practice of including children who are developmentally, culturally or linguistically diverse in integrated settings and ensuring full acceptance into the learning community

## SETTING THE STAGE FOR DEVELOPMENTALLY APPROPRIATE PRACTICES

Early childhood educators have scores of responsibilities as they go about their work with young children and families. Chief among these responsibilities is preparing the environment for the children. The way a classroom is arranged, the centers that are available to children, and the materials provided in each center are critical to the teaching and learning that goes on in that classroom. A substantial portion of a teacher's work is done each morning when the children enter the classroom *if* the teacher has created a learning environment that meets the needs of the group and individual students.

### Child-Centered Environments

Child-centered environments are planned around certain physical features. These include child-sized furniture and age-appropriate learning materials and toys all thoughtfully arranged (Clayton, 2001). In addition to the physical environment, teachers of child-centered classrooms also consider the **physiological** and **psychological environment**. These are equally important to young children's learning.

Children who are cold or hot, hungry or thirsty simply cannot learn as well as they can when their physiological needs are met by the adults in their lives. In addition to the many dynamics of teaching, early childhood educators also take care to oversee the classroom temperature and try to ensure that children have sufficient food to eat while they are in their care. When needed, these educators work with local social service agencies to help provide children with other necessities such as clothes and medical and dental care. This follows the thinking of Abraham Maslow (1970), whose theory of the hierarchy of human needs suggested that basic needs must be met before higher needs can be met (Figure 6–1).

**physiological environment** the manner in which furnishings and equipment are arranged to help meet needs for security and safety as well as to facilitate learning.

**psychological environment** affective dimensions of child/child and adult/child relationships in the group.

FIGURE 6–1
**Maslow's Hierarchy of Needs** *In Maslow's hierarchy of needs, the needs at lowest level have the most potency—they must be fulfilled before a person is motivated to try to fulfill higher needs.*

Psychologically, children need to feel safe and secure before they can learn. They have a need to feel acceptance from adults and peers. Children must also feel a sense of competence and approval before they can learn to their fullest potential (Maslow, 1970). In an effort to add to a child's sense of psychological security, adults who work with young children encourage the child to choose activities that interest him or her, support them as they acquire new knowledge and skills, respond quickly to their distress or frustration, and provide for predictability and routine structures throughout the day.

## The Active Nature of Learning

Early childhood educators recognize children's need to be active most of the time, knowing that during this activity, children are learning (Bickart, Jablon, & Dodge, 1999). People of all ages learn best from active involvement in whatever they are trying to learn. No one learns to bake a cake from just being told what to do. They must read the recipe, combine ingredients one at a time, and experiment with baking. Teenagers don't learn how to drive a standard transmission car through someone's description of how to coordinate the clutch, the accelerator, and the brake. They need to sit in the driver's seat and be given many opportunities to practice. Children do not learn how to ride a two-wheeler from verbal instruction. They need experience on the bicycle. The need for active involvement in learning experiences is particularly important for young children.

Young children require a variety of experiences every day with concrete materials, such as blocks, art materials, sand or water, math manipulatives, puppets, and books. Direct experiences with these types of open-ended materials are an important source of learning for children. Much of what they are learning is not readily apparent to the untrained observer. For example, in a single class of four- and five-year-olds where several children are painting at easels, different children will be learning different things from the same activity. Some may be learning hand-eye coordination, which is important in learning to write. Some may be learning to distinguish shapes and to create shapes purposely. Still other children may be using the paint to name colors they already know or to make new colors by combining the paints. At the easel, children also learn to develop their emerging creativity, express their feelings or ideas in a different way, and begin to understand the concepts of symmetry, balance, and design. This same breadth and depth of learning is available to young children at learning centers provided throughout the classroom.

*Centers, by the nature of their design, allow each child to work at his or her individual development level.*
*—Rebecca Isbell*

## PHYSICAL CHARACTERISTICS OF THE ENVIRONMENT

One of the first considerations of the physical environment is the amount of space provided indoors and in the outdoor play environment. The

*Different children learn different things from the same activity.*

*Every aspect of the physical environment, from the general arrangement of furnishings to the smaller details of color and texture, communicates something to the children using that space.*

*–Candice Bowers*

accreditation criteria of the National Academy of Early Childhood Programs stipulates a minimum of thirty-five square feet per child indoors and seventy-five square feet per child outdoors (NAEYC, 1998). It should be noted that these are minimum requirements and that larger spaces for young children are preferable. Children need ample room to move and play.

While they need sufficient space, large open spaces are not particularly conducive to organized or self-controlled classrooms. Smaller, well-defined areas help children focus on specific activities and help them understand behaviors that are expected in those areas. Early childhood classrooms are typically organized by learning centers that encourage distinctive play in each of the areas. Because all children develop at different rates, appropriately designed learning centers are able to meet the needs of children functioning at a wide range of abilities. The versatility of centers allows children to interact with center materials at their own developmental level. Children with different abilities can work in the same center and be learning very different concepts.

Several centers are commonly found in early childhood classrooms. These include the following:

- Art center
- Block center
- Dramatic play center
- Listening center
- Math center
- Music center
- Reading center
- Sand and water center
- Science center
- Writing center

Given available space in the classroom, most of these centers are available to children throughout the year. However, the materials in those centers do not remain the same. They are changed periodically according to the children's interests and needs. Learning centers are not limited to these common ones. Early childhood educators can expand children's learning by introducing centers' such as these:

- Puppet center
- Camping center
- Mechanics center
- Grocery store or pharmacy center
- Doctor's or dentist's office center
- Post office center
- Fast food center
- Home repair center
- Electronics repair center
- Astronaut/space shuttle center

Teachers provide a variety of centers based on children's interests so that children can expand their exploration of those interests.

## Furnishings

All furniture used in early childhood classrooms should support the organization of centers. Tables, chairs, and shelving should be child-sized, not just smaller than adult furniture, but appropriately sized for the age group that will be using it (Clayton, 2001). Furniture that would be appropriate for first-graders would be inappropriate for toddlers. The size of tables, chairs, cubbies, shelving, easels, puppet stages, and any other permanent furniture should be the proper size for the children in that room.

The furnishings for an early childhood classroom ought to help establish a warm, inviting place for young children. In addition to tables and chairs typically found in classrooms, other furniture could be used to create this atmosphere: small couches, end tables with lamps, and groupings of cushions and pillows on the floor. Other considerations for permanent furnishings in the classroom could include raised carpeted platforms, lofts, low tables so that children can kneel beside them to work, low cabinets so that children can use them as counters, and small cozy areas that provide private spaces. To help soften the classroom, teachers often add upholstered furniture, tablecloths, curtains, green plants, silk or dried flower arrangements, fabric-covered walls, quilted wall hangings, and warm colors. They also consider adding different textures within the room as well as attending to horizontal and vertical spaces.

## Configuration

There are many factors to contemplate when arranging the placement of centers in a classroom. Figures 6–2, 6–3, and 6–4 illustrate how classrooms might be effectively arranged. A teacher cannot truly know how well an arrangement will work until children actually work in those centers, but there are some general guidelines to follow:

- Centers should be clearly defined. Shelving, pegboard or other dividers, and throw rugs or carpet pieces can be used to define center boundaries.
- Center materials should be organized with a place for everything. Pictures and simple word labels encourage children to return materials to their designated space.
- Pathways between the centers should promote smooth movement of children from center to center. Too much open space lends itself to running in the classroom. Relatively narrow paths between centers are acceptable for most children, but must be widened if any students in that classroom have movement disabilities.
- Noisier centers, such as blocks and dramatic play, should be grouped away from quieter centers, such as reading and writing.
- Safety must be an ongoing consideration, and the classroom should be inspected on a regular basis for hazards that could cause falls or other injuries.
- Rules for getting in and out of the centers (taking turns, number of people to be in a center at the same time, and so on) should be posted and discussed.

Some centers have specific considerations:

- A science center requires light, so it should be positioned near windows; access to water would be preferable.

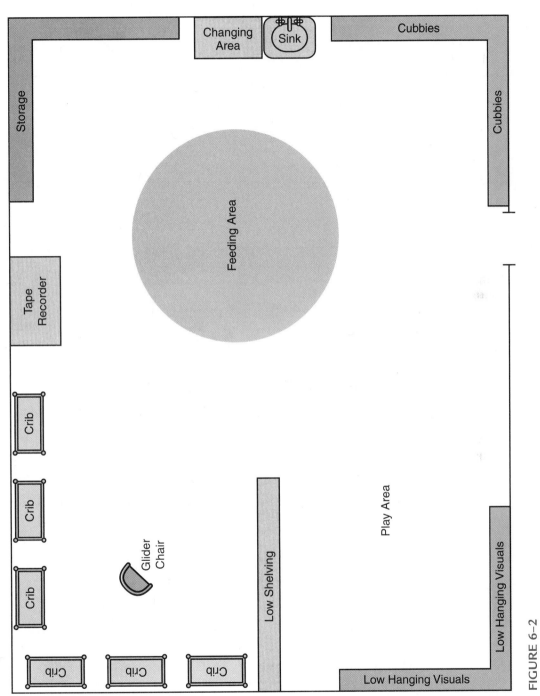

FIGURE 6–2
Sample Floor Plan for an Infant Classroom

211

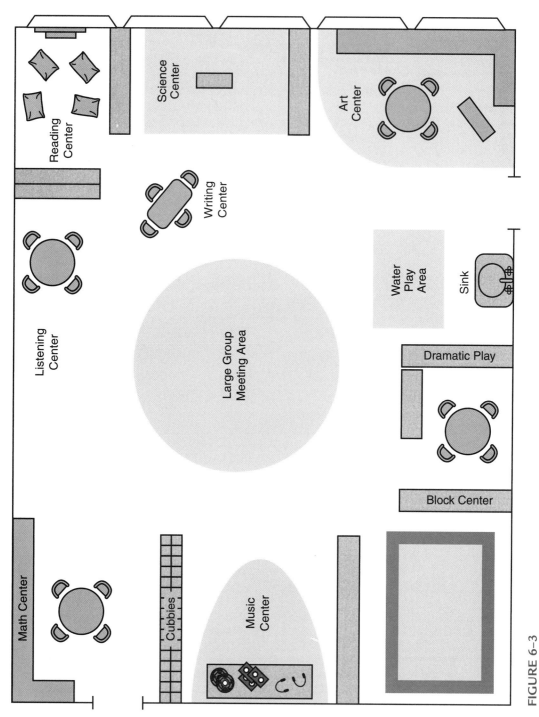

FIGURE 6–3
*Sample Floor Plan for a Three-year-old Classroom*

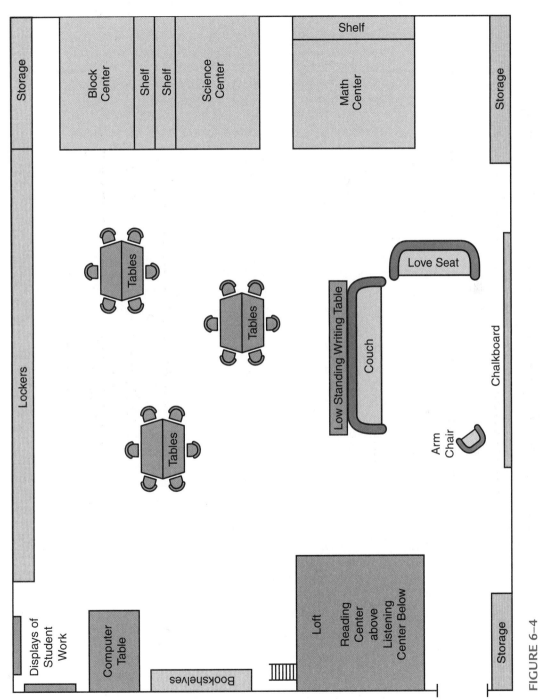

FIGURE 6–4
*Sample Floor Plan for a Second Grade Classroom*

213

- A sand and water center needs to be located near a source of water and placed on a tile or vinyl floor for easy cleanup.
- An art center needs to be positioned near water and on tile or vinyl, if possible. (If this is not possible, carpet can be covered with thick plastic, secured with strong tape.) A well-lighted space aids children's art production.
- Language arts-related centers such as reading, writing, and listening centers should be located near each other and the listening center near an electrical outlet.
- A math center should have sufficient space for children to spread manipulatives out on the floor or large, child-sized tables.
- A block center needs sufficient room for children to build large block structures but should be self-limiting by being enclosed on two or three sides.

As children begin to work in centers, some changes may be required. An observant teacher will notice children's traffic patterns, how they move when they are changing centers, and how they use the materials in the centers. Teachers make changes from time to time based on children's behaviors.

### Choice of Materials

With the increasing national interest in early childhood, manufacturers of toys, equipment, and learning materials are no exception. The market is saturated with materials for children birth through age eight; however, not everything labeled for young children is appropriate for them. Early childhood educators should take care to purchase items that are appropriate for the children with whom they work. Several factors need to be considered: children's ages, levels of development, abilities, needs, and interests. The materials listed in appendix A are a general guideline for materials appropriate for young children. Materials must be safe, durable, and attractive.

It is important that early childhood educators bring a broad representation of people and cultures into the classroom. This can be done in a variety of ways. Photographs of children and families that represent different cultures can be displayed in the classroom. Carefully selected children's books that represent many different cultures can be available in several centers, and books and poetry by people of diverse backgrounds should be available in the reading center. Multicultural books are being published in greater numbers recently. These are widely available in alphabet and counting books, and their numbers are growing in the area of family life.

Teachers can also display drawings, paintings, sculpture, and textiles created by artists of different cultures. To help children understand how family life differs in different cultures, the teacher can offer culturally diverse objects in the home center related to cooking, eating, tools, and personal objects. To reinforce that different skin tones and facial features are

*Literacy Links : Books with Aspects of Family Life from around the World*

Morris, A. (2000). *Families*. New York: HarperCollins.
Morris, A. (1998). *Shoes, shoes, shoes*. New York: Mulberry.
Morris, A. (1995). *Houses and homes*. New York: Mulberry.
Morris, A. (1994a). *On the go*. Glenview, IL: Scott Foreman.
Morris, A. (1994b). *Loving*. New York: Mulberry.
Morris, A. (1993a). *Hats, hats, hats*. New York: Mulberry.
Morris, A. (1993b). *Bread, bread, bread*. Glenview, IL: Scott Foresman.

valued, dolls representing the major cultural groups in the United States could be available in the home center, and multicultural paints, markers, and crayons made available in the art and writing centers. The music available to children in the listening and music centers can represent various cultures.

## Display and Use of Materials

How children interact with materials also affects which learning materials the teacher places in centers and how they are displayed. Children need opportunities to be independent at all ages. Learning materials in every center need to be well organized and accessible to all children. Usually materials should be arranged on low shelves so that children can reach all choices. If any children in the group have physical disabilities, this arrangement may have to be modified. Children in wheelchairs will need materials placed at an appropriate level so they can reach them. Typically the older the child, the more choices of materials there should be. Teachers can also modify the materials themselves. Containers and sacks that can be opened and released easily are practical in many applications, and reusable sticky material can be added to the backs of laminated letters and numbers so children can stick them to felt boards, for example. Handles can be bent to make them more easily grasped.

Children need to make decisions about how they will interact with the materials offered in learning centers. In most instances, items that can be used in different ways should be selected for centers. Materials like blocks, math manipulatives, clay, paints, sand, and dramatic play props can be used in numerous ways as children desire. Some single-use learning materials, such as puzzles, do belong in early childhood classrooms (Maldonado, 1996), but the vast majority of materials should allow children to interact with the objects in different ways.

Well-organized learning centers filled with a variety of materials offer a rich learning environment for young children (Isbell, 1995). However, centers are only as good as the way that children are encouraged and allowed to use them. Children need to interact with peers as they interact with the materials. Children talking to other children is an important part of their learning. Children need the opportunity to verbalize what they are doing and thinking. They learn as they are expressing themselves. If a teacher requires a hushed classroom, children's learning is restricted. Teachers also need to talk with children about their work in centers. The extent to which a teacher talks with children and facilitates their use of materials is also important. A teacher who prepares a stimulating environment and sits back merely to watch what happens is limiting the extent of teaching possibilities. Teachers should move from center to center engaging children in conversations about what they are doing and how they are interacting with the materials, and the teacher should model and describe different ways in which to interact with the learning materials.

## INTEGRATED LEARNING

Experiences for young children should be integrated. Traditionally, school experiences have been divided into different content areas. Reading, writing, math, science, and social studies were the major curriculum areas. Several other areas, such as music, art, and health, were also included in the school day. In this traditional form of schooling, learning in one content area rarely had any connection with another. This kind of discrete schooling is not appropriate for young children (Bredekamp & Copple, 1997).

Young children do not mentally separate learning into distinct categories or subject areas. As they try to make sense of their world, they make connections between what they know and what they are learning. For this reason, early childhood educators integrate activities and experiences for young children.

There are numerous ways a teacher can integrate curriculum. A fundamental way to integrate curriculum is through the materials offered in centers. While the names of learning centers imply discrete content areas, such as math center or reading center, materials in these centers are not content specific. For example, books should not be limited to the reading center nor should writing materials be limited to the writing center. These should be incorporated into all the centers in the classroom.

Children can learn almost any concept in almost any center. Some children choose the same centers over and over. That does not limit their learning, but it does challenge teachers to integrate learning into the centers more than they might otherwise.

The purpose of integrated learning is to help children make connections between what they know and what they are learning and to help them remember what they have learned (Wolfe, 2001). Young children are much less likely to remember isolated bits of information than information linked to prior knowledge. Teachers help children make connections with other information by the way they arrange centers, by the books they read and the songs they sing with the class, and by the way they interact with children in large and small groups.

## LEARNING CENTERS

The next section of this chapter briefly describes some of the common centers found in early childhood classrooms for children who are approximately three years old through first grade. Adaptations for infants and toddlers and second and third graders are discussed following the general discussion of learning centers.

For each center, suggestions are offered about center setup, and the materials that could be included in each of these centers are listed in appendix A. After the center description, a few books related to that center are listed as "literacy links." Literacy-related activities are such a critical component of early childhood classrooms that books and other types of printed materials should be a part of every center. While the eleven centers described below typically comprise the foundation of the early childhood classrooms, other centers can and should be offered to children (Isbell, 1995).

### Art Center

The art area of any early childhood classroom is a dynamic place. A wide variety of activities and media should be available so that children can experiment and refine their art exploration. Children will become bored if the same art experiences are offered day after day. Painting is not limited to painting at the easel with brushes. Children can—and should—experiment with sponge painting, sand painting, screen painting, cotton swab paintings, and so on. Art activities are not limited to painting. Opportunities are offered for drawing with different media such as chalk, colored pencils, charcoal, and pastels. Children also work with clay and play dough and create works of art through collage and print making. For younger children, these opportunities may be offered on different days, but for older children, several different media choices can be available every day. For toddlers, a teacher might offer finger painting one day, colored chalk on dark-colored construction paper the next day, and sponge painting the next. For kindergarten students, all of these art activities might be offered on the same day.

Art experiences for young children should focus on the process of a creation rather than how the final product looks. Young children should be encouraged to experiment with different media and make their own creative decisions rather than be told to reproduce a teacher's example or follow directions for a predetermined model.

*Incorporating Literacy into All Centers*

**Art Center**

Children's books illustrated using the media currently offered in the center, i.e. when collage is offered to children, display books by Ezra Jack Keats or Eric Carle; prints of master artists displayed along with biography books about the artists.

**Block Center**

A spiral-bound blank book entitled *The Block Book* (photographs of children's block structures accompanied by children's dictation); books that might inspire new construction; newspaper ads for building supply stores.

**Home Center**

Books focusing on family life; empty cans and boxes of food; grocery circulars; recipe books; labels; telephone and telephone book; newspapers, magazines, and catalogs; paper for writing notes and making grocery lists.

**Listening Center**

A menu of books/tapes available.

**Math Center**

A collection of counting books or books that relate to shapes, patterns, or numbers; word and picture labels for math manipulatives.

**Science Center**

Nonfiction books and themed nature magazines about class pets, labels for pets, plants, or collections of seeds, rocks, fossils, magnets, or other science-related objects.

---

*Literacy Link : Art*

Agee, J. (1990). *Incredible painting of Felix Clousseau*. New York: Sunburst.

Anholt, L. (1998). *Picasso and the girl with a ponytail: A story about Pablo Picasso*. New York: Barrons Juveniles.

Catalanotto, P. (2001). *Emily's art*. New York: Antheneum.

de Paola, T. (1989). *The art lesson*. New York: Putnam.

Hurd, T. (1996). *Art dog*. New York: HarperCollins.

Mayhew, J. (1999). *Katie meets the impressionists*. New York: Orchard Books.

---

This center can be a messy place, but children quickly learn that cleanup is a part of working in the art center when the teacher carefully explains and models cleanup procedures. Work surfaces covered with plastic or newspapers allow easier cleanup, and cleaning supplies such as paper towels, sponges, and child-sized mops are stored close to the art center.

## Block Center

The block center is a favorite of young children. Whether toddlers are stacking blocks one on top of another or first graders are creating complex cities, children are usually attracted to block building. One reason for this popularity is the open-ended nature of blocks. Blocks are versatile. With children's imaginations, blocks can become anything they wish them to be. Children make all the decisions about what they will do with the blocks.

*With children's imaginations, blocks can become anything they wish them to be.*

*Literacy Link: Blocks*

Chessen, B., & Chanko, P. (1998). *Building*. New York: Scholastic.

Hunter, R., & Miller, E. (1998). *Into the sky*. New York: Holiday House.

Lewis, K., & Cartwright, R. (2001). *Big machines! Big buildings!* New York: Hyperion Books for Children.

Macaulay, D. (2000). *Building*. New York: Houghton Mifflin.

Merriam, E., & Yaccarino, D. (1966). *Bam bam bam*. New York: Henry Holt.

Tarsky, S., & Ayliffe, A. (1997). *The busy building book*. New York: G.P. Putnam.

With little teacher involvement, children enhance visual perception, hand–eye coordination, and motor skills. As teachers spend time in the block center, describing children's actions or commenting about their own block construction, blocks become the elements for an assortment of learning experiences. They can be math materials as they are sorted, classified, counted, or used for patterning. Blocks can be literature extension materials as they are used to recreate settings for stories. They can be social studies materials as children reproduce field trip sites or their home and school neighborhoods. Blocks can also be used to experiment with science concepts such as balance or gravity. Adding accessories, like animal figures, people figures, and vehicles, enhances children's dramatic play in the block center.

Blocks should be offered to children in sufficient numbers so that their play is not restricted. Some early childhood educators suggest that one hundred to three hundred blocks should be available for a preschool class. Older children need even more. A large space for block constructions should be available to children, but this center should be somewhat self-restricting (by walls or dividers) or block building can take over the entire classroom. Storage of blocks is also a consideration for this center. They can be organized by sorting them into containers for each block shape or they can be placed on low shelves marked with identifying shapes so that children know where on the shelves to place each type of block.

## Dramatic Play Center

"One of the best ways children have to express themselves is through creative dramatic play."

–Mary Mayesky

Children's dramatic play involves much more than just having fun. Children learn through the pretending they do in this center. As children act out play themes, they are learning to share ideas, make group decisions, and cooperate with each other. Dramatic play also provides multiple opportunities for children to practice language and literacy skills and to enhance cognitive development.

Many teachers begin the year with a "home center" or "housekeeping center" because children's first play themes usually focus on home and family. Children replay familiar experiences such as preparing meals, doing

*Children often act out familiar experiences such as preparing meals and caring for younger children in the dramatic play area.*

laundry, or caring for young children. This type of play can be supported by child-sized furniture that represents a kitchen, living room, or dining room, dress-up clothing, and materials such as cooking utensils, dishes, food containers, and dolls.

The dramatic play center should be arranged so that children have sufficient space to move around easily. Teachers often use the child-sized furniture such as a refrigerator, a stove, and a sink, and rugs to define this area. Because the dramatic play center tends to be a noisy one, it should be placed near other noisy centers and away from the quieter centers.

While the play theme of home and family is a common theme that occurs in the dramatic play center, it is not the only one. Children may bring math manipulatives into the "home" and play "restaurant." Sometimes teachers may provide new props to support play themes they see emerging or may put new materials in the dramatic play center to encourage new play themes. At still other times, teachers and children work together to recreate the center into a new play theme.

Teachers often collect items that could be used for one play theme and store them in a clearly labeled box, generally referred to as a prop box. For example, a prop box for beach-related play might contain beach towels, old swimsuits, flip-flops, empty suntan lotion containers, old sunglasses, and magazines. Another prop box meant to encourage dramatic play about bakeries could contain rolling pins, mixing bowls, measuring spoons and cups, an old mixer with the electrical cord removed, cookie cutters, aprons, and baker's hats. Items for prop boxes can be collected from surplus household items, garage sales, thrift shops, or by sending notes home to students' families to let them know what you need. Prop boxes expand children's play and are only as limited as a teacher's imagination.

### Listening Center

The listening center provides essential experiences that promote language and literacy development. This center requires very little equipment or floor space. Setting up a listening center can be as simple as arranging a tape recorder and headsets among a group of pillows to create a cozy area. A basket or plastic container can serve as storage for audio tapes or tapes and books and be placed nearby. In this center children can listen to stories, poetry readings, environmental sounds, and musical tapes. Prerecorded tapes offer children the opportunity to hear stories read over and over. They can listen to favorite songs and not disturb children in other centers. They can listen to tapes recorded by the class or by individual children. Time spent in the listening center can offer a oasis for children who need quiet time in an active early childhood classroom.

### Math Center

Children working in the math center interact with each other and with many different types of learning materials. Materials offered to young children in this center range from buttons or seeds that children have collected to commercially produced math manipulatives such as pattern blocks and colored pegs. In the math center, children sort, classify, order, count, com-

*Literacy Link: Listening*

Any book can be added to the listening center. If commercially produced audio tapes are not available, teachers can audio-tape themselves reading a book. Better still, for many books, especially those with repeated texts, teachers can record a group of children choral reading a book.

*Time spent in the listening center can offer an oasis for children who need quiet time in an active early childhood classroom*

pare, and graph collections of objects. These objects should be meaningful to children, and the reasons that children engage in these activities should be specific and real. Young children should not be asked to perform contrived mathematical tasks such as those typically related to math

*Materials offered to young children in the math center range from buttons or seeds that children have collected to commercially produced math manipulatives such as pattern blocks and colored pegs.*

---

*Literacy Link: Math*

Lesser, C., & Regan, L. (1999). *Spots*. Orlando, FL: Harcourt.

McMillan, B. (1989). *Time to. . .* New York: William Morrow.

Murphy, S., & Remkiewicz, F. (1999). *Rabbit's pajama party*. New York: HarperTrophy.

Murphy, S., & Dunbar, F. (1997). *Every buddy counts*. New York: HarperCollins.

Pallotta, J., & Bolster, R. (2002). *The Hershey's kisses subtraction book*. New York: Scholastic.

Soderberg, E., & Koblish, P. (2001). *Counting to 100 with the NBA*. New York: Scholastic.

Williams, R. L. (2001). *The coin counting book*. Watertown: Charlesbridge.

worksheets. The concrete materials and meaningful experiences support children as they construct their own mathematical information (DeVries & Kohlberg, 1990).

The math center can become noisy if several children are working in the center. If the center is located on a carpeted area, some of the noise from dropped materials can be reduced. Some noise can be controlled if children have more than one place to work with math materials. Children should have the choice of using math materials at a table or on the floor. The floor space for this center should be relatively large. The floor and table space should be nondescript, without patterns of any kind. Storage of materials for this center should be organized and clearly labeled.

## Music Center

Children are naturally drawn to music. They march to the beat, move to action songs, and wave streamers or scarves as the music leads them. While many music-related activities, such as performing action songs or listening to relaxing sonatas during rest time, will often occur during large-group times, children enjoy directing their own musical experiences.

A tape recorder, a collection of audio tapes, rhythm instruments, and movement props (such as streamers, scarves, and costumes) can provide the basis for a music center. There should be enough room for children to choose their own creative movement activities, and this center should be located away from the quieter centers.

## Reading Center

The reading center can be one of the coziest centers in the classroom. It should be located in a quiet part of the classroom and the traffic pattern near this center should be negligible. Pillows, soft chairs, and carpeting or

---

*Literacy Link: Music*

Christelow, E. (1989). *Five little monkeys jumping on the bed*. New York: Houghton Mifflin.

Cooper, F. (1998). *Cumbayah*. New York: William Morrow.

Guthrie, W., & Jakobsen, K. (1998). *This land is your land*. New York: Little, Brown & Co.

Johnson, J. W. (1995). *Lift ev'ry voice and sing*. New York: Scholastic.

La Prise, L., Macak, C., Baker, T., & Hamanaka, S. (2001). *The hokey pokey*. New York: Scholastic.

Priceman, M. (2000). *Froggy went a-courtin*. New York: Little, Brown, & Co.

*The reading center is most appealing to children when they can see the front covers of books.*

rugs help create a relaxing atmosphere. Some teachers build lofts or use items such as row boats to help create the idea that the reading center is a special place in the classroom.

A wide variety of books should be available for children to choose among: class favorites, predictable texts, wordless books, concept books, classic fairy tales, poetry, and class-created and child-made books. Children are more likely to choose a book when they can easily see the front cover. Books spines are not particularly appealing to young children. Therefore several books should be placed so that children can see the front covers of the books. Books of similar genre can be stored together in baskets or plastic containers on low bookshelves.

The primary purpose for the reading center is for children to interact with self-selected books for the sheer pleasure of it. However, to expand children's exploration with the printed word, teachers often add flannel boards with a selection of storybook characters, letters of the alphabet, or other objects. Magnetic board and letters can also be placed in the reading center. Even a puppet stage can be set up nearby.

## Sand and Water Center

Sand and water play offer children the opportunity to enhance all areas of development. As they carry and lift containers of sand and water, they are strengthening large muscles. As they pour and measure, they are strengthening small muscles. They compare, observe, measure, predict, and make discoveries about sinking, floating, and mixtures as they work with these materials. In so doing, children learn important concepts. They learn to cooperate as they share materials and work together and are constantly using language as they discuss their actions.

The sand and water centers can be set up in the classroom or outdoors. If the center is indoors, it is best placed on a tile or vinyl floor so that the area can be mopped or swept easily. If this is not possible, thick plastic sheeting, even an old plastic shower curtain, can be taped to the floor to protect carpeting. If the center is placed outdoors, it should be in a shady area that can be supervised easily. Vinyl smocks should be available to protect children's clothing during water play and materials for cleaning stored close to this center.

## Science Center

Young children seem to be drawn to science if their curiosity is encouraged and they are allowed to interact with real objects related to science. Sometimes this center is neglected by teachers who do not feel qualified to "teach" science. However, with young children, an in-depth knowledge of botany and biology is not a prerequisite to having live plants and animals for children to care for and learn about. Teachers can learn the basics of caring for plants and animals by reading children's books.

Science is not just a body of knowledge, it is a way of thinking. Interesting, concrete materials to observe and explore encourage the natural curiosity of young children. Through interacting with objects from nature, children learn to observe. By talking with each other about science center materials, they learn to communicate what they are observing. With teacher-collected materials such as magnets, rain gauges, and balance scales, children learn to experiment. By interacting with teacher-made science objects, children learn to

---

*Literacy Link: Science*

Allen, J. (2000). *Are you a spider?* New York: Larousse Kingfisher Chambers.
Berger, M., & Berger, G. (2001). *Is a dolphin a fish?* New York: Scholastic.
Cannon, J. (2000). *Crickwing.* Orlando, FL: Harcourt.
Gibbons, G. (1993). *Frogs.* New York: Holiday House.
Legg, G. (1998). *From chicken to egg.* New York: Franklin Watts.
Rockwell, A. W. (1999). *One bean.* New York: Walker & Co.
Titherington, J. (1986). *Pumpkin pumpkin.* New York: Greenwillow Books.

analyze information and make predictions. These materials could include smelling jars—each of which has a separate smell (vanilla or almond extracts, lemon or orange juice)—or sound jars—opaque containers filled with items to make different sounds. The science center can offer rich experiences for children.

The science center should be placed near a window so the plants and animals can have the light they need. Low tables or shelves can be used to organize science materials.

## Writing Center

Writing materials are available in most centers, but a writing center is still an important area for early childhood classrooms. For young children, writing is a social experience. They need a shared area to experiment with writing and to talk about what they are creating.

Young children of all ages express themselves on paper in different ways. All stages of writing, including drawing and scribbling, invented letters, strings of random letters, invented spelling, and conventional spelling, should be accepted and valued.

The writing center is a central area in the room. It is filled with several types of paper, a variety of writing utensils, and other items that children might use in the process of creating drawings, stories, books, poems, letters, notes, signs, invitations, greeting cards, and anything else they decide to create. Equipment used to produce text can also be included in the writing center. A typewriter will add a different dimension to children's work. While a computer offers many opportunities for reading, math, and science learning, a simple word-processing program and child-friendly graphics software open endless possibilities for children's writing. Frequently teachers include a tape recorder in the writing center. Some verbal children find this a useful way to recall what they want to write. They record their thoughts, then they can stop and start the tape as they need to, so that their motor abilities can record all of their ideas.

## Computers as a Center

Not every program can afford computers in the classroom, but the presence of technology in early childhood classrooms is increasing. Computers were mentioned earlier in the discussion of the writing center. This is one use of computers that emphasizes the use of technology as a tool for learning, a way to integrated them into the curriculum (NAEYC, 1996; Samaras, 1996). Computers can also be used in early childhood classrooms as a separate center. So that they are an appropriate learning experience for young children, teachers are careful to select appropriate software (Shade, 1996). Children should be able to explore computer programs, determine the pace

*Suggestions for Selecting Appropriate Software for Young Children*

Children should be able to access programs independently or with minimal help.

Directions should be easily understood by children.

Keyboard functions should be simple.

Graphics should be appealing, appropriate to the content, and not distracting.

Audio component should be clear.

Spoken vocabulary of the software program should be age-appropriate.

Programs should encourage choice, decision making, problem solving, and creative thinking.

Programs should foster social and intellectual interaction with peers.

Programs should support the current curricula theme.

The content is age-appropriate and individually appropriate.

Adapted from Puckett, M.B., & Black, J.K. (2000). Authentic assessment of the young child: Celebrating development and learning (2nd ed.). Upper Saddle River, NJ: Merill/Prentice Hall.

and direction of the experience, and be creative. Developmentally appropriate software involves children in an active way. While computer programs can offer children some new experiences, computers should never replace hands-on experiences for children; for example, creative arts software should not replace actual drawing (NAEYC, 1996).

Not every early childhood classroom will have all the centers discussed in this section. Financial constraints and physical restrictions, such as the size of the room and configuration of the space, may force teachers to choose among these centers. But centers can be combined or changed out periodically through the year so that children can participate in a variety of learning activities. Whatever the physical restrictions, the primary consideration in arranging an early childhood environment is offering children many different developmentally appropriate activities within well-defined areas in the room.

*Literary Link: Writing*

Gibbons, G. (1982). *The post office book mail and how it moves.* New York: HarperTrophy.

Keats, E. (1968). *A letter to Amy.* New York: Penguin.

Langen, A., & Droop, C. (1996). *Felix explores planet Earth.* New York: Abbeville.

Leedy, L. (1991). *Messages in the mailbox.* New York: Holiday House.

## Meeting the Needs of Infants and Toddlers through the Environment

Obviously an environment for the youngest of our young children would look very different from the centers described in this chapter. An infant room requires different furnishings than rooms for preschool and older children. Infants require cribs, changing areas, high chairs in special feeding areas, and separate space for play. Toddlers require climbing equipment, small pushing and riding toys, and thick board books. But some of the same principles apply in planning an environment for infants and toddlers as they do in arranging space for older children. The rooms should be clearly divided into distinct areas.

For infants, the crib area should be separate from the play area so that sleeping infants are not disturbed by those who are playing. The changing area should be separate from both these areas, positioned near a sink for easy cleanup and near storage for diapers and other supplies. The caregiver should be able to reach all supplies without moving away from the infant. Low shelving should be near the play area so that crawling infants can choose their own toys and large foam cubes should be placed nearby for infants who are crawling or climbing. Visuals can also be placed on or near the floor for crawlers and toddlers.

Toys and materials in the play area should be well designed especially for infants and toddlers. Adults should take care to select crib toys wisely, considering toys such as specially designed crib mirrors, activity boards, washable soft toys, and pictures posted on the ceiling above cribs. Tape-recorded music can be located near cribs and play areas.

A room designed for toddlers has some of the same areas found in an infant room: a changing area located near a sink, a gross-motor area with low climbing structures, and a manipulative center containing toys and large puzzles. Additional centers for toddlers might include an art area with age-appropriate supplies such as large paper, nontoxic markers, crayons, and fresh play dough; a home center with dolls and stuffed animals; and an area featuring transportation toys such as trucks, planes, and cars. Toddlers are the least capable of all ages to share materials, so duplicate materials are essential. Because toddlers are increasingly mobile, they require large, open spaces and low tables and shelves for standing and balance. Special care should be taken to avoid sharp edges or small parts that can be swallowed and to cushion floors (Bronson, 1995).

In family child care homes or centers that use the same room for children of different ages, special care should be taken to arrange materials meant for older children in places where mobile infants and toddlers cannot reach them and to supervise closely their use. The home or center should be "childproofed" for all safety hazards, such as eliminating hanging electrical cords, covering electrical outlets, gating stairwells, and placing cleaning supplies and medicines out of reach.

## Classrooms for Elementary School Children

Just as rooms should be specially designed for infants and toddlers, the primary-grade classrooms should be specially designed for this particular age group as well. All the centers discussed above may not be used in classrooms for six-, seven-, and eight-year-olds. Some may be used, but with modifications to challenge older children.

Student choice of learning activities is still critically important, but the room may be arranged with academic priorities in mind. For example, developing proficient readers is a priority in early elementary school grades. Rather than having a single reading center as in a preschool class, an elementary classroom may have multiple reading centers, each offering a different activity related to reading: poetry, audio taping, magnetic letters, flannel board story retelling, interactive charts of familiar poems and songs, and author centers. Rather than one math center, elementary teachers may organize several math centers based on math concepts they are addressing: geometry, computation, and problem solving. A writing center may house all the materials, but children may choose to write in different parts of the classroom.

Elementary school children need less center definition than preschool children. Reading or math materials may be centrally located in centers, but these older children are more capable of gathering materials they need to accomplish a task and then choosing the place in the classroom where they wish to work.

For elementary teachers who have limited space and a room full of desks, the classroom can still be arranged in appropriate ways. Desks can be grouped together to create centers or learning areas, rather than assigning one desk to each student. Center materials can be stored in stacking crates about the room and near other related supporting materials. For example, math manipulatives can be placed near a bulletin board related to math or a chalkboard that children can use for math computation. Couches can be added to the classroom to add a homelike touch, as well as to add another working space for children. Alternatives are possible to the desks-in-rows approach to elementary school classrooms as with small groupings of three or four desks so children can work together, interacting and scaffolding each other's learning.

Whatever age group an early childhood educator is working with, the physical environment is critically important to the success of the program. The environment should be planned to be age appropriate and appealing to the children. However, when children begin to work in that environment, teachers should carefully observe how they interact in the centers and with the center materials. Changes in centers should be made periodically. Materials should be replaced and added as children's interests wane, themes change, and skills advance.

*Elementary teachers can group desks together to create learning centers.*

### Creating a Dynamic Physical Environment

It is common for some centers to be available to children throughout the year. For example, reading, writing, and listening centers should always be accessible to young children. This does not mean these centers would have the same materials in March that they did in August. Centers that remain in the classroom throughout the year should be examined by the teacher on a regular basis to determine if materials should be added or removed. The writing center needs almost daily attention to keep a selection of paper and writing instruments available to children. The art center also needs this kind of constant attention. Other centers are more generally reviewed on a weekly or biweekly basis.

There are particular times when center materials should be examined and rearranged. One of the most obvious reasons for scrutinizing a center is when children stop choosing that center. That should be a strong clue to the teacher that children are bored with the choices available. At this time, some of the materials should be stored away and others offered.

A second reason to remove materials from centers is when they become worn or broken. These materials should be removed from centers immediately and be repaired or discarded. Young children tend not to take care of materials when they are not in good condition.

Another reason to reorganize a center is to support children's new interests. Early childhood educators should pay close attention to interests emerging among students. If a teacher notices children digging for worms during recess, books and other learning materials about worms can be gathered and placed in appropriate centers. If children show an increased interest in cooking, items used to cook or bake and cookbooks can be placed into centers. Teachers follow the lead of students in deciding what materials should be put into different centers. An observant teacher who identifies new interests and provides materials for children to explore is meeting many needs of students through the way she rearranges the classroom environment.

## Managing Children's Center Choices

Children engage for longer periods of time in activities that they choose for themselves. For this reason, children need to make decisions about where they will spend center time and which materials they will work with. Obviously, every child cannot work in the art center at the same time. So a system for managing center choice should be put into place early in the year.

Early childhood educators implement different systems for managing how many children can work in each center. Many teachers decide how many children can work in each center before the children arrive. Some centers may allow only two children to work there because the space for the center is small. Typically centers are large enough to accommodate three or four children. As teachers are planning how many children will be allowed in each center, they ensure that there are sufficient number of choices for children. There should be at least twice the number of places to work in centers as there are children in the classroom. Next, teachers arrange centers so that this limit is clearly understood by children.

Some teachers glue library pocket cards to center signs, as many pocket cards as children allowed in that center at one time. At center time, each child is given an index card on which their name is printed. When a child chooses a center, he places that card in one of the pockets. If there are no pocket cards into which he can place his card, he must select another center. Other teachers place colored dots on center signs and distribute clothespins labeled with a child's name. As they choose a center, children clip their clothespin to a colored dot. Like the pocket-card system, if no colored dot is showing, children must choose another center. Another center-management system that has been used by teachers is necklaces that the teacher creates for each center. The correct number of necklaces hang near the entrance to the center. Children can choose a center only if a center necklace is available for them to wear. Each of these systems is self-managing for young children. If the teacher carefully explains the procedure and demonstrates what she expects from the children, they will be able to make center choices with few conflicts. Some children will need continued adult support in remembering center-choice procedures.

## ADDRESSING CHILDREN'S NEEDS THROUGH CHOICE OF DIVERSE EXPERIENCES

Children in a classroom have many different needs. One adult cannot directly meet all the developmental needs of all the children all of the time. A teacher could easily become overwhelmed if she had to think through the physical, psychosocial, cognitive, and language and literacy needs of twenty or more children. If she had to write out specific plans for meeting all those needs on a daily basis, it would be almost impossible.

Thinking about trying to meet such a diversity of needs underscores the necessity for a carefully planned physical environment. Learning centers, properly organized with appropriate materials, meet many of children's needs without the teacher's immediate intervention. Given sufficient numbers of appropriate choices of activities, children choose to work with materials that meet their own needs.

Many of the materials in an early childhood classroom can be used by children to meet different developmental needs. Children can work with the same set of materials and yet be learning very different things. This was apparent in a kindergarten home center. After listening to their teacher read *Pet Show* by Ezra Jack Keats (1972), several students transferred class pets from the science center and wooden animal figures from the block center into the home center. They used these real and pretend animals to create their own "pet show." Two children spent thirty minutes sorting and resorting the wooden animal figures into two groups: animals that could be in the pet show and animals that were too dangerous to be in the show. They argued over each animal, redefining their criteria for deciding which animals could be included in the show with each decision. Another child spent the first part of the hour in trying to gather the courage to hold the pet snake for the first time and the second half of the hour showing everyone how brave she was to let the snake wrap around her arm. One child spent most of the hour making a list of animals in the show by copying pet names from the labels on the cages. In the same center and acting out the same play theme, four children were working on and learning very different things.

The teacher's role in this dramatic play theme is not apparent. However, without the materials that the teacher had placed in the classroom or the choice of the book to read aloud, this play theme would not have emerged. This story underscores the importance of the role of the environment in supporting and initiating children's learning and the early childhood educator's responsibility in establishing that environment.

A second, equally important role of the teacher is that of observer. The teacher carefully noted what the children were saying and doing as they played. She knew which children were engaging in different activities during their "pet show." An experienced teacher will note skills the children are using, knowledge they are displaying, language they are using, and ways they interact with each other.

*Many of children's needs can be met in learning centers.*

The teacher will use the information she learns through this observation in a number of different ways. She may decide to add new materials to centers, locate new books, or plan specific activities for individual children. She will also use the interests that children demonstrate to plan future learning experiences for them.

One kindergarten teacher noticed that her students were not choosing the science center as frequently as they had before. The science center had been carefully organized over time and she felt good about its activity choices available to her students. The classroom pets were housed in this center: a guinea pig, a rat, a gerbil, a turtle, and a snake. There were also books about these animals, study skins and skeletons of rodents borrowed from a local museum's teaching collection, plants the children had grown from seeds, magnifying glasses, and a collection of magnets. But she knew from the apparent lack of interest in choosing the science center that she needed to reorganize the materials already there and add new materials. As she was considering this challenge, she noticed several children following a line of ants on the playground during recess. At that moment she believed she had found a possible solution to the problem of the science center. The next morning when the children arrived in the classroom, the science specimens and books about rodents had been moved from the science center table to the floor beside the rodent cages. The center table now housed an ant farm, some enlarged photographs of ants, and several books: *The Icky Bug Alphabet Book* by Jerry Pallotta (1986), *Ant Cities* by Arthur Dorros (1987), and *Ant* by A. Soutter-Perrot (1993). The interest in the science center was greater than ever as the children observed the ants, looked through the books and at the pictures, and began to ask questions about ants. There was even a renewed interest in the other learning materials that had been in the science center all along.

## RESPONDING TO EMERGING CURRICULA

The curriculum for early childhood classes should not be planned months in advance. While developmental needs of the children in the class are the framework for center materials and class activities, children's experiences and current interests should drive the curriculum for young children. These interests can come from a variety of sources. Some are spontaneous and some can be planned (Jones & Nimmo, 1994). Even in elementary schools, where most of the curriculum is driven by state and district mandates, teachers can use children's interests in deciding when and how to present mandated learning experiences.

Children may bring some ideas into the classroom from their experiences at home and in the community. If several children attend a circus performance, "circus" could easily become the class theme for a week or two. If one child captures a lizard and brings it in to share with the class, lizards may become the focus of several centers. In one kindergarten classroom, a month-long investigation into amphibians began when one child found a large toad on the school playground. At first the children put the toad into an empty aquarium so they could observe it more closely. Class discussions led to how they could prepare an environment so the toad would be happier in their science center. Children found books about toads and wrote letters to a veterinarian they had consulted before. From what they learned, they collected crickets for the toad to eat, found rich dirt and moss to create a better micro-habitat, and found a low dish to hold water for the toad. They drew pictures of the toad in observation logs and used developmental spelling to describe what they saw the toad doing. They charted how many crickets they put into the aquarium and how many the toad ate. They began writing stories that featured toads and started writing "toad facts" on index cards to post in the science center. Interest in the toad did not wane. Every morning as children arrived in the classroom, each child checked on the toad as soon as he or she put his or her personal things in cubbies. From this obvious interest, the teacher expanded children's investigation into a study of frogs and a comparison of frogs and toads. One parent bought an aquatic frog for the classroom. Another parent bought several books about frogs and toads as a gift for the children and the amphibian unit continued.

Some interests can be introduced to the children by the teacher. Children's interests might be piqued by a field trip to a farm or a museum. The teacher might bring in artifacts from the days of their great-grandparents or tools used by paleontologists and an entire unit of study might begin. The topic might be one of particular interest to the teacher. The teacher of a first-grade class attended a performance of Andrew Lloyd Webber's *Phantom of the Opera*. She loved the music and decided to share it with her class. One day she wore her *Phantom* sweatshirt to school and told the children during the morning meeting that she had a special tape to share with them. The class fidgeted as she played the overture and she wondered if she was expecting too much from six- and seven-year-olds. She decided to continue and explained the first scene to the children. They settled in and started listening carefully for the words she told them they would hear in the next excerpt of the musical. By the fourth scene, the children were recognizing the voices of Christine, Carlotta, Raoul, and the Phantom. After they had listened to the final scene, the children begged their teacher to "play it again," just as they did for favorite storybooks. For weeks, the children would start the tape as soon as they came into the classroom. Their dramatic play frequently featured the characters from *Phantom*. They wrote about the Phantom, made Phantom masks in the art center, and sang the lyrics as they worked in other centers. In this case, an interest of the teacher's became an interest of the children.

Learning centers and an observant and responsive teacher provide the flexibility for responding to children's changing interests and keeping the classroom active and vibrant. Children in classrooms learn much more than content. They learn their questions are important. They learn to find resources to answer their questions. They learn they can be in charge of their own learning. They begin to understand that learning is a life-long process.

## BIOGRAPHY BOX  *Joe Frost*

Joe Frost was born and reared in the Quachita Mountain area of Arkansas. He graduated from Waldron (Arkansas) High School and attended Oklahoma State University and the University of Maryland before receiving a doctorate in elementary education with a specialty in child development at the University of Arkansas. His teaching experience includes primary, elementary, and junior high levels and demonstration teaching with Head Start and nursery-school children. From public school he moved to university teaching at the University of Arkansas, Iowa State University, University of California at Davis, and the University of Florida. He is presently Catherine Mae Parker Centennial Professor Emeritus at the University of Texas at Austin.

Frost has lectured in most U.S. states, Canada, Mexico, Europe, and Asia. He has authored and edited eighteen textbooks and more than one hundred articles and research reports. *The Disadvantaged Child* co-edited with Glenn Hawkes, was selected by Pi Lambda Theta as one of the outstanding education books for 1966. His most popular book, *Early Childhood Education Rediscovered*, has been adopted by colleges and universities in all fifty states and in more than twenty foreign countries. His most recent books are: *Playgrounds for Young Children* (American Alliance for Physical Education, Recreation and Dance, 1990); *Play and Playscapes* (published by Delmar Learning in 1992), and *Play and Child Development* (Merrill/Prentice-Hall, 2001), and *Children and Injuries* (Lawyers and Judges Publishing, 2001).

He has served as a consultant to the U.S. Department of Education, the U.S. Consumer Product Safety Commission, the U.S. Department of Justice, and numerous other agencies, universities, and corporations. Frost participates in several professional organizations concerned with young children. He was president of the Association for Childhood Education International and was U.S. president and representative to the international Playground Association. His current research interests are children's play and play environments and family relations. He was selected Texas Educator of the Year in 1989 by the Texas Association for the Education of Young Children.

## EVALUATING CENTERS

Informal evaluation of how well centers are set up can be done simply by observing how often the center is selected by children and the types of interactions children have with the materials in the center. If children are not choosing to work in a particular center, then the adult needs to consider the materials that are offered in that center. Do materials need to be exchanged or new materials added to that center? Do the materials reflect the current interests of the students in the class? Are the materials presented in an organized, attractive way? Can the children in the class reach all the materials that are available in that center? Answering these questions can give the teacher some ideas about reworking the center to make it more appealing to children.

More formal evaluation of centers can be done by teachers. Rating scales (Harms, Clifford, & Cryer, 1998) and checklists (Puckett, 2002) are available to evaluate how well the environment has been constructed to meet the needs of young children.

# THE EXPANDED OUTDOOR PLAY ENVIRONMENT

Curriculum and learning do not occur only within the four walls of a classroom. Early childhood educators view the out-of-doors as a second classroom. While some educators view the outdoor play environment as "recess time," a time for children to run and expend excess energy, teachers of young children see the outdoors as another environment for children to explore and to learn.

Very few experiences are offered in the classroom that cannot be offered outdoors. Most center materials can be transferred from the classroom to outdoor play environments. Easels can easily be set up near the playground so that children can paint nature scenes that they see. Blankets, pillows, and baskets of books allow children to share reading in the shade of a tree. A battery-operated tape player and a small container of streamers allow movement activities to occur in the open air. These everyday experiences probably should be offered outdoors from time to time. None of these things are difficult to transfer from the classroom to the outdoor environment and the new surroundings elicit new perspectives about common experiences.

Teachers would probably not want to move large pieces of equipment outdoors, then back inside, on a regular basis. It would be preferable if extra sand and water tables were permanently available outdoors. Tricycles and other vehicles should probably be stored outside. Just as in the classroom, the depth of children's learning in the outdoor environment strongly relates to the types of concrete materials they can use to manipulate and explore (Frost, 1992).

*Rating Scale for Block Center*

|  | Apparent |  |  | Needs Work |  |
|---|---|---|---|---|---|
| Block center clearly defined | 5 | 4 | 3 | 2 | 1 |
| Sufficient space for complex block building | 5 | 4 | 3 | 2 | 1 |
| Adequate number of blocks for number of children allowed in center | 5 | 4 | 3 | 2 | 1 |
| Blocks stored in an organized manner | 5 | 4 | 3 | 2 | 1 |
| Accessories for block building available in sufficient numbers | 5 | 4 | 3 | 2 | 1 |
| Accessories to support different types of block building | 5 | 4 | 3 | 2 | 1 |
| Accessories stored in an organized manner so that children can access them independently | 5 | 4 | 3 | 2 | 1 |

*Checklist for Outdoor Play Area*

1. The play yard is free from hazards and equipment is safe.
2. Adults plan outdoor activities with as much care as they plan indoor activities.
3. During outdoor play time, adults interact with children to further their learning.
4. The play yard is organized into separate play areas and centers, offering children a variety of activities and types of play.
5. Outdoor activities are based on children's developmental needs.
6. Outdoor activities promote children's creativity and thinking skills.
7. Outdoor activities promote active movement and physical coordination.
8. Outdoor activities encourage children to make choices and initiate their own actions.
9. Children understand and help set safety rules.
10. Adequate storage is available for storing riding toys, portable equipment, and other outdoor materials.
11. The children have easy access to drinking water and a bathroom.

*Source:* From *Room to grow: How to create quality early childhood environments*, (p. 147). Edited by Linda Ard and Mabel Pitts (Eds.), 1995, Austin, Texas. Copyright 1995 by Texas Association for the Education of Young Children. Reprinted with permission.

Not all outdoor experiences should be organized by the teacher. Young children need plenty of opportunities to play in gravel, dig in the dirt, and gather rocks, twigs, and acorns. If your school is fortunate enough to have natural areas nearby, these areas can be cleared of poison ivy or other less-than-desirable plants and made available for children to explore (Rivkin, 1995).

## THE ENRICHMENT OF COMMUNITY RESOURCES

Because early childhood educators provide concrete, hands-on experiences for children, they tend to see the entire community as a plethora of opportunities for learning experiences. Every community offers an endless number of field trip opportunities for real learning.

### Field Trips

Virtually every community has grocery stores, post offices, public libraries, and restaurants. Even though children may go to these places with their parents on a regular basis, a shared field trip with classmates adds a new dimension to the familiar place. A child may go to the grocery store once a week, but when they accompany their class on a field trip to purchase ingre-

*Children need time to explore their environment in unplanned activities such as digging in the sand.*

dients for a cooking activity, the experience is different. Occasionally, construction sites are close enough to schools or child care centers for walking field trips.

Most large cities have a wealth of cultural and educational institutions that can be accessed for learning opportunities: science, history, or art museums; art galleries; children's theaters; puppet shows; symphony or ballet performances; libraries or bookstores that have special children's story times; and zoos and nature centers.

## Classroom Visitors

If it is too difficult to organize many field trips, teachers invite visitors to come to the class. This can be a wonderful way to help children come to view people as resources for learning what they want to know. If the children are planning a garden, experts from nurseries or parents or other family members who maintain a garden could be invited to the classroom to share their knowledge with the children. If the class is trying to decide what pet to add to the science center, pet store personnel or zoo staff could be invited to talk with the children. Older students could also be brought in as

*Early childhood educators can enrich the classroom routine by inviting guests to visit the classroom and share their knowledge.*

"experts" on animals they have raised as pets. Involving other people in the life of the class can be an enriching experience.

## REVISITING CHERYL'S CLASSROOM

Four months have passed, and a walk through Cheryl's classroom indicates that many changes have happened since she and Joy first arranged the learning centers and placed materials in them. Cheryl had placed many more pillows in several centers and had hung textured wall hangings to absorb some of the normal noise associated with active young children. She had discovered that controlling the noise level of the room helped maximize the use of hearing by the child who was visually impaired.

The science and dramatic play centers are no longer separate learning centers. The children had suggested combining the two centers to make a pet shop, so now all the furniture had been rearranged by the children themselves. A cash register and receipt book sat on a table near the opening of the center. The sharp edges of this table are padded so that the visually impaired student would not hurt himself during the time of adjusting to the new arrangement of the room. There are seven aquariums—also with edges padded—one for each of the class pets: a guinea pig, a family of mice, a rat, a hamster, a tarantula, a rat snake, and a box turtle. On each aquarium a price tag is posted alongside labels identifying the animal and its name. Containers of food are also labeled and priced. Child-dictated and child-illustrated booklets about each of the animals are in a display shelf along with nature magazines and commercially published books about the animals that are "for sale."

Each center has many more materials than Cheryl offered at the beginning of the year. The math center has many more manipulatives and several collections of objects that the children have gathered as a class—keys, buttons, seashells, fossils, and mini cars. The art center now offers at least ten different media from which children can select on a daily basis. The reading center is filled with more than two hundred books, all organized by child-written labels that read "Eric Carle," "Dr. Seuss," "true animals," "pretend animals," "poems," "families," "babies," and so on. The listening center has a large wicker basket filled with dozens of zip-top bags that contains two copies of the same book and either a professionally recorded or classmade audio tape. The water center has several lengths of rubber tubing to support the children's new siphoning play. The block center has several different kinds of blocks and eight baskets of different accessories to stimulate different types of block structures.

The most distinct difference in the classroom now is that the room has taken on the look of being occupied by active, interested children. Paintings, drawings, and dictated stories fill the room. Above the bookshelves containing math materials are sentence strips on which children have drawn patterns. Near the art center, several paintings have been matted and hung in what the children refer to as "our art museum." The reading center offers class-made and child-created books as well as commercially published trade books. The listening center has book reviews posted that children have dictated and illustrated. Near the water center are children's drawings that give directions on how to siphon water from one container to another, and hung on the wall near the block center are laminated drawings and photographs of block structures created in previous weeks. Cheryl has also taken photographs of children working in different centers and posts those around the room near signs that explain to adults visiting the classroom what children are learning as they are working in the different learning centers. Clearly the children have assumed ownership of this classroom. It reflects their interests and their work.

## Summary

The physical environment is critically important in early childhood as it supports young children's learning and helps meet their developmental needs. The learning of young children is integrated, thus well-planned centers enhance integrated learning at its best. Early childhood educators use what they know about child development and room arrangement to create a stimulating, age-appropriate environment. They must also rearrange the room and provide additional center materials to support the development and personal interests of individual children in the class. It is also important that teachers plan appropriate learning experiences for centers as well as for large and small groups of children. Planning learning activities will be discussed in the following chapter.

## Reflections

**1.** Choose one learning center and a particular age group of children. List the materials that could be placed in that center and describe the learning that could occur in that center with those materials.

**2.** Think about one child you know well who is between the ages of three and eight. Consider his or her needs in the following developmental areas: physical/motor, emotional and social, cognitive, and language/literacy. Determine how those needs could be met in a classroom.

**3.** Develop a list of possible learning centers beyond the more common ones. State what learning or experiences these centers might provide. How would you set up these centers? What materials or activities might be included?

**4.** List educational and cultural institutions in your community that would be appropriate for young children. Choose one of these and describe what types of learning might be stimulated by a field trip. Make your own preliminary visit, obtain literature about this resource. Write about what preparation you would plan for a group of young children before the trip and what follow-up experiences you would provide after the field trip.

## Field Experiences

**1.** Find four classrooms that serve the four following age groups: toddlers, preschool-aged children, kindergarten, and primary grades. Sketch the floor plan of each room and write suggestions about how the room could be rearranged to enhance the environment for each age group.

**2.** Visit a kindergarten classroom and select one center. Observe for two or three center times in that classroom. Keep detailed notes of the children's behaviors and conversations as they work in that center. Analyze what the children do and say and list the types of learning that occurred in that center.

**3.** Visit a public school that has prekindergarten and kindergarten classes and go outside with one of those classes. Make notes about the types of play you observe. Reflect on how that outside play environment could be enriched. Make notes about the types of play you might observe in the improved play environment.

**4.** Visit a center or family day home of high quality. How are the unique needs of infants (or toddlers) being met? What types of growth-enhancing materials and interactions are provided?

# Case Studies

## Teaching with Nothing

Andrea had been a part of a "grow your own" program in a large urban school district for three years. During the day, she worked as a secretary for a middle school. Three nights a week, she attended classes at a nearby university. Andrea was so excited when she finished all the required coursework during two summer sessions. She was ready to get into the classroom full-time and was looking forward to student teaching.

The week before school was scheduled to begin, an upper-level administrator called Andrea with disturbing news. Andrea was the first secretary to go through this program. All other participants had been teachers' aides, so no program participant had ever done a student teaching assignment. There was no mechanism in place for Andrea to student teach. The administrator explained that Andrea would have to begin the year as a classroom teacher and that he would call her soon with her specific school assignment.

The first day of school came and went with no call from the administrator and no teaching assignment. The same with the first week of school and the second week. Andrea continued to work in the middle school office, functioning as the main secretary. Her numerous calls of inquiry were not returned. She was beginning to wonder if she would ever have her own class.

Finally, on the Monday of the third week of school, Andrea received a call telling her to report to an elementary school the following day. She learned that the kindergarten enrollment was over state mandate in each of the four classes at this school. Andrea would be teaching the fifth kindergarten class at her new place of employment.

Andrea did as she was told. The next morning, she met with the principal of the elementary school. That day, the other kindergarten teachers were choosing the five students they would send to the new class. The principal introduced Andrea to each of the kindergarten teachers. Each of their classrooms were on the same hall. The principal took Andrea outside and showed her the portable building where she would start teaching the next day.

Andrea was so surprised at what she saw that she could not think of anything to say. In the small portable building, there were four tables, twenty child-sized chairs, one short bookshelf, and a teacher's desk. There were no books, no furniture to use to set up centers, no math manipulatives, no science materials. There was not even a box of crayons or a ream of paper. The principal left Andrea alone in her room so she could plan. After thirty minutes of making notes, Andrea returned to the principal's office to ask a few questions about supplies and materials. She was told that she would be given a ream of paper and 20 pencils, and that was it. There was no money in the current budget to buy anything. The new budget would not go into effect for six more weeks. At that time, Andrea would have $250 to buy "what she needed."

**What to Do?**

In this virtually impossible situation, what should Andrea do first? What could she pull together in a few hours on Tuesday night? What materials and supplies would be most important? What should she purchase with her own money? What might she be able to beg or borrow from the other kindergarten teachers who were strangers to her? What time should she get to school on Wednesday morning, and what could she set up in that time? What would she need for her "first day" of kindergarten? What would she need to gather for those first six weeks? What things would she be able to purchase with only $250?

**One Young Male Teacher vs. Three Older Wiser Female Teachers**

Kevin Lind was excited about his first year of teaching. He felt lucky that he was going to teach first grade. First grade was his grade of choice. That was what he asked for during his interview with the personnel department. As soon as he received the assignment, he went to the school. The principal and a few teachers were working that week before school was to start. Kevin followed the principal's directions and found his classroom. It was filled with desks and little else.

Based on his college courses, Kevin had assumed that first and second grade classes would be considered early childhood and taught as if they were early childhood classes. All of those desks did not send the message that first grade was early childhood at this school.

Kevin peeked into the other first-grade rooms. All three were set up with desks in rows. On top of each desk was a stack of textbooks and workbooks. At the front of each room, the same set of rules were posted. Kevin could not see any learning centers or any areas that would support small group work.

Totally uncomfortable with his observations, Kevin found a teacher who was working in a second grade classroom. He introduced himself and chatted for a few minutes before asking about the other teachers on his grade level. The second grade teacher told him the three first-grade teachers were all over fifty-five, and they had taught at this school since it opened twelve years ago. They were friends as well as colleagues. They planned together and had taught the same topics in the same order for the last twelve years.

**What to Do?**

It is difficult to be different from others on a grade level team. Kevin is younger than the other teachers. He has just graduated and this will be his first year to teach. He is the only male, and it appears that he is the only one who thinks developmentally appropriate practices belong in first-grade classrooms. What should Kevin do? How should he approach the other first-grade teachers? Should he share his beliefs with them? Should he arrange his class like the other teachers or as he believes a first-grade classroom should be set up? When school starts, how should Kevin handle the grade level team meetings?

## Further Reading

Bronson, M. B. (1995). *The right stuff for children birth to 8: Selecting play materials to support development*. Washington, DC: National Association for the Education of Young Children.

Clayton, M. K., with Forton, M. B. (2001). *Classroom spaces that work*. Greenfield, MA: Northeast Foundation for Children.

Isbell, R. (1995). *The complete learning center book*. Beltsville, MD: Gryphon House.

Mayesky, M. (2002). *Creative activities for young children* (7th ed.). Clifton Park, NY: Delmar Learning.

Puckett, M. P. (Ed.). (2002). *Room to grow: How to create quality early childhood environments* (3rd ed.). Austin, TX: Texas Association for the Education of Young Children.

## Helpful Web Sites

### ECE Web Guide
www.ecewebguide.com/learning_centers.htm
*This page on the ECE Web Guide lists eleven learning centers: Art Area, Block Area, Computer Center, Cooking and Nutrition, Dramatic Play, Language and Literacy, Math and Manipulatives, Music and Movement, Science and Gardening, Sensory Table, and Woodworking, as well as three early childhood related issues: Nap Time, Outdoor Fun, and Transitions. Click on any of the fourteen topics and several Web sites related to that topic will be displayed.*

### Northwest Educational Technology Consortium
www.netc.org/earlyconnections/
*This Web site connects technology with the way young children learn. In addition to the full text of the publication, Technology in Early Childhood Education: Finding the Balance, the Web site offers information related to Learning & Development, Learning & Technology, Technology in Child Care, Classroom Arrangement, Software Selection, Health & Safety, Hardware, and resources for child care, preschool, kindergarten, primary grades, and before/after school programs.*

Check the Online Resources™ for expert practitioners' responses to each case study.

For additional information on teaching young children, visit our Web site at **http://www.earlychilded.delmar.com**

# CHAPTER 7

## *Creating Curriculum*

*Early Childhood Principle* Professional early childhood educators provide a wide variety of experiences and activities for children.

In every group of children, a variety of background experiences and developmental levels can be found. Adults who work with young children acknowledge these differences in children and plan curriculum accordingly so that they meet these diverse needs. Teachers plan experiences that help build a sense of community among the entire group of children—shared experiences such as read-alouds, singing songs, reciting poetry, and going on field trips. Other needs of children are best met through small group experiences or one-on-one interactions. Teachers concurrently provide activities that allow success for children functioning at different developmental levels. In high-quality early childhood programs, teachers offer a sufficient number and variety of activities and experiences so that the needs of all the children in that program are met.

*After reading this chapter, you should be able to:*
- Discuss why activities must be meaningful to young children.
- Define curriculum in high-quality early childhood programs.
- List the four perspectives that inform transformational curriculum.
- Discuss emergent literacy and how adults can support children's language and literacy learning.
- Describe the active nature of mathematical and scientific learning for young children and how adults can support this learning.
- Discuss social studies learning in young children.
- Describe the integrated learning provided by units, themes, and projects.
- Discuss activities that best lend themselves to large and small groups or working with individuals.
- List factors early childhood educators should consider in creating a daily schedule for young children.

As you walk through a developmentally appropriate early childhood classroom, you will observe children actively involved in an assortment of activities. The types of centers, the nature of learning materials, and the experiences you observe will depend on the ages, abilities, and interests of the children in the classroom.

## THE TODDLER CLASSROOM

The classroom in this vignette demonstrates several characteristics evident in high-quality programs for toddlers. Pleasing instrumental music is playing in the background as the children and their parents enter the room. With parental assistance, children put personal items in cubbies and then select an activity. Some of the children choose to play in centers as one of their teachers, Ms. Chastain, observes and interacts with them. Two children choose between three of the simple four-piece puzzles that are placed on low shelves. Another child finds his favorite stacking toy in its place by the puzzles and takes it to the corner of the room where he likes to work. Two children snuggle in the beanbag chair in the reading center and watch other children in the room. A boy chooses to play in the art area, which offers large pieces of butcher paper and chunky chalk in a variety of colors that day.

Other children gather around the other teacher, Mrs. Donaldson, who is sharing a smelling activity with the children. She has sprinkled vanilla and almond extracts, lime and orange juice, and vinegar on cotton balls. Each cotton ball is in a separate plastic bottle so the toddlers can easily handle the smelling jars. This activity lasts about twenty minutes as some children leave the group activity and go to a center and children who initially started in centers decide to join Mrs. Donaldson. When all children are playing in the learning centers, Mrs. Donaldson begins to circulate through the centers talking with the children, describing what they are doing, and redirecting children whose behaviors become problematic.

After an hour of allowing children to choose their own activities, Ms. Chastain and Mrs. Donaldson encourage the toddlers to join them on a circleshaped rug for storytime. Mrs. Donaldson rereads a book, *Guinea Pigs Don't Read Books* (Bare, 1985), and plays along with the children as they imitate the sounds that guinea pigs make. Ms. Chastain tells the children she will hold the class guinea pig in the science center so they can pet it. With this announcement, group time ends and children spend more time choosing their own activities with Mrs. Donaldson supervising center activities.

As the children begin to lose interest in the guinea pig, Ms. Chastain puts it back in the cage. She joins Mrs. Donaldson, who is moving from center to center interacting with children. The teachers frequently mention

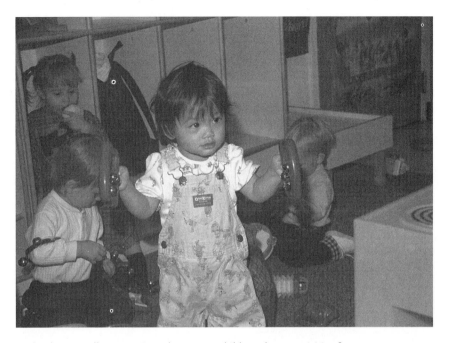

*In developmentally appropriate classrooms, children choose activities from an assortment of learning centers.*

toileting needs to the children who are developing self-control of their bladders or offer to change diapers for those children who are still wearing diapers. As a teacher changes a diaper, she describes the process as they proceed. She talks about photographs of children in the class that are posted beside the changing table.

A nutritious snack and extended outdoor play follow the second center time, which is then followed by lunch and nap time. The afternoon activities for the toddlers look similar to their morning activities—large periods of self-selected activities interspersed with short group times of reading, singing, and rhythm and movement activities.

## THE FIRST-GRADE CLASSROOM

In another early childhood classroom at the end of September, Mr. Cervantez begins the day by reading aloud to his first-grade class and talking with them briefly about how the author used dialogue to make the story more interesting. Following this shared reading, the children write and illustrate their own stories during writing workshop, working individually or in pairs. As a transition between writing and math, the class

**choral reading** a group reading experience when the entire group reads in unison.

**echo reading** a reading experience when one person, usually the teacher, reads a poem or short story one phrase at a time and the students echo each phrase.

participates in **choral reading** of familiar poetry and an **echo reading** of a poem new to them. Before lunch children select a game from the math menu and play together in small groups. After lunch they sing songs together as a group and conduct their class meeting. Then each child selects an activity to begin the afternoon. Some students choose tempera paints, watercolors, colored pencils, or markers to create drawings and paintings. Others write poems for the class poetry anthology being created. Some children care for class pets, nurture an assortment of plants, or sort fossils. A few children work to put together a floor puzzle about the planets while others find drawings in space books that help in assembling the puzzle. Other students work on the script for the video about space or an announcement for their class service project—the Lost and Found for their school.

In the first-grade class, as well as the toddler class, each teacher planned specifically for the children in their care. As they planned, Ms. Chastain, Mrs. Donaldson, and Mr. Cervantez considered each child in their class, what they already knew, and what experiences they had already had. The

*Following shared reading, children write and illustrate their own stories during writing workshop.*

teachers knew that it was important that each child have successful experiences. Therefore they provided many different types of activities to meet the range of needs of the children. They also recognized that children needed to be involved in activities that were meaningful to them, so as they planned they also considered children's interests.

## PLANNING FOR MEANINGFUL ACTIVITY

Early childhood educators know that young children learn, understand, and remember those things that are meaningful to them personally (Bredekamp & Rosegrant, 1992). Given this premise, adults who work with young children purposefully get to know the children in their care so that they can offer activities and learning experiences that will be meaningful to them.

Not every experience is equally meaningful to all children, so teachers are careful to plan multiple experiences that help children construct their own knowledge. There may be specific knowledge and skills that teachers believe children should develop, but not every child will learn these in the same way. For example, learning to recognize numerals 1 through 10 is a skill typically expected that kindergarten students will develop. Early childhood educators realize that this skill, although mandated by many school districts, is only surface knowledge about numbers. Children need to have many mathematical experiences so they can develop number sense. A teacher would provide many different activities that would help children construct mathematical knowledge. These mathematical activities would be offered within the context of everyday class activities rather than taught in isolation.

Despite the best efforts of a teacher to provide many different ways to encourage development of a skill, some children will not be particularly interested in the activities that she has selected or see an immediate need for learning that bit of knowledge. An experienced teacher will continue to look for opportunities that arise during the course of everyday activities or those that can be arranged to stimulate the interest level of specific students.

In Mrs. Jackson's kindergarten class, learning numerals 0 through 9 was a mandated skill. She incorporated many different ways to use numbers into the class routines, but Morgan showed no interest in learning this specific skill. After four months of kindergarten, the only numeral he consistently recognized was 1. He did not particularly care about using numbers to record game scores, to document the number of children who were absent, or to track how many children were allowed in a center. When the class voted on which snacks to have or which book to read, Morgan did not seem to pay attention to the numerals that were written down to record the votes. He did not seem to care about the dates on the calendar, numbering pages when he wrote books, or assembling number puzzles. Morgan could count objects to ten and it was important to him that other people knew he could count. He was forever counting rocks or buttons or blocks and showing his group to Mrs. Jackson, but he showed no interest in learning the symbols that represented the numbers he was counting. It was not until Mrs. Jackson introduced the card game War to the class that Morgan found his reason for learning numerals. He found that he could not win the game if he could not call out the numerals on the cards. An important part of playing the game was that each player announced the numeral of the card turned over. For example, a player might call out, "I got an 8. My 8 is higher than your 5."

Morgan wanted to play War. Every turn he would take the time to count the hearts or spades on his card and then say the number, but other children in the class wanted to play faster. They did not want to play with Morgan because they did not want to wait while he counted the objects on his card. Within two weeks of beginning to play War, Morgan had learned to recognize numerals 2 through 9. He learned a skill that previously he had not learned because he wanted to play a game with other children in the class. Morgan discovered a reason for recognizing numerals and consequently learned the skill. Learning to recognize numerals had become meaningful to him.

This same principle applies throughout every activity in the early childhood classroom. Children find personal meaning and learn more when their activities and experiences make sense or are useful to them. A teacher provides multiple activities and a variety of materials around a specific skill so that children can construct their own knowledge. She is diligent to observe the children closely so that she knows the particular knowledge and skills each child is acquiring. From this observation, watching how children approach their work, and listening carefully to what they say to each other, the teacher is able to make wise decisions about what kinds of activities to offer children.

When an early childhood program is meaning centered, it

- Provides enriched meaning and understanding, layers of understanding with depth and texture.
- Starts where the children are—children can engage immediately.
- Is informed by children's interests, both cultural and individual.
- Engages the child firsthand with concrete referents available.
- Provides ways of organizing information—classifying and categorizing— that make sense and help children connect the learning to what they already know.
- Places learning in context—experiences occur in natural or actual settings (Bredekamp & Rosegrant, 1992, p. 67).

Early childhood educators consider all these factors in creating activities that are meaningful to children. Taken together as a group, all the activities offered to children in an early childhood program form the basis of its curriculum.

## DEFINING CURRICULUM

There are several different definitions of the term *curriculum* in early childhood programs. In one sense, curriculum is simply what happens in the classroom (Tomich, 1996). It is the activities teachers plan, along with the play themes that children conceive as they interact with learning materials and with each other, and the unplanned moments that emerge when teachers follow children's leads during the day. These comprise an **emergent curriculum**.

A second definition for the term *curriculum*, used by some people in early childhood education, refers to commercially produced packages that delineate what children should be doing at particular ages. These prepackaged curricula can be used as references for early childhood educators, but should not be followed like a teacher's guide for a high school class. There are too many important factors that publishers cannot take into account: the strengths and needs of individual children in classes, the values and goals of the parents, and the expectations of the community. Early childhood educators know the children in their care like no publisher can. They can—and should—be responsible for creating appropriate curriculum designed for their specific group of children.

In a broader sense, **curriculum** in early childhood programs is viewed more holistically as "the organized framework that delineates the content that children are to learn, the processes through which children achieve the identified curricular goals, what teachers do to help children achieve these goals, and the context in which teaching and learning occur" (Bredekamp & Rosegrant, 1992, p. 10). This definition looks at curriculum in a more purposeful manner and encompasses all the components of an early childhood program.

### Transformational Curriculum

For more than a decade, the definition of early childhood curriculum has been presented by nationally recognized early childhood experts as a **transformational curriculum** (see Figure 7–1) (Rosegrant & Bredekamp, 1992). The transformational curriculum also encompasses all components of the early childhood program. In this type of curriculum, teachers make curricular decisions with specific knowledge as the basis for those decisions. Teachers use their knowledge about child growth and development; what they know about the individual development of each child in the group; the knowledge of curriculum disciplines such as language and literacy, math, science, and social studies; and the use of conceptual

**emergent curriculum** activities and experiences that teachers plan for children based on interests and the play themes of children that they observe.

**curriculum** all the components of an early childhood program.

**transformational curriculum** units, themes, and projects that teachers plan for children based on what they know about child development, the disciplines, and their own students.

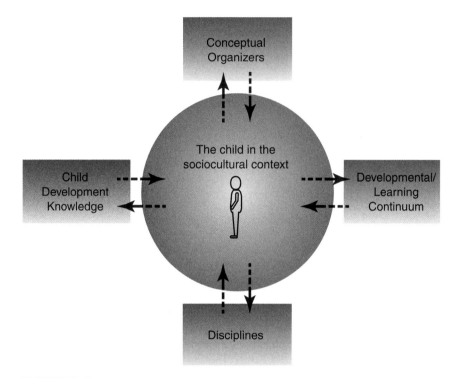

**FIGURE 7–1**

*Transformational Curriculum*

*Source:*From Bredekamp, S. & Rosegrant, T. (Eds.), (1992). *Reaching potentials Appropriate curriculum and assessment for young children*, Vol 1, pg. 71. Washington, DC: National Association for the Education of Young Children. Reprinted with permission from the National Association for the Education of Young Children.

organizers; or other meaning-centered approaches, such as themes, units, or projects (Bredekamp & Rosegrant, 1992).

When all of these knowledge bases are used to make curriculum decisions, the curriculum is stronger than it would be if one perspective was dominant. If knowledge about child growth and development is the primary informant for curriculum, the curriculum may be age appropriate, but not individually appropriate for many of the children in the group. If the individual development of children is the primary informant, the curriculum may lack integrity. If the disciplines are the primary emphasis, the curriculum may be unrelated to the children's needs or interests. If conceptual organizers are the primary focus, the curriculum "may be too idiosyncratic, lacking in direction or focus, or limited to 'fun' activities that lack integrity"

(Bredekamp & Rosegrant, 1992, p. 72). All four factors should be weighed carefully in making curriculum decisions.

A beginning understanding of child development can be developed by studying chapter 3 of this text, while an understanding of specific children can be learned only through close observation of those children. Observation techniques and methods of documenting those observations are described in chapter 4 of this text. Discussions of curriculum disciplines and conceptual organizers follow.

## Play-Based Curriculum

In each of the age groups of young children, high-quality programming requires that play be an integral part of the children's day (Fox, 1996). Play is important to early childhood programs for the fundamental reason that children learn as they play. From an infant who drops a spoon repeatedly off the high chair tray to the floor to the eight-year-old who spends two hours constructing a space station out of interlocking blocks, play is child centered, active, and meaningful to children. Play enhances all areas of development: physical/motor, emotional, social, language and literacy, and cognitive (Fox, 2000; Jambor, 2000; Piaget, 1962; Vygotsky, 1967; Yang, 2000). Nationally recognized play expert Joe Frost (1992) explains that play is the ". . . chief vehicle for the development of imagination and intelligence, language, social skills, and perceptual-motor abilities in infants and young children" (p. 48).

The importance of play in the lives of children is supported by theorists, researchers, and practitioners. Theorists Piaget and Vygotsky both wrote about the critical nature of play in the lives of children. Piaget (1980) wrote: "Play is a particularly powerful form of activity that fosters the social life and constructive activity of the child" (p. vii). In this statement he underscored his belief that play is closely related to cognitive development. He saw play as a method for children to refine what they were learning. Vygotsky defined play from a different perspective. He viewed play as a vehicle used by children to develop new areas of learning and believed that play actually led development (Vygotsky, 1978). Although Piaget and Vygotsky viewed the role of play in children's learning differently, both acknowledged its importance for young children (Thomas, 1992).

Many researchers have studied children as they play and found that play affects many different areas of skills and general development. Research confirms that play helps children expand their experiences, facilitate the development of mental processes (Yang, 2000), refine motor skills, enhance social skills (McClellan & Katz, 2001), increase their problem-solving abilities (Sylwester, 2000a, 2000b; Rivkin, 2001), gain information about objects and people (Chaille & Silvern, 1996), enhance creativity (Mellou, 1995), and develop greater competence in language (Heath, 1983; D'Arcangelo, 2000), literacy (Bodrova, Leong, Hensen, & Henninger,

*Playing is a fundamental process of creative thinking, allowing the child to construct and reconstruct the imagery of rich, early experiences, and thus to grow and develop.*

*—Joe Frost*

2000), and comprehension (Strickland & Morrow, 2000). These researchers generally agree that play is essential to the healthy development of young children.

Early childhood educators who have had extensive experiences with young children also know the value of play. They regularly observe children developing new knowledge and skills as they play. See "Learning through Play" box on the following pages for a list of some of young children's learning that educators have observed as children play in high-quality early childhood settings.

Young children do not distinguish play activities that enhance cognitive development from those that enhance physical development. Neither do they separate play activities that promote mathematical learning from those that promote literacy learning. Learning, for young children, is an integrated experience that occurs most optimally during their play. Doris Fromberg (1990) described play as the "ultimate integrator of human experience" (p. 223). Play serves as a way for children to develop understandings about their world and their experiences. Teachers in high-quality programs recognize the valued role of play in the learning and development of children and plan accordingly.

While theorists, researchers, and teachers value play in the early childhood curriculum, many parents find it disturbing to have their question "What did you do at school today?" answered by their child with the one-word answer: "Play." Teachers need to help parents understand what children are learning as they play. Play is not just entertainment for children. It is a valid and important method of learning (D'Arcangelo, 2000). Through play children learn the social skills of cooperating with one another in play themes or to create things new and original. Children learn to put parts together to form a whole when they work a puzzle. Through play children learn specific information related to content areas. For example, a teacher wanting to teach the concepts of liquid and solid could provide concrete materials such as sand and water and materials that would encourage children to experiment with these materials rather than spend time in verbal instruction. After children had several opportunities to work with these materials on their own, he would extend the children's sand and water play using comments about the work at hand and pose questions about what might happen if a child changed his or her experiment in a certain way. In another example of content-area learning, a teacher might use logos and forms of real print to support young children's interests in literacy skills. Rather than using direct instruction to teach children to read the logos, the teacher would place them in learning centers where the children could incorporate them into their play. The teacher would then continue to comment on the ways the children use the logos in an effort to extend their play. By using open-ended questions about related subjects, the teacher would stimulate the children's creative use of the print. In a further example relating to math, the teacher who believed the students

*Many researchers have studied children as they play and found that play affects many specific skills and general development.*

### Learning through Play

When children play in the **music center**, they are learning:

- To be conscious of rhythm in music.
- Concepts of fast and slow, loud and soft.
- To express themselves in new ways.
- Listening skills and auditory discrimination.
- Awareness and identification with their own culture and the cultural heritage of others.

When children play in the **home center**, they are learning:

- To be flexible in their thinking.
- To express themselves in sentences.
- To experiment with different adult roles.
- To sort and organize things.
- To make decisions.

*(continued)*

*Learning through Play (continued)*

· To improvise and use things in a symbolic way to represent something else.
· To carry out ideas with the cooperation of others.

When children play in the **block center**, they are learning:
· Concepts of shape, size, length, location, space, and angles.
· To create and repeat patterns.
· To cooperate with others.
· To solve problems.
· To make a plan and implement it.

When children play in the **water center**, they are learning:
· Hand–eye coordination as they pour.
· That some things sink and some things float.
· About wet, dry, and evaporation.
· Relative capacity of different sizes of containers.
· What happens when you add different items such as soap.

When children play in the **art center**, they are learning:
· To express imagination and creativity.
· Concepts of shape, size, and location.
· That their ideas have value.
· To distinguish shapes and to purposefully create shapes.
· The names of colors and how to make new colors.

When children play in the **science center**, they are learning:
· New vocabulary.
· Concepts of texture, color, weight, size, and characteristic.
· To group objects into categories.
· To observe likenesses and differences.
· To appreciate nature.

When children play in the **puppet center**, they are learning:
· To express ideas with words.
· To take on the role of someone else.
· To communicate with voice tones as well as words.
· To retell familiar stories.
· To use imagination to create their own stories.

When children play in the **math center**, they are learning:
· To notice details and likenesses and differences in objects.
· Concepts of color, size, and shape.
· Numerical concepts of more than and less than.
· Concepts of groups or sets.
· Logical reasoning.

needed additional experiences with concepts like one-to-one correspondence could incorporate skills to encourage this understanding into a play situation. Again, rather than lecturing on mathematical concepts or giving students worksheets for practice, the teacher might offer a game that would require the children to count dice dots and squares on the game board as a part of playing the games. In this way the children would be practicing one-to-one correspondence, working to sequence their thoughts, following directions, and taking turns, thus developing foundations for mathematical thought. All these important things can be learned through play.

### Different Types of Play

As children develop, their play looks very different. The play of infants and toddlers is vastly different from the play of older young children. Mildred Parten (1932) first described the development of children's play. She identified six different types of play: unoccupied behavior, onlooker behavior, solitary play, parallel play, associative play, and cooperative play.

In *unoccupied behavior*, children watch whatever happens to capture their attention. This behavior is typical of infants. They observe the world around them and when there is nothing that catches their attention, they typically turn to playing with their fingers or toes. While infants engage in unoccupied behavior much of their waking hours, it is common to observe this type of behavior in preschool and primary-age children, especially when they are adjusting to new situations.

*Onlooker behavior* is similar to unoccupied behavior in that the child is not actively involved with objects or other people. In onlooker behavior, children observe others more closely than in unoccupied behavior. They watch what others are doing, but with greater interest. They listen carefully to what other children are saying, but do not actually join in the play.

In *solitary play* children interact with objects alone. They show little or no interest in children who may be playing near them. This type of play is typical of infants and is frequently observed in young preschool children, but older children may also choose to play alone and still benefit from this type of play.

*Parallel play* is often observed in the play habits of toddlers. In parallel play, children play side by side. They are playing independently, but their play brings them into contact with other children. While they are playing with their own objects, they are aware of the children around them and appear to like the company of children near them.

*Associative play*, first seen in young preschool children, is the first type of group play. Pairs and small groups of children play in the same area; maybe even use the same materials, but are not truly interacting with each other. Two children can be playing in the block center, sharing the unit blocks, but one is building a house and the other is building a zoo. They may both be building zoos, but each child would be building his or her own zoo.

*Cooperative play* is the most social form of group play. This is usually observed in older preschool and kindergarten children, as well as primary-aged children. They work together in a play theme that they create and coordinate. One of the first forms of cooperative play is when children agree "who will be the mommy and who will be the daddy and who will be the baby and who will be the dog." Children can create elaborate play themes. Some continue for days, especially when teachers provide the raw materials needed to extend the play theme (Fayden, 1997).

Early childhood educators who carefully observe children at play realize that this is the natural way for children to learn. They support children's play by supplying the time, space, equipment, and materials for play (Clements, 2000). Children must have blocks of time so that they can engage in play. They must have sufficient spaces in which to play. They must have age-appropriate equipment and organized materials with which to interact. Young children also benefit from scaffolding provided by adults during their play. In one four-year-old classroom, the teacher had set up the dramatic play center as a lemonade stand with props such as pitchers, plastic glasses, a cash register, and play money to support this play theme. The children in the class had expanded the play to a short-order restaurant by gathering food, plates, forks, napkins from the home center and bringing in paper and markers from the writing center to use to create menus and order forms. Following the children's play, the teacher ordered food from the person taking orders. When no one asked for money to pay for her food purchases, the teacher made the decision to expand the children's play by introducing the issue of prices for the food, giving change if the person purchasing the food did not have the correct amount of money, and putting prices on the child-created menus. In this teacher's support of the dramatic play, he was able to raise the level of the play and integrate several mathematical concepts into an ongoing play theme.

### Integrated Learning

Children learn best when their learning is integrated. While the disciplines of language and literacy, math, science, and social studies will be discussed separately in this chapter, these should not be presented to children as distinct topics (Jaeger & Davenport, 1996). Just as the teacher integrated math into an ongoing play theme, knowledge and skills of the disciplines are best learned by young children when they are integrated. Reading, writing, math, science, and social studies should not be taught in isolation, but should be incorporated into every part of a child's day. Even preschool children can respond to literature by dictating what they liked about a story then illustrating the dictated comments or drawing a picture to show what they learned while observing the class rabbit. Most concepts related to a discipline can be integrated into center activities and incorporated into the children's daily activities.

Some activities naturally lend themselves to integrated learning. Cooking is one such activity. In the process of cooking, children are involved in learning reading, writing, math, science, and social studies concepts (Dahl, 1998). They can "read" and follow rebus recipes. They can dictate or write about their experience, what they smelled, tasted, and felt as they worked. They can count items; sort ingredients; begin to understand words like "bigger," "smaller," "more," and "less" and start to learn measuring words. They can observe, predict, compare, measure, and note similarities and differences throughout the cooking experiences. And they can work together as a group to achieve a common goal. In one cooking activity all the curriculum disciplines are integrated. This is an example of how to integrate the disciplines into one activity, but early childhood educators work to integrate the whole curriculum in ways that make sense to young children. Some early childhood teachers push this concept to the extreme, forcing strained connections that are not meaningful to children. Multiculturalism does not have to be forced into a unit on rocks nor the water center used as a focus during a unit on poetry. The guideline for natural integration of curriculum versus contrived integration is in the connections children make.

## Multicultural Experiences

Multicultural experiences need not be integrated into every part of the curriculum. However, today's children are growing up in a world comprised of culturally diverse people regardless of the makeup of their individual class or the children's immediate neighborhoods. It is important that early childhood educators bring a broad representation of people and cultures into the classroom. Multicultural aspects should be integrated into the existing curriculum rather than being taught in isolation.

In attempting to bring an awareness of different cultures into the classroom, teachers are careful to avoid what is often referred to as a "tourist curriculum." Hispanic heritage encompasses much more than eating tacos and dancing the Mexican Hat dance. The Chinese culture offers much more than New Year's dragons and rice. African Americans do much more than celebrate Kwanzaa. There is nothing inherently wrong with participating in any of these activities as long as they are not the only culture-related experiences offered. Young children need to experience relevant day-to-day events, customs, goals, family life, and traditions of a variety of cultures.

If cultural diversity exists in a class, beginning with those cultures makes sense. Families of students can make unique contributions to support the curriculum. If this is not possible, teachers can bring cultures into the class in myriad ways. Photographs of children and families that represent different cultures can be displayed in the room. Carefully selected children's books that represent many different cultures can be available in several centers, and books and poetry by people of diverse backgrounds should be read aloud on a regular basis. Teachers can also display drawings, paintings, sculpture, and textiles created by artists of different cultures. To help children understand how family life differs among cultures, the teacher can offer culturally diverse objects in the home center. To reinforce that different skin tones and facial features are valued, dolls representing the major cultural groups in the United States are placed in the home center, and multicultural paints, markers, and crayons are available in the art and writing centers. The class can also listen to music that represents various cultures and learn to sing simple songs in different languages.

Language is a fundamental component of culture. At the very least, teachers should learn to pronounce each child's name correctly. To show they value each child's home language, teachers make the effort to learn simple words and phrases of the languages represented in the class and help all the children learn some of these phrases. Teachers accept attempts at communicating in English from linguistically diverse children and offer time to acquire, explore, and experience second language learning (Nieto, 1999).

## Content Areas

One of the four primary informants of the transformational curriculum is knowledge of curriculum disciplines—the content areas. Early childhood educators need to be knowledgeable about the fields of language and literacy, math, science, and social studies. They need to learn what current research in these fields is indicating about how young children best learn the concepts in each of the disciplines and how adults can best support children's learning.

### Language and Literacy

Young children begin to learn about language and literacy from the moment they are born. They learn language from the language they hear. Infants begin to construct their own knowledge about language in the first few days of life. As parents and caregivers talk to the child, the child begins to understand that language can be comforting.

All young children need to be surrounded with language. Parents and caregivers interact verbally with infants and toddlers throughout the day. They describe daily routines, such as diapering, eating, and playing, when the infant is engaged in those activities, in calm simple language (White, 1995). As soon as infants begin cooing and babbling, adults respond in kind to these initial attempts at verbal communication. This type of response supports the infant's attempt to communicate with others. Parents and caregivers continue this type of support as children grow and expand their oral language. Adults extend toddlers' use of one- or two-word sentences by using entire sentences to rephrase what the young child has said. When a toddler says, "Juice," the caregiver acknowledges the verbal request and extends the child's language. She might respond, "You want a glass of juice. Do you want orange juice or apple juice?" As children continue to mature and expand their own use of language, early childhood educators continue to support this language use. They encourage children to use language throughout their daily activities: in centers, outdoors, or in group activities. Conversations between children, as well as conversations with adults, are encouraged throughout the day.

Literacy, both reading and writing, also begin to develop very early in life. The term for what children learn about reading and writing between the time they are born and the time that they become conventional readers and writers is **emergent literacy** (Sulzby & Teale, 1991; Teale & Sulzby, 1986). How much children learn about the written word in the stage of emergent literacy depends on the experiences they are provided by the adults who care for them.

Children who are cared for by literate adults have many experiences to develop understandings about the written word. Books are read aloud to them; signs are pointed to and read as they drive; newspapers, magazines, and catalogs are in the house or center. Children see adults reading and writing for adult purposes. And through these direct and indirect experiences children construct their own knowledge about the written word. The toddler who yells, "French fries, French fries" when she sees the fast food restaurant with the large, yellow "M" is demonstrating just how much she already understands about getting meaning from print. She is not reading in a conventional sense, but she thinks she is reading and *is* reading emergently. When a three-year-old scribbles on a piece of paper and reads those scribbles as "I love you, Mommy," she thinks she is writing and *is* writing emergently. There are many stages of emergent reading and writing that most children go through before they learn to read and write conventionally. These stages are described in the accompanying two boxes. Adults should respond to these stages just as they do with a child who is using one- or two-word sentences. They should treat these early attempts of reading and writing as important attempts and support the child's approximations. They should celebrate the learning that the child demonstrates.

Adults can best support children's literacy learning by providing a literacy rich environment and by reading and writing with children on a regular basis. Children should find books and written messages throughout the classroom and be encouraged to interact with print. There should be multiple opportunities for them to write messages, create signs, and dictate or write their own stories. Adults should show how much they value reading and writing by reading aloud to children several times a day and by writing in front of the children frequently. When children hear books read aloud, they begin to understand that reading has to make sense and develop an appreciation of books. When children observe adults writing for their own purposes or taking dictation from them, they begin to understand how writing is used to communicate. Adults should also acknowledge and support children's early attempts at communicating through reading and writing. Through multiple experiences, children gained the knowledge and skills necessary to become conventional readers and writers. Even at

**emergent literacy** the knowledge about reading and writing that children construct from birth until they become conventional readers and writers.

*When children hear books read aloud, they begin to understand that reading has to make sense, and then they develop an appreciation of books.*

this stage of literacy, children still need effective instruction with reading and writing presented as integrated experiences that are meaningful to them (Button, Johnson, & Furgerson, 1996).

*Stages of Emergent Reading*

| | |
|---|---|
| Listens | The child listens to books read aloud by an adult or older child. For infants and toddlers, this may only last a couple of minutes, but listening to stories is the first stage of emergent reading. |
| Looks at the Book's Illustrations while Listening | Looking at the pictures in the book being read aloud is a separate stage of emergent reading. |
| Talks about the Illustrations | Talking about the illustrations and asking and answering questions about the pictures are a natural extension to the read-aloud experience between adults and young children. |

*(continued)*

| | |
|---|---|
| Recognizes Logos | Young children may read Crest® as "toothpaste" or Cheerios® as "cereal," but these early attempts at reading demonstrate the child's attempt at getting meaning from print. |
| Pretends to Read | Another stage of emergent reading occurs when the child turns the pages of a familiar book and "tells" the story that he has heard. |
| Memorizes Text and Pretends to Read | Referred to as "voice-print matching," it appears that the child is reading conventionally because she has heard the book read aloud so many times that she has memorized the sequence of words in the text. Children can verbalize the words on each page and turn the pages at the appropriate times, but cannot recognize the text out of the context of that particular book. |
| Recognizes Some Words in Context | The child begins to recognize a few words that are particularly important to him or that he sees frequently. |

## Stages of Emergent Writing

| | |
|---|---|
| Drawing | Children draw and "read" their drawings as a form of communication. They may draw an unrecognizable form and say, "I played in the home center today with my friends," or may draw a tree like form and say, "This says remember to take me to the park." |
| Scribbling | Young children scribble on a piece of paper but they believe they are writing and often "read" what they have just written. Many times children will move the pencil like adults and make the scribbles from left to right. |
| Invented or Pseudo-Letters | Many young children make up their own letters. A circle with a line drawn down from the circle is a common invented letter. Again, children believe they are writing. |
| Random Letters | As children become more aware of the alphabet, they often write these letters in long strings of letters, but usually write them randomly. |
| Emergent Spelling | Emergent spelling takes many forms, but is related to the sounds the child hears in each words. At the beginning of this stage, children may write one letter to represent one word. Later words are represented by two letters, the initial and ending letter sound. As the child's writing continues to mature, most sounds are represented in their emergent spelling. |

## Math

Young children also begin to develop mathematical concepts very early in life when they are offered opportunities to be actively involved in experiences related to math. An infant who reaches out to pick up a rattle is learning something about the concepts of space and distance. The toddler who helps put away toys by placing trucks in one container and blocks in another is learning the fundamental math concept of classification. The three-year-old who is asked to get three crackers for snack time and then counts 1–, 2–, 3 as she places them on her napkin is learning one-to-one correspondence. The four-year-old who strings a bead necklace by alternating blue and green beads is learning patterning. Each of these concepts is an important early math concept.

Adults can support mathematical learning by providing an environment rich with mathematical materials and experiences. Math-related materials can be available to children at home and in virtually every learning center. Adults can also use mathematical language to describe what children are doing as they interact with the wooden beads and colored cubes in the math center, the measuring cups in the water center, the collections of nuts and bolts or seashells in the science center, the matching games in the puzzle center, or unit blocks in the block center. Comments from teachers or parents such as "I see you've put all the large bolts in one group and the small ones in another," or "You stacked three green cubes," or "Two of the small cups filled the bowl," begin to introduce mathematical language into the lives of young children. This math language is meaningful to the children because the words are directly describing the child's efforts. Adults can also talk about time, dates, ages, amounts, size, money, and other math ideas as a natural part of the child's day.

Children who have had many concrete experiences with math materials and have had these experiences labeled with appropriate math language begin to see math as a part of their everyday lives. Experts contend that children's understanding of math concepts evolves over time and with concrete experiences (National Council for Teachers of Mathematics, 2000). Children who explore classification and one-to-one correspondence as toddlers and preschoolers develop into children who begin to understand number sense, estimation, measurement, patterns and relationships, working with data, and geometry—as described by the National Council for Teachers of Mathematics (2000)—as kindergarteners and primary-grade students (Anderson, 1996).

## Science

Science for young children is a matter of exploration and experimentation as they try to make sense of the world around them (Harlan & Rivkin, 1996). For infants, early science exploration can be seen as they examine their fingers and toes or as they repeatedly drop a spoon from their high

*Rather than doing math because the teacher says it is math time, children should be encouraged to think about quantities when they feel a need and interest.*

*-Constance Kamii*

**BIOGRAPHY BOX** *Constance Kamii*

Constance Kamii is professor of early childhood education at the University of Alabama at Birmingham. A major concern of hers since the mid 1960s has been the conceptulization of goals and objectives for early childhood education on the basis of a scientific theory explaining children's sociomoral and intellectual development. Convinced that the only theory in existence that explains this development from infancy to adolescence was that of Jean Piaget, she studied under him for many years, first as a postdoctoral research fellow and later on a joint appointment with the University of Geneva and the University of Illinois at Chicago.

She has been working closely with teachers for thirty years to develop practical ways of using Piaget constructivism in the classroom. The outcome of this work can be seen in *Physical Knowledge in Preschool Education* and *Group Games in Early Education,* which she wrote with Rheta DeVries. Since 1980, she has been extending this curruculum research to the primary grades and wrote *Young Children Reinvent Arithmetic* (about first-grade arithmetic), *Young Children Continue to Reinvent Arithmetic, 2nd Grade,* and *Young Children Continue to Reinvent Arithmetic, 3rd Grade.* In all these books, she has emphasized the long-range, overall goal of education envisioned by Piaget, which is children's development of moral and intellectual autonomy.

chairs. For preschoolers, science concepts are learned as they play in mud puddles, pour water from container to container in the water center, or mix paints in the art area. For primary-grade children, science concepts can be enhanced and refined as they care for class pets and plants or begin to explore the scientific process by conducting experiments to see if meal worms prefer apples, potatoes, or carrots. As in the discipline of mathematics, children learn science concepts best when they are actively involved in experiences.

Certainly, science concepts are not limited to these experiences. Young children are fascinated by hands-on science. They can develop their own theories about the world of life, physical, and earth science and learn through exploring and experimenting with a variety of things they can touch and manipulate.

The adults' primary role in facilitating science learning is to encourage the natural curiosity of young children and to work together to find the answers to children's questions through observation, research, and experimentation (Ross, 2000). Adults should provide an environment that is intellectually stimulating. Children cannot act on their curiosity in a vacuum. Early childhood educators should have plants and animals in the classroom and use the outdoors as an equal science resource. They can help children collect rocks and fossils that can then be sorted, identified, and labeled (Diffily, 1996). They can connect children's literature to scientific concepts

*Science is what children do every day as they ask questions, observe ants, make ice cubes, ride a bicycle, sharpen a pencil, push a chair out from a desk, make a snowball, feed a cat, pound a nail, or turn on a light.*

*-Sally Kilmer & Helenmarie Hofman*

(Barcus & Patton, 1996). They should offer objects such as pendulums, magnifying glasses, rubber tubing, sieves, tweezers, and scales to extend children's scientific exploration. Even materials typically found in other centers can be used to teach science concepts. Sand, water, blocks, and rolling things are items common to the early childhood classroom. If teachers look at these materials in new ways, ask open-ended questions to extend children's thinking, and help children record their experiments and observations, everyday activities can be turned into science (Sprung, 1996). The outdoor playground also provides other opportunities for science learning through exploration of inclines and pendulums—slides and swings (Fox & Tipps, 1995). And, as in the other disciplines, adults should talk with children as they explore and discover, providing the language that describes what the child is doing.

### Social Studies

Social studies is a large field of study that encompasses many specialties, including anthropology, archeology, civics, economics, geography, history, philosophy, political science, psychology, religion, and sociology (Seefeldt, 1995). It is obvious that young children are not cognitively able to understand many of the abstract concepts associated with these areas of study, but they can develop important knowledge, skills, dispositions, and feelings (Katz & Chard, 2000) related to social studies. They begin to understand, accept, and handle feelings. They begin to develop an understanding of themselves and others. They learn to function as part of their class, their neighborhood, and their community. All these concepts are part of social studies for young children (Seefeldt, 1995).

Social studies concepts can be learned by children as they work in learning centers with some extra planning by the teacher. In the home center alone, children can learn the basics of economics by using play money and a cash register, weighing groceries on a scale, and writing in blank receipt books. They can explore jobs and careers by adding props to turn the home center into a dentist office, an airport terminal, or advertising agency. Children working in the block center can use the blocks to create buildings they have observed in their community: houses, apartment buildings, an airport, a mall, or the zoo. Children can also be encouraged to recreate what they have seen on field trips.

When teachers involve children in managing their own behavior, children have many opportunities to learn concepts relating to social studies. They can learn to formulate a set of rules, observe those rules, recognize the need to finish a task, identify property that belongs to themselves and others, classify acceptable and unacceptable behavior, discuss ways people can help each other, and use social skills appropriate to group behavior. Through storybook reading and group discussions, children can learn to identify the concept of a family and describe sequences in basic family and school routines. Many social studies concepts are a natural extension of life

*It is during early childhood, those years before the age of 8, that children are gaining the knowledge, skills, and attitudes required of citizens of a democracy.*

*—Carol Seefeldt*

in a group setting. Early childhood educators can integrate these concepts into the daily life of the group with a little thought and advance planning.

## Teaching through Questioning

Each content area includes specific knowledge and skills that early childhood educators teach and young children learn. Many of these skills are learned over time, through direct teacher modeling and hands-on learning experiences. For example, most young children learn to count from 1 to 10 by hearing adults count and learn the one-to-one correspondence of 1 to 10 through the experience of counting objects that are meaningful to them.

Another important teaching strategy for young children is teacher questioning, the type of questioning beyond those that have single right answers. When the teacher asks, "How many hearts are on this card?" she is posing a closed-ended question. There is only one right answer. However, using open-ended questions encourages children to think about their answers. Examples of open-ended questions related to math would be:

- How do you know that?
- How could you figure out if that is more or less than last time?
- How did you sort the _____ (shells, buttons, keys, etc.)?
- How could you keep score for that game?

Other open-ended questions are suggested in the box with the heading, Open-Ended Questions.

## Units/Themes

One of the best ways a teacher can integrate content areas is through units of study or themes. The words *units* and *themes* are often used interchangeably

---

*Open-Ended Questions*

- Would you tell me about your _____ (drawing, story, block structure, etc.)?
- What does that remind you of?
- How do you think you could find out the answer to your question?
- Why did you choose that book?
- What is special about those illustrations? Why do you like them?
- How does this story remind you of any other stories?
- How could you work on this with another person?
- What else do you need to build that?
- What do you think will happen if you add more blocks to this tower?

or even referred to as "thematic units." Whatever term is used, this is a way of organizing information and experiences in the classroom. Most often a teacher will select a topic she believes will be of interest to her students and plans many different experiences around this single topic. She examines each learning center and determines how information about that topic could be offered in as many centers as logically as possible. She considers all disciplines and all developmental areas.

Units and themes are organized around children's shared experiences or experiences that can be provided the children through hands-on experiences or field trips. Units or themes can also be organized around experiences that children in the group bring with them to the classroom—such as grocery stores, forms of transportation (car, bus, subway, or airplane), people who help us (parents, teachers, doctors, dentists), or families (Dorl & Dizes, 1999). Units can be organized around experiences that the teacher provides children in the classroom—such as planting seeds and caring for plants, experiments with the children's senses, or observing and caring for classroom pets.

Once the teacher has decided on the unit topic, she then begins to determine specific goals and the major understandings that she wants the children to grasp as a result of this unit of study. She brainstorms topics and activities that might be incorporated into the unit and collects resources that will be needed to support the unit such as books and learning materials for the centers.

Following a field trip to a farm, a teacher might add materials to different centers to expand children's exploration of the topic of farm animals (see Figure 7–2). For example in the art center, the teacher could put prints of masters' paintings that feature farm animals and offer easel painting. Farm animal figures and materials that can be used for fencing could be added to the block center. Denim overalls, straw hats, and bandannas could be added to the dress-up clothes available in the dramatic play center. The games and puzzles center could feature puzzles of farm animals and card-matching games with adult and baby animals. *The Very Busy Spider* by Eric Carle (1984), with accompanying audiotapes, could be added to the listening center. The teacher could add fast-growing plants to measure, along with charts to record the growth; she could add plastic animals to sort and classify to the math center and soil, containers, and a variety of vegetable seeds to the science center. A collection of fiction and nonfiction books about different farm animals could be added to the science center or the reading center and plastic gardening tools could be added to the sand center. With some thoughtful consideration and gathering of materials, a theme can be represented in almost every center.

Another way a teacher might organize a unit is by selecting one book to serve as the primary book for a week, integrating experiences and activities based on its story. To begin planning a unit like this, a teacher might use a **curriculum web** (Cassidy & Lancaster, 1993; Workman & Anziano, 1993).

---

*I cannot always predict what will happen. I take my cues from the children almost all the time. If a theme doesn't spark interest I stop and try something else.*
    -Mimi Chenfeld

**curriculum web** an organizational tool teachers use to view a single topic by different centers or by children's developmental areas.

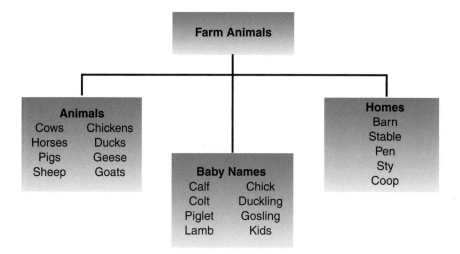

**FIGURE 7–2**
*Example of Curriculum Web for Farm Animals.*

Frequently teachers select one book as the focus book for a short, week-long unit. The teacher rereads this book several times and uses concepts in the book as ideas for mini-lessons for the whole class or as center activities. In one kindergarten class, the teacher uses *The Very Hungry Caterpillar* (Carle, 1969) to begin each year. The centers and activities he offers during that first week of school are all centered around themes that were in Eric Carle's book, like learning the days of the week, sequencing the events of the story, counting to five, and charting the fruits eaten by the caterpillar.

Some of the most effective units and themes are those that arise from children's inquisitive natures. There are infinite topics that might capture children's attention. Weather, storms, or seasonal changes might spark children's interest, and several themes could be created around what they want to know about these topics. Spontaneous scientific observations such as a bird's nest, an anthill, bird feathers, fossils, or budding flowers might initiate a theme. Other ideas might come from class field trips or vacation trips taken by the teacher or a member of the class, a community event, or even an object that a child brings to school (Church, 1995).

When making decisions about topics for units or themes, teachers should consider the children's previous experiences and they must consider what is worth knowing. Because so many things happen in the lives of young children that are worth studying and experiencing, there is no need to contrive topics for units. It is very important to approach topics for themes realistically. The younger the child, the more important it is that units for them be based on what can be actually experienced by the child within their own surroundings. Very young children in Arizona, for example, should probably not study the sea. Children in Florida should probably not study snowy winters, and children in New York City should probably not study rural topics. Units and themes for two-, three-, and probably four-year-olds should be based on their own personal experiences. Older children are better able to learn from experiences that are less direct.

Tara, a teacher of two- and three-year-olds, understood this concept and often created units from her observations of her students. She noticed many of her students spending a great deal of time carrying boxes around the classroom. They loved carrying all kinds of boxes. She used this interest to create an integrated unit of study. With assistance from the children's families, Tara collected empty food boxes, gift boxes, and packing boxes. She placed them in several centers and watched to see what the children would do spontaneously. Children began fitting the smaller boxes inside larger ones. Expanding on this behavior, Tara sorted some of the boxes by size, putting all the same-sized boxes in groups. Following her lead, several toddlers worked to sort the boxes by size. Soon they were also sorting boxes by their shape or by the box's primary color. After talking about logos, some of the children worked to find the boxes they could "read." Every child decorated individual boxes as their own private sculptures, then grouped them to create a box "city." The toddlers painted an empty refrigerator box Tara put into the art center and the next day began using it for a private reading area. Tara encouraged each child to select their own large box to paint. After the boxes dried, she asked the children to hide in their boxes and the group played "jack in the box." All the children would stay hidden in their boxes as Tara played familiar music. When she stopped the music, they would all pop out of their boxes. At other times during the day, they tossed bean bags into their boxes. They took boxes outside and used them as vehicles. They flattened other boxes and practiced sliding on a gently sloping hill on their playground. Over a period of two weeks, Tara followed the lead of her students, expanded their interactions with the boxes, and offered experiences to them they might not have otherwise discovered. She integrated boxes into virtually every center and used boxes as a vehicle to help the children discover mathematical concepts such as sorting and seriation, expand their creativity, and enhance large- and small-motor skills. Good teachers can take one interest expressed through the play of students and create integrated units of study that are meaningful to the students.

## Projects

Projects are another way to help organize and integrate curriculum (Diffily & Sassman, 2002). Projects are different from units and themes in that projects are generally more child-directed than units or themes. Teachers make fewer decisions about the topic or the activities related to the project. Instead the teacher facilitates decisions made about the project. The children decide what kinds of projects they will do as well as direct the manner

## BIOGRAPHY BOX *John Dewey*

John Dewey (1859–1952) was an American educator and philosopher. He believed that children's educational experiences should be related to their lives outside the classroom. He opposed the traditional method of teaching children to memorize information by rote methods and favored educational environments where children were encouraged to explore and discover information on their own. He saw the teacher's role as a facilitator of learning as opposed to a dispenser of information. Dewey was a professor of education at the University of Chicago from 1894 to 1904 and at Columbia University from 1904 to 1930. A prolific writer and speaker, his books, articles, and presentations supported the United States's progressive education movement during the early part of the twentieth century. His education philosophies continue to influence school reform movements today.

Photo © Bettmann/CORBIS.

in which the project will be carried out. Teachers may make suggestions along the way, but the children make the decisions. At the end of the project the children choose one or more ways to share what they have learned with others.

Using projects has been encouraged by educators for almost one hundred years (Dewey & Dewey, 1915; Dewey, 1938; Kilpatrick, 1925, 1936). John Dewey was one of the first educators to suggest that children learned best from planning their own activities and implementing their own plans. Dewey rejected the traditional subject-centered curriculum in favor of a child-centered curriculum. He believed that learning came through experience and encouraged teachers to have children engaged in real-world learning activities that connected to their homes and neighborhoods. While he did not label these activities projects, the principles were the same.

The use of projects has been recently popularized by the Italian early childhood program in Reggio Emilia (Edwards, Gandini, & Forman, 1998) and the American authors Lilian Katz and Sylvia Chard in their book *Engaging Children's Minds: The Project Approach (2000).*

In Reggio Emilia, publicly funded preschools serve almost half of the city's preschool-aged children. Projects represent the basis for the curriculum at these schools. The projects may last several days or several months. They may involve an entire class or only a small group of children. The projects come from three primary sources: those resulting from a child's natural encounter with the environment, those reflecting mutual interests on the part of the teacher and children, and those based on teacher concerns regarding specific cognitive and/or social concepts (New, 1990). These projects represent an opportunity for children and teachers to investigate a mutually chosen topic in-depth. One example of a Reggio Emilia project involved examining the city in the rain. The project started with typical

> *Differences between Units/Themes and Projects*
>
> | **Units/Themes** | **Projects** |
> |---|---|
> | · Selected by teacher based on children's interests | · Selected by the children themselves |
> | · Are integrated | · Are research based |
> | · Directed by the teacher with child choice | · Directed by the children with guidance from the teacher |
> | · Usually last one or two weeks | · Are conducted over a long period of time |
> | · May have an end product or a culminating event | · Have an end product |

preschoolers' questions about where the rain comes from. Children speculated about the answer to this question and drew pictures of rain. These drawings served as the basis for the beginning of the project that lasted for several weeks as the children became involved in such activities as audio-taping rain sounds on different surfaces, taking field trips into different parts of the city to observe changes that occurred when it rained, drawing city scenes before and during a rainfall, photographing the changing sky during a rainstorm, and researching and sketching what happens to rain water from the time it falls to earth until it is piped into homes (Forman, 1998). Reggio Emilia has led the way in the use of projects with young children and now many early childhood educators in the United States are now using projects in their programs (Edwards, Gandini, & Forman, 1998). Lilian Katz has visited Reggio Emilia multiple times and uses what she learned in Italy and what she has learned from American classroom to write and lead seminars on how to use the project approach in early childhood classrooms.

In one kindergarten class in Texas, the students decided to create a museum exhibit about reptiles (Diffily, 2000). They had seen exhibits created by older students at their school and wanted to do the same type of work. After the initial vote to construct an exhibit and the decision that the focus of the exhibit would be reptiles, the next eight weeks were filled with research, planning, and implementation of those plans.

The students read and responded to many different fiction and nonfiction books about reptiles, but their reading and writing experiences were much broader than experiencing literature and responding to it. Some children wrote memos to administrators and families to coordinate field trips to see how real professionals create museum exhibits. Some wrote letters to a local museum and a zoo to schedule field trips. Later they wrote thank-you letters to those staff members who had shared live reptiles with the class. They also wrote business letters and e-mailed questions they had about reptiles to experts in several different cities.

**BIOGRAPHY BOX** *Lilian G. Katz*

Lilian G. Katz is Professor Emerita of Early Childhood Education at the University of Illinois (Urbana-Champaign) where she is also co-director of the ERIC Clearinghouse on Elementary & Early Childhood Education. She is a past president of the National Association for the Education of Young Children and is editor of the journal *Early Childhood Research & Practice*.

Dr. Katz is the author of numerous publications about early childhood education, teacher education for the early years, child development, and parenting of young children. She was the founding editor of the *Early Childhood Research Quarterly*. She is currently chair of the editorial board of the *International Journal of the Early Years*, published in the United Kingdom. Her most recent book, coauthored with J. H. Helm is *Young Investigators: The Project Approach in the Early Years*. Her book *Talks with Teachers of Young Children*

(1995) is a collection of her essays. The second edition of her well-known book, *Engaging Children's Minds: The Project Approach*, coauthored with S. C. Chard, was published in 2000.

A popular and much sought-after presenter, Dr. Katz has lectured in all fifty states and in more than forty countries. She has held visiting posts at colleges and universities in Australia, Canada, England, Germany, India, Israel, the West Indies, and many parts of the United States. She is the recipient of numerous honors, including two Fulbright Awards and an Honorary Doctor of Letters degree from Whittier College, Whittier, California, and an honorary Doctor of Philosophy from the University of Goteborg, Sweden. Born and raised in England, Dr. Katz became a U.S. citizen in 1953. She holds degrees from San Francisco State University and Stanford University. She and her husband, Boris Katz, have three grown children, four grandsons, and one granddaughter.

They wrote notes to older students asking them to come to the classroom at particular times to read parts of expository text that they could not read but had marked with sticky notes as something they wanted to hear read aloud.

They dictated facts they had learned and identified whether they learned the information from books, from observation, or from experts. After collecting these facts for two weeks, they sorted the facts by source. Using published fact cards as models, they sketched reptiles and created fact cards of their own.

They decided to make their own reptile alphabet books based on Jerry Pallotta's *The Yucky Reptile Alphabet Book* (1989). When they began having difficulty remembering which letters they had already done, they created an alphabet chart. This chart helped them keep up with which letters of the alphabet they had created pages for and which ones they still needed to do. With only a little encouragement from their teacher, they quickly learned to use indices of some of the reference books about reptiles to locate reptiles to use in their own alphabet book.

After seeing a photo essay during the field trip to the museum, they decided to make their own photo essay about their study of reptiles. Using photographs taken on field trips and during class project time, they drafted label copy for each photograph and asked for peer response to be sure their copy described the photograph to ensure that other people would understand. Finally they typed the label copy in final form and mounted the photograph and label copy onto poster board.

In small committees, they examined the brochures they had picked up at the zoo and the museum and talked about what made those brochures good ones. After listing characteristics of a good brochure, they drafted their own exhibit brochure, asking other committees for input, before finalizing their parts of the brochure.

As it came closer to the deadline for the museum opening, the students decided they needed more reptiles. They had already decided to take the turtle and snake from the class's science center to the museum exhibit, but two live specimens weren't enough for their exhibit. They wrote to the museum staff member who had talked with them earlier about the three orders of reptiles and asked to borrow specimens from each of the orders he had discussed.

They designed an invitation for the museum opening to which they invited all the adults related to the classroom: parents, grandparents, friends, and volunteers. With help from older students, they looked up addresses in the telephone book and in the school directory and addressed their own envelopes. Some students worked on a memo to all the teachers in the school that invited all classes to schedule a tour of the exhibit. They also developed a system for keeping up with which classes had responded to the memo and when different tours were scheduled.

The day of the exhibit opening for their families, more than sixty adults crowded into the museum exhibit. The excitement of the kindergarten students was evident as they acted as docents for their family members and other guests who came to the opening. The rest of the week was spent with class docents giving tours to other students in the school and visitors to the building.

Throughout the weeks of planning, working on different components of the exhibit, and giving tours, the children in this kindergarten class continued their typical schedule minus one hour of center time. The project replaced this time. However, during project time, they learned things they might not have learned without this project. They learned that they could find out fascinating facts about reptiles by having someone read to them from a variety of books. They learned that they could record these facts and read them to other people. They learned that they could write letters and actually have adults write back to them, agreeing to show them live reptiles, answering questions, and loaning specimens. They learned that they could create important products that adults took seriously. Through their involvement in real-world reading and writing and by creating a museum exhibit that people came to tour, they learned that they could do important work.

The children involved in this project did not drop all other activities during the time they were researching reptiles and creating the exhibit. They still listened to their teacher read books and poetry. They created paintings, sang songs, and moved to music. They took care of class pets and plants. They continued to have daily opportunities to choose center work and to play outdoors. This project provided children with opportunities to engage in activities they chose, in work that was meaningful to them, and in activities that were integrated.

Young children do not have to wait until they are in kindergarten to begin working on projects. Some early childhood educators have successfully facilitated projects with children as young as two and three years old (LeeKeenan & Edwards, 1992; LeeKeenan & Nimmo, 1993). One such project was called "Looking at Each Other" and arose from the children's increasing interest in peer relationships. This was an attempt to integrate multicultural and anti-bias experiences into the classroom. Teachers prepared photograph face puppets for each child to play with, laminated photographs of children and hid them in different places in the classroom, and provided copies of the photographs of children so that children could use them in different art activities throughout the project. At the end of the project, the children were much more aware of each other and were fairly adept at describing similarities and differences among their peers (Lee-Keenan & Edwards, 1992). This project not only gave the teachers a way to provide meaningful activities for the toddlers and integrated multicultural and anti-bias experiences into the children's daily activities, it also motivated a group of young children who typically worked alone to begin working together in small groups.

---

*Learning Embedded in One Kindergarten Project Creating a Museum Exhibit about Reptiles*

**Processes Used throughout the Project**
- Learning to plan and work as a team member
- Learning to work independently
- Learning to use multiple resources
- Learning to help others find resources
- Learning to set work priorities
- Learning to allocate time
- Brainstorming ideas and options
- Negotiating solutions and decisions

**Doing Research on Reptiles**
- Learning characteristics and names of specific reptiles
- Learning that scientific information can be learned from observation, books, and experts

*(continued)*

*Learning Embedded in One Kindergarten Project Creating a Museum Exhibit about Reptiles (continued)*

- Observing classroom pets (snake and turtle) and keeping observation logs
- Learning the three primary orders of reptiles and sorting reptiles by orders
- Distinguishing fact and fiction accounts of reptiles
- Dictating questions prompted from read-alouds
- Writing letters to experts to get those questions answered
- Dictating or writing facts and sorting facts by sources
- Counting "facts" and comparing quantities
- Drawing and painting reptilian pictures

**Field Trips to Zoo and Museum**

- Writing letters to museum and zoo personnel
- Charting parents who volunteer to drive for each field trip
- Dividing class into field trip cars
- Sketching reptiles from close observation
- Taking notes about label copy

**Reptile Alphabet Books**

- Using adult model: *The Yucky Reptile Alphabet Book* (Pallotta, 1989)
- Using charts to organize information
- Finding a reptile for each letter of the alphabet
- Drawing reptile and writing facts about that reptile
- Using the index of expository books

**Photo Essay**

- Deciding which photographs should be taken to chronicle project
- Taking photographs
- Drafting and finalizing label copy
- Mounting photograph and label copy

**Hanging Items in Museum**

- Sorting facts, drawings, and photographs by source or order deciding what could be added to the exhibit to show what has been learned

**Creating Exhibit Brochure**

- Examining brochures from zoo or museum to determine important components
- Working in small groups on different parts of the exhibit brochure
- Drafting, assessing peer response, editing, and revising brochure
- Counting and adding groups to determine number of brochures needed

**Invitation to Families and Friends of the Class**

- Drafting and typing invitation copy
- Counting and adding groups to determine number of invitations needed
- Using telephone book to find addresses
- Practicing format of addressing envelopes
- Mailing invitations

*(continued)*

*Learning Embedded in One Kindergarten Project Creating a Museum Exhibit about Reptiles (continued)*

**Giving Exhibit Tours**
· Keeping track of scheduled tours and time that tours lasted
· Sharing what was learned about reptiles and creating a museum exhibit
· Fielding questions and responding to written questions submitted to the class

**Self-Evaluation**
· Dictating what they had done to help create the museum
· Choosing their best exhibit work and providing a rationale for that decision

## GROUPING CHILDREN

Children in early childhood programs are cared for in groups. While young children need individual attention and care, they also need to begin learning how to function as a members of a group. The project previously described offers a strong motivation for children to begin considering the needs of others and working with peers. At other times, children need to gather as a large group for activities such as the teacher reading aloud to the class. Children need time every day in all three types of interaction: individual attention, small-group experiences, and large-group activities. Varying the groupings of children, the control a child has over his or her day, and the ratio of children to adults who care for them are important considerations in early childhood programs.

The younger the child, the more flexible the schedule should be. The younger the child, the more they should be able to direct their own activities. Infants should be able to regulate when they want to eat and sleep, when they want to be active and when they want quiet time. This kind of individualized care requires low child-to-staff ratios. For young children, birth through twenty-four months, it is recommended that an adult be responsible for no more than three or four children (NAEYC, 1998). Three-, four-, and five-year-olds should have scheduled eating and resting times with flexible group, individual choice, and outdoor play times. It is recommended that children in this age group have between 8:1 and 10:1 child-to-adult ratios (NAEYC, 1998). For elementary school children, schedules should be routine and predictable and 10:1 to 12:1 ratios are recommended (NAEYC, 1998). See appendix B for these ratios.

### Planning Large-Group Activities

Whole-group instruction is generally ineffective with young children. There is almost always a wide range of previous experience and abilities in groups of young children. Few "lessons" can be taught that will benefit all of the

*Children need time every day in all three types of interaction: individual attention, small-group experiences, and large-group activities.*

children equally. Typically large-group instruction benefits approximately one-third of the group. Some children will already know the information that is presented and a few will not have the background experiences to permit them to understand the information. However, this does not mean that early childhood educators never bring children together as an entire group. Shared experiences are important in helping build a sense of community among the students.

Several activities are conducive to whole-group experiences. One of these is shared reading. Experienced early childhood educators know how important it is to read aloud to children and typically plan several shared reading experiences every day. Many teachers begin each morning by reading a book aloud to the entire group of children and use shared reading as a transition before or after lunch or recess, or as a way to end the day.

There are other valid reasons to bring children together as a whole group: singing; performing finger plays, action songs, or creative movement activities; sharing a visitor with the class; playing group games; planning activities; solving problems; or reviewing the day's experiences.

Early childhood educators need to be especially observant of children during large-group experiences. Excessive wriggling, chatting with other children, lying down, or just standing up and walking away from the group should be signals to the teacher that something is wrong. Children may have had to wait too long for the group activity to begin. They may not be interested in the activity or the timing may be off. If children are not being attentive, it is probably best to end the activity and try it again at another time. Learning to respond to the cues of the group takes time and experience, but successful group experiences can be orchestrated when the teacher learns to follow the children.

Toward the end of a prekindergarten year, Mr. Russo's students had developed attention spans that permitted group times to last as long as twenty minutes. He always began their group meeting times with the same action song that directed children to turn around, reach up "and touch the sky," turn around again, and then quietly sit down. The moment the song ended, Mr. Russo started a finger play with the children and then introduced the book he had prepared to read aloud to the group. He varied his reading voice throughout the reading time, using character voices to keep the children's attention as he read the book. He encouraged children to predict what was going to happen next in the story and frequently asked them if something that was happening with the story's characters had ever happened to them, helping them relate the story to their own lives. After finishing the book, Mr. Russo asked the children to tell him their favorite part of the story. As they shared this with the group, they were individually dismissed from the group to find materials in the writing or art center so they could draw the "favorite part" they had just mentioned. This group meeting had been very effective. The children were attentive throughout the song, the finger play, and the read-aloud. There were few wiggles and almost no discussion between children. The song had become part of their daily routine. The finger play was one they all knew and enjoyed doing. The book Mr. Russo selected was appropriate for this group of children, and they sat totally engaged in listening to the story as he read to them. When asked about their favorite part of the story, every child had an answer and was eager to draw a picture about this.

Group meetings had not always run this smoothly for Mr. Russo's class. Early in the year, he had had to keep whole-group experiences to less than ten minutes, some days less than five minutes. During action songs and finger plays, only a few children were interested in learning the words to the song and the movements that accompanied those words. Read-alouds had to be very short books, and even then, not every child listened to the teacher read. Several children in this class had never had group experiences and simply chose not to participate in these activities. These four-year-olds had to learn what was expected of them during group meeting. Their compliant behavior and interest in group activities had to be developed. Mr. Russo was patient with the children, knowing that with careful planning of high-interest activities and repeated opportunities, they would learn how to function as a group—for age-appropriate lengths of time. Even at the end of the year, Mr. Russo kept large-group meetings relatively short and planned activities for small groups and individual decision for most of their school day.

## Planning Small-Group Activities

While there are legitimate reasons for working with large groups of children, much of young children's learning occurs in small groups or in pairs. In smaller groups, children do not have to wait to participate in activities. They can interact more easily with each other and with the materials. An adult working with a group of four to six children is able to more easily adjust lessons to these specific children and to provide the appropriate scaffolding for the students. With smaller groups, it is easier to observe each child, get to know what each child is learning, and learn how best to support each child.

Group size, typically between two and ten, depends on the activity. These smaller groups are best for reading stories when the teacher wants to encourage every child in the group to participate in a discussion, for working with manipulatives when children might need teacher assistance, or when introducing new concepts to the class, such as a new game, conventions of writing, or working on parts of a project. Typically when the teacher is working specifically with a small group of children, other children in the class are working in self-selected activities.

In a first-grade classroom, Jordan had analyzed the work in her students' writing folders. She realized that five of the students were ready for some specific work on punctuation. Many of the children were already using periods appropriately and were beginning to use quotation marks and even commas in their writing. Other children in the class were still working hard to encode initial and ending consonant sounds for the words they wanted to write. None of the children in these last two groups would have benefited from instruction in using periods at the end of sentences. One group had already mastered that skill. The other group was not yet ready to focus on punctuation. Jordan called the five children together, as other children worked on their own levels during writing workshop, and talked with them about how published authors used periods and how they could make their writing more readable for other people if they also used periods in their writing. This was an appropriate grouping of these children for this reason.

## Planning Individual Activities

Had only one child in Jordan's class been "ready" to learn about using periods, it would have been appropriate that she spend some time with that one child discussing punctuation. Many of the most important teaching moments with young children occur one on one. A few minutes spent between a teacher and one child can be extremely productive. In an individualized focused moment, an observant teacher is able to determine how much the child understands about a particular issue and can immediately decide how much support or direct instruction needs to be given. Working with just one child gives the teacher an opportunity to listen intently and focus on what the child says or does. With this concentrated attention, a teacher can assess a child's perspectives and respond in supportive and affirming ways. The teacher can then provide materials, experiences, and feedback commensurate with the child's interests and needs. One-on-one grouping is most appropriate when helping children learn a new skill or refine a skill, for dictation of stories or information, for individual discussions about literature, or for teacher/child interviews.

In third grade, Kathey scheduled two reading conferences with each student every week. Kathey facilitated a self-selected reading workshop in her classroom (Roller, 1996). In order to track what the students were reading and to keep up with the children's reading development, Kathey conducted reading conferences with her students. Twice each week, she discussed with individual students the plot of the book they were reading, personal and literary allusions, and how they were reacting to the piece of literature. She listened to them read aloud from their book or their reading response journal and commented on progress they were making or areas they needed to focus on. Kathey firmly believed that this short time spent with individual students was much more effective than whole-group or small-group reading instruction, and the progress of her students confirmed her belief.

While primary-grade teachers may choose to work with individual students in a conference-type format, early childhood teachers also work with individual children throughout the age groups. Caregivers work with individual infants by talking to them or conversing by echoing the infant's cooing sounds. Teachers who work with toddlers might work with one child in seriation or classification activities or by transcribing a child's dictation or story retelling. Teachers who work with preschoolers might work on early math or literacy concepts. This one-on-one time spent between child and early childhood educator is instructive for the child and informative for the adult.

Young children should spend time every day in different groupings. The balance of time spent in child-selected activities and in teacher-led experiences will vary based on the age of the children and in the individual characteristics of the children. Early childhood educators must use the knowledge they have about child growth and development and what they know about their own group of children to make these decisions.

## PLANNING CHILD-CENTERED SCHEDULES

*We should establish routines that are reasonable and make sense to children.*

*-Marianne Gareau and Collean Kennedy*

In planning groupings of children and in setting daily schedules, early childhood educators follow a few basic guidelines. Young children have a need to know what will happen in their lives. Routines and group rituals offer predictability, and young children find security in the routine of a schedule. They need to know what to expect when they first enter the classroom in the morning. They need to know what will occur throughout the morning, when the teacher will read aloud, when they will eat, what to expect from afternoon activities, when they can make choices and when they need to comply with teacher requests, when they can talk and when they need to listen to others, and they need to know how the day will end.

Early morning routines set the tone for the day. Many teachers play soft music as children arrive. This helps children begin the day in a relaxing mood. Early childhood educators greet each child as he or she arrives, spending a few moments talking with the child about his or her evening and his or her morning. Young children usually are brimming with stories they want to share with someone important to them, and teachers know that they need to take the time to really listen to these stories. Looking directly into a child's eyes, listening to the stories of their lives, and responding in a

---

*Sample of a Two-Year-Old Schedule*

| | |
|---|---|
| 8:00 A.M. | Child Choice of Center Activities |
| 9:00 A.M. | Shared Storytime |
| 9:10 A.M. | Movement-Finger Plays-Music |
| 9:20 A.M. | Snacks |
| 9:40 A.M. | Center Choice |
| 10:30 A.M. | Outdoor Time |
| 11:30 A.M. | Lunch |
| 12:15 P.M. | Nap/Rest Time |
| 2:00 P.M. | Shared Storytime |
| 2:10 P.M. | Outdoor Time |
| 2:40 P.M. | Center Choice |
| 3:20 P.M. | Snacks |
| 3:40 P.M. | Center Choice until Family Picks Them Up |

caring, interested manner sets another tone for the day, one that lets each child know that they are valued.

Children need to know what the morning routines are in their classroom. Some teachers elect to place three or four specific activity choices on certain tables and let children know what they can choose to do as soon as they arrive and are settled with their belongings put away. Other teachers decide that early morning is a time when the children may choose from of all classroom centers. In kindergarten or elementary school classrooms, many teachers choose to begin the day with **journal writing** or DEAR (Drop Everything And Read) time. Any of these morning activities will work well for children as long as they know beforehand what to expect when they enter the room.

**journal writing** drawings or emergent/ conventional spelling created by a child to record events in his or her life.

After the early morning choice time, teachers may opt to begin the day with a singing time or a shared story time or maybe a whole-group sharing time in which topics of interest are discussed, even debated. Some teachers choose this time to review yesterday's activities, projects, and events or to go over the plans for the day.

Schedules need to provide sufficient time for children to truly engage in their activities. Most children need large blocks of time, as much as thirty to forty-five minutes, to fully involve themselves in dramatic play themes, block building, or writing projects. This factor should be considered in developing the daily schedule.

Children need many opportunities every day to choose what they will do. There should be a balance of structured times when the children function as a group and open-ended times when the children choose their

---

*Sample of a Kindergarten Schedule*

| | |
|---|---|
| 8:00 A.M. | Child Choice of Center Activities |
| 9:00 A.M. | Shared Storytime |
| 9:20 A.M. | Literature Extension Activities |
| 9:45 A.M. | Writing Workshop |
| 10:30 A.M. | Math Menu |
| 11:20 A.M. | Poetry Reading |
| 11:30 A.M. | Lunch |
| 12:00 P.M. | Rest Time |
| 12:30 P.M. | Shared Storytime—Action Songs |
| 12:45 P.M. | Child-Choice of Center Activities |
| 2:00 P.M. | Outdoor Play |
| 2:45 P.M. | Class Meeting |
| 3:00 P.M. | Shared Storytime/Action Songs/Review of the Day |
| 3:20 P.M. | Get Ready for Dismissal |
| 3:30 P.M. | Dismissal |

*Sample of a Second-Grade Schedule*

| | |
|---|---|
| 8:00 A.M. | Individual or Paired Reading |
| 8:30 A.M. | Group Meeting Time |
| 9:00 A.M. | Shared Reading |
| 9:30 A.M. | Reading Response/Writing Workshop |
| 10:30 A.M. | Music and Movement |
| 10:45 A.M. | Author's Chair |
| 11:00 A.M. | Recess |
| 11:30 A.M. | Poetry Shared Reading |
| 11:45 A.M. | Lunch |
| 12:15 P.M. | Chapter Book Shared Reading |
| 12:30 P.M. | Math Menu |
| 1:30 P.M. | Project Time (science or social studies based) |
| 3:00 P.M. | Clean Up |
| 3:10 P.M. | Review and Planning Meeting |
| 3:30 P.M. | Dismissal |

activities. Children should not make all the decisions about their day. Because children are naturally active, they often do not realize on their own that they need to slow down and have some quiet time. Teachers need to be aware of children's needs for a balance of energetic activities and tranquil ones and plan for this in the daily schedule.

An observer can often recognize a truly skilled early childhood educator by the way he or she assists children making transitions from one activity to another. A standard rule for early childhood educators is that they should never ask children to "do nothing." They should always ask children to "do something." As children are gathering for a story time, those who arrive promptly should not be expected to sit still and wait until everyone comes to the meeting area. The teacher could start reciting a finger play, singing a song, or begin a game of "follow me," making different hand or arm gestures, while waiting for everyone to gather. For children who are a bit older, these transition times could include learning sign language, counting in another language, or reciting a poem. For the very youngest children— infants and toddlers—transitions can be facilitated by the adult verbalizing for the child what is about to occur. Children need support from their teacher in making successful transitions from one activity to another.

## REVISITING THE OPENING VIGNETTES

If you were to visit Ms. Chastain and Mrs. Donaldson's toddler classroom or Mr. Cervantez's first-grade classroom again later in the year, you would note many changes. In both classes, the students would seem more independent. As they moved from center to center, their decisions would appear more purposeful. They would be making more of their own decisions. The teachers would have gotten to know all of the students very well and would be using the children's interests more in determining the curriculum for the children. As in the beginning of the year, they still use what they know about child growth and development, the individual children, the disciplines, and themes and units, but they are making these decisions more easily.

The toddlers are working on a unit about families while the first-graders are studying their community. The classroom itself has changed, representing the current themes that were negotiated between the teachers and the students. The addition of materials to support the themes is evident. The walls and bulletin boards are filled with the work of interested, active young children and photographs of their field trips and work in the classroom. The students in these classrooms have become successful learners.

## Summary

Young children need to feel successful in what they do. Early childhood educators plan carefully to ensure this success. They learn as much as they can about their students and use that information, along with knowledge of child growth and development and the curriculum disciplines, to plan a wide variety of integrated activities within some form of curriculum organizers, such as units, themes, and projects. Just as early childhood educators work to integrate language and literacy, math, science, and social studies into learning centers and group experiences, they are aware of multicultural and anti-bias issues and also integrate these into the curriculum. Teachers provide many opportunities during the day so that children can self-select their own activities, but also schedule opportunities for children to work in small groups and share whole-class experiences. The way in which a teacher schedules children's activities during the day helps support positive behaviors from young children. This and other methods of guiding young children are discussed in the next chapter.

## Reflections

**1.** Choose one topic common to young children and create your own curriculum web of activities related to that theme that will ensure that children's physical, psychosocial, cognitive, and language and literacy needs are being met.

**2.** Select a children's book. Talk with another person about the story and the possible activities that could be generated from different parts of that book.

**3.** Think about a particular group of children you have observed and discuss your thoughts about how the teacher of those children might assure that the curriculum, activities, and materials are relevant, meaningful, and mind engaging to a particular class.

**4.** In a small group, talk about factors that would distinguish infant/toddler programs that are merely good baby-sitting or custodial in design and those that provide growth, development, and language opportunities.

**5.** Compare the primary-grade suggestions in this chapter with your own experiences in your first-, second-, and third-grade classes.

## Field Experiences

**1.** Choose one of the following age groups: toddlers, preschoolers, kindergarten, or primary. Observe a classroom of children this age. Make notes about activities offered to children and the way the teacher arranges the room to accommodate their emerging capabilities.

**2.** In the same setting, make notes about activities the teacher provides children through large- and small-group activities. Notice how learners respond in both large- and small-group times.

**3.** In the same setting, make notes about activities the teacher provides individual children. How and why has the teacher chosen these activities, materials, instruction, and so on for this particular learner?

## Case Studies

### Change Curriculum or Not?

Josie had planned a long-term thematic unit for her second-grade class on plants. It was late spring, and all of her previous classes had loved the gardening activities she had offered to them. It seemed like a perfect way to spend the last month of school. That would be just long enough for seeds they planted to become seedlings, and children would be able to take the seedlings home to transplant into their gardens. Over the last few months, Josie had located more than a dozen new children's books about how vegetables and flowers grow and how to garden. The reading level of the books covered the range of reading abilities in her classroom. She located several Web sites that she knew the children would find informative and interesting. She made arrangements for field trips to a local nursery and the city gardens. She arranged for several friends who were avid gardeners to come to her class each Friday to work with the children. She purchased seeds, potting soil, and containers. She also purchased several plants for experiments about water and light, several varieties of plants to observe, and a few less familiar plants such as Venus fly-traps. Josie was ready for this unit.

On the very day she planned to introduce the plant unit, Josie's students came in from recess having collected grasshoppers and crickets. All they wanted to talk about was grasshoppers and crickets. The next day several children brought in books about insects and the discussion about grasshoppers and crickets expanded to include ants, beetles, ladybugs, butterflies, and all kinds of other insects.

### What to Do?

Despite all her preparation, should Josie switch the topic for her final unit of the school year? Should she try to pull children's interest away from insects and proceed with the curriculum she had planned to follow for the last month of school? Should she drop half of what she planned for the plant unit and research and plan a shorter unit on insects? With only a month remaining in the school year, what would Josie's best option be?

### Meeting Standards versus Integrated Learning

Mr. Lorenzo, a prekindergarten teacher, has just left the first faculty meeting of the school year. Mrs. Josco, the new principal of the elementary school, has announced that *her* school is going to be a leader in the school district's new standards initiative this year. She lays out her plan about how each grade level will meet the standards that have been mandated by the district. She shares a schedule for each grade level that delineates specific times that each content area will be taught every day. Mrs. Josco concludes by telling the faculty that there will be no variation from her plan and that there is no room for negotiation.

### What to Do?

Mr. Lorenzo strongly believes in developmentally appropriate practices and is convinced that young children learn best through active, integrated learning experiences. He knows that he can not just ignore Mrs. Josco's mandate. He has heard from faculty where Mrs. Josco served as principal the past five years that she spends time in classrooms every day. He knows he cannot refuse to follow her mandates. That would be insubordination, grounds for being fired. Given his beliefs and her mandates, what should Mr. Lorenzo do?

## Further Reading

Bergen, D., Reid, R., & Torelli, L. (2001). *Educating and caring for very young children: The infant/toddler curriculum*. New York: Teachers College Press.

Bickart, T. S., Jablon, J. R., & Dodge, D. T. (1999). *Building the primary classroom: A complete guide to teaching and learning*. Portsmouth, NH: Heinemann.

DeVries, R., Zan, B., Hildebrandt, C., Edmiaston, R., & Sales, C. (2002). *Developing constructivist early childhood curriculum: Practical principles and activities* Washington, DC: National Association for the Education of Young Children.

Gallenstein, N. L. (2003). Creative construction of mathematics and science concepts in early childhood. Olney, MD: Association for Childhood Education International.

Helm, J. H., & Beneke, S. (Eds.). (2003). *The power of projects: Meeting contemporary challenges in early childhood classroom—Strategies and solutions*. Washington, DC: National Association for the Education of Young Children.

Neuman, S. B., Copple, C., & Bredekamp, S. (2000). *Learning to read and write: Developmentally appropriate practices for young children*. Washington, DC: National Association for the Education of Young Children. (Available in Spanish)

Puckett, M. B. (Ed.). (2002) *Room to grow: How to create quality early childhood environments*. (3rd ed.) Austin, TX: Texas Association for the Education of Young Children.

Richey, D. D. (2000). *Inclusive early childhood education*. New York: Delmar Learning.

## Helpful Web Sites

### Teaching Strategies

http://www.teachingstrategies.com/

*The mission of Teaching Strategies, Inc., is to enhance the quality of early childhood programs by offering the highest quality curriculum materials, training programs, parenting resources, and staff development services. With separate pages for educators and parents, Teaching Strategies features printed resources about active learning and developmentally appropriate practices for children birth through grade three. Excerpts from most resources are available for viewing online.*

### North Central Regional Educational Laboratory

http://www.ncrel.org/sdrs/areas/stw_esys/5erly_ch.htm

*NCREL is a nonprofit organization that provides research-based resources for teachers, administrators, and policy makers. This particular page describes guidelines for early childhood curriculum and assessment.*

**Early Childhood.Com**
http://www.earlychildhood.com
*This Web site offers ideas for activities and curriculum for young children and a selection of articles from* Early Childhood News.

Check the Online Resources™ for expert practitioners' responses to each case study.

For additional information on teaching young children, visit our Web site at **http://www.earlychilded.delmar.com**

# CHAPTER 8

## Guiding Young Children

*Early Childhood Principle* Professional early childhood educators use instructive guidance to help children develop healthy personalities and social and moral competence.

The critical foundations for healthy personality development are laid during infancy and early childhood, and the strength of these foundations determines the extent to which individuals continue to develop and sustain a healthy personality throughout their lives. There are three important psychosocial goals of early childhood development and indeed all human development.

1. A healthy personality
2. Social competence
3. Moral competence

Becoming socially and morally competent depends on interactions with others who help children construct social and moral meaning. Positive interactions help children view themselves as accepted and decent and guide them toward more mature behaviors and constructive relationships with others. Developmentally appropriate expectations and constructive guidance facilitate early development of healthy personalities and the construction of social and moral meaning. This chapter is about facilitating such development.

*After reading this chapter you should be able to:*
- Discuss the major goals of developmentally appropriate guidance of young children.
- Define and explain the concept of emerging development.
- Distinguish between instructive guidance and discipline.

- Discuss the importance of the early stages of personality development and self-esteem to the development of social and moral competence.
- Describe how prosocial development emerges and is nurtured and supported.
- List ways early childhood educators and caregivers facilitate work and play behaviors that lead to positive self-regard, wise decision making, self-control, prosocial interactions, and a sense of community.

## UNDERSTANDING EMERGING DEVELOPMENT

Christalyn, now eight months old slaps at her caregiver's face, throws objects from her crib and cries when they are not retrieved, cries upon separation from her parents, and turns away from people she does not know.

Two-year-old Luke is very physical in his play behaviors with others in his child care group. He takes what he wants, does not share, cries when others take his toys from him, has been known to bite, gets frustrated easily, clings to his parents, and resists nap times.

Four year-old LaDonna loves dramatic play and spends most of her prekindergarten morning in the sociodramatic center. She assumes the lead role and establishes rules for who can and can't play and what roles will be assigned to whom. Sometimes she is very assertive in this activity. When classmates rebel, she becomes angry. When an adult intervenes, she cries.

Regelio, a kindergartener, tattles incessantly. He is watchful of behaviors of others, is easily frustrated when others do not follow group rules, and is often in a verbal "tête-à-tête" with a classmate over how things are supposed to be.

Seven-year-old Patrice is very self-critical, has developed feelings of being treated unfairly if others receive privileges that she does not get. Her friendships are often transient, though she forms strong attachments to her current "best friend." She prefers to play with girls. She appears anxious when separated from familiar people and places. She is slow to get started after arrival at school. Patrice is a child with juvenile rheumatoid arthritis (JRA).

What do the behaviors of Christalyn, Luke, LaDonna, Regelio, and Patrice have in common? Do these behaviors represent inappropriate parenting practices or ill will on the part of the child? Should these behaviors be corrected? . . . punished? Is there cause for concern?

Actually all of these behaviors are, in a developmental sense, "good" behaviors. You are probably asking, "How can hitting, bossing, tattling, refusing to share, resisting nap times, and crying when adults intervene possibly be labeled as 'good' behavior?" These can be thought of as "good" behaviors because they indicate **emerging development** or increasing maturity. These behaviors are age appropriate and represent expected social and emotional development. These behaviors can segue into more socially acceptable forms when met with sensitive, developmentally appropriate, and instructive guidance techniques.

We begin this chapter with the concept of emerging development because we want to stress that growth and development are ongoing and that immature behaviors, some of which are often troublesome, are for the most part indications of progress toward more mature behaviors. Successful guidance of young children depends on this understanding.

As well, basic to guidance of young children is an understanding of parental goals and expectations and the diversity of these goals represented in any one group of children. Setting developmentally appropriate social and moral goals always takes into consideration the socialization context of the home and family.

The concept of emerging development helps early childhood educators view what might otherwise be thought of as inappropriate (or misbehavior) as healthy signs of progressing growth and development. Developmentally appropriate guidance of young children conveys acceptance and respect and is instructive. Appreciating emerging development helps early childhood educators to maintain focus on the "big picture" and long-term outcomes while assisting children with their immediate needs. Responding appropriately to age-related behaviors helps children build the foundations of a healthy personality (trust, autonomy, initiative, and industry), positive self-concepts, and more mature forms of interacting with others.

Often adults, failing to recognize emerging development such as that which Christalyn, Luke, LaDonna, Regelio, and Patrice exhibit, respond in corrective rather than in instructive and supportive ways. They may believe

**emerging development** growth and development that is appearing and represents a point or stage in a continuous process that moves from immature to mature forms.

*Knowledgeable adults respond appropriately to young children's negative feelings.*

that these behaviors call for some form of discipline through reprimand or punishment. Inappropriate correcting or reprimanding of "normal" behavior such as these mitigates against the development of trust, autonomy, initiative, and industry and interferes with the development of self-directing behaviors, positive self-regard, and social and moral competence in the long run (Bronson, 2000; Katz, McClellan, Fuller, & Walz, 1995). Negative responses can actually impede this forward growth and development, while positive, affirming interactions that *teach* and offer *alternatives* facilitate it. Understanding emergent development helps early childhood educators keep long-term goals in the forefront while responding to immediate child behaviors in instructive and supportive ways (Sylwester, 2000a).

Healthy personality development is a life-long process building upon each preceding foundational accomplishment from birth through adult life (Revisit Figure 3–2). Becoming socially and morally competent is also a long-term process. These are goals that will not be fully realized during the course of a year, but progress toward them will be evident to early childhood educators as they observe and work with young children on a day-to-day basis.

## Connecting in Meaningful Ways with Families

Planning for individual and group emotional and social well-being entails communicating with parents about their desires and goals for their children, what they expect their children to achieve during their early care and education, and how they guide (or discipline) their children at home. As discussed in chapter 5, the more we know about family expectations, life circumstances, interests, and cultural values, the more effectively we interact with children and their families.

That home and early childhood programs constitute different social environments for children is a given. Understanding that parents often differ from teachers in their deeply held views, child-rearing practices, and behavior expectations is important to establishing positive family-school or family-center relationships.

Developing collaborative relationships with parents begins when children enter the early childhood program. Communicating and collaborating on how best to meet mutual goals, communicating school policies and procedures relating to guidance techniques, and planning for ongoing communications help parents to understand and support the guidance goals of the early childhood program. When children experience continuity in their guidance in both settings they feel a greater sense of predictability and security and can grow more readily toward self-control.

## Understanding the Cultural Contexts of Child Behaviors

There are cultural differences in behavior expectations of children. Some cultures stress cooperation over competition; others, competition and winning. Some stress unquestioned obedience to authority figures. The manner in which respect is communicated varies among cultures. Some cultures stress independence and self-determination. Most cultures have gender-related social rules and norms; most have expectations regarding contexts in which emotions may or should not be expressed. Social conventions and skills are derived from one's culture.

Professional early childhood educators are not required to know about all cultural social norms. However, in interacting with the young children in one's group or class, it is important to respect cultural expectations, while facilitating each child's integration into the group and the culture of the center or school (Katz, McClellan, Fuller, & Walz, 1995; Small, 2001).

## HEALTHY PSYCHOSOCIAL DEVELOPMENT

In chapter 3, you were introduced to Erik Erikson's (1963) theory of psychosocial development. Erikson's stages of personality development are particularly relevant to our discussion of guidance of young children. While Erikson outlined eight stages (or critical periods) that advance from birth through adulthood, for our discussion, the first four states—trust, autonomy; initiative, and industry—are described.

### Erikson's Early Stages of Personality Development

Erikson proposed that each stage of personality development presented a psychological "crisis" in which there are two opposing personality potentials. Think of these opposites as resting on a balance scale. The goal of healthy personality development is to tip the scale in favor of trust, autonomy, initiative, and industry over their polar opposites, mistrust, shame and doubt, guilt, and inferiority. Certainly there may be elements in each of these polar opposites that are necessary, such as mistrust of strangers, skepticism that avoids gullibility, guilt that nudges the conscience, and discomfort with performance that causes one to try harder next time. The point of Erikson's theory is to stress the need for a tipped scale in favor of the positive characteristics over the negative ones.

### Trust versus Mistrust

Trust, the first "step" in healthy personality development, is an outgrowth of early bonding and attachments in infancy. Trust relies on predictable, reliable, supportive, warm, and nurturing care. Adults who respond readily to infant cues for nourishment, attention, warmth, playfulness, and discomfort help the infant develop a strong sense of trust. From these nurturing and supportive interactions, the infant develops trust in others as well as himself and his ability to communicate and elicit responses. A basic sense of trust is fundamental to healthy intra- and interpersonal relationships.

*A healthy sense of trust develops when infants can depend on caring and supportive adults to meet their needs.*

Infants who do not develop a healthy sense of trust do not form strong attachments with parents and primary caregivers during infancy and early childhood. Nor do they later form attachments or strong relationships with extended family members, friends, and playmates. Mistrust interferes with all human relationships, including spousal and workplace relationships later on. Individuals who mistrust are less open to new experiences and ideas, risk taking, and creative thinking. As such, learning is affected. A strong sense of trust in self and others paves the way for the next stage of psychosocial development, that of developing a sense of autonomy.

### Autonomy versus Shame and Doubt

Between ages one and three years, children are gaining increasing motor, language, cognitive, and social abilities. They have mastered fundamental motor skills of walking, climbing, and running; they can feed themselves; they have some ability to handle their clothing; and they may be gaining bladder and bowel control. At this point in growth and development a sense

*By encouragin*

It is also
psychosocia
carry them (
cute their (
Including cl
giving and a
behaviors a
Out-of-b
perhaps agg
bounds init
constructive
hurts or en(
and promp
exploring o
out-of-boun
perspective
ing and offe

of autonomy emerges and becomes an overriding psychosocial issue for the child. This period of development is often tumultuous as the toddler begins to assert his or her will. Determined yet still unskilled attempts to dress and undress, to turn the door knob, to fasten the seat belt, to turn on and off a light, to make decisions about what to wear, to decide whether to be carried or to walk independently, for example, signal a healthy and growing sense of autonomy.

The toddler's sense of autonomy is enhanced through guidance that encourages choices and independence and avoids power struggles in which the child is frequently disempowered by a bigger and stronger person who insists on compliance. The child's successes in locomotion and other motor coordinations build a sense of competence and self-determination. Mealtimes that respect food preferences, hunger, and satiety (feeling of having had sufficient food) support an emerging sense of self as independent. Supportive experiences in toilet learning are particularly important as toddlers assume control over their bodies. Pretend play and opportunities to interact with other children encourage autonomy. Guidance that is overrestrictive, overprotective, or unclear, unpredictable, or too permissive interferes with the developing sense of autonomy. Rather, guidance needs to be firm with clearly stated, predictable limits or boundaries and consequences that relate to misdeeds. We will discuss these characteristics of guidance later in this chapter. Upon a firm foundation of trust and autonomy, a sense of initiative emerges.

The opposite of autonomy is a sense of shame and doubt. When toddlers are squelched in their attempts to develop a sense of autonomy, the scales can tip too far in the opposite direction, resulting in a potentially debilitating sense of shame or doubt. When this occurs, children may exhibit feelings of guilt and penitence, self-consciousness, reluctance to try new things, overdependence on adults, and overreliance on the will and wishes of others. These feelings and behaviors, if allowed to persist, interfere with success with the ensuing stages of personality development and can remain a part of the personality into adulthood.

### Initiative versus Guilt

Children between the ages of three and six years are eager to master new skills. It is a period during which children ask many questions and exploit their new sense of autonomy. Social play becomes more intense and focused, as do conversations with others. Children during this period enjoy involvement in planning and anticipating special events such as a holiday celebration, special projects, family outings, and class field trips. Play during this period becomes more social and elaborate. Dramatic play particularly is complex and creative, with sociodramatic scenarios that are rich with fantasy and imagination.

Adults support this emerging sense of initiative through their encouragement of play and the provision of play-based curricula. Because this is a

> Psychoanalytic theo-
> rists have highlighted
> the emotionally integra-
> tive function of pre-
> tense, pointing out that
> anxiety-provoking
> events—such as a visit to
> the doctor's office or
> discipline by a parent—
> are likely to be revis-
> ited in the young child's
> play but with roles
> reversed so that the
> child is in command and
> compensates for
> unpleasant experiences
> in real life.
>
> *-Laura E. Berk*

their own behaviors in subsequent similar situations. It is also important at this stage to engage children in rule making, being certain that the reasons for the rules are logical and clearly explained. When children have a hand in developing class rules for which they have a clear understanding of their purposes, they are more inclined to remember and follow the rules. Children who are developing a sense of initiative need many opportunities to engage in new and challenging activities and to participate in decision-making group projects and cooperative activities.

An inadequate sense of initiative can lead to feelings of guilt. When feelings of guilt are persistent, children begin to seek undue assurances and permission from adults and playmates. They do not take personal risks, try new activities, or reach out to others. They may derive little satisfaction or joy from their own emerging capabilities. Feeling thwarted in initiating their own ideas, interests, and activities is a deterrent to the developing sense of initiative. When children have been unduly teased, ridiculed, or treated with disrespect, and when others respond to their ideas and questions off-handedly or perhaps impatiently, the developing sense of initiative is deterred.

### Industry versus Inferiority

Erikson's fourth stage of psychosocial development is marked by the development of a sense of industry. Industry begins to emerge around age six and is associated with mastering social and academic skills. The rich fantasy and make-believe of earlier years turns to more reality-based endeavors. The developing sense of industry is exhibited in the child's desire to learn how things work and how to do real tasks. While process was important during the three preceding stages of psychosocial development, product becomes important during this stage. Children begin to take pride in their writings, artwork, and block constructions as products of their own efforts. Interest in learning "real" skills carries over into interests in succeeding in school. Meaningful and relevant experiences with classmates, teachers, curricula, and assessments set the stage for the development of a healthy sense of industry.

Self-confidence and feelings of competence are particularly vulnerable to schooling experiences, as children are forming images of themselves as learners. Children who experience unachievable expectations or too many failures (academic or social) develop the opposite of a sense of industry, that of a sense of inferiority. Confidence and self-worth suffer and social and academic efforts are less industrious.

## Elkind's Additional Psychosocial Challenges

David Elkind, a psychology professor and well-known scholar and author of *Miseducation: Preschoolers at Risk* (1987), identified two additional psychosocial developmental challenges (1987). He describes these as *belonging versus alienation* and *competence versus helplessness*. According to Elkind, during the period in which initiative is developing, children are interacting more and more with their peers, and therefore experience the need to belong. The sense of belonging versus alienation is an associated psychosocial crisis to be resolved. In the same way, Elkind associated the competence versus helplessness crisis with the developing sense of industry.

## Belonging versus Alienation

From infancy, children acquire a sense of belonging within the family when parents include them in their activities such as shopping for groceries, washing the car, taking care of household chores, engaging in meaningful conversations, and playful interactions. Frequent visits or communication with extended family members also provide a sense of belonging within the extended family. Where neighbors are mutually supportive and connected, children may also find a context in which they feel a sense of belonging. As children extend their social interactions to playmates, they are confronted with learning how to make and maintain friends, enter play groups, and function in a manner that elicits positive responses and continued inclusion.

While a sense of alienation interferes with social interactions and learning, Elkind suggests that the sense of belonging that is too strong leads children to unquestioning conformance, yielding too willingly to the wishes and demands of the group or groups to which they wish to belong. The resolution of this psychosocial crisis should lead the child to productive membership in the group, while remaining sufficiently autonomous to neither overly conform nor become overly alienated.

## Competence versus Helplessness

Elkind's second psychosocial challenge is the development of a sense of competence versus helplessness. He suggests that attaining a sense of competence that is stronger than a sense of helplessness can be related to the match between school curricula and expectations and a child's modes of learning. He mentions "push-down" curricula as causing feelings of helplessness in young learners. Tying a sense of helplessness to inappropriate curricula, Elkind explains that during the cognitive development period of concrete operations, children should not be subjected to formal instruction that fails to respect the child's need for concrete materials and firsthand experiences in order to learn. (Parenthetically, recent brain research, mentioned in chapter 3, suggests that premature formal instruction [worksheets, flash cards, memorization of decontextualized material] actually interferes with the brain's ability to make the neurological connections necessary for such learning). Inappropriate instructional practices ignore children's natural capabilities and leave the learner feeling frustrated, helpless, and incompetent.

Play is also very important to the young child's developing sense of competence. Through play, children practice social interaction skills, apply new concepts to their play themes, and grow in social awareness. Play can do for young children what ego-defense mechanisms do for older children and adults. It can protect the ego from undue insult by providing a medium for role-playing assertive behaviors, pretending to be strong and powerful and in control (Elkind, 1987). In effect, through play, children test and practice their social abilities and growing sense of competence. Successful resolution of these psychosocial crises depends not only on parents but also on caregivers and teachers as well. Elkind (1987) said it best:

> Schooling practices become as important as parenting practices in the outcome of the crises of personality potentials. Just as we know what parenting practices encourage and support trust, autonomy, initiative, and belonging, so do we know what schooling practices encourage industry and competence.
>
> When we recognize the young child's unique modes of learning and adapt educational practices to them, we engage in healthy education. When we ignore what we know about how young children learn, and expose them to teaching practices appropriate to children at older age levels, we miseducate them and put them at risk for a sense of inferiority and helplessness. (pp. 157–158).

## Self-Esteem

**self-esteem** one's positive or negative self-evaluation.

**Self-esteem** is a by-product of these earlier accomplishments along with the child's continual self-evaluations and assessments of how others respond to him or her, particularly their most important others—parents, siblings, grandparents, caregivers, teachers, and playmates.

Professional early childhood educators understand the critical importance of positive self-concepts and self-esteem. They know that self-esteem in young children is fostered when adults recognize the young child's need for acceptance, self-determination, and authentic accomplishment. Self-esteem is also enhanced when adults provide challenging yet achievable tasks and curricula for young children. Self-esteem is supported through guidance that builds a sense of autonomy and competence, a sense of belonging and worth, and the knowledge that one's contribution to the family and classroom group is valued.

### Self-Esteem and Children with Special Needs

Children who are physically, emotionally, or cognitively challenged face numerous obstacles in growing up. They share the same needs for affection, acceptance, belonging, achievement, respect, and dignity as do other less challenged children. A common issue for young children with disabilities is the feeling of being different or being singled out for special treatment. Sensitive early childhood educators provide comfortable, accessible, user-friendly classroom environments, materials, and activities. These teachers structure the environments and play and work groups to facilitate dialogue, interaction, peer assistance, and mutuality. Promotion of group sensitivity,

*In inclusive classrooms, all children learn about disabilities and develop mutual respect.*

understanding, and acceptance is an important part of the teacher's inter-actions with class members. Setting age- and individually appropriate social and academic expectations is particularly important for the development of healthy self-concepts and positive self-regard.

## SOCIAL COMPETENCE

A definition of social competence is difficult to construct. The socialization process through which social competence emerges begins in the home and includes the values, beliefs, customs, and expected social behaviors of a particular culture. These cultural norms have been handed down from one generation to the next. Children are exposed to many socializing agents: family, siblings, extended family members, neighbors, caregivers, teachers, and the media. Socialization is influenced through observation of role models in many contexts. Awareness of cultural socialization values assists caregivers and teachers in relating respectfully to individual children and guides collaborations with parents when social behavioral issues arise.

## Social Cognition

**social cognition** the ability to understand the thoughts, intentions, and behaviors of oneself and others.

A major component of social competence is that of **social cognition**, which includes the ability to think intelligently about the effects of one's words and actions on others. The development of social cognition is a key focus in the guidance of young children. Helping aggressors understand that aggression hurts is essential to their ability to think about the feelings and perspectives of others. By the same token, when children behave in empathic and considerate ways, the positive feedback they receive from others facilitates their perspective taking.

In the vignette at the beginning of this chapter, Luke's attempts to interact with playmates reveal his emerging social interest. However, at this very early age, toddler egocentrism and lack of language necessary to negotiate social interactions deter his success. He obtains what he wants by simply taking it. Lacking language, his approach is physical. As yet, he has no notions of property rights or the effects of his behaviors on others. Because biting is faster than formulating words, it can become the toddler's means to an end, and it works!

While Luke's actions were hurtful and socially unacceptable, his intentions were not. Early childhood professionals recognize Luke's inability to ask for what he wants and his need to learn a more socially acceptable strategy. Luke's teacher addresses him firmly yet nonjudgmentally, "Biting hurts. I cannot let you hurt others (and she could add, . . . "nor will I let others hurt you"). Jeremy is playing with the truck now. When he is finished, I will help you ask for the truck. Here is a truck for you; or perhaps you would like to paint" (offering an alternative). Turning to Jeremy, who is still crying from the confrontation, "I know that hurt, Jeremy. I will help you wash your arm. You may play with the truck until you have finished. Luke did not mean to hurt you; he was trying to ask for the truck." After tending to the wound, the teacher coaches Jeremy, "When you have finished with the truck, give it to Luke to play with." The teacher then monitors and follows through on her promise to Luke, asking him if he wishes to play with the truck now. If he says "no," she accepts his choice without further ado.

As children get older they rely on social cognition in solving social interaction problems. Patrice, age seven, has been creating a school-safety poster with a small group of her classmates. Unfortunately, there is only one red marker, and the group has decided that the poster letters should all be red. Two members of the group begin to argue over who will use the red marker first. Disturbed over the delay, Patrice makes her way to another group whose poster is being created with finger paints. She asks, "May we borrow some of your markers?" to which the others who have no need for them at this time reply, "Yes." Jubilantly, proud of having solved a problem, Patrice returns to her group announcing, "I found some more red markers!" In this case, Patrice not only found a socially competent way to resolve the problem, but also relied upon her sense of initiative to do so. Patrice demonstrated emerging social competence. Had the teacher had to intervene, she may have asked the students to stop and think about a possible solution and then assisted as they forwarded various possibilities: turn taking, borrowing, or perhaps, negotiating another color scheme. In both Luke's and Patrice's case, the teacher plays an important role in facilitating social cognition, the ability to think about the problem and consider the needs and feelings of others.

## Making and Sustaining Friendships

Becoming socially competent with peers involves the additional skills of (1) initiating interactions, (2) maintaining ongoing relationships, and (3) resolving interpersonal conflicts (Asher, Renshaw, & Hymel, 1982; Ladd, 1990). While the goal of learning to interact successfully with others is not to gain popularity (in the adult sense of the term), there is something to be learned from studies of popular and unpopular children about their interaction strategies. Research has described characteristic interactions of these two groups of children (Roopnarine & Honig, 1985; Kemple, 1991).

Studies have found that children who are popular with their peers initiate entry into play groups by suggesting a joint activity or engaging others in conversation. They are better at perspective taking as demonstrated by their sense of timing and ability to unobtrusively find a role or place for themselves in the ongoing activity of others. On the other hand, children who are less popular tend to use vague approaches in an attempt to call attention to themselves as they move closer in proximity to a play group's ongoing activity. They may simply smile, stare, or gesture. They may taunt, brag, or act silly to call attention to themselves. These children need coaching and mediating assistance from adults who can help them find more effective strategies for initiating friendships. Central to this coaching is to help them consider the situation and the perspectives of others.

## Taking the Perspective of Others

The ability to take the perspective of others is a cognitive skill that develops slowly. Opportunities to play with others and to work in small cooperative groups expose children to different points of view and engage them in resolution of a variety of social problems. Social interactions engage children in dialogue and disputes and in comparison of viewpoints, and they provide the impetus for acknowledging that others have needs and wishes, often as strong as their own.

In this sense, there is value in conflict among children. Social interactions, both cooperative and conflicting, are essential if children are to develop autonomous thinking and the ability to take the perspective of another. Of course, when conflict is destructive or dangerous, adults intervene immediately, but disagreements between children provide a teachable moment in which children can test and refine their own skills in conflict resolution (Kohn, 1996). Professional early childhood educators become discerning about when to intervene, when to allow the children to "work it out," and when to mediate or coach. When allowed to resolve their own conflicts, children generally arrive at a mutually agreed upon solution. When adults intervene, one or more participants feel unfairly treated no matter how helpful the adult tried to be. Friendships can be cultivated through resolutions of conflicts (Rizzo, 1992). These friendships are often thwarted when adults are too eager to simply stop a conflict.

A number of studies have verified a link between peer relationships in early childhood and later adolescent and adult social adjustments and relationships (Hartup & Moore, 1990; Parker & Asher, 1987; Wentzel, 1991). Ladd (1990) found that kindergarten children who were rejected by their peers during the first two months of the school year developed less favorable perceptions of school, had higher levels of resistance to school attendance, and lower levels of school performance. This study and subsequent research underscores the need for early childhood professionals to support and mediate social interactions from the beginning as children are becoming integrated into group experiences (Birch & Ladd, 1997). We have discussed healthy personality development and social competence; we turn now to the third major goal of guidance—that of helping children develop moral competence.

## MORAL COMPETENCE

Moral competence in young children involves the ability to take the perspective of others; understanding intentions; developing notions of negligence, responsibility, and restitution; and assuming prosocial behaviors (empathy and altruism).

Children under age six are in a premoral stage in which they have little understanding of rules and their reasons. Play with others is presumed to be just for fun with no framework of rules for winning or agreements to cooperate. Around age four and five years, with increasing cognitive development and expanded opportunities to observe others, children become more conscious of rules and indeed, between the ages of six and ten years, become quite rule bound. They believe that rules are established by some superior power (God, parent, policeman, "the boss" [of the child care center or school, or other setting]), and must always be obeyed. At this age, children believe that breaking these absolute rules is reason for punishment and punishment should be swift.

At this stage, children do not understand intentions; therefore, they view most misdeeds on the basis of observable consequences, as in Piaget's example. Young children view the child who broke fifteen cups while doing a good deed as naughtier than the child who broke one cup while stealing jam (Piaget, 1932/1965). The young child's view of rules is egocentric and idiosyncratic. Young children have little notion that others might perceive the rule differently. Recall Regelio at the beginning of this chapter. Regelio's tattling is indicative of his rule-bound perceptions and level of emerging moral development. Piaget referred to this stage of moral development as one of **heteronomous morality** in which the individual follows the rules and wishes of others. The individuals are, in fact, governed by others.

Heteronomous morality (or absolutist reasoning) is due in part to typical egocentrism in young children and to their inability to separate their own subjective experiences from external events. In Regelio's instance, the teacher, after determining that no harm is forthcoming, can acknowledge Regelio's concern with something like "Thank you for remembering the rules" or "When we remember the rules, our class time together is more pleasant." With four- and five-year-old children and younger, who need more direct, concrete feedback, the teacher might respond, "You remembered the rule about drawing on your own paper. I will help Luke remember that rule, too." In responding in a manner that acknowledges the child's emerging moral development, the adult fosters moral thinking. When a child tattles, the opportunity to assist the child in perspective taking arises. Taking time to discuss the "infraction" from other points of view helps children formulate more prosocial understandings.

Unfortunately, many children in the United States are subjected to heteronomous classroom management practices from early childhood through high school. In heteronomous classrooms, the teacher establishes and enforces the rules and doles out rewards and punishments. Children are expected to conform blindly to the rules or suffer predetermined consequences. Rules and consequences are frequently posted in a prominent location in the classroom as a constant reminder. Such discipline practices run the risk of arresting moral development at its most immature stage and can result in adults whose behaviors lack autonomy, initiative, and prosocial relationships with others. In these classrooms, children learn to behave for external and tangible rewards (favor with teacher, stickers, stars, checks, smiley faces) rather than for intrinsic satisfaction. They often rebel, testing and challenging the rules and the rule makers. Clever children learn to "work the system" in their favor. Classroom management schemes based

**heteronomous morality** a morality that is led and governed by others rather than oneself.

**autonomous morality**
the ability and desire
to make moral deci-
sions based on one's
own convictions.

on rewards and punishment and on heteronomous expectations do not help
children become autonomous thinkers in which they make wise choices
based on internal convictions of the right thing to do (Kohn, 1996).

The move from heteronomous morality to **autonomous morality**
depends on cognitive maturation and the types of socializing experiences
children have had. As we shall see later in this chapter, when children are
treated with respect, given logical reasons for rules, have more egalitarian
(rather than power-assertive) relationships with their parents and teachers,
progress toward autonomous morality is fostered and children experience
the values of a democratic society. As Dewey proposed long ago, democratic classrooms provide the laboratory in which children practice the
tenets of democracy (Dewey, 1916/1966).

Autonomous morality emerges in environments in which respect and
cooperation are continually practiced and where children are engaged in
activities in which they construct their own moral convictions about relations with others (DeVries & Zan, 1995). If the long-term goal of moral
competence prevails, a better approach than the heteronomous classroom
described above is one in which children are provided many opportunities
to construct moral meaning from their experiences.

Setting the stage for the mental construction of moral meaning entails
the following:

- Reflective planning
- Taking the time to engage children in the establishment of class
  rules
- Discussing and understanding the reasons for each rule
- Guiding dialogue that leads to perspective-taking
- Helping children distinguishing between intent and accident
- Establishing relevant consequences that relate to the misdeeds them-
  selves
- Holding class meetings to discuss and resolve class issues
- Developing a climate that fosters mutual respect and prosocial
  behaviors
- Allowing choices and individual and group decision making
- Preserving the dignity and integrity of each participant

Only through these strategies do children have the types of experiences
that lead to autonomous thinking and the development of moral convictions. Through these types of classrooms, children learn to participate as a
constructive member of a group.

This type of teaching may seem like a very large order at first.
However, there are many opportunities each day for this type of teaching
to occur. Early childhood educators who focus on behaviors in this constructive way and create climates where social and moral competence can
emerge make a choice between creating peaceful, child-development-

oriented classrooms or classrooms in which they must focus their energy on monitoring misbehaviors and disagreements, enforcing the rules, and meting out consequences.

## Prosocial Development

Prosocial development is integral to social and moral competence. Research is plentiful on this topic. Studies have stressed that the more highly trained and stable the preschool staff is the lower the levels of aggression are among children in their classes (Park & Honig, 1991). According to Hartup (1989), children who are aggressive and disruptive, who are unable to sustain close relationships with other children, and who have difficulty finding acceptance among their peers are seriously at risk for adult maladjustments. Children who experience constructivist classrooms in which social and moral development are fostered resolve more of their conflicts and enjoy more friendly interactions with peers than do children who experience authoritarian classroom atmospheres (DeVries, Haney, & Zan, 1991). Where adult-directed classrooms were compared with classrooms that emphasized child initiations, more socially competent behaviors and fewer juvenile delinquency convictions were found at age fifteen years (Schweinhart, Weikart, & Larner, 1986).

Just these few illustrative studies point out the life-long value of providing opportunities for children to experience and develop prosocial behaviors. **Prosocial behavior** is defined as any action that benefits others. It includes behaviors such as showing compassion and providing comfort; sharing time, information, and resources; cooperating; helping by rescuing; and defending and removing cause for distress (Marion, 1999). Prosocial behaviors are altruistic and empathic. Altruism is defined as intentions to help others without expectation of rewards. Empathy is the ability to vicariously experience the feelings of others.

Children become prosocial when:

- They themselves are treated with respect, warmth, and caring.
- Adults use authoritative guidance to instruct and inform their behaviors.
- Expectations for prosocial behavior are clearly stated and in words that convey what prosocial behavior is, such as "share," "cooperate," "help," and "comfort."
- Classroom rules and guidance emphasize cooperation over competition.
- Anger management and conflict resolution are modeled and coached in a constructive way.
- Materials are developmentally appropriate and in sufficient supply.
- Group consensus is sought in rule making and issues that involve the whole class.

*The only way for us to live together successfully as a human species is to figure out how to deal with diversities of all sorts. If young children learn to do this in their small classroom group, perhaps they will be able to expand it to larger groups in society. By giving children at an early age opportunities to develop sociomoral competence, we may avoid their development into adults who know only how to mindlessly submit to or rebel against the rules of people in power. By fostering early sociomoral development of children, we may put them on the path to becoming the kinds of adults who can take up the responsibilities of democratic citizenship and work toward equity in human relationships.*
*—Rheta DeVries & Betty Zan*

**prosocial behavior** actions intended to benefit others without expectation of rewards.

- They are engaged in acts of altruism through class projects, such as drawing pictures and writing notes to children absent due to illness or planting flowers in the school or center yard.
- Discussions of diversity and special needs are frank, yet sensitive, positive, unbiased, and informative.
- They are exposed to many prosocial models through literature and audio and video media, class visitors, and school or center personnel.
- They are assigned authentic responsibilities that contribute to the well-being of the class, such as assisting a new class member in becoming acquainted with others or learning the routines; mentoring and assisting a classmate who needs help with a task; assuming responsibility for watering and caring for plants, feeding and caring for class pets, watching for unsafe materials or surroundings, such as crayons on the floor that someone could slip on, chairs that are askew that could create a traffic hazard, broken toys or equipment that could injure someone, and so on.
- They are provided authentic feedback relating to the benefits and pleasure of others when prosocial behaviors occur.

There are obviously long-term advantages to the group when prosocial behaviors are encouraged. Children themselves benefit from the positive responses and interactions that result from their prosocial efforts, which, in turn, encourages further positive interactions with others. Ultimately society itself benefits when its citizens are more prosocial.

## STYLES OF CAREGIVING

By observing preschool children and rating their behaviors according to degree of impetuosity, self-reliance, aggressiveness, withdrawal, and self-control, Diana Baumrind (1966, 1967, 1971, 1972) has classified them into three groups:

1. *Competent* children, who are self-reliant, self-controlled, explorative, cooperative, happy, and content
2. *Withdrawn* children, who are distrustful, fearful, slow to warm up to other children, solitary in their play, often aimless, and frequently sad
3. *Immature* children, who are impulsive, lacking self-control and self-reliance, often aggressive, and the least inclined to explore their environments

When Baumrind observed these same children at ages eight and nine, she found that these characteristics tended to persist overtime. She interviewed their parents to determine how their child-rearing practices dif-

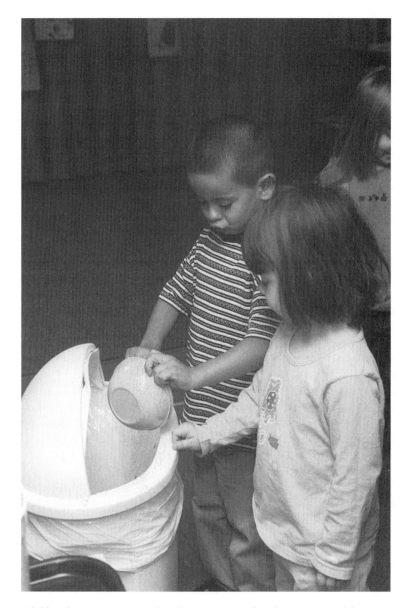

*Children become prosocial when they are assigned authentic responsibilities such as cleaning up after meals.*

fered. She found three patterns of parent control that corresponded with the patterns of behavior observed in the preschoolers and in their later behaviors.

Baumrind found that children who were categorized as *competent* had parents who were controlling and demanding, yet warm, rational, responsive, and receptive to their child's communications; These parents were encouraging and valued verbal give-and-take and respected, their children's interests and individual capabilities. These parents encouraged autonomy, independence, and self-control. Baumrind referred to this type of parenting as **authoritative**.

Parents of children classified as *withdrawn* tended to be detached, controlling, less warm and encouraging to their children. These parents attempted to shape and control children's behavior and attitudes along a set of standards for conduct that were often absolute. Unquestioning obedience; respect for authority, and accepting parents' or teacher's word as always right was expected. She labeled this type of parenting **authoritarian**.

Parents of *immature* children were noncontrolling and nondemanding though they were warm and communicative most of the time. These parents made few demands for responsibility and orderly behavior. Children were given greater latitude in regulating their own behaviors with little guidance by which to learn appropriate behaviors. Baumrind labeled this group of parents as **permissive**.

While these represent dominant patterns of parenting (caregiving and teaching), no one adult fits a particular category all of the time. There are probably elements of each of these in all of us. Hence, adults need to be reflective about their own ways of interacting with children. This is important on two fronts: (1) adults can assess more critically their expectations and responses to children and their families and determine if modification is needed, and (2) adults can consider the long-term effects of certain caregiving and teaching styles on child behavior and competence. Developing an authoritative style of caregiving contributes to a psychologically safe learning environment for young children and fosters the types of social and cognitive development that leads to social and moral competence.

## Facilitating Social and Moral Competence through Constructive Guidance

Authoritative guidance is commensurate with the types of interactions described throughout this textbook. It is developmentally appropriate, and it leads to the types of social and moral thinking fostered in constructivist classrooms. As such, we refer to this type of guidance as **constructive guidance**, for it both *instructs* and sets the stage for individual children to *construct* meaning from their experiences. When guidance issues arise, early childhood professionals engage children in thoughtful and meaningful discussion of the problem and exploration of possible solutions. They guide children toward self-control as children begin to think about their actions and the actions of others.

**authoritative caregiving** guidance that provides reasonable, age-appropriate expectations and logical explanations for expected behaviors; differs from authoritarian or permissive caregiving.

**authoritarian caregiving** guidance in which adults expect unquestioning obedience and apply rigid standards for behavior; relies on punishments and rewards.

**permissive caregiving** a noncontrolling, undemanding relationship with children, in which they are given little guidance and few rules of conduct.

**constructive guidance** developmentally appropriate adult-child relationships that facilitate the construction of social and moral meaning, leading to higher levels of understanding and competence in interacting with others.

Children learn to behave, not because they anticipate rewards or punishment, but because they enjoy the outcomes of positive interactions and they have learned that certain behaviors serve the best interest of self and others while other behaviors do not.

We distinguish constructive guidance from **discipline** because the latter often denotes external control of child behaviors that may employ negative and harmful ways of interacting with young children. By the same token, the term *classroom management* is somewhat troubling in that it also implies preconceived negative notions about children. *Classroom management* carries the connotation of *controlling* rather than *instructing*, as though children cannot be taught appropriate behaviors and to arrive at acceptable rules through guided class meetings and consensus. Discipline and classroom management, as conceptualized here, generally address short-term goals.

Classroom management often implies rigid rules and the use of rewards and punishment to coerce children into following them. While quick action

**discipline** adult-child relationships that may or may not be positive, developmentally appropriate, or instructive; generally infers external control of child behavior.

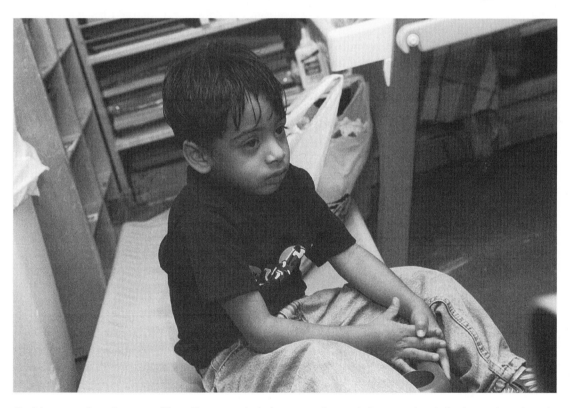

*Punishment such as time-out seldom, if ever, results in long-term changes in inappropriate behaviors and can impede the child's development of self-control.*

and firmness may be needed to stop behaviors that are dangerous or to assist children with out-of-bounds emotional outbursts or perhaps serious behavioral disturbances, such approaches are not as effective in building self-control that emanates from within the child (Kohn, 1996). Experts suggest that certain reward and punishment strategies typical in today's classrooms, while they may address immediate issues and short-term goals, fail to achieve appropriate child development goals (Kohn, 1996; Nelsen, Erwin, & Duffy, 1995). Instructive guidance addresses short- and long-term emotional, social, and moral goals and enlists the child's emerging cognitive abilities.

It is the authors' opinion that children are not well served when guidance is perceived as a set of rules to which all must blindly comply or as a system of rewards and punishments from which children are supposed to extrapolate "correct" behaviors. Nor are children well served when adults seek simple recipes for the handling of specific types of behaviors ("What do you do if a child . . . ?") Rather, professional educators ask, "How might I help shift the **locus of control** from me (the adult) to the child?" Constructive guidance then places greater responsibility on the child to learn and control her behaviors and interactions with others. Shifting the locus of control helps adults focus on helping children grow in social cognition and prosocial behaviors rather than correcting or reprimanding.

Constructive guidance is nurturing, supportive, and satisfying to both children and their teachers. A relationship between adults and children that accepts childhood behaviors for what they represent—a particular age and stage, level of understanding, portrayal of past experiences, and indications of emerging capabilities—is essential in early childhood care and education programs.

By contrasting the different approaches of two early childhood teachers, the following illustrates how one teacher shifts the locus of control from the adult to the children. In this contrast you will also see some of the differences between constructive authoritative guidance and authoritarian/power assertive approaches.

### Classroom A

The children in Teacher A's prekindergarten class have just finished their lunch, and she is gathering them around her in preparation for story reading time. As the children assemble, she instructs each one to sit "with your legs crossed, put your hands in your lap, and look at me. Then I'll know when you are ready to listen." Children wait in this position until all have assembled, then she begins to read the story. Taylor, a bit sleepy, stretches his legs behind him and assumes a tummy down, head resting on his hands and elbows position, yet continues to listen to the story. Teacher A says to him, "Taylor, how do we sit to listen to the

**locus of control**
relates to whether an individual is led or controlled by others or by oneself.

story?" Taylor reluctantly resumes an "upright, legs crossed" position. However, as Teacher A resumes the story, he begins to lean on Mandy, who is seated next to him. Mandy resists angrily, saying, "Get off of me!" and Taylor retorts, "I'm not going to be your friend." Teacher A firmly puts the story book down, stands and walks over to Taylor, takes him by the arm, and pulls him toward the timeout chair. "If you can't listen to the story with the rest of us, you will just sit here until I tell you when you can get up."

*Classroom B*

The children have just completed lunch and are putting away lunch boxes, discarding trash, and wiping the tables clean, then washing their hands. As the children are busy, cleaning up after lunch, Teacher B stations herself near the tape player on which she is playing familiar songs for sing-along while the tasks are completed. As children assemble for story time, she continues to sing along and leads a few finger plays until everyone has assembled. Early in the year, Teacher B taught the children about surrounding themselves with personal space and respecting the personal space of others. Today, Megan had a book request, and so Teacher B read her choice, *The Very Hungry Caterpillar* (Eric Carle, 1969). The children assumed comfortable positions for listening, some sat with feet out in front of them, others with legs crossed, others in a reclining position with a pillow, still others chose to sit in chairs around the periphery of the group. Jackson wandered over to a window and stared dreamily through it, but seemed to maintain interest in the story. Soon, he became interested in the story's pictures and the group's happy chanting of the repetitive refrain, ". . . but he was still hungry!" and wandered back to take a place where he could also participate. In the meantime, Regan began to talk to a classmate, distracting others around her. Teacher B, continuing to display the book's pictures, said firmly but warmly, "Regan, talking disturbs others. Please wait until we have finished the story to visit with Chandra." Teacher B continues the story without incident.

What contrasts do you see in these scenarios? If you were four years old, which class would you prefer? If your child were to be in one of these settings, which would you choose? Why? Let us talk about each.

> Teacher A allowed her needs for order and control to supersede children's need for physical comfort and a mind-engaging, pleasant storytime.
>
> Teacher A expected Taylor's unquestioning compliance and did not take into consideration what his body language might be conveying, such as an uncomfortable sitting position, fatigue or sleepiness, or perhaps boredom with the story.
>
> Teacher A failed to assist children in managing their own behaviors by maintaining the role of "instruction giver."

Teacher A did not consider the effects of public reprimand on both Taylor and the other members of the group.

Teacher A allowed anger to enter into her interaction with Taylor, presenting a negative model for handling emotions.

In contrast, Teacher B demonstrated a higher level of competence in guiding her class:

Teacher B placed more emphasis on facilitating individual and group behaviors and placed no undo emphasis on seating. Having taught the children to respect personal space of others, the children had learned how to seat themselves comfortably without disturbing their classmates.

Teacher B used an effective transition technique to guide children from lunch cleanup to storytime. By stationing herself in the story-reading area and singing familiar songs and reciting familiar finger plays, the children could pick up on familiar cues and redirect their own behaviors toward the next routine.

Teacher B acknowledged Jackson's need for time to perhaps reflect and to make his way to the next routine. Sometimes it just takes a little longer to make a transition.

Teacher B employed perspective-taking instruction by reminding Regan that talking disturbs other listeners.

By allowing Megan to hear the story of her choice, Teacher B demonstrated her encouragement of and respect for child choice.

## PRINCIPLES OF CONSTRUCTIVIST APPROACHES TO GUIDANCE

Constructive guidance takes time, planning, knowledge, and skill. The following principles of constructive guidance help describe knowledge and skills essential to instructive guidance with young children. Think again about Christalyn, Luke, LaDonna, Regelio, and Patrice, whose behaviors were described at the beginning of this chapter, as we work through what teachers need to know and be able to do in order to facilitate healthy personality and social and moral competence:

*Early childhood professional educators and caregivers are empathic and are able to view situations from each child's point of view.*

Luke's inability to share has little to do with selfishness, but a lot to do with how he perceives his personal belongings or objects that are in his possession when he is being urged to share. Infants and toddlers view their belongings as extensions of themselves. Expecting them to share their toys or other possessions is like asking them to give up a part of themselves. This perception of toys as extensions of themselves explains why young children frequently fight over toy possession. The question the adult must ask is, "Is it absolutely essential for Luke to share his toy?" Usually the answer is "No." More helpful in developing friendly interactions among toddlers is providing duplicate items to facilitate play and shared experiences. Where providing duplicates is not a practical choice, the empathic adult mediates with a potential solution: "Luke wants to hold his teddy bear. Let's see if we can find you another stuffed animal to hold. We have several and you can choose the one you like." Then, "Know what?, . . . The two of you can sit in the rocking chairs together, and talk or sing to your teddy bear and bunny."

*Early Childhood professionals understand egocentrism in young children.*

Young children believe that others see the world from the same point of view as they do. When Christalyn throws objects from her crib and they are playfully retrieved and returned to her to throw again, she has created a pleasurable game that brings others to her in a playful mode, while at the same time she has discovered what happens to toys when they are dropped from the crib and an understanding of cause and effect is emerging. She does not understand the adult's point of view should they tire or be unable to retrieve the thrown object. Hence, she cries in frustration when the game is terminated. By the same token, when three-year-old Jason proudly announces to his nursery school teacher, "We have a new television at our house," she responds with enthusiasm, but before she can ask him to describe the new television set, he asks, "Did you see it, too?" He does not realize that the teacher has not just had his same experience. This egocentrism explains the young child's early inability to take the perspective of others.

*Early childhood professionals understand the young child's limited capacity to take the perspective of another.*

In LaDonna's situation, she has mentally created a sociodramatic play theme in which she wants others to participate. Her inability to perceive the perspectives of her playmates who do not hold her same mental scheme interferes with the free flow of their sociodramatic play. Thoughtful adults who understand LaDonna's frustration and that of the other participants mediate the play theme by first observing and listening to each participant's point of view, then offering suggestions on how each might fit into the play theme more successfully. Perhaps additional props are needed, or a reshuffling of individual roles, or a new direction for the unfolding "story."

*Early childhood professionals understand the young child's limited memory capacity.*

Memory includes two abilities: to recognize and to recall. Young children are better able to recognize than to recall. For instance, it is easier for very young children to retell a story just read to them if the pages of the book are slowly turned to reveal the pictures in sequence. Kindergarten and first-grade students may recognize their name in print, but not be able to write their names with all of the letters in correct sequence without a print model.

For young children to remember daily routines such as cleanup times, storytimes, rest or nap times, outdoor play, and certain rules of behaviors, they need prompts and repetition before these routines are stored in long-term memory. Frequent reminders, daily group planning, restating expectations, rebus charts depicting daily schedules and routines, picture and print labels for storage and display of materials, and songs and finger plays associated with particular events or expectations, are child-friendly ways of helping children remember.

Thoughtful early childhood caregivers and teachers provide various visual, auditory, and other sensory information to help children remember. They give directions in small increments at a time; for example, instead of saying, "Put your books away now, and go to the restroom, wash your hands, get your lunch, and line up," moments before, the teacher might say, "We need to prepare to go to lunch; finish reading your books." Moments later, she will instruct "Put your books away and go to the restroom." This is subsequently followed with "Be sure to wash your hands, then get your lunch." She then walks to the classroom door to signal where to line up and summons children to her as they have completed the previous tasks. As children get older, they develop mental strategies for remembering, such as repeating something to themselves over and over until they have memorized it or associating new information with prior knowledge or experience, at which time they will be able to recall a series of three to five instructions.

The ability for children to retain information in short- or long-term memory increases with age. Information of the past few minutes is stored in short-term memory and usually lasts only a few seconds. When children have little or no knowledge of or prior experience with the new information, they seldom store it in long-term memory unless it has had a strong impact on their sensory perceptions or their emotions or has created some form of **cognitive dissonance**. For instance, when a parent asks a preschooler, "What did you do at preschool today?" the most likely answer is "Nothing," or "I don't know," or "We played." There may have been some very important learning events that took place, and over time these events will, indeed, be stored in long-term memory. But let's say a child who has been forbidden to play in the

**cognitive dissonance**
a mental dilemma in which new information is discordant or at variance with one's current understanding.

creek behind his home finds that another child brought some tadpoles to school to share with the class. At the end of the day the child would most likely volunteer the information about what happened at school today before asked. Cognitive dissonance caused this event to be stored in long-term memory.

As well, young children need a lot of repetition. Daily routines and transition signals that are predictable, behavior expectations that are frequently reiterated, teachers who are consistent role models, and learning events that are extended over several days, or perhaps, weeks help children to develop a store of remembered information.

*Professional early childhood educators understand that young children do not make distinctions between intent and accident.*

Grant, stumbling over a stray crayon on the floor, accidentally knocked over Tyrone's block building. Tyrone reacted by angrily wrestling Grant to the floor. Tyrone, at an early level of social cognition, did not understand that Grant had no intentions of knocking over his block building. Incidents such as this occur frequently during the course of the day in a group of young children, providing opportunities for the teacher to help children make distinctions between accident and intent. Again, learning to take the perspective of others—in this case, recognizing that a crayon on the floor caused Grant to stumble—can be taught by a skilled adult who then can help both boys regain their composure and positive feelings toward one another. Certainly, forbidding hurtful, aggressive behavior is called for in this incident; but at the same time, understanding of Tyrone's perspective helps the teacher know to teach him to look for other causes for the mishap and how to respond differently when such accidents occur. In addition, the teacher can help both students learn to verbalize what happened to each other and the importance of considering the feelings and perspectives of others. It is a teachable moment for practicing conflict resolution. You will be introduced to additional conflict resolution strategies in chapter 9.

*Professional early childhood educators understand the role of authentic feedback.*

Previously, we suggested that young children develop self-esteem from authentic achievement. Individual and group achievements deserve honest and authentic responses. Too often the praise children receive is artificial, contrived, and manipulative, conveying inappropriate messages that fail to foster genuine feelings of self-esteem or lasting behavior changes.

Indeed, the wrong types or overuse of praise undermines self-esteem, respect, and moral competence (Kohn, 1996). Children do not need smiley faces, stickers, class applause, hollow praise, "Good job," or manipulative "I like the way . . ." and other shallow types of feedback. Far more effective in facilitating self-directing behavior and motivation is

*Skilled early childhood educators help children learn to negotiate and verbally resolve their conflicts.*

feedback that is connected and reasoned: "You worked at that a long time, and you succeeded in finding out what floats and what doesn't float. Perhaps tomorrow, I can find for you some other experiments to try." "That was really challenging, managing to stay on the balance beam all the way across, but you did it." "You have a good start there on your clay sculpture. What do you plan to do next to your sculpture?" "Look at Josh's face; he is so pleased that you let him play with your truck for a while. It makes people feel good when others share. I bet it makes you feel good, too." "I am concerned about the way you are using the hula hoop. You could hurt yourself or someone else. How can you play with it safely?" Authentic feedback considers the child's feelings and the message they take from it. It is respectful, constructive, and nurturing. Most importantly, it is ethical: it does not threaten, punish, embarrass, or manipulate. Authentic feedback facilitates the three main goals of guidance: healthy personality development, social competence, and moral competence.

*Professional early childhood educators recognize that children with and without disabilities need classroom social and emotional climates that build acceptance, a sense of belonging, and psychological security.*

In an inclusive class, all children can learn about disabilities and develop mutually respectful interactions. Patrice, whose juvenile rheumatoid arthritis often causes severe discomfort, has difficulty maintaining attention and is often rejected by her classmates. On an occasion when several children were dancing to the music of a new recording, Patrice attempted to join them. Megan watched her a moment, then said, "You can't do this. You can't turn around like we do." Mr. Martinez, their teacher, observed this encounter and joined the group in following the music for the remainder of the dance. Afterwards, in Patrice's presence, he said kindly to Megan, "I noticed that you thought Patrice could not turn around. It is true that Patrice cannot turn around the way you do. It hurts her legs when she tries to turn too fast. She enjoys dancing just like all of us do. Do you want to ask Patrice what types of music she enjoys when dancing?" Patrice responds matter-of-factly, "I can't do the Hokey-Pokey, but I like that music where we play with the scarves." The conversation continues between the two girls after Mr. Martinez moves away:

**Megan**: Do your legs really hurt?

**Patrice**: Sometimes. Sometimes, I'm afraid I will fall down.

**Megan**: You want to play with clay now?

Mr. Martinez will make it a point to select several developmentally appropriate books to share with the whole class about disabilities. Through constructive guidance Mr. Martinez allowed Megan to express her curiosity about Patrice's physical disability in a sensitive way and one that helped both girls communicate in a positive way. By realizing that others in the class may also have curiosities and misunderstandings, he created a positive atmosphere in which learning about special needs could occur.

The next time a group of children were dancing, some of the children took the initiative to move chairs out of the way to make more room. Mr. Martinez created small cooperative groupings from time to time to give class members opportunities to get to know Patrice and for her to know them. In time Patrice became less concerned about alleged privileges others were receiving and developed a stronger sense of belonging. She was more enthusiastic upon arrival each morning, and her social interactions increasingly became more positive. As the days went by, Mr. Martinez continued to provide opportunities for children to know one another in more personal and empathic ways.

*Professional early childhood educators foster self-control in children through instructive and positive interactions.*

Early childhood professionals recognize that self-control develops gradually and unevenly. They provide coaching, assistance, positive guidance, and cognitive engagement to facilitate the development of self-control.

Five-year-old Regelio was having difficulty getting along with other children in the kindergarten class. He took toys away from other children, pushed children out of his way, and interrupted whoever was speaking during group times whenever he had something to say. As an only child, he had had few experiences with other children. For Regelio, learning to exist in an environment with fifteen other children was not easy. Ms. Sanchez understood that Regelio was not purposefully being mean to his classmates. He simply did not know what to do in many situations. Ms. Sanchez decided to do whatever possible to help Regelio develop social and moral competence.

Every morning as Regelio entered the classroom she reminded him of the behaviors that were expected during morning group time. This verbal reminder helped Regelio begin to think about the children who sat near him during morning share time. Just before center time, Ms. Sanchez reminded Regelio privately that she expected to see him cooperating with other children and they discussed what cooperation would look like in the center that he chose. When Regelio did get angry with others, Ms. Sanchez took the time to talk with him about the emotions he was feeling. She helped Regelio label those emotions and acquire new, more verbal ways of expressing feelings of anger and frustration.

Initially, Regelio's behaviors toward the other children did not change much. By the third week of school, he could echo Mr. Sanchez's words, "I don't like it when you won't let me have the blocks" or "Cooperating means I let other people play the 'daddy' sometimes." In a few more weeks, Regelio's behaviors were becoming more acceptable to his classmates. He repeated the words his teacher used to describe acceptable behavior to regulate his own behavior. Regelio's teacher could have used time-out to punish him for pushing children and taking toys away from them, but this would not have helped him learn alternative strategies or to regulate his own behavior. Ms. Sanchez will continue to observe Regelio's behaviors and provide supportive feedback for his efforts—a nod, wink, smile, or private word of constructive praise.

## Summary

Young children do not come into the world knowing how to interact with others. Healthy personalities and social and moral competence emerge in fairly predictable stages that often include unacceptable behaviors. Difficulties in managing emotions and engaging in meaningful interactions with others reflect individual personalities and temperaments, immaturity and inexperience, and often suggest possible mitigating circumstances that have interfered with healthy development. The reasons for unsuccessful social interactions are as numerous as are the behavioral difficulties emanating therefrom. However, most social difficulties result from age-related characteristics including egocentrism and the inability to take the perspective of others, age-related perceptual abilities, faulty reasoning, limited impulse control, and inadequate language skills. Most social difficulties relate to reactive behaviors in which children act before they think, difficulties in negotiating and communicating requests and needs, and difficulties in initiating and maintaining friendships.

Any discussion of developmentally appropriate programs for young children cannot ignore the critical importance of interactions that promote healthy personality development and social and moral competence. As early childhood education professionals assess their goals for both individuals and the group, they consider the social and emotional context(s) in which interactions among children and between children and adults take place. Theories of personality development, social cognition, and social competence are helpful to professional early childhood educators as they think about appropriate guidance techniques. Contemporary research on learning affirms the importance of healthy personality, social cognition, prosocial orientations, and social and moral competence to optimal learning. Finally, numerous research studies reveal that the types of caregiving and interactions that infants and young children experience can have lasting effects that influence later adult social behaviors and relationships with others.

## Reflections

**1.** Reflect upon the types of guidance you received both at home and in school contexts. What types of positive and negative experiences did you have? What effect do you think these had on your self-concept, self-esteem, self-confidence, and interactions with others?

**2.** If children must learn self-control from within, how successful can external rewards and punishment be? What types of adolescent and adult behaviors might emerge from a childhood guided primarily by external controls?

**3.** What is your definition of moral behavior? Discuss your definition with others. How many different definitions of morality were identified in this discussion?

## Field Experiences

**1.** Select five children ranging in age from infant/toddler to age eight, as with the opening vignette. Observe their behaviors in various contexts: home, baby-sitter, caregiver, classroom, playground, or wherever possible. Write several anecdotes that portray the observed child's ways of interacting with others, both adults and children. What emerging psychosocial development could you discern?

**2.** Visit several early childhood classrooms and observe how caregivers and teachers establish rules and limits and how these are taught to children. Describe several situations in which adults used constructive guidance to facilitate social and moral competence. How did teachers support healthy personality development as defined by Erikson and Elkind?

**3.** Interview several families to determine their styles of caregiving. How do parents describe their behavioral (or social and moral) goals for their children? What are the common social and moral goals shared by the families you interviewed? How compatible are these goals with the goals outlined in this chapter?

## Case Studies

### "... Just Hit Him Back!"

Derek is in lay terms "a scrapper." He is quick to anger and quick to blame others for conflicts and mishaps. Today, Derek has spent considerable time and effort building an elaborate roadway with the blocks in the block center. It has bridges and ramps, a service station, an office building, ("... where my Daddy works"), and a fast food drive-in restaurant. He is intense, focused, and proud of his work.

Jason, who has been working with play dough at a nearby table notices that the hermit crab across the room has managed to reach the top of a branch in its aquarium and is about to fall to the floor. He rises so quickly from his chair that it falls backward knocking over Derek's office building and scattering his roadway blocks. As Jason is rushing to rescue the hermit crab, Derek "tackles" him, bringing him to the floor hitting and shouting "You broke my building!"

Yesterday, Derek hit a classmate for getting in the lunch line in front of him; and the day before he threatened a classmate with "I'm going to beat you up if you don't let me play with you."

Derek's teacher requests a conference with his parents. She asks for guidance and insights into Derek's angry, aggressive behaviors. The conversation reveals that Derek has a teen-age brother whom he greatly loves and admires, but who teases him often and intensely. The older brother seldom allows Derek to "win" when they play games or sports together and taunts Derek when he loses. Further, Derek's older brother has advised him "... not to let anyone pick on you . . ." and ". . . if someone hits you — you just hit them back."

## What to Do?

How can or should Derek's teacher respond to this information? What does Derek's behavior reveal about his social conventional understandings? What can Derek's teacher do within the classroom context to help Derek learn more appropriate interaction skills?

### Age Two and Misunderstood

When Kari was two years old, she was frequently punished by her parents for her negative behaviors, toileting accidents, inability to share her toys with playmates, and frequent spills. Her behaviors caused her parents extreme frustration, and she was frequently reprimanded and sent to her room or a time-out place. Her behaviors did not improve over time; instead she began to burst into tantrums and crying with little provocation.

In preschool her teacher found Kari's unhappy and negative behaviors particularly frustrating and she too punished Kari often, sometimes reprimanding her in front of her classmates and having her "sit out" of special projects and activities. Her social skills were awkward and strained, and consequently, Kari was not a sought-after playmate.

When Kari entered kindergarten she had difficulty making friends and was quite slow establishing a trusting relationship with her teacher. She displayed a tendency to avoid or ignore adults and exhibited extremes in behavior from giddy and silly to morose and negative.

Kari's psychosocial needs are profound and her chances for success with school related tasks and behavior expectations are at risk.

## What to Do?

What does this scenario reveal about the effects of early experiences on development and later behaviors? How might the parents have applied child development knowledge to their interactions with their two-year-old? Did the preschool teacher make mistakes in her interactions with Kari? What might she have done to advance more positive psychosocial outcomes? What types of experiences need to be provided for Kari to help her learn and use more positive and productive interaction behaviors? Can Kari's psychosocial difficulties interfere with her cognitive development and learning? If so, in what ways?

## Further Reading

Beaty, J. J. (1999). *Prosocial guidance for the preschool child*. Columbus, OH: Merrill/Prentice Hall.

Beaty, J. J. (1995). *Converting conflicts in preschool.* Fort Worth, TX: Harcourt Brace.

Brazelton, T. B., & Greenspan, S. I. (2000). *The irreducible needs of children: What every child must have to grow, learn, and flourish.* Cambridge, MA: Perseus Publishing Books.

Kohn, A. (1993). *Punished by rewards: The trouble with gold stars, incentive plans, A's, praise and other bribes.* Boston: Houghton Mifflin.

Levine, M. (2002). *A mind at a time.* New York: Simon & Schuster.

Nelsen, J., Lott, L., & Glenn, H. S. (2000). *Positive discipline in the classroom: Developing mutual respect, cooperation and responsibility in your classroom* (3rd ed.). (The Positive Discipline Series). Roseville, CA: Prima Publishing.

Oddone A. (2002). Promoting resilience in an "at-risk" world. *Childhood Education, 78,* 274–277.

Sylwester, R. (2000). *A biological brain in a cultural classroom: Applying biological research to classroom management.* Thousand Oaks, CA: Corwin Press.

Vance, E., & Weaver, P. J. (2002). *Class meetings: Young children solving problems together.* Washington, DC: National Association for the Education of Young Children.

## Helpful Web Sites

### Child Abuse Prevention

http://childabuse.com
*An Internet center for professionals working in the field of child abuse and neglect. Provides information on prevention and intervention of child abuse and an index of services and related organizations.*

### Frank Porter Graham Child Development Center

www.fpg.unc.edu/
*A multidisciplinary center for the study of young children and families, child care, child health and suggests educational strategies with a focus on risk factors and developmental problems.*

### Child Mental Health Foundations and Agencies Network (FAN)

www.nimh.nih.gov/childhp/collabor.html
*The Web site provides access to the report, A Good Beginning: Sending America's children to school with the social and emotional competence they need to succeed.*

### National Center for Early Development and Learning

www.ncedl.org
*Located at the University of North Carolina at Chapel Hill, under the Research and Development Centers Program administered by the U.S.*

*Department of Education Office of Educational Research and Improvement, this site provides articles and research briefs on numerous topics of importance to the early childhood profession.*

Check the Online Resources™ for expert practitioners' responses to each case study.

For additional information on teaching young children, visit our Web site at **http://www.earlychilded.delmar.com**

# CHAPTER 9

## *Creating Communities of Learners*

*Early Childhood Principle* Early childhood educators recognize that young children learn best within a community of learners where every member is valued and treated equitably and accepts responsibility for creating this community.

Learning to work and play in large and small groups is an important task for young children during the early childhood years. Adults help facilitate this learning process in many different ways. In high-quality early childhood programs, adults purposefully model the behaviors they want to foster in young children—prosocial behaviors, respect for everyone, assisting others who need help, and learning together. Early childhood educators use different strategies to help children learn how to treat each other, how to speak respectfully to each other, and how to function as a community. In learning to work as a community of learners, children develop close relationships with each other and learn to help each other socially and cognitively.

*After reading this chapter, you should be able to:*
- Discuss the concept of a community of caring learners.
- Describe the adult's role in helping foster relationships among children.
- Discuss how early childhood educators help young children learn to resolve conflict.
- Describe the multiple uses of class meetings.
- Discuss shared learning among young children and how adults facilitate this learning.

**S**ix people sit around a kitchen table finishing a breakfast of toast and scrambled eggs. Ricardo, the eighteen-month-old, wants his toast cut into little squares. Joyce and Jessica, the two two-year-olds, won't eat their eggs without catsup. The four-year-old, Mario, wants grape jelly, and the five-year-old, James, wants strawberry jam. One woman, Toni fields all the food requests and generally tries to keep the peace as five young children eat breakfast and talk most of the time. The conversation—although disjointed with comments about the food—is centered on going to the park later that morning. The children talk about who is going to slide, who wants to swing, and who will climb on the climbing equipment. The older children talk about climbing the cargo nets and playing pirates from their ship—the platforms linked with steps. The two-year-olds talk about playing in the big sand box and keep repeating, "We'll take shovels and buckets." They go as a group to the park twice a week and are always excited about these outings.

As Toni clears the table and cleans the kitchen, James pushes the play button on the tape player and sounds of Raffi fill the den. All the children choose something different to do: pull up to the window and look out at the flower garden, look through a tub of books, dance to the music, put together a puzzle, and string beads. These first choices change quickly and children are on to other activities. This hum of activity continues for forty-five minutes as Toni interacts with the children as they play. She "drinks" a cup of pretend coffee that Jessica brings to her, sings the familiar tune of "Baby Beluga" with the two older children, and helps build a block tower. She cuddles the younger children when they climb into her lap and reads *Pat the Bunny* (Kunhardt, 1968) with two of the younger children. She changes diapers, helps Joyce and Jessica settle a disagreement on who could play with the nesting cups, and turns the tape over when it stops. She helps Mario turn puzzle pieces until they fit together, talking about what she is thinking as she turns puzzle pieces and looks for spaces the piece might fit. She rolls a large ball to Ricardo and pushes it back after he has tried to push it to her, chanting "First to you, then to me." It is a busy morning, filled with a myriad of activities that meet the needs of the age ranges of the children in her care.

This could be a typical morning of a mother and a large family. However, the mother in this home only has one child, Mario. She is a family child care home provider who cares for four children while their parents work. Her work day begins at 7:00 A.M. when the first parent brings her child to the private residence that serves as a child care facility and continues until 6:00 P.M. when the last parent arrives to pick up his child. Throughout the day, this family child care home provider feeds, comforts, and cares for five children. Because she has chosen child care as her work, she is more aware of how children learn and purposefully creates environments with the five children in mind. She also selects learning materials to place in the environment for the children to choose and facilitates the children's play with those materials and with each other. She is particularly careful to work on strengthening her relationship with each child and the relationships that were forming among the children. Toni's emphasis on relationships helps create a sense of community among the children for whom she cares.

## COMMUNITIES OF LEARNERS

A community of learners is more than just a group of children who spend time together. In a community of learners, relationships between adults and children are respectful and caring. The ways that people treat each other are considered to be just as important as any other component of the program. The adults take an active role in helping children develop these special relationships (Charney, 2001).

### Adult Leadership in Creating Communities of Learners

A community of learners does not develop without purposeful work by teachers. From the first day of school, teachers behave in certain ways in order to model the behaviors they want to foster in their students. They help children see each other as resources. They teach language that supports respectful relationships among adults and other children. They offer multiple opportunities for children to learn how to solve problems and make decisions that are good for the whole group.

### Modeling Behaviors

Teachers are always modeling behaviors whether they are conscious of this or not. In almost everything early childhood educators do during the time they are with children, the children are observing what they do and how they do it. A teacher models prosocial and learner behaviors in the way she talks to children and other adults, by joining children as they work in centers, and by using and commenting on specific skills that children in the age group could learn.

#### Prosocial Behaviors

In chapter 8, prosocial behaviors were discussed from a developmental perspective. In this discussion, prosocial behaviors are discussed from the perspective of how teachers encourage these behaviors in young children. Teachers encourage social competency in young children by modeling the behaviors of a socially competent person. Teachers model ways of interacting with children and adults alike. They actively listen when children speak to them. They look directly at children and make comments about what the child has shared, demonstrating that they were indeed listening.

*Early childhood teachers model prosocial and learner behaviors when they join children as they work in learning centers.*

They participate in the children's work at the learning centers and take turns as an equal person in that group. They follow all the rules established by the class and generally demonstrate the behaviors of a person who works at getting along with others.

Toni, the caregiver in the opening vignette, constantly models social behaviors she wants to encourage in the children for whom she cares. When she enters the dramatic play area, she asks permission of the children playing there, "I'd like to shop in your grocery store this morning. Is that okay with you?" When one of the two-year-olds offers her a "cup of coffee," Toni comments, "Why thank you. I was wishing I had a cup of hot coffee." When the four-year-old is painting at the easel, she says, "I would like to paint a picture myself. When you are finished with your painting, would you let me know so I can be next?" The respectful language Toni uses with the children when she speaks to them models for them the ways in which she wants them to speak to each other.

*Learner Behaviors*

Teachers also model learner behaviors. To examine this modeling, look closely at how Toni models behaviors of someone who is literate. Sometimes this caregiver models specific skills she wants children to learn. In the larger sense of development, she wants the children to become literate people who enjoy reading and writing. She is aware that literate people share certain characteristics. They read for pleasure. They read a variety of types of books. They use books to find out the answers to questions they have. She models these behaviors even with the very young children in her care. She shows how much she loves reading by having a shared reading time several times each day with the entire group and with small groups of children. She talks about how much she loves books and shows that she values books by the way she handles, stores, and shares books. She shares a wide range of high-quality reading materials with children: fiction by a variety of authors, nonfiction, poetry, magazines, newspapers, and brochures. And instead of always answering children's questions, she models how to find the answers to questions by helping them find appropriate books.

In addition to general attitudes about books, literate people have basic skills that all early childhood educators model. Adults know how to hold a

*Instead of always answering children's questions, the teacher models how to find the answers to questions by helping students consult appropriate books and resources.*

book and turn the pages from the front to the back. They can identify the front and back covers of the book. They know the differences between text and illustration and that the pictures are related to what the print says. They know where to begin reading on a page. They know what a title, an author, and an illustrator are. Early childhood educators model these skills every day. Holding a book and turning the pages correctly is such a basic skill that older children and adults do not think about it, but for a young child, these behaviors should be modeled and labeled. Teachers of toddlers, young preschoolers, and older preschoolers who have had little experience with books often comment about how they hold a book and how they carefully turn its pages. This is not direct instruction, but a more casual modeling of the behavior with verbal labeling of what they are doing. Teachers often point to the text as they read and point to the illustrations as they comment or ask questions about the pictures. This modeling helps children develop the concept of the difference between text and illustration and the knowledge about where to start reading on each page. Teachers also read the title and author of a book as an introduction before reading the book. Repeated experiences of a teacher modeling and discussing these skills related to concepts about books will help the child assimilate this information.

All of the behaviors described here are related to literacy, but the idea of modeling learner behaviors can occur in any center at any time. If a group of children in the math center are sorting pattern blocks into color groups, the caregiver might use this moment to introduce new ways of sorting. She would ask if she could join the group then sort the pattern blocks by a different attribute—by the shape or by the number of sides on each shape. She might choose to talk through what she is doing as a model, commenting as she sorts, "This is a diamond so I am going to put this diamond with the squares and the diamonds because it has four sides. This is a hexagon with six sides, so I can't put it with the three-sided blocks or the four-sided blocks. I'll have to start a new pile of blocks with six sides." Or she may choose to sort pattern blocks without comment and listen to what the children say as they watch her go through the sorting process. In each case, she is modeling learner behaviors that she wants to encourage in children. In modeling social and learner behaviors and in discussing these behaviors with children, the teacher is developing her relationship with children. Teachers also work to help develop relationships between and among children.

## Fostering Interdependence

In a community of learners, children come to depend on each other when they need help. Young children often look to adults to help solve their problems, but when teachers try to establish a community of learners, they help the children learn to look to each other for assistance. Even very young children can help each other as they go about their day. They can share toys and books, help other children build the kind of block structure they want,

*Children learn to look to each other for assistance.*

find the puzzle they are looking for, or offer words of comfort when another child is upset or hurt—and teachers can help foster this type of interdependence.

In one prekindergarten class, Kevin, the teacher, had a special technique for helping children learn to depend on each other. He identified "experts" in the class very early in the year and would facilitate children helping each other in the areas where they were "experts." The first week of school, the names of those children who could tie shoes were posted on a chart entitled "I can help tie shoes." Instead of tying the shoes of a child who asked him for help, Kevin would take the child to the chart and read the names listed, suggesting that "one of his friends" could help him. Tying shoes was a skill that some children knew before coming to class. Other "helping" skills that Kevin looked for were the ability to open milk containers, sort blocks, construct puzzles, and string beads. He would note children's names who could perform particular tasks and ask them to help other children who could not do those things. He also looked for skills he could teach children so that they, too, could become an "expert" in the classroom.

One morning of the second week of school, Kevin asked two students if they would like to become listening center experts. He showed them how to check to see if the pause button on the tape recorder had been pushed and how to release that button. On subsequent days if a child in the class had a problem with the recorder not working, the teacher directed the child to one of the listening center "experts." Kevin watched children as they worked and noted any skill or bit of knowledge that he could help a particular child share with another. Instead of answering a child's question about how to put water in the class guinea pig's water bottle or where to find more construction paper for the writing center or more glue for the art center, Kevin would suggest the name of a child who could answer that question. In time, the children learned who in the class was an "expert" in these areas and would turn to each other for help, rather than depending on the teacher for "all the answers."

### Fostering Respectful Relationships among Children

Beyond learning to help each other and rely on other children for help, teachers help young children learn to treat each other respectfully. Much of this comes in helping children learn to talk to each other in respectful ways. Even very young children can be coached into asking others to join in their play themes, saying "please" when they ask for help or saying "thank you" when another person helps them. The adult should always model respectful language and suggest specific words to young children at appropriate times.

Jace, a four-year-old, was having some trouble getting along with other children in the dramatic play center. He tended to be boisterous and would typically enter the center and try to take over. The other children were getting tired of his directives about how they should play and began to exclude him. One morning he went into the dramatic play center, which was set up as a fast food restaurant. He announced that he was going to cook the hamburgers and that everyone else should get away because they might get hurt. The other children simply told him to go away. This reaction hurt his feelings and tearfully he found his teacher and explained to Mr. Batts that the other children were being mean to him. The teacher asked Jace to tell him everything that had happened, which Jace truthfully recounted. Mr. Batts responded, "Perhaps the other children already had someone who was cooking the hamburgers and you forgot to ask if you could do that. Remember when other children are playing, it is more respectful to ask if you can join their play. Why don't you try asking if you can play in the restaurant and ask what they need you to do?" Jace, apparently not convinced, just shrugged his shoulders and wandered over to the writing center. Moments later, Mr. Batts heard Jace shouting his name. The teacher looked up and saw Jace standing in

*Very young children can be coached to invite others to join in their play.*

the dramatic play center. At eye contact, Jace shouted, "It worked, Mr. Batts. It worked. I'm doing the cash register!"

Young children often need specific suggestions about language they can use to "get what they want" from others. Sometimes adults can do what Mr. Batts did with Jace in offering a sentence or two for a particular child related to one situation. Other times the teacher might lead group conversations about how to be respectful to each other. Puppets are a good medium for involving young children in conversations about acts of kindness and appropriate language to use with each other. Books can be read to the group and the teacher can lead a discussion about how the characters in the book helped each other. Role-playing is another good method to use in helping children think about how to treat others. Children learn about helping each other and cooperating with other children by observing models, by reminders and suggestions about specific language to use, and by talking about this type of behavior.

### Helping Children Resolve Conflicts

Children also learn about solving interpersonal problems in several different ways. In every group of people, it is inevitable that conflicts will arise. Some adults who work with young children view conflict as something that should be stopped immediately. However, early childhood educators who are fostering a sense of community among children view conflict as an opportunity to help children learn how to treat each other in more respectful ways. It is perhaps hardest for people to maintain respectful language toward another person during moments of conflict, and this is particularly true for young children. A young child intent on getting his or her own way during a conflict often resorts to shouting or using physical actions. Teachers should intervene during these conflicts and support children as they work through times of conflict. Adults can help children understand another's point of view, learn how to express their feelings, and use questions and suggestions to solve problems.

*Adults can help children understand another's point of view.*

In the family child care center in the opening vignette, James and Mario, the four- and five-year-olds, were arguing loudly one morning about who could paint at the easel first. Toni stepped closer to the two boys and asked them to sit down for a moment beside her. They stopped arguing for the moment and sat down. She explained that yelling at each other was probably not going to solve their problem and that their loud voices were upsetting the younger children. She also explained that she was sure that they could come up with a solution that they would both be happy with and that she wanted to help them find what solution. Toni asked James to explain his side of the story first. "I want to paint. I wanted to paint yesterday and I forgot, so today, I want to." Then Mario got to tell his side of the story, "I got out the paints. I was careful and didn't spill any paints at all and Jessica wanted to paint and I helped her and now it's my turn."

Toni then asked the boys to tell each other what they wanted. Mario said, "I want to paint first," and James said, "And I want to paint first." Toni stated, "I hear you both saying that you want the same thing. You can't both paint first, so what are some of the possible solutions?" Both boys were silent. Toni continued, "Well, it seems to me that Mario could paint at the easel first or James could paint first or maybe there are other solutions. What could those be?" Quietly, Mario responded, "Maybe we could paint together like a mural that we did before," and James said, "Since Mario got out the paints, I could get out the watercolors and do those." Toni smiled at both boys and told them what great solutions they had come up with. She suggested that they talk about the solutions while she checked on the younger children. In just a few minutes, the boys were laughing and talking about what kind of painting they could create together.

Resolving this conflict seems rather easy, but this conversation was the result of many conflict resolution conversations between Toni and Mario and James. Over time, the boys had learned that they could state their opinions to each other, that there were multiple ways of solving a problem between them, and that they could come up with solutions and pick the one that made the most sense to them.

With the younger children, Toni was usually the one who came up with possible solutions to a conflict between children and typically led them to a decision. When Joyce and Jessica, the two two-year-olds, were both trying to ride on the same car push-toy and were trying to push each other away from the car, Toni was more suggestive than she was with the older children. Toni put her arms around each child and said, "I can't let you push each other. Someone might get hurt if you push. I can see that you both want to ride on the car but it is not big enough for two children. Joyce can ride it or Jessica can ride it. We have to decide what we are going to do. Joyce, instead of pushing Jessica, use your words to tell her what you want. Jessica, I need you to do the same thing—use your words." Both children emphatically stated that they wanted to ride the car. Toni then reminded the girls, "We have a car that you can ride and we have a fire truck that you can ride. Joyce, will you ride the fire truck first and then you and Jessica can change?" Simply by having duplicate materials, reminding the children about their options, and asking for a desired behavior, Toni was able to help even very young children begin to learn how to solve conflicts.

## Conducting Group Times and Class Meetings

These types of conflict resolution meetings can occur between one adult and two children—as described—or the entire class can be involved in helping children solve problems (Nelsen, Lott, & Glenn, 2000). Group times in early childhood classrooms are not always focused on solving problems.

One way teachers help develop relationships among children is through shared experiences during group times. The early childhood educator is a part of the group and usually sits on the floor with the children. Groups often gather in a circle, which allows everyone to see each other. This is a

*Teachers help develop relationships among children in the way that they conduct group times.*

good configuration for group discussions, but it is not necessary for read-alouds or action songs, which often take place during group times.

The teacher is part of the group, but is much more than just one of the group. She is the one who orchestrates this time. Group times should always be of high interest to the children, and the times of coming together should be kept relatively short. Typically group times should be approximately five to ten minutes for children under three, ten to twenty minutes for children three and four years old, and thirty minutes for children five and older (DeVries & Zan, 1994), although these times are only general estimates. If children appear restless, the time should be reduced, but if children are engaged, group time can last a bit longer. This time spent with the whole group helps build a sense of togetherness as children share experiences. Group times can consist of read-alouds, action songs and finger plays, dramatizing stories, and daily routines such as attendance and snack times.

As mentioned earlier, in classes where the teacher is trying to develop a sense of community among the children, group times take on additional meaning. All of the activities mentioned previously still occur, but at other times during the day the teacher and the children meet together to talk and to make decisions about things that affect them as a group. The teacher helps children learn to talk about how they want their class to be, reflect on classroom situations that have been disruptive, and find solutions to problems (Developmental Studies Center, 1996; DeVries & Zan, 1994).

In the same prekindergarten class discussed earlier, Kevin and the children met together every day for a special group time they came to call "Our Class Meeting." The class meeting had two purposes: to help each other and to solve problems that affected the class (Nelsen, 1996). As an integral part of the meeting, the children were also learning to identify problems, listen respectfully as others in the group talked, propose possible solutions, and come to a consensus about the best possible solution. When children meet together and solve problems, the sense of community—the feeling that "we are all in this together" and that we can work together to make our class what we want it to be—is enhanced.

During one class meeting, Kevin brought up something he noticed during morning center time. It was the same problem that occurred in the family child care center between James and Mario. Children in Kevin's class were arguing over whose turn it was to paint at the easel. When Kevin intervened in the argument, he reminded those children that they had agreed at a previous class meeting that arguing was not respectful and asked them to think about ways they might avoid arguing. Now, in the class meeting, Kevin asked the children who had been arguing to present the problem to the whole class. Michael said that the girls were taking too long at the easel, that they were painting two or three paintings, and that that wasn't fair. Marques and Ismael agreed that this was the truth. Matthew claimed that he never got a chance to paint, never, never, and that wasn't fair either.

Stephanie and Breanna, who had been involved in the argument, said there was no agreement that they couldn't paint as many paintings as they wanted to and if they got there first, they should be able to stay as long as they wanted. With the problem defined, the teacher asked if they had thought of any solutions to the problem. None of the children involved in the argument had any ideas, so the teacher asked if anyone else in the class could think of a possible solution. Katherine said she thought the easel should be closed if people were going to argue about it. Jordan said that wouldn't be fair to the people who were not arguing and suggested that everyone should just take turns at the easel. From that comment, Julia proposed that there be a sign-up sheet for the easel, just like the sign-up sheet posted in the science center so everyone knew who was supposed to feed the class pets. Marques repeated his earlier comment and said that he thought that if you were painting, that one was enough, and then it should be someone else's turn. With further discussion, the children agreed that they would try the sign-up sheet idea and paint only one painting at a time. Other than introducing the problem, Kevin had little input into this class meeting. The students described the problem, brainstormed possible solutions, and agreed on how they wanted to handle the issue.

The conflict in both situations was the same one—children arguing over who could paint at the easel—but the solutions were different. That is perfectly fine. Solving problems like this helps foster the sense of community among children. But class meetings are not only for conflict resolution. Class meetings can also be used to make decisions about the learning experiences of the class.

### Helping Children Learn to Make Decisions through Voting

One way to help young children solve problems or make decisions as a class is through voting. Voting on issues that are important to the group is one way to help children learn to discuss several sides of one issue, to make an individual decision and to learn to accept a vote that does not go their way (DeVries & Zan, 1994).

It is an important part of the decision-making process to vote on issues that mean something to the children. Children care about issues such as the books the teacher is going to read aloud, action songs the group is going to perform, whether outdoor play happens before or after poetry reading, and what snack to have on a particular day. When introducing voting to a group of children, the teacher should make the options clear and the outcome of the vote should not be something that is going to upset children. Learning to accept that your choice "lost" is not an easy task for young children. The teacher might offer two books and ask the class which one they want to read first. The children would then discuss their reasons for choosing one over the other and then vote. Knowing that the book that received fewer votes would be part of group time later the same day reduces the sadness that losing a vote sometimes brings. This type of neutral voting process helps prepare children for later votes that might evoke more emotion.

After some experience with voting on simpler issues such as which book to read or which snack to have, children can begin to use voting to make more important group decisions. In Mrs. Gonzalez's first-grade class, on the first day back from winter break, she began by asking children to make a list of things that they wanted to learn during the rest of the year. She wrote the children's suggestions on a chart tablet as they brainstormed. Some of the topics the children mentioned were space, dinosaurs, hurricanes, rocks, fossils, tigers, sharks, rocks, plants, and elephants. During the next two weeks of school, Mrs. Gonzalez read one book about each of the topics and led the children through discussions about what they knew about each topic and what they wanted to learn about it. At the end of the second week, the class conducted a class meeting to discuss which topic they wanted to start with. A lively discussion was held with different children telling their reasons for wanting one topic over the others, then a vote was held. The topic of fossils won by two votes. While some children were disappointed in the vote, their previous experiences with voting had taught them that just because they lost one vote did not mean that they could not do their own research about the topic that interested them. It just meant that the group would focus on fossils first and that they might be able to persuade the group to vote for their preference during the next vote about what to study.

Creating a community of learners is not something that happens quickly. Just as it takes time for relationships to develop, it takes time for a group of children to learn to depend on each other, to learn to solve problems in small and large groups, to make decisions about their learning as a group, and to feel like a "community." A leader in the area of helping teachers create communities of learners is Rheta DeVries. She conducts extensive research in this area, makes national presentations on the topic, and coauthored *Moral Classrooms, Moral Children* (DeVries & Zan, 1994), which contrasts communities of learners with classrooms led by more traditional teachers.

*The educational objective of voting is principally to promote children's self-regulation by giving them real power to make decisions about what happens in their class.*
*-Rheta DeVries & Betty Zan*

## SHARED LEARNING IN GROUP SETTINGS

Shared learning is a natural outgrowth of the relationships that children form when adults encourage the sense of community. Teachers affect the degree to which children help support each other's learning in many different ways. Helping facilitate peer relationships to foster interdependence and solve group problems—as described previously—is one way. Teachers can also encourage shared learning through materials offered in learning centers, the way the classroom is set up, and even through the curriculum.

Materials that encourage children to create things together can encourage shared learning. Unit blocks and large blocks are obvious examples of this type of material. Offered sufficient numbers of blocks, groups of children can create large, complex block structures. Props in the dramatic play center encourage cooperative play themes where children use the props to take on different roles related to that play theme. Art materials that encourage group creativity are also examples of materials that can help facilitate children working together in groups.

Even the way the classroom is arranged can facilitate shared learning. Materials that are placed where children have easy access to them encourage them to help one another find and return materials rather than ask for adult help. In classes where a community of learners is encouraged, children help each other in many ways. A child having trouble putting a puzzle together will be helped by a friend. A child struggling with a coat will be assisted by another. A child who cannot see the pattern created by another student will have the pattern explained to her. A student struggling with how to represent what he wants to write can find someone to help him "sound out" words. Children in environments in which shared learning is valued and encouraged will help less competent peers and help them learn.

Another way of looking at shared learning has been espoused by cognitive psychologists. Expanding on Vygotsky's theory of scaffolding discussed in chapter 3, Collins, Brown, and Newman (1989), Gardner (1991), and Bayer (1990) have described the concept of apprenticeship in the learning process. In essence, in an apprenticeship two people work beside each other: one, an expert in a certain area, the other person, a novice in that area. Apprenticeships are formally arranged by adults so that they can learn something from an expert. These relationships are formed to learn everything from auto mechanics to practicing medicine. When children are encouraged to work together, apprenticeships occur naturally as children of differing abilities work beside and with one another. Children who regularly work in pairs or small groups tend to share what they know with those around them. A child who knows how to sort pattern blocks will help another child struggling with the task by demonstrating what he is doing as he explains the process. A child who has mastered climbing to the top of the playground equipment will show another child how to accomplish this goal and talk the novice climber through the process. Older children can be encouraged to act as models for younger students.

Howard Gardner (1991), Harvard University professor, has written about the benefits of apprenticeships in the classroom. Recognizing that all individuals within a group have particular areas of strength and areas that still need to be strengthened, it seems logical that those who are accomplished at a particular skill or concept assist those who are still developing that skill. Often a child can explain things to another child in ways that an adult cannot. This type of shared learning experience promotes increased understanding for both children. In assuming the role of a teacher, the more

*Shared activity forces the participants to clarify and elaborate their thinking and to use language.*

*-Elena Bodrova &
Deborah Leong*

## BIOGRAPHY BOX *Howard Gardner*

Howard Gardner is professor of education and adjunct professor of psychology at Harvard University, adjunct professor of neurology at the Boston University School of Medicine and co-director of Harvard Project Zero. The recipient of many honors, including a MacArthur Prize Fellowship, Gardner is the author of eighteen books and several hundred articles. In 1990, he was the first American to receive the University of Louisville's Grawemeyer Award in education. Gardner is best known in educational circles for his theory of multiple intelligences, a critique of the notion that there exists but a single human intelligence that can be assessed by standard psychometric instruments. During the past decade, he and colleagues at Project Zero have been working on the design of performance-based assessments, education for understanding, and the use of multiple intelligences to achieve more personalized curriculum, instruction, and assessment. Most recently, Gardner has been carrying out intensive case studies of exemplary creators and leaders; he and colleagues have launched an investigation of the relationship between cutting-edge work in different domains and a sense of social responsibility.

Gardner's A. B. in social relations was obtained from Harvard College and his Ph.D in social psychology from Harvard University. Some of Gardner's publications include most recently, *The Disciplined Mind* (1999), *Intelligence Reframed* (1999), and *Good Work: When Excellence and Ethics Meet* (with M. Csikszentmihalyi and W. Damon, 2001). Others include *Artful Scribbles: The Significance of Children's Drawings; Art, Mind, and Brain: A Cognitive Approach to Creativity; Frames of Mind: The Theory of Multiple Intelligences, Leading Minds: An Anatomy of Leadership,* and *Extraordinary Minds,* (1997).

competent child deepens his knowledge as he or she strives to put into words the understanding, and the less competent child learns from the more competent child. Sometimes these apprentice relationships occur naturally. More often the adult facilitates the apprenticeship relationships in the classroom.

In the kindergarten classroom, the idea of apprenticeship is perhaps most noticeable in the writing center. Writing abilities of typical kindergarten students range from drawing and scribbling to using rather sophisticated developmental spelling. Eavesdropping on conversations between five-year-olds in the writing center will often reveal apprenticeship relationships.

- "If you want to write about guinea pigs and you can't write guinea pigs, just look on the cage. It says it right there."
- " 'Dad' starts like 'Darriel.' Look at Darriel's name on his locker and you'll know how to start 'Dad.' "
- "Just find the book about snakes and I'll help you find 'reptiles.' It starts 'ruh' like a 'R.' We can find it if you want to write it."

*Older children can be encouraged to act as models for younger students.*

Children who are encouraged to help each other will usually do so. However, it is the responsibility of the teacher to help children understand how they can help each other.

The comments overheard in the writing center grew out of the teacher's deliberate facilitation of children working together. From the first day of school, the teacher observed children's writing behaviors so that he would know what skills and knowledge each child brought to the classroom. From the second day of school, he began referring children to each other by subtly suggesting, "Matthew, if you want some help writing an 'S,' why don't you ask Sarah? Her name starts with an 'S' and she already knows how to write that," or "Krista, you can spell 'the,' can't you? John Michael wants to write that word and he can't quite figure out how to start. Would you be willing to take a moment and help him spell 'the'?"

This method of referring children to each other for assistance and support can occur throughout early childhood programs, not just during the setting of a kindergarten writing center. In a toddler classroom, Janda was having a difficult time separating from her mother. After a week in the program, Janda was participating in center-choice times well, but would begin to cry during the quieter times of storytime, singing circle, and rest time. One morning as Janda began to weep during storytime, Mrs. Moncrief suggested that Marques go to Janda's cubby and find her special blanket for her. Marques found the blanket and brought it to Janda, who cuddled it and stopped crying. That afternoon as the toddlers gathered for storytime, Marques stopped by the cubby area and brought Janda's blanket to her again, saying, "For not crying." Even with very young children, when teachers suggest specific ways in which children can help each other, they do.

This form of helping each other grows into shared learning where children help each other learn some of the important tasks of childhood. They can show each other how to use scissors from the art center to cut open their plastic package of fruit snacks, how to put together puzzles, how to play new games, how to build taller, more complex buildings in the block center, how to conquer climbing equipment, and how to hop and skip and jump. Children are usually eager to share what they know and what they are able to do. Adults can facilitate this shared learning by creating an environment that encourages children helping other children and by making carefully timed suggestions.

## REVISITING THE FAMILY CHILD CARE CENTER

Throughout the chapter we've seen how Toni modeled the social and learner behaviors she wanted to encourage among the children in her care. We have seen her help children solve conflicts. Now let's look at some of the shared learning that occurs in this home as a result of the community of learners that Toni encourages.

Mario is sitting beside Ricardo helping him place shape blocks into the sorting container. Because Mario is four years old and Ricardo is only eighteen months old, this is a natural apprenticeship relationship. Mario has had many experiences with this toy since he was a toddler, so as he puts one shape into the container, he talks about its color and its shape, just as he has heard Toni do with Ricardo. Mario feels like he is doing important work as he helps Ricardo play and Ricardo loves Mario's attention.

In the kitchen, James explains to Jessica how she needs to wear a smock when she plays in the water center. He tells her that the water will make her clothes wet when she pours water from one measuring cup to another and that the smock will help keep her clothes dry. He does this as he helps her put the smock over her head and fastens it at the sides.

In both cases, an apprenticeship relationship was active. The older, more experienced child was acting as the expert and the younger child was the novice. Shared learning was occurring as the older children used what they knew to help others.

### Summary

Children do learn from each other, but adults play crucial roles in the learning processes of young children. These roles are varied, complex, and essential. In high-quality programs, adults recognize the importance of developing a sense of community among the children. A community of learners is characterized by children who treat each other respectfully, who rely on each other for help, and who solve problems together. The adult takes the lead in helping children develop these relationships and in facilitating children working and learning together. The following chapter discusses the opportunities for early childhood educators and the challenges that lie ahead for the profession.

## Reflections

1. Think about your own experiences in early childhood educational settings. Were you a part of a community of learners or was the teacher "in charge" of the class? How did you feel about these experiences?
2. In small groups, discuss how young children might feel if they were in a class where community of learners was encourage. Make a list of these feelings, then contrast those feelings to those children might have in a teacher-controlled classroom.

## Field Experiences

1. Find a classroom that has regular class meetings and ask permission to attend one of them. Note the ways in which children speak to each other. Note the role that the teacher takes in the meeting and the problem-solving skills encouraged throughout the meeting. How does the teacher maintain cordial, helpful, and nonhurtful interactions.
2. Observe a group of preschool children and look for examples of ways that children help each other. Look for a child assisting another with puzzles, math manipulatives, block building, or creating artwork. How does the teacher encourage mutual respect and helpful behaviors?
3. Observe in several different early childhood classrooms focusing on the behaviors of the teachers' interactions with the children. Keep a log about how teachers model prosocial behaviors.

## Case Studies

### What Should Our Class Rules Be?

This is Marta's fifth year of teaching, but her first year to teach kindergarten. For the four years she taught third grade, one of her primary goals was to keep early childhood principles as the basis for her educational decisions. She worked to establish child-centered classes each year and always started the year by leading her students in creating class rules. Marta saw no reason to change this procedure just because her new students would be five years old instead of eight.

On the first day of kindergarten, Marta started the school year just as she had the preceding four years. She began a group meeting by telling her students how happy she was that each one of them was in this class. She talked about some of the wonderful things they would do that first week, such as learning new songs, listening to new books, and playing with new friends. Then she told the children that to do all these things, they needed to agree on how everyone would act in the classroom. Marta was not prepared for the answers that children had when she asked what they thought some of the class rules should be.

The children's first few suggestions were:

- No hitting and if anyone hits anyone, you should call their mother
- No pushing and if they do, send them to the principal
- No punching and if it happens, they can't stay in our class

**What to Do?**
It had not occurred to Marta that the third graders she was used to working with had had three years of experience with school rules and that most of them had been involved in creating some or all of those rules. Her new kindergarten students probably had not been asked to set their own rules. Instead of stating how they should treat each other, which was what Marta was hoping for, the kindergartners relied on their past experience with rules and listed things that they had been told not to do. For every rule, these children thought there had to be punishment. What can Marta do to turn this situation around? She wants the rules to come from the children, but also wants the rules to be stated in terms of what children should do instead of what they should not do.

**Home Rules vs. School Rules**
In this same kindergarten class, one boy stood out among all the others as a challenge to Marta's patience and her beliefs about working with young children. Marta felt Caleb's aggressive nature undermined her attempts at establishing a community in the class. Caleb pushed children aside so he could sit beside her in group meetings. He hit children to make them drop toys when he wanted to play with them. He even bit children to get his way.

It was only two weeks into the school year, and already Marta was feeling helpless. When she called Caleb's parents to talk about working together to help him, his father answered the telephone. The father insisted that he was teaching Caleb to be a man and that a man stands up for what is his. Despite her explanations about hitting not being allowed in school, the father remained firm. Without support from home, she knew it was going to take more time for Caleb to change the ways he treated other people. In class, Marta continued responding every time Caleb was aggressive, comforting the person he hurt and reinforcing with Caleb that hitting, pushing, and biting were wrong. Already, the children were excluding Caleb from their play. When he came into a learning center, other children would leave. During outside games, the children would stop playing a game before they would let Caleb be a part of it.

### What to Do?

Marta realizes that Caleb's actions are causing the other children to exclude him. But a community of learners includes everyone in the class. Marta knew that she had to get Caleb to the point where he used words instead of actions to get what he wanted from other children. She recognized that it would take weeks, maybe longer, to change his automatic responses. Still she wanted Caleb to be an accepted member of the community. What should Marta do?

### Further Reading

Bodrova, E., & Leong, D. J. (1996). *Tools of the mind: The Vygotskian approach to early childhood education.* Englewood Cliffs, NJ: Merrill/Prentice Hall.

Developmental Studies Center (1996). *Ways we want our class to be: Class meetings that build commitment to kindness and learning.* Oakland, CA: Author.

DeVries, R., & Zan, B. (1994). *Moral classrooms, moral children: Creating a constructivist atmosphere in early education.* New York: Teachers College Press.

Nelsen, J. (1996). *Positive discipline.* New York: Ballantine.

Nelsen, J., Erwin, C., & Duffy, R. (1995). *Positive discipline for preschoolers.* Rocklin, CA: Prima Publishing.

Nelsen, J., Lott, L., & Glenn, H. S. (2000). *Positive discipline in the classroom: Developing mutual respect, cooperation, and responsibility in your classroom* (3rd ed.). Roseville, CA: Prima Publishing.

Perlmutter, J., & Burrell, L. (2001). *The first weeks of school: Laying a quality foundation.* Portsmouth, NH: Heinemann.

Vance, E., & Weaver, P. J. (2002). *Class meetings: Young children solving problems together.* Washington, DC: National Association for the Education of Young Children.

### Helpful Web Sites

### The Project Approach

http://www.project-approach.com/foundation/class.htm
*This Web site describes a community of learners within a project-based learning class.*

**Northwest Regional Educational Laboratory**
http://www.nwrel.org/msec/images/resources/justgood/06.00.pdf
*While this Web site emphasizes communities of learners in math and science*
*classes, the principles regarding how to build this sense of community are*
*the same no matter what content is being taught.*

Check the Online Resources™ for expert practitioners'
responses to each case study.

For additional information on teaching young children,
visit our Web site at **http://www.earlychilded.delmar.com**

## PART FOUR

# Early Childhood Careers in the Twenty-First Century

▶ CHAPTER 10

*Opportunities and Challenges
in the Early Childhood Profession*

# Opportunities and Challenges in the Early Childhood Profession

*Early Childhood Principle* Early childhood educators continue professional development through participation in the profession at large.

Becoming a professional early childhood educator is a dynamic process with both challenges and opportunities. The demands of the profession to provide highest quality developmentally appropriate experiences for children, and the parallel emerging issues associated with an ever-changing society, create an amalgam of choices for those who enter the profession. Regardless of setting or age of children served, professionalism is measured by the extent to which the early childhood caregiver or educator makes thoughtful and wise choices on behalf of children and families.

*After reading this chapter, you should be able to:*
- Discuss what it means to be a professional in early childhood education.
- Reflect on and discuss an early childhood educator's professional code of ethics.
- Reflect on the early childhood educator's relationship to the larger body of professionals.
- Discuss challenges confronting contemporary and future professional early childhood educators.
- Develop a plan for continuing professional development and involvement.

**M**ARLYN, the mother of five-year-old Brian, took a day off from work to observe him for an entire day of kindergarten near the beginning of the year. At the end of the day, she asked the teacher to talk about what she had seen. She had a page of notes about Brian's behaviors during the day, comments like "rocks back and forth during storytime," "does not do the motions to songs—just jumps and swings arms," "dashes when changing centers." She added some questions she wanted Brian's teacher to discuss with her: "When does the real school work begin?" "Will Brian be learning to read? He seemed very interested in the books, but he didn't stay in the library center long." She was concerned that Brian had "wasted" an entire day at school and "knew" that he could not be learning anything important until he learned to sit still and pay attention. She was curious about the curriculum. "Would it challenge Brian?" The teacher visited with Marlyn for an extended period of time about the kindergarten program, its goals and methodology, and then about Brian in particular and his need to move around. She assured Marlyn that Brian was indeed learning. Marlyn was still unconvinced. She was concerned that her son would fall behind the other more self-controlled children.

The teacher then asked Brian to join them. She asked Brian about *Swimmy* (Lionni, 1963), one of the stories she read to the class that day. Brian was able to retell the story from start to finish, including relating the moral of the story about being able to accomplish more by groups of people working together. Brian was able to sing the chorus of the new song they had learned that day and recite a finger play the class had performed. With appropriate questioning, he was able to recall which centers he had chosen that day and what he had done in those centers. Marlyn truly believed that Brian's constant movement during group times and short attention span in centers indicated a lack of learning, but his ability to recall information and answer questions about his day proved her wrong. Not all young children have the need for constant movement like Brian, but all young children do have needs for teachers who understand their unique ways of learning.

## DEFINING THE EARLY CHILDHOOD PROFESSIONAL

Marlyn, like many parents, is not as trusting of the play mode employed by children as they learn as are early childhood professionals. Many parents and lay persons think early education should look more like "real" school, something more formal, more structured, with learning outcomes that are more observable and easily measured. Yet, confident in her knowledge about child growth and development and assured that her practices are developmentally appropriate, Brian's teacher was able to effectively allay this misperception and share her knowledge with his mother. Brian's teacher

*Requirements: Nursery School Teacher*

Must have 4 hands, 4 feet, patience of a saint, medical training, Bachelor's degree. Must also be a trained furniture mover, expert carpenter, fine pianist, neat, tidy, expert housekeeper, trained psychiatrist, and an artist. Must be able to see around corners, to fly, to run as fast as a slow gazelle, to move slowly and calmly, to sing and dance, to see each child as an individual and children as a group.

Martha Koiro
*The 2-to-5 News*, October 1956, p. 7

is confident because she knows that she shares a common body of knowledge and competencies with other professionals in her field. In this chapter we will explore the defining characteristics of professionalism in early childhood education.

## Core Knowledge and Skills

Most professions are undergirded by a shared body of knowledge and a set of requisite skills or competencies. The early childhood profession is no different. As the "poetic" descriptors in the accompanying box suggest, professionals in early childhood education have assessed and described their roles and responsibilities variously over the years. The basic skills, however, are probably less changed than is the language used to articulate them, as is illustrated in Figure 10–1 in which the National Association for the Education of Young Children lays out its most recently adopted standards for the early childhood teaching profession (Hyson, 2002).

The evolution of the education and early childhood profession and its professional organizations over the decades have brought focused and scholarly attention to the needs of children and the concomitant knowledge and skills necessary to care for and teach them. Further, research has repeatedly demonstrated the important and critical nature of the teacher-child relationship and its potential for positive or negative long-term outcomes. With increasing numbers of children in out-of-home child care arrangements, and increasing preschool enrollments, today perhaps more than ever, the profession must take a focused look at the qualifications and training requirements for early childhood educators.

Through research and consensus building, standards for the profession have evolved. The NAEYC standards articulated in Figure 10–1 have been approved by the National Council for the Accreditation of Teacher Education (NCATE) and will be applied when institutions of higher education seek

**FIGURE 10–1**
*NAEYC Standards: What Should Tomorrow's Teachers Know and Be Able to Do?*

1. **Promoting child development and learning**

   Well-prepared early childhood professionals
   - understand what young children are like;
   - understand what influences their development; and
   - use this understanding to create great environments where all children can thrive.

2. **Building family and community relationships**

   Well-prepared early childhood professionals
   - understand and value children's families and communities,
   - create respectful, reciprocal relationships; and
   - involve all families in their children's development and learning.

3. **Observing, documenting, and assessing**

   Well-prepared early childhood professionals
   - understand the purposes of assessment;
   - use effective assessment strategies; and
   - use assessment responsibly, to positively influence children's development and learning.

4. **Teaching and learning**

   Well-prepared early childhood professionals
   - build close relationships with children and families;
   - use developmentally effective teaching and learning strategies;
   - have sound knowledge of academic disciplines or content areas; and
   - combine all of these to give children experiences that promote development and learning.

5. **Becoming a professional**

   Well-prepared early childhood professionals
   - identify themselves with the early childhood profession;
   - are guided by ethical and other professional standards;
   - are continuous, collaborative learners;
   - think reflectively and critically; and
   - advocate for children, families, and the profession.

The complete document, "NAEYC Standards for Early Childhood Professional Preparation: Baccalaureate or Initial Licensure Level" (revised 2001), with detailed explanations and references, may be downloaded from **www.naeyc.org/profdev.**

*Source:* Hyson, M. (2002). Preparing tomorrow's teachers: NAEYC announces new standards. *Young Children, 57*(2), 78–79. Reprinted with permission from the National Association for the Education of Young Children.

accreditation. These standards represent a set of shared values highlighting the importance of preparing early childhood teachers to:

- "work effectively with young children with disabilities in inclusive settings;
- promote the learning of children from many cultures and language groups;
- build strong relationships with all families and in all communities;
- use more in-depth knowledge of early childhood assessment practices and issues;
- integrate essential content knowledge in literacy, mathematics, and other disciplines with knowledge of child development and learning; and
- go beyond textbook knowledge to demonstrate real competence in making a difference for children." (Hyson, 2002, p. 78).

Addressing content areas typically included in public school curricula, the Association for Childhood Education International (1997) sets forth a broad base of general knowledge and subject areas taught by early childhood and primary-grade teachers. It is expected that early childhood educators (prekindergarten through third grade) will have:

- An acquaintance with great music, art, and literature
- Knowledge of health, safety, and nutrition
- Understanding of the physical and biological aspects of the world and the universe
- Knowledge of mathematical concepts
- Ability to read with comprehension, then to analyze, interpret, and judge a wide range of written material
- Knowledge of technology as an educational resource, instructional tool, and curriculum component
- Comprehension of the variety and complexity of communication patterns as expressed by people of differing cultural and socioeconomic backgrounds in a global context
- Knowledge and understanding of differences and similarities among societies and cultures, both at home and abroad
- Awareness of the social, historical, and political forces affecting children and the implications for education within individual nations and world contexts (pp. 164–165)

Projecting the needs for a "quality early care and education system," scholars list a number of recommendations, but important among them for this discussion is the recommendation to expand the content of training and education of practitioners in child care and early education.

*Early childhood educators know how to use technology to enhance classroom learning.*

Recommendation V of the *Not by Chance* report (Kagan & Cohen, 1997) states:

> By the year 2010, the content of education and training for early care and education staff will be expanded to (1) address the needs of diverse children and families; and (2) implement effective approaches to instruction, management, and leadership.

In responding to this report, Jensen (1999) observes that:

> ". . . for early childhood practitioners in the 21st century a child development, teacher competency, or apprenticeship orientation is insufficient. Instead, early childhood practitioners will need broad-based knowledge and skills derived from transdisciplinary approaches to pedagogy, curriculum, and human services. For example, they will need knowledge of ethics and values and a disposition not to judge or make assumptions too quickly. They will need an

understanding of the functioning of social groups, friendship, and belonging. They will need knowledge of aesthetic expression and appreciation of beauty. They will need to exhibit curiosity and a capacity for inquiry. They will need knowledge of communication and appreciation for expressive language. Moreover, to become professional leaders in the 21st century, they will need field-based preparation experiences as well as work environments that nourish the development of their leadership capacities." (p. 173–174)

Acquiring a broad base of knowledge in one's field takes time. It begins with an introduction, such as this text has attempted to provide, proceeds through early training and course work, and continues throughout one's career.

In setting personal career goals and planning a career path, the early childhood professional considers both the range of topics and the areas of knowledge that can enhance or are particularly germane to their immediate circumstance. As with young learners, the "teachable moment" often occurs when there is a felt need to know. A classroom experience, a puzzling child behavior, a parent's concern, a debate with a colleague, or an ethical dilemma directs one's focus to a particular body of knowledge from which guidance might be found.

On the other hand, professional educators do not dwell within their immediate circumstance, but also pursue knowledge and skills with long-range goals in mind—goals for individual children, for the program or setting in which they work, goals for the profession itself, and personal career goals. From this journey through the existing and emerging early childhood knowledge universe, professionals over time learn to

- Contrast and assess different points of view,
- Discover ways to enhance the learning experiences of their students,
- Develop greater attunement with children's developmental needs, and
- Reflect on their own thinking and practice.

The outcome from these processes is a professional educator who is always in a state of improvement. The benefits to children, families, the educator, and the education process itself are significant.

## Responding Appropriately to New Knowledge and Emerging Research

You may have noticed many citations throughout this text. The early childhood profession is guided by an enormous body of research that validates our efforts to define and provide developmentally appropriate experiences for young children. Professional early childhood educators read the professional literature. Through explorations of the literature, educators become discerning consumers of research and new information. Being well grounded in philosophy and theory relating to early education steers professional educators toward the most valid and reliable new information and

*It is not the amount of experience or the degree of education that determines quality. Only an early childhood knowledge base makes a distinguishable difference (Bauch, 1988). Doctors do not walk into surgery with an instructional manual. Attorneys do not defend clients using prescribed dialogues that are guaranteed for all cases. These professionals interpret cases individually, and then apply the most appropriate interventions. Each patient is unique, each client an individual.*
*-Kathleen Glascott*

away from sensational or faddish directions the literature might take. The more one reads in his or her field, the more discerning and selective one becomes in the use of information. Discerning consumers of professional literature are more discerning in their practices. Often confronted by parent and peer pressure to offer programs or engage in practices of questionable value to children, the informed early childhood professional is less likely to be easily, or unnecessarily swayed.

### Articulating State of Knowledge and Best Practices to Others

Keeping abreast makes one an educator with credibility, who garners respect of students, parents, colleagues, and policy makers. By the same token, the better informed caregivers and educators are, the more accurately and helpfully they can interpret their programs to parents. They display an assuring self-confidence to others. Marlyn, in the opening vignette, was fortunate to have a professional educator to help her understand the unique ways children learn and the accompanying unique ways early childhood classrooms support that learning.

Perhaps this text has encouraged you to seek more information about certain topics of special interest to you. Staying abreast of emerging research and new knowledge is an important responsibility assumed by professional early childhood caregivers and educators. We have all known individuals who stopped enriching their knowledge base at some point in their careers. Educators cannot afford to do this, as they have a moral and ethical responsibility to provide the most current and relevant education for their students, whose lives will be touched by a different era with different demands than those of the teacher's life experience.

### Committing to a Professional Code of Ethics

In addition to a knowledge base and competencies in working with young children and their families, professional early childhood educators must be able to make wise choices and decisions, often with little time to reflect. Katz (1995) describes our profession as one in which there is "commitment to standards of practice for which members are—at least theoretically—held accountable" (p. 185). In the early childhood education profession, standards of highest quality are defined through consensus of members of the profession and expressed through a professional **code of ethics** (Feeney & Kipnis, 1989; NAEYC, 1998). As do other professions, the early childhood profession subscribes to a code of ethics that is based on a set of core values held by its members. A professional code of ethics sets the framework for professional behaviors and decision making. Think about the following professional dilemmas:

**code of ethics** a set of standards that outline professional responsibilities and terms of behaviors and conduct.

> You are a preschool teacher who runs into one of your parents at the grocery store, and in the course of your conversation, she inquires

about the progress of a neighbor's child who, along with her own, is in your class. How should you answer?

You are in the teacher's lounge and the conversation turns to the alleged poor reputation of one of your student's parents. What should you say or do?

A child has revealed to you that the jacket he is wearing was shoplifted by his father at a local department store. How must you respond?

When taking your state licensure test, you notice that the person at another table has brought notes. What should you do?

A child in your class becomes quite ill with a communicable disease. The child has exposed the other children to the disease. What is your responsibility?

You have been asked by your director to offer a curriculum that in your opinion is clearly beyond the capabilities of the age of the children to whom you have been assigned. The director insists that parents expect it. How should you respond?

Early childhood caregivers and educators are faced daily with similar ethical dilemmas. Sometimes it is clear to us how to respond or what to do. Other times, it is not so clear. We must rely on professional judgment to respond appropriately. What guidelines are available to support the development of sound professional judgments?

The NAEYC Code of Ethical Conduct (Feeney & Kipnis, 1989; NAEYC, 1998) addresses four areas of relationships in which professionals are engaged: (1) children, (2) families, (3) colleagues, and (4) community and society. The code sets forth exemplary standards for professional practice and decision making in each of these areas. The early childhood professional's responsibility to children and families is emphasized in the following statement:

> Above all, we shall not harm children. We shall not participate in practices that are disrespectful, degrading, dangerous, exploitative, intimidating, psychologically damaging, or physically harmful to children. This principle has precedence over all others in this code. (P-1.1)

Faced almost daily with ethical dilemmas, professional educators find guidance in a code of ethics. The NAEYC and DEC codes of ethics are included in appendix C and D.

## Relating to the Early Childhood Profession at Large

Professional early childhood educators are themselves a community of learners through the at-large profession. Through membership and participation in local, state, regional, and national professional organizations, early childhood caregivers and teachers share experiences, build a cadre of colleagues, and access professional information and resources.

*Professional workshops and conferences provide opportunities to learn about the profession at large and to form friendships with others in the field.*

Professional associations are committed to raising the quality of lives for young children. The following mission statements of some of the leading professional early childhood associations describe this commitment in different ways and with varying areas of emphasis:

### Association for Childhood Education International

"ACEI shares a dual commitment to the fulfillment of every child's potential and to the professional development of classroom teachers." ACEI's purpose is:

- To promote the inherent rights, education, and well-being of children in their home, school and community.
- To work for desirable conditions, programs, and practices for children from infancy through early adolescence.
- To bring into active cooperation all individuals and groups concerned with children.
- To raise the standard of preparation for those actively involved with the care and development of children.
- To encourage continuous professional growth of educators.
- To focus the public's attention on the rights and needs of children and the ways various programs must be adjusted to fit those rights and needs (ACEI Membership Brochure, 1997).

## National Association for the Education of Young Children

"NAEYC exists for the purpose of leading and consolidating the efforts of individuals and groups working to achieve healthy development and constructive education for all young children. Primary attention is devoted to assuring the provision of high-quality early childhood programs for young children" Further, "NAEYC's work to accomplish its mission focuses on three broad goals:

> Goal 1—Facilitating improvements in the professional practice and working conditions in the field of early childhood education—by creating professional development opportunities/resources and by setting and promoting standards of professional practice
>
> Goal 2—Improving public understanding, support, and funding of high-quality programs in centers, homes, and schools serving young children and their families—through public policy initiatives and public awareness and engagement activities
>
> Goal 3—Building and maintaining a strong, diverse, and inclusive organization that enables NAEYC to achieve Goals 1 and 2" (NAEYC mission and philosophy statement, July 1996)

## Division for Early Childhood of the Council for Exceptional Children

The Division for Early Childhood of the Council for Exceptional Children states as its mission:

> 1. Promoting parent-professional collaboration in all facets of planning, designing, and implementing early childhood intervention services (for children with special needs birth through age eight)
> 2. Advocating for policy planning and best practice in prevention and intervention. DEC supports full access for young children with special needs and their families to natural settings and service-delivery options. Respect for family values, diverse cultural and linguistic backgrounds, and family circumstance are integral considerations in DEC's prevention and intervention efforts
> 3. Supporting those who work with or on behalf of infants and young children with special needs and their families (DEC/CEC membership brochure, 1997)

These mission statements provide insight into the philosophy and purpose of the organizations and the types of programs and services the organizations provide. This information helps individuals select professional organizations most compatible with their own philosophy and career goals.

Professional organizations host local, state, regional, and national workshops and conferences. You can begin participation in professional organizations by simply attending local meetings (if there is a local affiliate in your area), special workshops, seminars, or conferences. Write to individual organizations for information about nearest affiliate groups or workshop opportunities (see appendix E). Become acquainted with the group's purposes and goals, volunteer to serve on local organization committees of special interest to you, or help organize special events such as literacy campaigns, child care quality awareness programs, early childhood educator workshops, fund-raising and toy-lending events, and so on.

Professional organizations publish journals and newsletters through which recent research and public policy events are reported, along with practical literature relating to classroom practices to enhance the professional's day-to-day planning and interactions with children and families. Many of these journals are refereed; that is, the articles are accepted for publication on the basis of approval standards established by the organization. This approval process helps to assure the reader of the accuracy, quality, and appropriateness of the information published in a particular journal.

### Forming Networks of Like-Minded Colleagues

Members of professional organizations represent many facets of the early childhood care and education field, caregiver and educators, public school teachers, Head Start personnel, child care and school administrators, social work professionals, counselors, play therapists, and many others. Through membership, caregivers and teachers form informal networks of friends who communicate throughout the year on topics and concerns germane to their daily work. Through these networks caregivers and teachers establish supportive relationships with one another, share experiences, learn what others are doing in their programs, debate issues, and keep informed of broad issues relating to their work. Through professional association networks, early childhood caregivers and educators learn about legislation and public policy affecting young children and families and can join efforts to support (or defeat, if need be) those policies. Sometimes this networking takes place through computer based networks.

### Technology and the Early Childhood Educator

We now have the technological ability to access an ever-expanding array of information. Virtually all schools and most classrooms have computer capabilities, some more sophisticated than others, and many teachers and students have personal computers in their homes. Not only do computers bring new dimensions to teaching and learning in classrooms, they also provide individuals with unlimited sources of information and opportunities to connect with others in the field.

The Internet, which had its origins more than twenty years ago in the U.S. Department of Defense, has evolved into a widespread communication system largely supported by the National Science Foundation. In recent years schools and colleges have been connecting to the Internet to bring current research and data into classrooms. Individuals can communicate through e-mail, sharing information and common interests with others on local, state,

*Technology makes it possible for teachers to access an infinite amount of information and to network with other early childhood professionals.*

national, and international networks. Today, many colleges, universities, and other training institutions establish class listservs whereby students can form links for sharing, collaborating, and reflecting on their classroom experiences both in the field (e.g., student teaching) and in their scholarly pursuits. Some select a specific topic or question to explore during a designated time frame. This provides students an opportunity to compare and contrast their different perspectives and readings. By communicating with colleagues and instructors through electronic media, students are enriched with both scholarship and support and become a part of a community of learners (Benson & Meyer, 2000). Of course, the Internet itself provides unlimited resources for scholars and practitioners in the early childhood profession.

As with other media—literature, computer software, and film—educators who access the Internet must become discerning consumers. There are wide ranges in the quality and accuracy of material available through cyberspace. Educators need to ask questions about who or what entity is the author of the Web site. Web site addresses offer clues as to the source of the information in the extension or the part of the address that comes after the "dot." For example, ".com" usually represents commercial businesses; ".gov" represents a government agency; ".edu" represents an education agency or institution; and

".org" represents some organization, such as faith-based, social, civic, philanthropic, education, or other group. Reliable Web sites provide information about the authors and how to get in touch with them by phone or postal address. Internet users must keep in mind that simply because text is available on-line does not assure accuracy, currency, reliability, or validity of the content. Nevertheless, learning to navigate the vast amount of information available to educators is a necessary skill and provides an invaluable resource.

Communicating with individuals and resource outlets means finding those who share a common knowledge and research base and seek the best interest of children and their families through high-quality early childhood care and education programs with a developmentally appropriate philosophy. As with all media, the range of topics is infinite. The accuracy of information is variable. Wise choices are as important here as with other sources of information. Most commercial computer outlets and bookstores provide helpful guides on how to get the most from Internet communications. (Many Web sites have been included with the list of professional organizations in appendix E.) Through networking, whether through professional association meetings and conferences or through electronic sources, early childhood educators learn about issues surrounding the early childhood field at large and become actively involved in seeking solutions to issues relating to the lives and experiences of children and families.

### Advocacy and the Early Childhood Educator

Throughout our careers early childhood educators are called upon to respond appropriately to a plethora of issues relating to high-quality experiences for children and families. For example, the most persistent issues early childhood educators face today is that of assuring that young children have the types of experiences that recognize known principles of child growth, development, and learning and that serve the best long-term interests of children and families. As you have read this text, you have probably identified the chief issues early childhood professionals are attempting to address: (1) providing developmentally appropriate interactions and learning experiences, (2) establishing class sizes that allow for optimal learning experiences for children, (3) making certain that those who care for and teach young children are well educated and trained to do so, and (4) establishing and maintaining highest quality child care programs that are affordable and accessible to parents. Helping others understand these issues and participating in the development of viable solutions is an ongoing responsibility of the early childhood professional.

Those of us who work with children and families on a daily basis have firsthand knowledge of their experiences and needs. We are in a unique position through which these needs might be communicated to others. Advocacy is about improving the lives of children and families through participation in decision-making processes. Sometimes that participation means simply sharing with others what we know about children's growth and development needs. Other times it means taking an active role in the political process itself.

Goffin and Lombardi (1989) identify three types of teacher advocacy:

- *Personal advocacy*, in which we address issues in our immediate work places (hygiene, safety, family involvement, developmentally appropriate curricula, and so on)
- *Private sector advocacy*, in which we communicate and collaborate with local businesses, corporations, foundations, and professional and civic organizations to bring awareness of child and family issues before a wider audience
- *Public policy advocacy*, in which we communicate with local, state, and federal policy makers in an effort to influence policies or legislation that serves the best interest of children and families

Because young children cannot speak for themselves, an important role of the early childhood professional is to be a spokesperson for high-quality early experiences for young children. On a one-on-one basis, we can do this in our schools and centers by sharing with colleagues recent professional journal articles, discussing their content, and exploring what new information may mean for daily practices and curriculum models in our own programs. It may mean sharing brochures and professional parenting literature published by our professional associations with parents and policy makers in our communities. Advocacy includes discussing this information in parent meetings and support groups, selecting appropriate professional literature to highlight in school or center newsletters or post on bulletin boards, and taking an active role in local events associated with state or national child-advocacy campaigns.

Through professional associations, large numbers of members can take a stand through awareness campaigns; position statements; representation on local, state, and national public policy task force groups and fact-gathering committees; and committees who monitor or help author legislation. Sometimes several professional, business, and community organizations join forces to raise awareness or promote certain issues or causes.

National, state, and local professional child development, family development, and early childhood education associations in alliance with one another play prominent roles in guiding and supporting high-quality early experiences for very young children. For instance, through the collaborative work of professional organizations, the Stand for Children and "I Am Your Child" campaigns launched in 1996 and 1997 respectively, focused public attention on the importance of the early years in an unprecedented manner. Television documentaries, news magazine special features, public forums, a gathering of thousands at the foot of the Lincoln Monument in

---

**BIOGRAPHY BOX** *Barbara Bowman*

Barbara Bowman is one of three faculty members who founded the Erikson Institute in 1966. She is an authority on early education and a nationally recognized advocate for improved and expanded training for practitioners who work with children and families.

Bowman, a past president of the National Association for the Education of Young Children, combines advocacy at the national level with a strong commitment to leadership and teaching. At Erikson, she teaches courses in early education and administration. She has also taught at universities in China and Iran. In addition, she has directed training projects for Head Start teachers, caregivers of infants at risk for morbidity or mortality, and preschool primary teachers and administrators. Her research has most recently focused on assessment practices. She is a frequent consultant on parent support programs.

Bowman has served on numerous national boards. She earned her B.A. from Sarah Lawrence College and her M.A. from the University of Chicago. Honors include DHL from Bank Street College of Education, Roosevelt University, Dominican University, and Governor's State University.

Photo courtesy of Kathy Richland Photography.

---

Washington, D.C., distribution of brochures, and the establishment of network Web sites throughout the country urged legislators, the voting public, and professionals in the field to focus on issues surrounding child life in America. Recent research on early brain growth and neurological development has precipitated a number of professional conferences, including a White House Conference on Early Childhood Development in April 1997. Instrumental in bringing about many of these advocacy efforts, and one of the nation's most outspoken and well-known child advocates, is Marian Wright Edelman, executive director of the Children's Defense Fund.

It has been said that the quality of a program is measured against the degree to which the program meets the standards of the profession (Koralek, Colker, & Dodge, 1993). National and regional professional organizations such as the Association for Childhood Education, International (ACEI), Association for Supervision and Curriculum Development (ASCD), National Association for the Education of Young Children (NAEYC), National Association of Early Childhood Teacher Educators (NAECTE), and Southern Early Childhood Association (SECA), to mention only a few, have led the way to establishing quality standards and articulating them to members of the profession and to the public.

Advocacy then is both an individual opportunity and a collaborative one. Each early childhood professional finds that certain niche in which he or she feels most comfortable promoting best practices and high-quality lives for children and their families. While working through groups gives clout and voice to professional concerns, advocacy need not be associated only with large or grand efforts. Perhaps the strongest advocacy is that which emulates best practices with young children on a day-to-day basis in high-quality programs that effectively serve the needs of children and families.

## A Summary Definition of Professionalism in Early Childhood Care and Education

From the foregoing, a definition of professionalism in early childhood education emerges. It is generally accepted that the early childhood professional is one who:

- Has had specialized education and training in child growth and development and early childhood education.
- Possesses a certain body of knowledge shared by others in the profession.
- Demonstrates a specialized set of skills essential to caring for and educating young children.
- Commits to providing the healthiest and most psychologically sound experiences for young children.
- Articulates the essentials of developmentally appropriate practices to others—families, colleagues, policy makers.
- Participates in the early childhood profession at large through membership in early childhood professional organizations.
- Commits to being accountable to a professional code of ethics.
- Expects professional development to be an ongoing career-long process.

Professionalism is not a static state; it is one in which the individual is always getting better. Commitment to high-quality lives for children and families is the central focus of the professional's career, and striving for best practices is an exercise in persistence.

## CHALLENGES CONFRONTING EARLY CHILDHOOD PROFESSIONALS

As we begin this discussion, our text has come full circle. High-quality early childhood care and education programs can make a difference in the lives of children and families. Perhaps the greatest challenge in early childhood profession is assuring that young children at home and in out-of-home programs have the kinds of environments and interpersonal experiences that promote optimal development. The research is quite clear about the importance of adult-child relationships during the early formative years. Challenges, then, confronting early childhood professionals center on:

- Meeting the early developmental needs of infants and young children as we learn more and more about human growth and development and diversity.

*"Neither loving children nor teaching them is, in and of itself, sufficient for optimal development; thinking and feeling work in tandem."*
*Barbara T. Bowman,*
*M. Suzanne Donovan,*
*M. Susan Burns*

## BIOGRAPHY BOX *Marian Wright Edelman*

Marian Wright Edelman, founder and president of the Children's Defense Fund (CDF), has been an advocate for disadvantaged Americans for her entire professional career. Under her leadership, the Washington-based CDF has become a strong national voice for children and families. CDF's mission is to educate the nation about the needs of children and encourage preventative investment in children before they get sick, drop out of school, suffer too-early pregnancy or family breakdown, or get into trouble. In this new century, CDF seeks to ensure that no child is left behind and that every child has a Healthy Start, a Head Start, a Fair Start, a Safe Start, and a Moral Start in life with the support of caring parents and communities.

Mrs. Edelman, a graduate of Spelman College and Yale Law School, began her career in the mid-60s when, as the first black woman admitted to the Mississippi Bar, she directed the NAACP Legal Defense and Educational Fund office in Jackson, Mississippi. In 1968, she moved to Washington, D.C., as counsel for the Poor People's March that Dr. Martin Luther King, Jr., began organizing before his death. She founded the Washington Research Project, a public interest law firm and the parent body of the Children's Defense Fund. For two years, she served as the director of the Center for Law and Education at Harvard University, and in 1973 began CDF.

Having received many honorary degrees and awards including the Albert Schweitzer Humanitarian Prize, the Heinz Award, and a Fellowship from the MacArthur Foundation, Edelman has served on the board of trustees of Spelman College which she chaired from 1976 to 1987. A prolific writer, she is the author of *Families in Peril: An Agenda for Social Change, The Measure of Our Success: A Letter to My Children and Yours*, and the 1995 book, *Guide My Feet: Meditations and Prayers on Loving and Working for Children*.

Marian Wright Edelman is married to Peter Edelman, a professor at Georgetown Law School. They have three sons: Joshua, Jonah, and Ezra.

- Communicating and collaborating with parents of many cultures, languages, and value orientations.
- Communicating and collaborating with a wide range of services for children and families, including health-care and nutrition programs, speech and hearing specialists, a variety of services for children with special needs, and family support programs.
- Maintaining a cadre of early childhood professionals who are committed to serving the best interests of children and families.
- Striving for higher, more stringently enforced standards of quality for programs serving children and families.
- Assuring that adults who work with young children are highly qualified and hold appropriate credentials.

Each of these challenges have been previously addressed in this text. However, the last two challenges seem to warrant attention here. Raising standards of quality for early childhood programs and assuring qualified personnel are two emerging issues of some urgency.

Recent studies have revealed some disturbing facts about the quality and developmental appropriateness of far too many early childhood programs. The Children's Defense Fund (1996, 2001) reported that "only one in seven child care centers and one in 10 family child care homes are of good enough quality to enhance children's development" (CDF, 1996, p. 26) and improvements have not been forthcoming (CDF, 2000). Further, it is reported by a study of 225 child-care centers' infant/toddler programs that only 8.4 percent of the classrooms were developmentally appropriate. The rest were of poor quality (40.4 percent) such that health and safety were jeopardized, or of mediocre quality (51.1 percent), which was thought to neither harm nor help children (Cost, Quality and Child Outcomes Study Team, 1995). Studies by the Families and Work Institute of family child-care homes and relative care found that 35 percent of the care children receive in these settings is of such poor quality that it harms children's development, finding that 56 percent of the care is merely custodial, and only 9 percent is good enough to have any positive influence on child development (Galinsky, Howes, Kontos, & Shinn, 1994). Studies of implementation of developmentally appropriate practices reviewed by Dunn and Kontos (1997) indicate that as few as one-third to one-fifth of the early childhood and primary programs studied exemplified developmentally appropriate practices.

The reasons behind these findings are multiple, relating to training requirements, high costs of providing quality child care, political issues in public schools relating to test-driven curricula that often mitigate against developmentally appropriate practices, and parent awareness of quality and developmental issues. There are no easy solutions to these multiple causes. However, early childhood training and credentialing and enforcing higher standards for licensure and accreditation are two major approaches spearheaded by professional organizations.

The National Association for the Education of Young Children has laid the groundwork for addressing these issues through its voluntary center accreditation program, and the publication of *Guidelines for Preparation of Early Childhood Professionals* (National Association for the Education of Young Children et al., 2002). These latter guidelines have been endorsed by the Association of Teacher Educators, the Division for Early Childhood of the Council for Exceptional Children, and the National Board for Professional Teaching Standards.

## Preparation of Early Childhood Professionals

Assuring well-qualified personnel to work with young children and their families represents a major challenge to the early childhood profession. The responsibility for this rests not only with individuals to assure their own

*The most important difference between professionals and nonprofessionals in any field goes far beyond being able to do the job without outside direction: It is that professionals are interested in [high] quality. The work they do themselves is [of high] quality, and, if they manage or teach others, it is important to them that they do [high] quality work. Getting the job done, even done well, is good enough for nonprofessionals, but continually improving the way the job is done both for themselves and others is the hallmark of professionals.*

*–William Glasser*

knowledge and skills, but with the early childhood professional collective to encourage only those best suited for work with young children to enter the profession. The qualities of individuals best suited for work with young children has been described throughout this text. The need for specialized training has also been emphasized. Avenues for obtaining appropriate training and credentials to work with young children exist through the national Child Development Associate Credential programs and through colleges, universities, and other certifying entities.

### Child Development Associate Credential

The Child Development Associate (CDA) credentialing program is a national effort to credential caregivers who work with children from birth to age five in center-based child care programs, family day-care homes, and as home visitors. The Council for Early Childhood Professional Recognition, Washington, D.C., operates the program. It is a performance-based program in that professional Child Development Associates are expected to demonstrate certain competencies in order to receive the credential to work with young children and their families. Performance is centered on the following competency goals:

1. To establish and maintain a safe, healthy learning environment
2. To advance physical and intellectual competence
3. To support social and emotional development and provide positive guidance
4. To establish positive and productive relationships with families
5. To ensure a well-run, purposeful program responsive to participant needs
6. To maintain a commitment to professionalism

Additional information about these goals and competencies can be found in Appendix F.

The CDA program offers endorsements in four areas: center-based preschool, center-based infant/toddler, family child care, and home visitor. In addition, individuals working in bilingual (Spanish/English) programs may obtain additional training toward a specialization in that area. The CDA credential is granted on the basis of direct assessment of knowledge and performance of individuals who meet certain criteria relating to prior training and experience, or through specialized training followed by performance assessment.

### Public School Teacher Certification

The last twenty years have been a period of rapid growth in public-education programs for young children. It is reported that in 1974 only thirteen states offered kindergarten to all their five-year-olds. Today every state provides full- or half-day kindergarten in some, if not all of their districts. Thirty-nine

**BIOGRAPHY BOX** *Carol Brunson Day (formerly Phillips)*

Carol Brunson Day is executive director of the Council for Early Childhood Professional Recognition, Child Development Associate National Credentialing Program in Washington, D.C. Day received her bachelor of arts degree in psychology from the University of Wisconsin, her mas-

ter of arts degree in early childhood education from the Erikson Institute, and her Ph.D in education from Claremont Graduate School. Day has been involved in the early childhood profession for many years. As a member of the Human Development Faculty at Pacific Oaks College in Pasadena, she specialized in early childhood education and cultural influences on development for thirteen years.

states and the District of Columbia provide state financed prekindergarten for selected populations of three- to five-year-old children, and three of these states and the District of Columbia provide prekindergarten to anyone. (Typically, states have made prekindergarten available to children of families whose incomes fall below the poverty level or who do not speak English.) In 2002, 11.9 million children younger than five were enrolled in some type of early childhood education program ("Quality Counts," 2002).

As early childhood programs, prekindergarten, kindergarten, and preschools for at-risk children have become more and more a part of public education, so has the need for well-qualified early childhood professionals. Recognizing that the manner in which young children are taught is quite different from that of older children, teacher preparation institutions have developed specialized preparation programs, field experiences, and certifications for persons entering the early childhood education profession.

All states have teacher certification requirements, though there is great variation in these requirements from state to state. Indeed, states vary in their definitions of early childhood. Some define the period for which certification might be granted from birth through anywhere from age five through age thirteen. Others limit the period from birth through age eight (as does the early childhood profession); still others do not include infant and toddler ages in their certification programs. Certificates then reflect the states' "definition" of early childhood and qualify teachers for assignment in grades commensurate with this definition.

By the same token, college and university training programs vary in the emphasis placed on the early years and on attention to the type of settings in which the early childhood professional will be employed. Traditionally, university departments and schools of education have trained individuals for positions in public schools. Two-year colleges, through vocational home economics and child development programs, have prepared individuals for work with children in child care settings. Today, there is greater collaboration among various training entities in which credits earned toward one type of training may well be applied to another, reducing appreciably the duplication of course work, and recognizing a common body of knowledge that can expand and can become more comprehensive with additional levels of education.

### Accreditation of Early Childhood Programs

The NAEYC launched a voluntary accreditation system in 1984 with the publication of *Accreditation Criteria and Procedures of the National Academy of Early Childhood Programs* (revised 2002). This accreditation system applies standards of quality that address all components of early childhood programs, including staff-child interactions, staff-parent interactions, administration, staffing, staff qualifications and continuing development, physical environments, curricula, health and safety, nutrition and food service, administration, and on-going program evaluation.

The NAEYC accreditation system has two major goals: "(1) to help early childhood program personnel become involved in a process that will facilitate real and lasting improvements in the quality of the individual program seeking accreditation, and (2) to evaluate quality for the purpose of accrediting those programs that demonstrate substantial compliance with criteria for high quality" (Bredekamp, 1984, p. 1). To assure the validity of the accreditation criteria, NAEYC obtained systematic reviews and input from thousands of early childhood professionals. NAEYC created a division known today as the National Academy of Early Childhood Programs to carry out the accreditation program. Since its inception, the NAEYC accreditation process has had a significant impact on raising consumer and employee awareness of quality in programs serving young children and families. Professional early childhood educators today support and encourage accreditation of all programs serving young children and their families.

## ANTICIPATING YOUR OWN CAREER PATH

Each of us comes into career decisions through different pathways. Some have known since childhood the career we want to pursue. Others have been encouraged by important role models in our lives: parents, teachers, counselors, mentors, friends. Still others have had experiences with children, either one's own or in working with others, that have sparked an interest in an early childhood career. Regardless of inspiration, each of us has a professional goal and can lay plans for achieving that goal.

A personnel director for our nearby school district has a standard question he asks candidates for teaching positions: "Where do you want to be in five years? . . . ten years? What do you hope to accomplish during those years?" Quite thought-provoking questions. How would you answer them? Perhaps you haven't thought about your plans beyond your present goals.

Now, however, is as good a time as any to think about your goals. Reflect on these questions:

- In what type setting do you feel most suited to work: family home setting; center-based child care, private preschool, public prekindergarten or kindergarten, parenting, adult education?
- What age children have you found most intriguing: infants, toddlers, three- to four-year-olds, five-year-olds, six-, seven-, or eight-year olds?
- To which age group do you feel you can most easily relate?
- What aspects of teaching have you found most interesting so far: classroom design, materials selection, curriculum planning, setting goals for individual children, planning for short- or long-term developmental outcomes, planning for children with special needs, collaborating with parents, learning about and relating to diverse cultures?
- What curriculum topics do you find particularly enjoyable: literacy, language arts, mathematics, science, social studies, art, music, drama, physical/motor activities, enhancing and mediating child play, or others?
- What areas of human growth and development have you found to be particularly interesting: neurological development and brain growth, physical/motor development, cognitive, language, social, emotional, moral development?
- What aspects of the early childhood education profession itself have attracted your interest: learning about early childhood education history, child growth and development in general, assessing student outcomes, working with parents, communicating with colleagues, learning about the professional organizations, child advocacy, political issues surrounding policy decisions in early childhood care and education?
- Have you identified other interests?

Reflecting on your own personal interests and strengths is the first step in anticipating a career path. Setting goals around these interests is the second step. Anticipating, as the personnel director requests, where you want to be in two, five, and ten years helps you to lay plans for getting there.

## From Goals to Plans and Experiences

According to NAEYC, a professional path requires completion of a professional preparation program that meets recognized guidelines leading to a degree (and sometimes certification), or ongoing participation in formal training leading to competencies that may be assessed for credit toward a degree or special credential such as the CDA described above (Willer, 1994). Table 10–1 identifies professional categories commensurate with levels of informal and formal training.

**TABLE 10–1**

*Definitions of Early Childhood (Professional Categories)*

*This table is designed to reflect a continuum of professional development. The levels identify preparation requirements for which standards have been established nationally.*

**Early Childhood Professional Level VI**

Successful completion of a Ph.D. or Ed.D. in a program conforming to NAEYC guidelines; OR

Successful demonstration of the knowledge, performance, and dispositions expected as outcomes of a doctoral degree program conforming to NAEYC guidelines.

**Early Childhood Professional Level V**

Successful completion of a master's degree in a program that conforms to NAEYC guidelines; OR

Successful demonstration of the knowledge, performance, and dispositions expected as outcomes of a master's degree program conforming to NAEYC guidelines.

**Early Childhood Professional Level IV**

Successful completion of a baccalaureate degree from a program conforming to NAEYC guidelines; OR

State certificate meeting NAEYC certification guidelines; OR

Successful completion of a baccalaureate degree in another field with more than 30 professional units in early childhood development/education including 300 hours of supervised teaching experience, including 150 hours each for two of the following three age groups infants and toddlers, 3- to 5-year-olds, or the primary grades; OR

Successful demonstration of the knowledge, performance, and dispositions expected as outcomes of a baccalaureate degree program conforming to NAEYC guidelines.

**Early Childhood Professional Level III**

Successful completion of an associate degree from a program conforming to NAEYC guidelines; OR

Successful completion of an associate degree in a related field, plus 30 units of professional studies in early childhood development/education including 300 hours of supervised teaching experience in an early childhood program; OR

Successful demonstration of the knowledge, performance, and dispositions expected as outcomes of an associate degree program conforming to NAEYC guidelines.

**TABLE 10.1 (continued)**

**Early Childhood Professional Level II**

II. B. Successful completion of a one-year early childhood certificate program.

II. A. Successful completion of the CDA Professional Preparation Program OR completion of a systematic, comprehensive training program that prepares an individual to successfully acquire the CDA Credential through direct assessment.

**Early Childhood Professional Level I**

Individuals who are employed in an early childhood professional role working under supervision or with support (e.g., linkages with provider association or network or enrollment in supervised practicum) and participating in training designed to lead to the assessment of individual competencies or acquisition of a degree.

*Source:* Johnson, J., & McCracken, J.B. (Eds.), 1994. *The early childhood career lattice: Perspectives on professional development.* (p. 16). Washington DC: NAEYC Reprinted with permission from the National Association for the Education of Young Children.

In addition to formal training, there are other opportunities to enhance professional growth. Working closely with a practicing early childhood educator through volunteer work, as an employed aide, or through formal or informal mentoring, you can gain valuable firsthand experience. Direct experience with a skilled professional early childhood educator provides the learner many opportunities to observe, explore, inquire, and experiment with ideas while receiving valuable instruction and feedback. Your course instructor can help you identify developmentally appropriate classrooms in which these types of opportunities are available.

Mentoring experiences should occur in different types of settings throughout your training so that an understanding of many facets of the early childhood profession is gained. In planning your career path, it is particularly enriching to experience children and teaching in many settings—child care, infant programs, school-age child care, public and private preschools—in order to gain a gestalt of the profession, enlarge your awareness of the needs of children and families, and to ascertain your particular areas of interests and skill. Again, selecting exemplary programs is important if observation and participation is to be truly helpful.

In addition to formal education opportunities, there are numerous opportunities to enrich your knowledge and experiential base. In addition to the professional development mentioned earlier in this chapter, such as keeping up with the literature and becoming active in professional associations, there are also serendipitous opportunities. Pay close attention to community endeavors that are associated with child and family life and education. Media public service announcements often highlight child and family issues and community events. Newspapers announce family life education and child development seminars. Bookstores sometimes feature authors of children's books or well-known authorities in education, child development, and related fields. Pediatricians' offices provide informational fliers and literature for parents of young children, as do local health departments. Hospitals often offer child-health, safety, nutrition, baby-sitting seminars, new parent classes, and other related topics of interest to early childhood educators. It is also enlightening to read the types of literature parents read (newsstand parenting magazines) and compare the content of the articles with professional literature in order to best respond to conversations about topics of interest to parents. Attend local school board meetings and visit with a city councilperson or state legislator who is interested in education and child and family issues; ask to be placed on their mailing lists. If you travel, seize the opportunity to arrange visits to child care and early childhood programs in the city, state, or country you are visiting. Becoming a skilled and knowledgeable professional early childhood educator means exploring many sources of information and availing oneself to many types of experiences. Do not limit yourself to a few textbooks or the graded assignments required in course work, as important as these are! The field is far too large and captivating.

One way to convert goals to plans is to begin the development of a personal professional planning and documenting portfolio. Portfolio development can begin at any point in one's career, but as you project a future in the early childhood profession, consider the talents, experiences, and interests that you currently bring.

### Beginning a Professional Development Portfolio

There is no one particular design for a professional development portfolio; it is often as unique as the individual creating it. Keep in mind that you are in control of your portfolio and its contents. Your portfolio can be a powerful motivation in that as you reflect upon its contents and its future contents, you can plan for your own ongoing professional enrichment. Indeed, perhaps the greatest value of portfolio development is the self-reflection that its contents can evoke.

For a beginner's purpose, the professional development portfolio is defined as a multifaceted assemblage of plans and products of student efforts toward professional development. It is necessary to distinguish this planning portfolio from a portfolio in which one might be assessed for admission to student teaching, for instance, or one presented during an interview for a child care or teaching position. The professional development portfolio is not as structured nor as rigidly assessed as performance portfolios might be.

This initial professional development portfolio helps the student set goals, reflect upon knowledge and skills needed to achieve those goals, and to anticipate opportunities for acquiring such knowledge and skills. Such a portfolio might contain, but is not limited to, the following:

- Student *professional goals statement*
- *Formal degree plan* or a competency achievement plan
- *Résumé* of prior experiences with young children
- *Two-, three-, four-year calendar* of expected formal course work and field experiences and classroom or center *visitations*
- File folder of upcoming *professional organization meetings*, conferences, seminars, or other professional development events to be scheduled when feasible
- *Selected works in progress*, such as research papers or sample lesson plans
- *Professional literature logs* (some students prefer to keep card files of professional literature; be certain to record complete bibliographical information so that you can find the document or book should you wish to return to it at a later date)
- *Field experience and observation logs* (sometimes these logs become dialogue documents as well, when student and mentor teachers share observations and comments about them)
- *Networking* and *electronic communications,* logs, and journals
- *Curiosity file:* concepts, vocabulary, contradictions, discrepancies, questions you wish to have clarified through self-study or class discussions
- A *videotape* of yourself teaching a lesson or working with a small group of children that can be viewed with a mentor or perhaps classmates whom you may trust to provide constructive feedback. Appendix H delineates suggested contents of a professional portfolio.

You may think of other planning items to include to help you self-assess and plan for your initial professional development. As you progress through your professional development program, your portfolio (which is a dynamic work in progress and changes over time) will become more focused, its contents more clearly related to actual performance and products.

In this section we have attempted to illustrate that professional development is an ongoing process. Early childhood professionals are responsible adults who continually seek opportunities to enhance their knowledge and skills in working with young children and their families. As you embark upon your studies and pursuit of a career in early childhood care and education, we, the authors, extend to you a warm welcome and wish for you a challenging and rewarding career path with many memorable and growth-enhancing experiences.

*A beginning teacher is also a beginning scholar. There are many years of study ahead. Learning does not end at the completion of student teaching. There are many important gaps in your grasp of the teaching profession. To be adequately informed will require continuous updating in the years to come.*

*-F. D. Kreamelmeyer*

## Summary

With increasing scientific emphasis on the importance of the early years in human growth and development, the early childhood education profession is in the spotlight. In the years to come child care and early education programs will probably come under more scrutiny than ever before. Like no other time in history, the demands for truly educated and qualified early childhood educators is mounting. Training programs will become focused as much on the biology of growth and development as on the pedagogy of teaching. Professional early childhood educators will be called upon to clarify and justify their practices on the basis of emerging information from the biological and psychological fields.

As parents and the general public become more aware of the long-term effects of early life experiences and as the need for child care mounts, we can anticipate greater demands for evidence of high quality through educator licensure and certification and stronger licensing standards and accreditation of programs serving children and families.

## Reflections

**1.** Advocacy takes knowledge and time. With your classmates, make a list of issues surrounding child development and family life to which early childhood educator advocacy might be addressed. Discuss how early childhood professionals might address these issues through advocacy efforts.
**2.** With your classmates, create a list of issues confronting families and children today. What implications do these issues have for early childhood caregivers and teachers? Will services and curricula necessarily need to be structured in particular ways in order to accommodate the needs of today's children and families? If so, how?
**3.** Form a small group of colleagues with whom you feel comfortable sharing your planning portfolio. Together discuss what types of experiences would enhance each of your plans and help each of you best achieve your goals.
**4.** After observing in a number of classrooms and child care centers, develop with a partner a composite profile of the professional early childhood educator. Make a list of characteristics and qualities. Compare your profile with that of others in your class. Discuss the training and experiential prerequisites to becoming an early childhood professional.

## Field Experiences

**1.** With the help of your instructor, identify one or more professional meetings or conferences you and several of your colleagues can attend. In class, share your insights gained with one another: what were the purposes of the meeting(s); what types of concerns or topics were addressed; what early childhood careers were represented among the participants; what did you learn that you did not know before you attended? Did you leave the meeting with concerns, questions, or resolve?

**2.** Interview at least ten early childhood educators. Ask what they find to be the most rewarding aspects of their work, and what they find to be the most challenging or frustrating aspects of their work. If they could give a beginner one piece of advice, what would it be?

## Further Reading

Bowman, B., Donovan, M. S. & Burns, M. S.(Eds.). (2000). *Eager to learn: Educating our preschoolers*. Washington, DC: National Academy Press. (www.nap.edu).

Cummings, C. (1995). *Creating good schools for young children: Right from the start: A study of eleven developmentally appropriate primary school programs*. Alexandria, VA: National Association of State Boards of Education.

Feeney, S., & Freeman, N. K. (1999). *Ethics and the early childhood educator: Using the NAEYC code*. Washington, DC: National Association for the Education of Young Children.

Kohn, A. (2000). *The schools our children deserve: Moving beyond traditional classrooms and tougher standards*. New York: Houghton Mifflin.

Nash, B. J. (1996). *"Real world" ethics: Frameworks for educators and human service professionals*. New York: Columbia University.

Odom, S. L. (Ed.). (2002). *Widening the circle: Including children with disabilities in preschool programs*. Washington, DC: National Association for the Education of Young Children.

Robinson, A., & Stark, D. R. (2002). *Advocates in action: Making a difference for young children*. Washington, DC: National Association for the Education of Young Children.

Shonkoff, J. P. & Phillips, (Eds.). (2000). *From neurons to neighborhoods: The science of early childhood development*. Washington, DC: National Academy Press. (www.nap.edu)

Tertell, E. A., Klein, S. M., & Jewett, J. L. (Eds.) (1998). *When teachers reflect: Journeys toward effective, inclusive practice*. Washington, DC: National Association for the Education of Young Children.

## Helpful Web Sites

### Child Trends

www.childtrends.org/

*A nonprofit, nonpartisan research center that studies trends relating to children and families. This organization tracks data on major indicators of children's well-being, analyzes trends, and provides timely data.*

**National Association for the Education of Young Children**
www.naeyc.org/profdev
*Describes the NAEYC Standards for Early Childhood Professional Preparation, providing the full text of the standards and accompanying research and theory relating to the standards.*

**National Child Care Information Center**
www.nccic.org
*This online library, developed in partnership with the ERIC Clearinghouse on Elementary and Early Childhood Education, makes accessible thousands of documents related to child care.*

**Wheelock College**
www.institute.wheelock.edu
*This is the site of the Wheelock College Institute for Initiatives in Leadership and Career Development program committed to creating equitable, accessible, and exemplary career development systems in early childhood education.*

**National Board for Professional Teaching Standards**
www.nbpts.org
*The National Board for Professional Teaching Standards (NBPTS) provides certification for experienced teachers who voluntarily go through extensive self-study, documentation, and assessment to demonstrate their expertise and skills.*

**Connect for Kids**
www.connectforkids.org
*Provides current information on many topics relating to children, families, education, and advocacy. Includes Web sites and contact addresses with new items and articles.*

## Epilogue

The information presented in this introductory text is just that—an introduction. There are so many facets to working with young children and their families that the study of early childhood education must be a lifelong endeavor. If you decide to stay in this field, you should be prepared to continue the study you've begun in this course. You should read teacher magazines and professional journals and books on a regular basis. You should join professional organizations and be active in them. You should attend conferences and go to in-service presentations. You should have frequent conversations with like-minded colleagues about how to implement best practice for young children and how to work effectively with families. Early childhood education is not a profession for those who are not willing to work hard.

Becoming an early childhood educator is not a decision to be taken lightly. Working with young children is demanding. It is physically, emotionally, and intellectually exacting and there are many responsibilities associated with working with young children. Too many people choose to study early childhood education because they love young children or because they think working with small children will be "so much fun." These reasons are not good enough for choosing this field of work.

However, if you are thinking about becoming an early childhood educator because you want to make a difference in this world and you are willing to work hard, you will find working with young children and their families fulfilling and rewarding. Every day you work with young children in developmentally appropriate ways, you can be confident that you are making differences in lives.

There are moments in the lives of every early childhood educator when the responsibility and the joy of this profession become very clear. For Margaret Puckett, a moment of great responsibility came to her through the words of a five-year-old boy. It was during a morning group meeting where her kindergarten students were sharing stories and things they had brought from home. Margaret always felt that these meetings offered opportunities for the children and her to grow closer to each other as members of a caring, sharing community. These times were always enjoyable, one of her favorite times of the day.

This particular morning, the conversation flowed easily from among Margaret and her students. She noticed one boy, Phillip, sitting quietly. He seemed both eager and reticent to join in the group conversation. She asked, "Phillip, did you bring a story or something you would like to share with the class?" Phillip stood as though ready to make an important announcement, but then he hesitated. He stood swinging his shoulders from side to side, looking up and around, and putting his fingers in his mouth. Gently, Margaret pressed, "Did you want to tell us what you brought to class today?" Finally, in a somewhat wry voice, grinning with mild embarrassment, he said, "I brought you me, Mrs. Puckett. I brought you me."

Phillip's words were more profound than he could know. In that moment, Margaret was reminded of the powerful responsibility that comes with working with young children. Every day we work with young children, they bring themselves to us. Teachers touch children's present and future lives in profound ways, though they may never know the outcomes. All of us who care for and teach young children leave imprints that will affect them for the rest of their lives. This critical responsibility weighs heavily on early childhood educators. But along with the realization of this responsibility comes the joy in knowing that high-quality early childhood experiences—provided by knowledgeable early childhood educators—positively affect the lives of young children now and in their adult lives.

For additional information on teaching young children, visit our Web site at **http://www.earlychilded.delmar.com**

# APPENDIX A

# LEARNING CENTER MATERIALS

## Art Center Materials

Easel with containers for tempera paints, including skin-tone tempera paints

Other paints: finger paints, watercolor sets, tempera markers

Paint brushes, paint rollers, foam brushes

Smocks or old adult-sized shirts

Crayons and markers, including multicultural crayons and markers

Colored chalk

Glue, glue stick

Pipe cleaners

Popsicle® sticks

Ribbon, yarn, sequins, glitter, confetti, feathers

Straws, pie plates, and other three-dimensional materials

Scissors

Masking and transparent tape

Clay

Play dough

Rolling pins and cookie cutters

Sponges

Manila, tissue, crepe, and opaque paper

Newsprint

Books that relate to art topics, biographies of master painters, picture books that use particular media as illustrations

## Block Center Materials

Unit blocks

Large hollow blocks

Brick blocks

Snap or bristle blocks (larger sizes for younger children)

Lego® or Duplos® and Lego® tables

Sets of wooden people, such as family members, airport crew

Sets of animals, such as farm animals or zoo animals

Cars, trucks, airplanes

Sets of small street signs

Wooden doll furniture

Rulers, yardsticks, and retractable tape measures

Collection of nuts and bolts for children who no longer put objects in their mouths

Books related to buildings and construction

## Dramatic Play Center Materials

Kitchen/dining room furniture, child sized

Cooking utensils

Empty cans of food or empty food boxes

Cookbooks

Dress-up clothes

Dolls representing different ethnicities

Cribs and items used to care for dolls

Telephone and telephone books

Prop boxes for several different play themes

Books about families or other play themes

## Listening Center Materials

Tape recorder with 3–4 headsets

Collection of age-appropriate books with accompanying audio tapes

Collection of various music tapes

Collection of environmental sound tapes

Tapes made by the class or individual students

## Math Center Materials

Collections of real objects (for older preschoolers and elementary school students) to use for sorting, classifying, and counting: buttons, shells, keys, pebbles, seeds, and nuts

Nesting cubes

Playing cards

Dice

Dominoes

Pattern blocks

Inch square tiles

Linking cubes

Two-color counters

Cuisenaire® rods

Stringing beads

Pegboards and pegs

Geoboards and rubber bands

Abacus

Rulers

Yardsticks

Cash register

Play money

Balance scales

Hourglass

Kitchen timer

Counting books and other books that have math themes

## Music Center Materials

Instruments such as drums, rhythm sticks, shakers, tone blocks, triangles, clackers, bells, cymbals, tone bells, and triangles

Child- and teacher-made instruments

Costumes and scarves for creative movement activities

Batons for conducting

Blank staff-lined paper

Pictures and books about famous composers and musicians

Song books

Books with musical themes

## Reading Center Materials

Wide variety of picture books, poetry, fiction, and nonfiction

Big books

Class-made and child-made books

Children's magazines

Pillows, cushions, or other items to make area cozy and inviting

Posters

## Sand and Water Center Materials

Sand or water (or other materials such as rice or birdseed)

Measuring cups and spoons

Small buckets and shovels

Sand molds

Spray bottles

Sieves, funnels, and plastic tubing

Plastic turkey basters and medicine droppers

Ladles, egg beaters, margarine containers

Sponges

Styrofoam, wood, plastic, and cork pieces

Water-works toys

Vinyl smocks

## Science Center Materials

Pets appropriate to classroom such as guinea pigs, hamsters, gerbils, rats, nonpoisonous snakes, turtles, rabbits, fish, birds

Live insects

Empty nests

Different types of plants

Seeds, small containers, and potting soil

Collections of rocks and fossils or seashells

Bark, twigs, leaves, feathers

Sound jars

Scent jars

Scales

Magnets

Magnifying glasses and binoculars

Eyedroppers and funnels

Locks and keys

Pulleys and levers

Charts and posters of science-related interests (purchased or made by children)

Books related to other items in the center

Magazines such as *Ranger Rick* or *ZooBooks*

## Writing Center Materials

Variety of paper types, including a variety of sizes, shapes, colors, and textures

Index cards

Markers, crayons, pencils, colored pencils

Pencil sharpeners

Paper clips

Envelopes

Tape, glue, glue stick

Rubber stamps and ink pads

Staplers

Hole punches

Tape recorder and blank audio tapes

Books that feature writing

# APPENDIX B

# ADULT: CHILD RATIOS RECOMMENDED BY NAEYC

The National Association for the Education of Young Children provides the following guidelines for staff-child ratios at child care centers.

### For Infants (Birth–12 Months)
A group of ten infants should be supervised by one teacher for every three infants (1:3). Twelve infants is the maximum number recommended and should be cared for by one caregiver for every four children (1:4).

### For Toddlers (12–24 Months)
A group of ten toddlers should have one caregiver for every three toddlers (1:3); for a group of twelve, one caregiver for every four children (1:4); for a group of fourteen, one caregiver for every five children (1:5); for a group of sixteen, one caregiver for every four children (1:4).

### For Two-Year-Olds
A group of ten two-year-olds should have one caregiver for every four children (1:4); for a group of twelve, one caregiver for every five children (1:5); for a group of fourteen, one caregiver for every six children (1:6).

### For Three-Year-Olds
For a group of fourteen three-year-olds, one caregiver for every seven children (1:7); for a group of sixteen, one caregiver for every eight children (1:8); a group of eighteen children by one caregiver (1:9); and for a group of twenty children, one caregiver for every ten children (1:10).

### For Four-Year-Olds
For a group of fourteen four-year-olds, one caregiver for every eight children (1:8); for a group of sixteen, one caregiver for every nine children (1:9); and for a group of twenty children, one caregiver for every ten children (1:10).

### For Five-Year-Olds
For a group of sixteen five-year-olds, one caregiver for every eight children (1:8); for a group of eighteen, one caregiver for every nine children (1:9); and for a group of twenty children, one caregiver for every ten children (1:10).

### For Six- to Eight-Year-Olds
For a group of twenty-two children, one caregiver for every ten children (1:10); for a group of twenty-four, one caregiver for every eleven children (1:11); and for a group of twenty-eight children, one caregiver for every twelve children (1:12).

SOURCE: From *Accreditation Criteria and Procedures*, (rev. ed., p. 47, 1998). Washington, DC: NAEYC. Copyright 1998 by the National Association for the Education of Young Children. Reprinted with permission from the National Association for the Education of Young Children.

# APPENDIX C

## CODE OF ETHICAL CONDUCT AND STATEMENT OF COMMITMENT

*A position statement of the*
National Association for the Education of Young Children

Revised November 1997

### Preamble

NAEYC recognizes that many daily decisions required of those who work with young children are of a moral and ethical nature. The NAEYC Code of Ethical Conduct offers guidelines for responsible behavior and sets forth a common basis for resolving the principal ethical dilemmas encountered in early childhood care and education. The primary focus is on daily practice with children and their families in programs for children from birth through 8 years of age, such as infant/toddler programs, preschools, child care centers, family child care homes, kindergartens, and primary classrooms. Many of the provisions also apply to specialists who do not work directly with children, including program administrators, parent and vocational educators, college professors, and child care licensing specialists.

### Core Values

Standards of ethical behavior in early childhood care and education are based on commit-ment to core values that are deeply rooted in the history of our field. We have committed ourselves to

- Appreciating childhood as a unique and valuable stage of the human life cycle
- Basing our work with children on knowledge of child development
- Appreciating and supporting the close ties between the child and family
- Recognizing that children are best understood and supported in the context of family, culture, community, and society
- Respecting the dignity, worth, and uniqueness of each individual (child, family member, and colleague)
- Helping children and adults achieve their full potential in the context of relationships that are based on trust, respect, and positive regard

### Conceptual Framework

The Code sets forth a conception of our professional responsibilities in four sections, each addressing an arena of professional relationships: (1) children, (2) families, (3) colleagues, and (4) community and society. Each section includes an introduction to the primary responsibilities of the early childhood practitioner in that arena, a set of ideals pointing in the direction of exemplary professional practice, and a set of principles defining practices that are required, prohibited, and permitted.

**The ideals** reflect the aspirations of practitioners. **The principles** are intended to guide conduct and assist practitioners in resolving ethical dilemmas encountered in the field. There is not necessarily a corresponding principle for each ideal. Both ideals and principles are intended to direct practitioners to those questions which, when responsibly answered, will provide the basis for conscientious decisionmaking. While the Code provides specific direction and suggestions for addressing some ethical dilemmas, many others will require the practitioner to combine the guidance of the Code with sound professional judgment.

The ideals and principles in this Code present a shared conception of professional responsibility that affirms our commitment to the core values of our field. The Code publicly acknowledges the responsibilities that we in the field have assumed and in so doing supports ethical behavior in our work. Practitioners who face ethical dilemmas are urged to seek guidance in the applicable parts of this Code and in the spirit that informs the whole.

## Ethical Dilemmas Always Exist

Often, "the right answer"—the best ethical course of action to take—is not obvious. There may be no readily apparent, positive way to handle a situation. One important value may contradict another. When we are caught "on the horns of a dilemma," it is our professional responsibility to consult with all relevant parties in seeking the most ethical course of action to take.

## Section I:
## Ethical responsibilities to children

Childhood is a unique and valuable stage in the life cycle. Our paramount responsibility is to provide safe, healthy, nurturing, and responsive settings for children. We are committed to support children's development, respect individual differences, help children learn to live and work cooperatively, and promote health, self-awareness, competence, self-worth, and resiliency.

### Ideals

I-1.1—To be familiar with the knowledge base of early childhood care and education and to keep current through continuing education and in-service training.

I-1.2—To base program practices upon current knowledge in the field of child development and related disciplines and upon particular knowledge of each child.

I-1.3—To recognize and respect the uniqueness and the potential of each child.

I-1.4—To appreciate the special vulnerability of children.

I-1.5—To create and maintain safe and healthy settings that foster children's social, emotional, intellectual, and physical development and that respect their dignity and their contributions.

I-1.6—To support the right of each child to play and learn in inclusive early childhood programs to the fullest extent consistent with the best interests of all involved. As with adults who are disabled in the larger community, children with disabilities are ideally served in the same settings in which they would participate if they did not have a disability.

I-1.7—To ensure that children with disabilities have access to appropriate and convenient support services and to advocate for the resources necessary to provide the most appropriate settings for all children.

## Principles

**P-1.1**—Above all, we shall not harm children. We shall not participate in practices that are disrespectful, degrading, dangerous, exploitative, intimidating, emotionally damaging, or physically harmful to children. This principle has precedence over all others in this Code.

**P-1.2**—We shall not participate in practices that discriminate against children by denying benefits, giving special advantages, or excluding them from programs or activities on the basis of their race, ethnicity, religion, sex, national origin, language, ability, or the status, behavior, or beliefs of their parents. (This principle does not apply to programs that have a lawful mandate to provide services to a particular population of children.)

**P-1.3**—We shall involve all of those relevant knowledge (including staff and parents) in decisions concerning a child.

**P-1.4**—For every child we shall implement adaptations in teaching strategies, learning environment, and curricula, consult with the family, and seek recommendations from appropriate specialists to maximize the potential of the child to benefit from the program. If, after these efforts have been made to work with a child and family, the child does not appear to be benefiting from a program, or the child is seriously jeopardizing the ability of other children to benefit from the program, we shall communicate with the family and appropriate specialists to determine the child's current needs; identify the setting and services most suited to meeting these needs; and assist the family in placing the child in an appropriate setting.

**P-1.5**—We shall be familiar with the symptoms of child abuse, including physical, sexual, verbal, and emotional abuse, and neglect. We shall know and follow state laws and community procedures that protect children against abuse and neglect.

**P-1.6**—When we have reasonable cause to suspect child abuse or neglect, we shall report it to the appropriate community agency and follow up to ensure that appropriate action has been taken. When appropriate, parents or guardians will be informed that the referral has been made.

**P-1.7**—When another person tells us of a suspicion that a child is being abused or neglected, we shall assist that person in taking appropriate action to protect the child.

**P-1.8**—When a child protective agency fails to provide adequate protection for abused or neglected children, we acknowledge a collective ethical responsibility to work toward improvement of these services.

**P-1.9**—When we become aware of a practice or situation that endangers the health or safety of children, but has not been previously known to do so, we have an ethical responsibility to inform those who can remedy the situation and who can protect children from similar danger.

## Section II:
## Ethical responsibilities to families

Families are of primary importance in children's development. (The term *family* may include others, besides parents, who are responsibly involved with the child.) Because the family and the early childhood practitioner have a common interest in the child's welfare, we acknowledge a primary responsibility to bring about collaboration between the home and school in ways that enhance the child's development.

## Ideals

I-2.1—To develop relationships of mutual trust with families we serve.

I-2.2—To acknowledge and build upon strengths and competencies as we support families in their task of nurturing children.

I-2.3—To respect the dignity of each family and its culture, language, customs, and beliefs.

I-2.4—To respect families' childrearing values and their right to make decisions for their children.

I-2.5—To interpret each child's progress to parents within the framework of a developmental perspective and to help families understand and appreciate the value of developmentally appropriate early childhood practices.

I-2.6—To help family members improve their understanding of their children and to enhance their skills as parents.

I-2.7—To participate in building support networks for families by providing them with opportunities to interact with program staff, other families, community resources, and professional services.

## Principles

P-2.1—We shall not deny family members access to their child's classroom or program setting.

P-2.2—We shall inform families of program philosophy, policies, and personnel qualifications, and explain why we teach as we do—which should be in accordance with our ethical responsibilities to children (see Section I).

P-2.3—We shall inform families of and, when appropriate, involve them in policy decisions.

P-2.4—We shall involve families in significant decisions affecting their child.

P-2.5—We shall inform the family of accidents involving their child, of risks such as exposures to contagious disease that may result in infection, and of occurrences that might result in emotional stress.

P-2.6—To improve the quality of early childhood care and education, we shall cooperate with qualified child development researchers. Families shall be fully informed of any proposed research projects involving their children and shall have the opportunity to give or withhold consent without penalty. We shall not permit or participate in research that could in any way hinder the education, development, or well-being of children.

P-2.7—We shall not engage in or support exploitation of families. We shall not use our relationship with a family for private advantage or personal gain, or enter into relationships with family members that might impair our effectiveness in working with children.

P-2.8—We shall develop written policies for the protection of confidentiality and the disclosure of children's records. These policy documents shall be made available to all program personnel and families. Disclosure of children's records beyond family members, program personnel, and consultants having an obligation of confidentiality shall require familial consent (except in cases of abuse or neglect).

P-2.0—We shall maintain confidentiality and shall respect the family's right to privacy, refraining from disclosure of confidential information and intrusion into family life. However, when we have reason to believe that a child's welfare is at risk, it is permissible to share confidential information with agencies and individuals who may be able to intervene in the child's interest.

P-2.10—In cases where family members are in conflict, we shall work openly, sharing our observations of the child, to help all parties involved make informed decisions. We shall refrain from becoming an advocate for one party.

**P-2.11**—We shall be familiar with and appropriately use community resources and professional services that support families. After a referral has been made, we shall follow up to ensure that services have been appropriately provided.

## Section III:
## Ethical responsibilities to colleagues

In a caring, cooperative work place, human dignity is respected, professional satisfaction is promoted, and positive relationships are modeled. Based upon our core values, our primary responsibility in this arena is to establish and maintain settings and relationships that support productive work and meet professional needs. The same ideals that apply to children are inherent in our responsibilities to adults.

### A—Responsibilities to co-workers

**Ideals**

**I-3A.1**—To establish and maintain relationships of respect, trust, and cooperation with co-workers.

**I-3A.2**—To share resources and information with co-workers.

**I-3A.3**—To support co-workers in meeting their professional needs and in their professional development.

**I-3A.4**—To accord co-workers due recognition of professional achievement.

**Principles**

**P-3A.1**—When we have concern about the professional behavior of a co-worker, we shall first let that person know of our concern, in a way that shows respect for personal dignity and for the diversity to be found among staff members, and then attempt to resolve the matter collegially.

**P-3A.2**—We shall exercise care in expressing views regarding the personal attributes or professional conduct of co-workers. Statements should be based on firsthand knowledge and relevant to the interests of children and programs.

### B—Responsibilities to employers

**Ideals**

**I-3B.1**—To assist the program in providing the highest quality of service.

**I-3B.2**—To do nothing that diminishes the reputation of the program in which we work unless it is violating laws and regulations designed to protect children or the provisions of this Code.

**Principles**

**P-3B.1**—When we do not agree with program policies, we shall first attempt to effect change through constructive action within the organization.

**P-3B.2**—We shall speak or act on behalf of an organization only when authorized. We shall take care to acknowledge when we are speaking for the organization and when we are expressing a personal judgment.

**P-3B.3**—We shall not violate laws or regulations designed to protect children and shall take appropriate action consistent with this Code when aware of such violations.

### C—Responsibilities to employees

**Ideals**

**I-3C.1**—To promote policies and working conditions that foster mutual respect, competence, well-being, and positive self-esteem in staff members.

**I-3C.2**—To create a climate of trust and candor that will enable staff to speak and act in the best interests of children, families, and the field of early childhood care and education.

I-3C.3—To strive to secure equitable compensation (salary and benefits) for those who work with or on behalf of young children.

## Principles

P-3C.1—In decisions concerning children and programs, we shall appropriately utilize the education, training, experience, and expertise of staff members.

P-3C.2—We shall provide staff members with safe and supportive working conditions that permit them to carry out their responsibilities, timely and non-threatening evaluation procedures, written grievance procedures, constructive feedback, and opportunities for continuing professional development and advancement.

P-3C.3—We shall develop and maintain comprehensive written personnel policies that define program standards and, when applicable, that specify the extent to which employees are accountable for their conduct outside the work place. These policies shall be given to new staff members and shall be available for review by all staff members.

P-3C.4—Employees who do not meet program standards shall be informed of areas of concern and, when possible, assisted in improving their performance.

P-3C.5—Employees who are dismissed shall be informed of the reasons for their termination. When a dismissal is for cause, justification must be based on evidence of inadequate or inappropriate behavior that is accurately documented, current, and available for the employee to review.

P-3C.6—In making evaluations and recommendations, judgments shall be based on fact and relevant to the interests of children and programs.

P-3C.7—Hiring and promotion shall be based solely on a person's record of accomplishment and ability to carry out the responsibilities of the position.

P-3C.8—In hiring, promotion, and provision of training, we shall not participate in any form of discrimination based on race, ethnicity, religion, gender, national origin, culture, disability, age, or sexual preference. We shall be familiar with and observe laws and regulations that pertain to employment discrimination.

## Section IV:
## Ethical responsibilities to community and society

Early childhood programs operate within a context of an immediate community made up of families and other institutions concerned with children's welfare. Our responsibilities to the community are to provide programs that meet its needs, to cooperate with agencies and professions that share responsibility for children, and to develop needed programs that are not currently available. Because the larger society has a measure of responsibility for the welfare and protection of children, and because of our specialized expertise in child development, we acknowledge an obligation to serve as a voice for children everywhere.

## Ideals

I-4.1—To provide the community with high-quality (age and individually appropriate, and culturally and socially sensitive) education/care programs and services.

I-4.2—To promote cooperation among agencies and interdisciplinary collaboration among professions concerned with the welfare of young children, their families, and their teachers.

I-4.3—To work, through education, research, and advocacy, toward an environmentally safe world in which all children receive adequate health care, food, and shelter, are nurtured, and live free from violence.

I-4.4—To work, through education, research, and advocacy, toward a society in which all young children have access to high-quality education/care programs.

I-4.5—To promote knowledge and understanding of young children and their needs. To work toward greater social acknowledgment of children's rights and greater social acceptance of responsibility for their well-being.

I-4.6—To support policies and laws that promote the well-being of children and families, and to oppose those that impair their well-being. To participate in developing policies and laws that are needed, and to cooperate with other individuals and groups in these efforts.

I-4.7—To further the professional development of the field of early childhood care and education and to strengthen its commitment to realizing its core values as reflected in this Code.

## Principles

P-4.1—We shall communicate openly and truthfully about the nature and extent of services that we provide.

P-4.2—We shall not accept or continue to work in positions for which we are personally unsuited or professionally unqualified. We shall not offer services that we do not have the competence, qualifications, or resources to provide.

P-4.3—We shall be objective and accurate in reporting the knowledge upon which we base our program practices.

P-4.4—We shall cooperate with other professionals who work with children and their families.

P-4.5—We shall not hire or recommend for employment any person whose competence, qualifications, or character makes him or her unsuited for the position.

P-4.6—We shall report the unethical or incompetent behavior of a colleague to a supervisor when informal resolution is not effective.

P-4.7—We shall be familiar with laws and regulations that serve to protect the children in our programs.

P-4.8—We shall not participate in practices which are in violation of laws and regulations that protect the children in our programs.

P-4.9—When we have evidence that an early childhood program is violating laws or regulations protecting children, we shall report it to persons responsible for the program. If compliance is not accomplished within a reasonable time, we will report the violation to appropriate authorities who can be expected to remedy the situation.

P-4.10—When we have evidence that an agency or a professional charged with providing services to children, families, or teachers is failing to meet its obligations, we acknowledge a collective ethical responsibility to report the problem to appropriate authorities or to the public.

P-4.11—When a program violates or requires its employees to violate this Code, it is permissible, after fair assessment of the evidence, to disclose the identity of that program.

## Statement of Commitment

As an individual who works with young children, I commit myself to furthering the values of early childhood education as they are reflected in the NAEYC Code of Ethical Conduct.

To the best of my ability I will

- Ensure that programs for young children are based on current knowledge of child development and early childhood education.
- Respect and support families in their task of nurturing children.
- Respect colleagues in early childhood education and support them in maintaining the NAEYC Code of Ethical Conduct.

- Serve as an advocate for children, their families, and their teachers in community and society.
- Maintain high standards of professional conduct.
- Recognize how personal values, opinions, and biases can affect professional judgment.
- Be open to new ideas and be willing to learn from the suggestions of others.
- Continue to learn, grow, and contribute as a professional.
- Honor the ideals and principles of the NAEYC Code of Ethical Conduct.

# APPENDIX D

# THE DIVISION FOR EARLY CHILDHOOD

## Code of Ethics
### The Division of Early Childhood of the Council for Exceptional Children

Adopted: September, 1996
Revised: April, 1999

As members of the Division for Early Childhood (DEC) of the Council for Exceptional Children (CEC), we recognize that in our professional conduct we are faced with choices that call on us to determine right from wrong. Other choices, however, are not nearly as clear, forcing us to choose between competing priorities and to acknowledge the moral ambiguity of life. The following code of ethics is based on the Division's recognition of the critical role of conscience not merely in preventing wrong, but in choosing among courses of action in order to act in the best interests of young children with special needs and their families and to support our professional colleagues.

As members of DEC, we acknowledge our responsibility to abide by high standards of performance and ethical conduct and we commit to:

1. Demonstrate the highest standards of personal integrity, truthfulness, and honesty in all our professional activities in order to inspire the confidence and trust of the public and those with whom we work;

2. Demonstrate our respect and concern for children and families, colleagues, and others with whom we work, honoring their beliefs, values, customs, and culture;

3. Demonstrate our respect for families in their task of nurturing their children, and support them in achieving the outcomes they desire for themselves and their children;

4. Demonstrate, in our behavior and language, that we respect and appreciate the unique value and human potential of each child;

5. Strive for personal professional excellence, seeking new information, using new information and ideas, and responding openly to the suggestions of others;

6. Encourage the professional development of our colleagues and those seeking to enter fields related to early childhood special education, early intervention, and personnel preparation, offering guidance, assistance, support, and mentorship to others without the burden of professional competition;

7. Ensure that programs and services we provide are based on law as well as a current knowledge of and recommended practice in early childhood special education, early intervention, and personnel preparation;

8. Serve as an advocate for children with special needs and their families and for the professionals who serve them in our communities, working with those who make the policy and programmatic decisions that enhance or depreciate the quality of their lives;

9. Oppose any discrimination because of race, color, religion, sex, sexual orientation, national origin, political affiliation, disability, age, or marital status in all aspects of personnel action and service delivery;

10. Protect the privacy and confidentiality of information regarding children and families, colleagues, and students; and

11. Reflect our commitment to the Division for Early Childhood and to its adopted policies and positions.

The Division for Early Childhood acknowledges with appreciation the National Association for the Education of Young Children, the American Society for Public Administration, and the Council for Exceptional Children, whose codes of conduct were helpful as we developed our own.

# APPENDIX E

# NATIONAL ORGANIZATIONS
# (ADDRESSES, PHONE NUMBERS, WEB SITES)

**Alexander Graham Bell Association for the Deaf**
3417 Volta Place, N.W.
Washington, DC 20007-2778
202-337-5220
Web site: www.agbell.org/

**American Academy of Pediatrics**
141 Northwest Point Blvd.
Elk Grove Village, IL 60007-1098
847-434-4000
Web site: www.aap.org

**American Council of the Blind**
1155 15th Street, N.W., Suite 1004
Washington, DC 20005
202-467-5081 or 800-424-8666
Fax: 202-467-5085
Web site: www.acb.org/

**American Montessori Society**
281 Park Avenue South, 6th Floor
New York, NY 10010-6102
212-358-1250
Fax: 212-358-1256
Web site: www.amshq.org

**American Society of Deaf Children**
P.O. Box 3355
Gettysburg, PA 17325
717-334-7922
Fax: 717-334-8808
E-mail: ascd@deafchildren.org
Web site: www.deafchildren.org

**Association for Childhood Education International**
17904 Georgia Avenue, Suite 215
Olney, MD 20832
301-570-2111 or 800-423-3563
Fax: 301-570-2212
E-mail: aceihq@aol.com
Web site: www.udel.edu/bateman/acei

**Association for Supervision and Curriculum Development**
1703 North Beauregard Street
Alexandria, VA 22311-1714
703-578-9600 or 800-933-ASCD
Fax: 703-575-5400
E-mail: member@ascd.org
Web site: www.ascd.org/

**Asthma and Allergy Foundation of America**
1233 20th NW, Ste. 402
Washington, DC 20036
202-466-7643
Fax: 202-466-8940
Web site: www.aafa.org/

**Autism Society of America**
7910 Woodmont Avenue, Suite 300
Bethesda, MD 20814-3067
301-657-0881 ext. 145
Fax: 301-657-0869
Web site: www.autism-society.org/

**Big Brothers/Big Sisters of America**
230 North 13th Street
Philadelphia, PA 19107
215-567-7000
Fax: 215-567-0394
E-mail: national@bbbsa.org
Web site: www.bbbsa.org/

**Candlelighters Childhood Cancer Foundation**
P.O. Box 498
Kensington, MD 20895-0498
301-962-3520 or 800-366-2223
Fax: 301-962-3521
E-mail: info@candlelighters.org
Web site: www.candlelighters.org/

**Children with Attention Deficit Disorders (CHADD)**
8181 Professional Place, Suite 150
Landover, MD 20785
800-233-4050 or 301-306-7070
Fax: 301-306-7090
Web site: www.chadd.org

**Children's Defense Fund**
25 E Street, NW
Washington, DC 20001
202-628-8787
E-mail: cdfinfo@childrensdefense.org
Web site: www.childrensdefense.org

**Child Welfare League of America**
440 First Street NW
Third Floor
Washington, DC 20001-2085
202-638-2952
Fax: 202-638-4004
Web site: www.cwla.org

**Clearinghouse on Disability Information**
U.S. Department of Education
Room 3132 Switzer Building
330 C Street SW
Washington, DC 20202-2524
202-732-1244
Fax: 202-401-2608
Web site: www.health.gov/nhic

**The Council for Exceptional Children (CEC)**
1110 North Glebe Rd. Ste. 300
Arlington, VA 22201
703-620-3660
Fax: 703-264-9494
E-mail: service@cec.sped.org
Web site: www.cec.sped.org

**Cystic Fibrosis Foundation**
6931 Arlington Road
Bethesda, MD 20814
301-951-4422 or 800-FIGHT-CF
Fax: 301-951-6378
E-mail: info@cff.org
Web site: www.cff.org

**ERIC/EECE**
University of Illinois at Urbana-Champaign
Children's Research Center
51 Gerty Drive
Champaign, IL 61820-7469
217-333-1386 or 800-583-4135
Fax: 217-333-3767
Web site: www.ericeece.org/

**Families and Work Institute**
267 Fifth Ave., Floor 2
New York, NY 10016
212-465-2044
Fax: 212-465-8637
Web site: www.familiesandworkinst.org

**Family Resource Coalition of America**
20 N. Wacker Drive, Ste. 1100
Chicago, IL 60606
312-338-0900
Fax: 312-338-1522
Web site: www.frca.org

**The Federation of Families for Children's Mental Health**
1101 King Street, Ste. 420
Alexandria, VA 22314-2971
703-684-7710
Fax: 703-836-1040
Web site: www.ffcmh.org/

**High/Scope Educational Research Foundation**
600 North River Street
Ypsilanti, MI 48198-2898
734-485-2000
Fax: 734-485-0704
E-mail: info@highscope.org
Web site: www.highscope.org/

**Intercultural Development Research Association**
5835 Callaghan Road, Suite 350
San Antonio, TX 78228-1190
210-444-1710
Fax: 210-444-1714
Web site: www.idra.org/

**International Reading Association**
800 Barksdale Road
P.O. Box 8139
Newark, DE 19714-8139
302-731-1600
Fax: 302-731-1057
Web site: www.reading.org/

**Learning Disabilities Association of America**
4156 Library Road
Pittsburg, PA 15234-1349
412-341-1515
Fax: 412-344-0224
E-mail: info@ldaamerica.org
Web site: www.ldanatl.org/

**March of Dimes Birth Defects Foundation**
1275 Mamaroneck Avenue
White Plains, NY 10605
914-428-7100 or 800-996-2724
Fax: 914-997-4537
Web site: www.modimes.org

**National Association of Child Care Professionals (NACCP)**
P.O. Box 90723
Austin, TX 78709
800-537-1118
Fax: 512-301-5080
E-mail: admin@naccp.org
Web site: www.naccp.org

**National Association of Child Care Resource and Referral Agencies (NACCRRA)**
1319 F Street Ste. 500
Washington, DC 20004-1106
202-393-5501
Fax: 202-393-5501
Web site: www.naccrra.org/

**National Association for the Education of Young Children (NAEYC)**
1509 16th Street, NW
Washington, DC 20036-1426
202-232-8777 or 800-424-2460
Fax: 202-328-1846
E-mail: naeyc@naeyc.org
Web site: www.naeyc.org/

**National Association for Family Child Care (NAFCC)**
5202 Pinemont Drive
Salt Lake City, UT 84123
801-269-9338
Fax: 801-268-9507
E-mail: nafcc@nafcc.org
Web site: www.nafcc.org/

**National Association for Gifted Children**
1707 L Street, Suite 550
Washington, DC 20036
202-785-4268
Web site: www.nagc.org

**National Association of Elementary School Principals**
1615 Duke Street
Alexandria, VA 22314
800-38-NAESP
Fax: 800-38-NAESP or 703-684-3345
E-mail: naesp@naesp.org
Web site: www.naesp.org/

**National Association of State Boards of Education**
277 South Washington Street, Suite 100
Alexandria, VA 22314
703-684-4000
Fax: 703-836-2313
E-mail: boards@nasbe.org
Web site: www.nasbe.org

**National Black Child Development Institute**
1101 Fifteenth Street, NW, Suite 900
Washington, DC 20005
202-833-2220
Fax: 202-833-8222
E-mail: moreinfo@nbcdi.org
Web site: www.nbcdi.org/

**National Center for Children in Poverty**
Columbia University School of Public Health
154 Haven Avenue
New York, NY 10032
212-304-7100
Fax: 212-544-4200
Web site: www.cpmcnet.columbia.edu/dept/nccp/

**National Center for Learning Disabilities**
318 Park Avenue South, Suite 1401
New York, NY 10016
212-545-7510
Fax: 212-545-9665
Web site: ncld.org/

**National Child Care Information Center**
243 Church Street NW, 2nd Floor
Vienna, VA 22180
800-616-2242
Fax: 800-716-2242
E-mail: info@nccic.org
Web site: www.nccic.org/

**National Clearinghouse on Child Abuse and Neglect Information**
330 C Street, SW
Washington, DC 20447
800-FYI-3366 or 703-385-7565
Fax: 703-385-3206
E-mail: nccanch@clark.net
Web site: www.calib.com/nccanch/

**National Coalition for Campus Children's Centers**
119 Schindler Education Center
University of Northern Iowa
Cedar Falls, IA 50614
800-813-8207 or 319-273-3113
E-mail: ncccc@uni.edu
Web site: www.campuschildren.org/

**National Council of Parent-Teacher Associations (PTA)**
330 North Wabash Avenue, Suite 2100
Chicago, IL 60611
312-670-6782 or 800-307-4PTA
Fax: 312-670-6783
E-mail: info@pta.org
Web site: www.pta.org/

**National Governors' Association**
Hall of States
444 North Capital Street
Washington, DC 20001-1512
202-624-5300
Web site: www.nga.org/

**National Head Start Association**
1651 Prince Street
Alexandria, VA 22314
703-739-0875
Fax: 703-739-0878
Web site: www.nhsa.org

**National Information Center for Children and Youth with Disabilities**
P.O. Box 1492
Washington, DC 20013-1492
800-695-0285
Fax: 202-884-8441
E-mail: nichcy@aed.org
Web site: www.nichcy.org

**National Organization for Victim Assistance (NOVA)**
1730 Park Road NW
Washington, DC 20010
202-232-6682
Fax: 202-462-2255
Web site: www.try-nova.org/

**National Resource Center for Health and Safety in Child Care**
UCHSC at Fitzsimons
Campus Mail Stop F541
Aurora, CO 80045-0508
800-598-KIDS (5437)
Fax: 303-724-0960
Web site: www.nrc.uchsc.edu

**National School-Age Care Alliance**
1137 Washington Street
Boston, MA 02124
617-298-5012
Fax: 617-298-5022
Web site: www.nsaca.org/

**Parents Anonymous Inc.**
675 West Foothill Boulevard, Suite 220
Claremont, CA 91711
909-621-6184
Fax: 909-625-6304
E-mail: parentsanonymous@parentsanonymous.org
Web site: www.parentsanonymous.org/

**Parents without Partners**
1650 South Dixie Highway Ste. 510
Boca Raton, FL 33432
561-391-8833
Fax: 561-395-8557
E-mail: pwp@iti.net
Web site: www.parentswithoutpartners.org

**Pediatric AIDS Foundation**
1140 Connecticut Ave., NW Ste 200
Washington, DC 20036
202-296-9165
Fax: 202-296-9185
E-mail: info@pedaids.org
Web site: www.pedaids.org/

**School-Age Child Care Project**
Wellesley College Center for Research on Women
106 Central Street
Wellesley, MA 02481
718-283-2547
Fax: 718-283-3657
Web site: www.wellesley.edu/WCW/CRW/SAC/

**Southern Early Childhood Association**
P.O. Box 55930
Little Rock, AR 72215-5930
501-227-5297 or 800-305-7322
Fax: 501-227-5297
Web site: www.southernearlychildhood.org

**Spina Bifida Association of America**
4950 MacArthur Boulevard, Suite 250
Washington, DC 20007-4226
202-944-3285 or 800-621-3141
Fax: 202-944-3295
Web site: www.sbaa.org/

**Stepfamily Foundation**
333 West End Avenue
New York, NY 10023
212-877-3244
Fax: 212-362-7030
Web site: www.stepfamily.org

**United Cerebral Palsy Association**
1660 L Street NW, Suite 700
Washington, DC 20036-5602
800-USA-5UCP
Fax: 202-776-0414
Web site: www.ucpa.org

**Women's Bureau, U.S. Department of Labor**
Work and Family Clearinghouse
200 Constitution Avenue, NW, Room S-3002
Washington, DC 20210-0002
202-693-6710 or 800-827-5335
Fax: 202-693-6725
Web site: www.dol.gov/dol/wb/welcome.htm

**Zero to Three: National Center for Infants, Toddlers, and Families**
200 M Street NW, Suite 200
Washington, DC 20036
202-638-1144 or 800-899-4301
Fax: 202-638-0851
E-mail: 0to3@zerotothree.org
Web site: www.zerotothree.org

# APPENDIX F

# CHILD DEVELOPMENT ASSOCIATE COMPETENCY GOALS AND FUNCTIONAL AREAS

### CDA Competency Goals and Functional Areas

| CDA Competency Goals | Functional Areas |
|---|---|
| I. To establish and maintain a safe, healthy learning environment | 1. Safe: Candidate provides a safe environment to prevent and reduce injuries. |
| | 2. Healthy: Candidate promotes good health and nutrition and provides an environment that contributes to the prevention of illness. |
| | 3. Learning Environment: Candidate uses space, relationships, materials, and routines as resources for constructing an interesting, secure, and enjoyable environment that encourages play, exploration, and learning. |
| II. To advance physical and intellectual competence | 4. Physical: Candidate provides a variety of equipment, activities, and opportunities to promote the physical development of children. |
| | 5. Cognitive: Candidate provides activities and opportunities that encourage curiosity, exploration, and problem solving appropriate to the development levels and learning styles of children. |
| | 6. Communication: Candidate actively communicates with children and provides opportunities and support for children to understand, acquire, and use verbal and nonverbal means of communicating thoughts and feelings. |

*(continued on next page)*

## CDA Competency Goals and Functional Areas

| CDA Competency Goals | Functional Areas |
| --- | --- |
| | 7. Creative: Candidate provides opportunities that stimulate children to play with sound, rhythm, language, materials, space, and ideas in individual ways and to express their creative abilities. |
| III. To support social and emotional development and provide positive guidance | 8. Self: Candidate provides physical and emotional security for each child and helps each child to know, accept, and take pride in himself or herself and to develop a sense of independence. |
| | 9. Social: Candidate helps each child feel accepted in the group, helps children learn to communicate and get along with others, and encourages feelings of empathy and mutual respect among children and adults. |
| | 10. Guidance: Candidate provides a supportive environment in which children can begin to learn and practice appropriate and acceptable behaviors as individuals and as a group. |
| IV. To establish positive and productive relationships with families | 11. Families: Candidate maintains an open, friendly, and cooperative relationship with each child's family, encourages their involvement in the program, and supports the child's relationship with his or her family. |
| V. To ensure a well-run, purposeful program responsive to participant needs | 12. Program Management: Candidate is a manager who uses all available resources to ensure an effective operation. Candidate is a competent organizer, planner, record keeper, communicator, and a cooperative coworker. |
| VI. To maintain a commitment to professionalism | 13. Professionalism: Candidate makes decisions based on knowledge of early childhood theories and practices. Candidate promotes high quality in child care services. Candidate takes advantage of opportunities to improve competence, both for personal and professional growth and for the benefit of children and families. |

# APPENDIX G

# DEC RECOMMENDED PRACTICES IN EARLY INTERVENTION/EARLY CHILDHOOD SPECIAL EDUCATION

## Parent Checklist

### Mary Louise Hemmeter • December 2000

This checklist is designed to be used by parents to aid in their selection or to help improve programs for their young child with special needs. While this checklist is based on the *DEC Recommended Practices in Early Intervention/ Early Childhood Special Education* (Sandall, McLean, & Smith, 2000), it does not include all of the practices. It is meant to give parents a general overview of the program by highlighting some of the salient practices. For more information on the DEC Recommended Practices and other resources, contact DEC (see contact information at the end of this checklist). Within the checklist, the term *professional* will be used to refer to teachers, therapists, classroom assistants, and others who work with children.

### How do professionals work together with families to meet the needs of the children?

❐ Teams of professionals and family members make decisions and work together.

❐ Professionals from various disciplines (e.g., physical therapy, speech therapy) teach skills to each other so that when they are working with children they can work on all of the child's goals.

❐ Services are based on the child's needs, involve the child's regular caregivers, and focus on the child's regular routines.

❐ Services are provided in ways that eliminate stress, are flexible and individualized for each child and family, and promote the well-being of families.

❐ Services are sensitive and responsive to the cultural, ethnic, racial, and language preferences and backgrounds of families.

### How does the program determine the strengths and needs of the child and family?

❐ Programs provide families with a primary contact person and easy ways to contact that person.

❐ Families and professionals meet together to talk about the child's strengths and needs.

❐ Professionals ask families to talk about their child's interests, abilities, and needs and demonstrate to the families that this information is critical and useful in terms of developing the child's program.

❐ Professionals ask families to talk about their resources, concerns, and priorities related to their child's development.

❐ Professionals use a variety of methods for determining the child's strengths and needs (e.g., observe the child in different settings, interview the primary caregivers, test the child).

❐ Professionals test children in settings that are comfortable for the child.

❒ Professionals become familiar with the child before testing him/her.

❒ Professionals and families assess children at different times during the year to measure progress. Modifications in the child's program are made based on these ongoing findings.

❒ Professionals report assessment results to families in a way that is understandable, sensitive, and responsive to the family's concerns.

❒ Families are given time to ask questions, express concerns, or make comments about assessment findings before decisions are made about the child's program.

❒ Professionals tell families about their rights related to assessment.

## What does the classroom look like (if it is a center-based program)? How is the day structured?

❒ The classroom is free of safety hazards (e.g., sharp objects, slippery rugs, hazardous materials).

❒ There are interesting materials that are appropriate to the children's ages and are adapted for the needs of children with disabilities.

❒ There are materials that represent different cultures.

❒ There are a variety of different types of activities (e.g., small group, large group, centers).

❒ Activities are structured such that children can learn through interaction with materials and other children in addition to interactions with adults.

## What are the teachers and other adults doing?

❒ Professionals provide children with different levels of support depending on their needs (e.g., physically assisting a child, asking questions, providing models).

❒ Professionals use teaching strategies and adaptations that promote the child's participation in classroom activities.

❒ Professionals encourage children to help each other.

❒ Professionals provide instruction to children that target their individual goals and objectives.

❒ Professionals attempt to prevent challenging behaviors by explaining class rules, planning activities that are interesting to children, minimizing the amount of time children have to wait without having something to do, and modeling appropriate social skills.

❒ Professionals provide parents with information about ways they can work on their children's goals during family routines and activities.

❒ Professionals use technology (e.g., switches connected to toys, choice-making boards, computers) to help children learn new skills.

❒ Professionals select technology that is available in all of the child's environments.

## What are the policies of the program, and how are they communicated to families?

❒ Families are involved in the development of program policies.

❒ Program policies ensure that families understand their rights.

❒ Program policies reflect and are sensitive to the diversity of children and families in the program.

❒ Program policies are communicated to families in ways that are understandable and clear to all families.

❒ Program policies require a family-centered approach in all phases of the child's program. Policies promote the family's active participation in all decisions about their child.

❏ Program policies promote the provision of services in naturally occurring settings and routines.

❏ Program policies ensure that the child's program is based on child and family needs.

❏ Program policies promote collaboration with other programs in terms of providing services and supporting the family's transitions between programs.

❏ Program policies ensure that families are involved in all aspects of the program (e.g., curriculum development, professional development, staff evaluation).

## Reference

Sandall, S., McLean, M.E., & Smith, B.J. (2000). *DEC Recommended practices in early intervention/early childhood special education.* Longmont, CO: Sopris West.

## Note

This checklist is also available free of charge from the DEC Web site: www.dec-sped.org

For more information on *DEC Recommended Practices in Early Intervention/Early Childhood Special Education:*

Division of Early Childhood/Council for Exceptional Children
1380 Lawrence St., Suite 650, Denver, CO 80204
Phone: (303) 556-3328   Fax: (303) 556-3310
Email: dec@ceo.cudenver.edu
Website: www.dec-sped.org

# APPENDIX H

# CREATING A PROFESSIONAL PORTFOLIO

## Suggested Contents

Name_____    Semester begun _____

Address _____    Semester completed_____

Classification _____    E-mail _____

Phone numbers: Home _____    Work _____

I. Career Goal Statement

II. Commitment to Learning
    A. Observation/Participation
        Observations Logs/Journal
        Observation Assignments
        Reflective Journals
        Diversity of Observation Locations
    B. Academic Course Work
        Degree Plan
          Initial
          Final
        Course Syllabi
        Test Performances and Other Grades
        Evidence of Improvement
    C. Course-Related Research
        Assigned
        Self-Selected/Self-Directed
        Topics of Special Interest
        Peer Study Group with Feedback
    D. Acquaintance with Professional
          Literature
        Textbooks
        Professional Books
        Trade Books
        Journals

        Research Studies and Reports
        Electronic Resources
    E. Student's Own Creative Work
        Essays
        Projects
        Teaching Materials
        Case Study Assessments
        Audio/Visual Presentations
        Other
    F. Recognition
        Honors
        Special Awards
        Letters of Appreciation
        Accolades

III. Professional Preparation and
    Development
    A. Experience Working with Young
          Children and Their Families
        Employed
        Volunteer
    B. Professional Associations
        Mentoring Teacher(s)
        Professional Association Meetings
        Professional Association
          Membership(s)

Subscription(s) to Professional
  Journal(s)
Professional Conference(s)
Professional Seminars/Workshops
Lectures
Professional Networking
Advocacy Efforts

C. On-Campus Academic and Social
   Involvement
   Mentoring Professor(s)
   Early Childhood Demonstration
    Teaching Lab

# GLOSSARY

## A

accommodation—Process by which ways of thinking (schemata) are modified to conform to new information.

advocacy—The work to educate decision makers about policies that are best for children and their families.

altruism—Helpfulness without the expectation of recognition or reward.

assessment—Evaluation of children's progress.

assimilation—Process of incorporating new motor or conceptual learning into existing schemata.

atrophy—To waste or wither away.

authoritarian caregiving—Guidance in which adults expect unquestioning obedience and apply rigid standards for behavior; relies on punishment and rewards.

authoritative caregiving—Guidance that provides reasonable, age-appropriate expectations and logical explanations for expected behaviors; differs from authoritarian or permissive caregiving.

autonomous morality—The ability and desire to make moral decisions based on one's own convictions.

axon—Long and slender, axons are the major communication link between neurons, sending messages that will be received by dendrites.

## C

child-centered programs—Early childhood programs that consider the individual and developmental needs of each child and provide curricula, materials, schedules, enrichment opportunities, and guidance strategies commensurate with those needs and with sound principles of growth, development, and learning.

child-directed speech—Also referred to as *motherese* and *fatherese*, a special form of speech used when talking to children that has special characteristics such as short sentences and higher and more variable intonation than speech used to communicate with adults.

**child study movement**—A period during the early 1900s in which the focus of interest in children moved from how to teach certain topics or skills to how children grow, develop, and learn.

**choral reading**—A group reading experience in which the entire group reads in unison.

**classification**—Ability to focus on one or more attributes of objects and group them according to various categories (color, shape, texture, etc.).

**code of ethics**—A set of standards that outline professional responsibilities and terms of behaviors and conduct.

**cognitive dissonance**—A mental dilemma in which new information is discordant or at variance with one's current understanding.

**compensatory education programs**—Early childhood programs designed to compensate for potential disadvantages of growing and living in poverty.

**concrete operations**—Ability to think logically only when problems that are posed can be visualized or considered in concrete terms.

**conservation**—The concept that physical attributes (mass, weight, shape, and configuration) stay the same even when the appearance changes.

**constructive guidance**—Developmentally appropriate adult-child relationships that facilitate the construction of social and moral meaning, leading to higher levels of understanding and competence in interacting with others.

**curriculum**—All the components of an early childhood program.

**curriculum-centered approaches**—Early childhood programs that ascribe primary importance to curriculum goals, including adherence to topic sequences, skill sequences, and time blocks for completion of segments of the curriculum.

**curriculum web**—An organizational tool teachers use to view a single topic by different centers or by children's developmental areas.

# D

**dendrites**—Bushlike, branching extensions of nerve cell that receive neurological messages.

**developmentally appropriate practices**—Pertains to age appropriateness (the predictable patterns of growth and development that occur in children) and to individual appropriateness (the uniqueness of each child in individual rates and patterns of growth and development in physical/motor, cognitive, language, literacy, learning styles, psychosocial development, family, and linguistic and cultural backgrounds).

**developmentalist**—A professional who bases his or her assumptions about children on principles of human growth and development.

didactic instruction—Instruction that presents information to children in a structured, drill and practice format, teaching discrete skills in small units or steps.

discipline—Adult-child relationships that may or may not be positive, developmentally appropriate, or instructive; generally infers external control of child behavior.

downshifting—A psychophysiological response to education expectations that the learner deems meaningless or threatening, resulting in less sophisticated use of the brain.

# E

echo reading—A reading experience in which one person, usually the teacher, reads a poem or short story one phrase at a time and students echo each phrase.

ecological systems theory—A theory emphasizing the concept that a variety of social and cultural systems influence the development of the child.

emergent curriculum—Activities and experiences that teachers plan for children based on interests and the play themes of children that they observe.

emerging development—Growth and development that is appearing and represents a point or stage in a continuous process that moves from immature to mature forms.

emergent literacy—The knowledge about reading and writing that children construct from birth until they become conventional readers and writers.

empathy—Ability to vicariously experience the feelings of others.

exosystem—Settings in which the child does not actively participate but that still affect him or her (e.g., parents' workplace, local government, local corporations).

# F

family systems theory—The belief and counseling practice that presumes that all family members' lives affect all others in the family.

# G

glial cells—Supportive cells found in the nervous system that play a role in myelinating axons and guiding the regrowth of damaged axons.

# H

heteronomous morality—A morality that is led and governed by others rather than oneself.

high stakes testing—Tests for which life-influencing decisions are made based on the student's score (e.g., retention, promotion, graduation, admission to special programs).

## I

**inclusion**—The practice of including children who are developmentally, culturally, or linguistically diverse in integrated settings and ensuring that each child is fully accepted as a member of the learning community in which he or she participates.

**inner speech**—Also referred to as *private speech*; silent inner verbal thought; speech to oneself that direct behavior and assists understanding.

## J

**journal writing**—Drawings or emergent/conventional spelling created by a child to record events in his or her life.

## K

**kidwatching**—Careful observation of children for assessment purposes.

## L

**locus of control**—Relates to whether an individual is led or controlled by others or by oneself.

**longitudinal studies**—Research that collects information about the same subjects at different ages over an extended period of time, sometimes spanning several years or even decades.

## M

**macrosystem**—Dominant beliefs of society.

**maturationist theory**—Theory suggesting that the origins of growth and development unfold from within the human organism.

**mesosystem**—Interrelationships and experiences among home, school, and the neighborhood.

**microsystem**—Relationships and experiences from the child's immediate environment.

**moral realism**—Morality that focuses on rules and consequences with little regard or understanding of intentions.

**myelin**—Fatty tissue that partially covers some axons. Myelin serves to increase the speed with which impulses travel along nerve fibers.

## N

**neural tube**—The vertebral canal from which the brain and spinal cord arise.

**neuron**—A nerve cell and its connections; the basic functional unit of the nervous system.

normal schools—The first teacher-training institutions, many of which became teacher colleges and later departments of education in colleges and universities.

norms—The average age of the emergence of certain behaviors or average scores on tests that are based on large representative samples of a population.

nursery school movement—A period during the early 1900s in which early childhood programs for infants, toddlers, and three- and four-year-olds were being developed; most early nursery schools were associated with university child-study departments.

## O

object permanence—The realization that objects and people exist even though they cannot be seen or heard.

## P

perceptual-motor development—Refers to the coordinations of perceptions (sensory learning) and motor abilities.

permissive caregiving—Noncontrolling, undemanding relationships with children, in which they are given little guidance and few rules or conduct.

physiological environment—The manner in which furnishings and equipment are arranged to help meet needs for security and safety and to facilitate learning.

premoral—Earliest stage of moral development in which the child is unaware of moral rules or values.

preoperational thought—The stage of cognitive development between ages two and seven in which the child has mental structures for sensorimotor actions but cannot engage in operational or logical thinking.

progressive education movement—A period during the late 1800s to the 1950s in which resistance to rigid, teacher-dominated practices of the past were challenged by more student-centered and democratic philosophies.

prosocial behavior—Actions intended to benefit others without expectation of reward.

psychological environment—Affective dimensions of child/child and adult/child relationships within the group.

## Q

qualitative assessment—Evaluation of children's progress that is reported descriptively, often in the form of a narrative report, as opposed to quantitative assessment, which is reported as number or letter grades.

# R

realia—Real items used in classrooms to provide concrete, first-hand concept development and knowledge, such as sea shells, magnets, and indoor gardens.

reversibility—Ability to reverse thinking and to return to an original or beginning point.

# S

scaffolding—A changing quality of assistance provided by a skilled partner (peer or adult) in which help is adjusted to less and less as the learner gains competence and autonomy.

schemata—Mental structures or categories of perceptions and experiences.

self-esteem—One's positive or negative self-evaluation.

seriation—Ability to arrange objects or events in sequential order according to selected attributes, such as large to small or first to last.

social cognition—The ability to understand the thoughts, intentions, and behaviors of oneself and others.

story grammar—Understanding of beginning, middle, and ending of stories, characters, plot, and problem.

synapse—The point of electrical or chemical interaction and contact between two neurons or between a neuron and a muscle fiber.

# T

test-driven curricula—Curricula that focus unduly on the content of achievement tests or other standardized test(s), severely restricting the range of content and experience essential to a well-balanced education.

transformational curriculum—Units, themes, and projects that teachers plan for children based on what they know about child development, the disciplines, and their own students.

# W

window of opportunity—Critical periods during which essential experiences have their greatest impact.

# Z

zone of proximal development—The distance between what a learner can accomplish independently and what he or she can accomplish with the help of a more skilled classmate or an adult.

# REFERENCES

Adamson, J. W. (1905). *Pioneers of modern education*. Cambridge, England: Cambridge University Press.

Ainsworth, M. D. S. (1973). The development of infant-mother attachment. In B. M. Caldwell & H. N. Ricciuti (Eds.), *Review of child development research, Vol. 3* (pp. 1–94). Chicago: University of Chicago Press.

American Educational Research Association. (2000). Position statement of the American Educational Research Association concerning high-stakes testing in preK-12 education. *Educational Researcher, 29*(8), 24–25.

Ames, L. B., Gillespie, C., Haines, J., & Ilg, F L. (1979). *The Gesell Institute's child from one to six*. Lumberville, PA: Modern Learning Press.

Anderson, S. R. (1998). The trouble with testing. *Young Children, 53*(4), 25–29.

Anderson, T. L. (1996). "They're trying to tell me something": A teacher's reflection on primary children's construction of mathematical knowledge. *Young Children, 51*(4), 34–42.

Asher, S. R., Renshaw, P. C., & Hymel, S. (1982). Peer relations and the development of social skills. In S. G. Moore & C. R. Cooper (Eds.), *The young child: Reviews of research, Vol. 3* (pp. 137–158). Washington, DC: National Association for the Education of Young Children.

Association for Childhood Education International. (1997). Preparation of the early childhood teachers: A position statement. *Childhood Education, 73*(3), 164–165.

Barcus, S., & Patton, M. M. (1996). What's the matter? *Science and Children, 34*(1), 49–51.

Bare, C. S. (1985). *Guinea pigs don't read books*. New York: Penguin Group.

Baumrind, D. (1966). Effects of authoritative parental control on child behavior. *Child Development, 37*, 887–907.

Baumrind, D. (1967). Child care practices anteceding three patterns of pre-school behavior. *Genetic Psychology Monographs, 75,* 43–88.

Baumrind, D. (1971). Current patterns of parental authority. *Developmental Psychology Monographs, 4* (no. 1, Pt. 2).

Baumrind, D. (1972). Socialization and instrumental competence in young children. In W. W. Hartup (Ed.), *The young child: Reviews of research* (Vol. 2, pp. 202–224). NY: Russell Sage Foundation.

Bayer, A. S. (1990). *Collaborative-apprenticeship learning. Language and thinking across the curriculum, K-12.* Mountain View, CA: Mayfield.

Beaty, J. J. (2001). *Observing development of the young child* (6th ed.). New York: Merrill/Prentice Hall.

Bebko, J. M., Burke, L., Craven, J., & Sarlo, N. (1992). The importance of motor activity in sensorimotor development: A perspective from children with physical handicaps. *Human Development, 35,* 226–240.

Bennett, W. (1986). *First lessons.* Washington, DC: U.S. Government Printing Office.

Benson, M., & Meyer, J. (2000). Student teachers' reflections and collaboration through electronic mail discussions. *Journal of Early Childhood Teacher Education, 21*(2), 20.

Berger, E. H. (1999). *Parents as partners in education: Families and schools working together* (5th ed.). Englewood Cliffs, NJ: Prentice Hall.

Berk, L. E., & Winsler, A. (1995). *Scaffolding children's learning. Vygotsky and early childhood education.* Washington, DC: National Association for the Education of Young Children.

Bickart, T. S., Jablon, J., & Dodge, D. T. (1999). *Building the primary classroom.* Washington, DC: Teaching Strategies; Portsmouth, NH: Heinemann.

Birch, S. H., & Ladd, G. W. (1997). The teacher-child relationship and children's early school adjustment. *Journal of School Psychology, 35*(1), 61–79.

Bloom, B. (1964). *Stability and change in human characteristics.* New York: Wiley.

Bodrova, E., Leong, D. J., Hensen, R., & Henninger, M. (2000). Imaginative, child-directed play: Leading the way in development and learning. *Dimensions of Early Childhood, 28*(4), 25–30.

Bowen, H. C. (1906). *Froebel and education through self-activity.* New York: Charles Scribner's Sons.

Bowlby, J. (1969/1982). *Attachment and loss: Vol. 1. Attachment* (2nd ed.). New York: Basic Books.

Bowlby, J. (1973). *Attachment and loss: Vol. 2. Separation: Anxiety and anger.* New York: Basic Books.

Bowlby, J. (1980). *Attachment and loss: Vol. 3. Loss: Sadness and depression.* New York: Basic Books.

Brazelton T. B. & Greenspan, S. I. (2000). *The irreducible needs of children: What every child must have to grow, learn, and flourish.* Cambridge, MA: Perseus Publishing.

Bredekamp, S. (1993). Redeveloping early childhood education: A response to Kessler. *Early Childhood Research Quarterly, 6*(2), 199–210.

Bredekamp, S. (Ed.). (1984). *Developmentally appropriate practice in early childhood programs serving children from birth through age 8* (Expanded ed.). Washington. DC: National Association for the Education of Young Children.

Bredekamp, S. (Ed.). (1987). *Developmentally appropriate practice in early childhood programs serving children from birth through age 8* (expanded ed.). Washington, DC: National Association for the Education of Young Children.

Bredekamp, S., & Copple, C. (Eds.). (1997). *Developmentally appropriate practice in early childhood programs* (Rev. ed.). Washington, DC: National Association for the Education of Young Children.

Bredekamp, S., & Rosegrant, T. (Eds.). (1992). *Reaching potentials: Transforming early childhood curriculum and assessment* (Vol. 1), Washington, DC: National Association for the Education of Young Children.

Bredekamp, S., & Rosegrant, T. (Eds.). (1995). *Reaching potentials: Transforming early childhood curriculum and assessment* (Vol. 2). Washington, DC: National Association for the Education of Young Children.

Bretherton, I., & Walters, E. (Eds.). (1985). Growing points in attachment theory and research. *Monographs of the Society for Research in Child Development, 50*(1–2, Serial No. 209).

Bronfenbrenner, U. (1979). *The ecology of human development: Experiments by nature and by design.* Cambridge, MA: Harvard University Press.

Bronfenbrenner, U. (1986). Ecology of the family as a context for human development: Research perspectives. *Developmental Psychology, 22,* 723–742.

Bronfenbrenner, U. (1989). Ecological systems theory. In R. Vasta (Ed.), Six theories of child development: Revised formulations and current issues. *Annals of Child Development, 6,* 187–249.

Bronson, M. B. (1995). *The right stuff for children birth to 8: Selecting play materials to support development.* Washington, DC: National Association for the Education of Young Children.

Bronson, M. B. (2000). *Self-regulation in early childhood: Nature and nuture.* New York: Guilford Press.

Button, K., Johnson, M. J., & Furgerson, P. (1996). Interactive writing in a primary classroom. *The Reading Teacher, 49*(6), 446–454.

Cahan, E. D. (1989). *Past caring: A history of U.S. preschool care and education for the poor 1820–1965.* New York: Columbia University.

Caine, G., Caine, R. N., & Crowell, S. (1999). *Mindshifts: A brain-based process for restructuring schools and renewing education* (Rev. ed.). Tucson, AZ: Zephyr Press.

Caine, R. N, & Caine, G. (1997). *Education on the edge of possibility.* Alexandria, VA: Association for Supervision and Curriculum Development.

Caine, R. N., & Caine, G. (1994). *Making connections: Teaching and the human brain.* Alexandria, VA: Association for Supervision and Curriculum Development.

Campbell, F. A., & Taylor, K. (1996). Early childhood programs that work for children from economically disadvantaged families. *Young Children 51*(4), 74–80.

Carle, E. (1969). *The very hungry caterpillar.* New York: Philomel.

Carle, E. (1984). *The very busy spider.* New York: Philomel.

Cassidy, D. J., & Lancaster, C. (1993). The grassroots curriculum: A dialogue between children and teachers. *Young Children, 48*(6), 47–51.

Chaille, C., & Silvern, S. B. (1996). Understanding through play. *Childhood Education, 72*(5), 274–277.

Charney, R. S. (2001). *Teaching children to care: Management in the responsive classroom.* Greenfield, MA: Northeast Foundation for Children.

Chess, S., & Thomas, A. (1987). *Origins and evolution of behavior disorders from infancy to early adult life.* Cambridge, MA: Harvard University Press.

Children's Defense Fund. (1996). *The state of America's children, 1996.* Washington, DC: Author.

Children's Defense Fund. (2001). *The state of America's children, 2001.* Washington, DC: Author.

Church, E. B. (1995). Creating curriculum together. *Scholastic Early Childhood Today, 9*(5), 32–33.

Clark, E. V. (1983). Meanings and concepts. In J. H. Flavell & E. M. Markman (Eds.), *Handbook of child psychology: Vol. 3. Cognitive development* (4th ed., pp. 787–840). New York: Wiley.

Clayton, M. K., with Forton, M. B. (2001). *Classroom spaces that work.* Greenfield, MA: Northeast Foundation for Children.

Clements, R. (2000). Playworkers: Creating opportunities for children's play. *Dimensions of Early Childhood, 28*(4), 9–13.

Coleman, M. (1997). Families and schools: In search of common ground. *Young Children, 52*(5), 14–21.

Collins, A., Brown, J. S., & Newman, S. E. (1989). Cognitive apprenticeships: Teaching a craft of reading, writing, and mathematics. In L. B. Resnick (Ed.), *Knowing learning and instruction: Essays in honor of Robert Glaser.* Hillsdale, NJ: Lawrence Erlbaum Associates.

Comenius, J. A. (1896). *The great didactic* (M. W. Keatinge, Trans.). London: A.C. Black. (Original work published 1628–1632).

Comenius, J. A. (1896). *The school of infancy. An essay of the education of youth during the first six years.* (W. S. Monroe, Trans.). Boston: Heath Co. (Original work n.d.)

Comenius, J. A. (1897). *Orbis sensualium pictus (The world of sensed objects in pictures)* (M. W. Keatinge, Trans.). London A.C. Black. (Original work published 1658).

Cost, Quality and Child Outcomes Study Team. (1995). *Cost, quality and child outcomes in child care centers. Public report* (2nd ed.). Denver: Economics Department, University of Colorado.

Dahl, K. (1998). Why cooking in the curriculum? *Young Children, 53*(1), 81–83.

Dana Alliance for Brain Initiatives. (1996). *Delivering results: A progress report on brain research.* Washington, DC: Author.

D'Arcangelo, M. (2000). The scientist in the crib: A conversation with Andrew Meltzoff. *Educational Leadership, 58*(3), 8–13.

DeCesare, D. (2002). How high are the stakes in high-stakes testing? *Principal, 81*(3), 10–12.

Developmental Studies Center. (1996). *Ways we want our class to be: Class meetings that build commitment to kindness and learning.* Oakland, CA: Author.

DeVries, R., & Zan, B. (1995). Creating a constructivist classroom atmosphere. *Young Children, 51*(1), 4–13.

DeVries, R., & Zan, B. (1994). *Moral classrooms, moral children: Creating a constructivist atmosphere in early education.* New York: Teachers College Press.

DeVries, R., Haney, J., & Zan, B. (1991). Sociomoral atmosphere in direct instruction, eclectic, and constructivist kindergartners: A study of teacher enacted interpersonal understanding. *Early Childhood Research Quarterly 6,* 449–471.

DeVries, R., & Kohlberg, L. (1990). Number and arithmetic. In R. DeVries & L. Kohlberg (Eds.), *Constructivist early education: Overview and comparison with other programs* (pp. 185–222). Washington, DC: National Association for the Education of Young Children.

Dewey, J. (1938). *Experience and education.* New York: Colliers Books.

Dewey, J. (1966/1916). *Democracy and education.* New York: The Free Press.

Dewey, J., & Dewey, E. (1915). *Schools of tomorrow.* New York: E. P. Dutton.

Diffily, D. (1992). The power of portfolios: A parent portfolio conference. *Portfolio News, 4*(1), 4–5.

Diffily, D. (1996). The project approach: A museum exhibit created by kindergartners. *Young Children, 51*(2), 72–75.

Diffily, D. (2000). Project reptile! *Science and Children, 38*(7), 30–35.

Diffily, D. (2001b). *Revisiting family involvement: Perspectives of teachers and families.* ERIC Clearinghouse on Elementary and Early Childhood Education. ED 453 961.

Diffily, D. (2001a). Family meetings: Building relationships between the teacher and families. *Dimensions of Early Childhood, 29*(3), 5–10.

Diffily D., & Fleege, P. O. (1993b). The power of portfolios for communication with families. *Dimensions in Early Childhood, 22*(2), 40–41.

Diffily, D., & Fleege, P. O. (1993a). *Portfolio assessment: Practical training in evaluating the progress of kindergarten and primary grade children in individualized portfolio formats.* Austin, TX: Annual Meeting of the Texas Association for the Education of Young Children. (ERIC Document Reproduction Service No. 354 082).

Diffily, D., & Morrison, K. (1996). *Family friendly communication in early childhood programs.* Washington, DC: National Association for the Education of Young Children.

Diffily, D., & Sassman, C. (2002). *Project-based learning with young children.* Portsmouth, NH: Heinemann.

Dorl, J., & Dizes, D. E. (1999). Your mop is my guitar: Emergent curriculum in our classroom. *Young Children, 54*(4), 14–16.

Dorros, A. (1987). *Ant cities.* New York: Harper & Row.

Dunn, L., & Kontos, S. (1997). Research in review: What have we learned about developmentally appropriate practice? *Young Children, 52*(5), 4–13.

Edwards, C., Gandini, L., & Forman, G. (Eds.). (1998). *The hundred languages of children: The Reggio Emilia approach to early childhood education* (2nd ed.). Norwood, NJ: Ablex.

Elkind, D. (1986). Formal education and early childhood education: An essential difference. *Phi Delta Kappan, 67*(9), 631–636.

Elkind, D. (1987). *Miseducation: Preschoolers at risk.* New York: Knopf.

Erikson, E. (1950). *Childhood and society.* New York: Norton.

Erikson, E. (1963). *Childhood and society* (2nd ed.). New York: Norton.

Fayden, T. (1997). Children's choices: Planting the seeds for creating a thematic sociodramatic center. *Young Children, 52*(3), 15–19.

Feeney, S., & Kipnis, K. (1989). The National Association for the Education of Young children code of ethical conduct. *Young Children, 45*(1), 24–29.

Fields, J. V. & Spangler, K. L. (2000). *Let's begin reading rights: A developmental approach to emergent literacy* (4th ed.). Columbus, OH: Merrill/Prentice Hall.

Forman, G. (1998). Helping children ask good questions. In B. Neugenbauef (Ed.), *The wonder of it: Exploring how the world works* (pp. 21–25). Redmond, WA: Exchange Press.

Fowell, N., & Lawton, J. (1993). Beyond polar descriptions of developmentally appropriate practice: A reply to Bredekamp. *Early Childhood Research Quarterly, 8*(5), 19–24.

Fox, J. E. (1996). Back-to-basics: Play in early childhood. *Early Childhood News, 8*(5), 19–24.

Fox, J. E. (2000). Constructive play in the art center. *Dimensions of Early Childhood, 28*(4), 15–20.

Fox, J. E., & Tipps, R. S. (1995). Young children's development of swinging behaviors. *Early Childhood Research Quarterly 10*(4), 491–504.

Frank Porter Graham Child Development Center. (1999). *Early learning. Later success: The Abecedarian study.* Chapel Hill: University of North Carolina at Chapel Hill.

Frankenburg, W. K. (2002). Developmental surveillance and screening of infants and young children. *Pediatrics, 109*(1), 144–146.

Froebel, F. (1905). *Mother play and nursery songs with finger plays.* Boston: Lothrop, Lee & Shepard Co. (Original work published 1878).

Froebel, F. (1926). *The education of man* (W. N. Hailman, Trans.). New York: Appleton. (Original work published 1887).

Fromberg, D. P. (1990). Play issues in early childhood education. In C. Seefeldt (Ed.), *Continuing issues in early childhood education* (pp. 223–243). Columbus, OH: Merrill/Prentice Hall.

Frost, J. L. (1992). *Play and playscapes.* Clifton Park, NY: Delmar Learning.

Galinsky, E., Howes, C., Kontos, S., & Shinn, M. (1994). *The study of children in family child care and relative care: Highlights of findings.* New York: Families and Work Institute.

Gallahue, D. L., & Gallahue, J. C. (1995). *Understanding motor development. Infants, children, adolescents, adults.* Dubuque, IA: Brown & Benchmark.

Gardner, H. (1983). *Frames of mind: The theory of multiple intelligences.* New York: Basic Books.

Gardner, H. (1991). *The unschooled mind: How children think and how schools should teach.* New York: Basic Books.

Gardner, H. (1993). *Multiple intelligences: The theory in practice: A reader.* New York: Basic Books.

Gardner, H. (1998). *Where to draw the line: The perils of new paradigms.* Paper presented at the annual meeting of the American Educational Research Association, San Diego, CA.

Gardner, H. (1999). *Intelligence reframed.* New York: Basic Books.

Genishi, C., & Dyson, A. H. (1984). *Language assessment in the early years.* Norwood, NJ: Ablex.

Gesell, A. (1925). *The mental growth of the preschool child: A psychological outline of normal development from birth to the sixth year.* New York: Macmillan.

Gesell, A. (1930). *Guidance of mental growth in infant and child.* New York: Macmillan.

Gesell, A. (1940). *The first five years of life: A guide to the study of the preschool child.* New York: Harper & Brothers.

Gesell, A., & Armatruda, C. S. (1941). *Developmental diagnosis: Normal and abnormal child development.* New York: Hoeber.

Gesell, A., & Ilg, F. L. (1949). *Child development.* New York: Harper & Row.

Gestwicki, C. (2000). *Home, school, and community relations* (4th ed.). Clifton Park, NY: Delmar Learning.

Goffin, S. G., & Lombardi, J. (1989). *Speaking out: Childhood advocacy.* Washington, DC: National Association for the Education of Young Children.

Goffin, S. G., & Meyers, M. (1989). *A landscape of concerns: A resource reference of position papers.* Washington, DC: National Association for the Education of Young Children.

Goodlad, J. (1983). *A place called school.* New York: McGraw-Hill.

Goodman, Y. (1978). Kid watching: An alternative to testing. *National Elementary Principal, 57*(4), 41–44.

Grace, C. & Shores, E. F. (Eds). (1992). *The portfolio and its use: Developmentally appropriate assessment of young children.* Litte Rock, AR: Southern Association on Children Under Six.

Gredler, G. R. (1984). Transition classes: A viable alternative for the at-risk child? *Psychology in the Schools, 21,* 463–470.

Greenberg, P. (1990). Before the beginning: A participant's view. *Young Children, 45*(6), 41–52.

Griffith, J. (1996). Relation of parental involvement, empowerment, and school traits to student academic performance. *Journal of Educational Research 90,* 33–41.

Grossman, S. (1999). Examining the origins of our beliefs about parents. *Childhood Education 76*(1), 24–27.

Hakuta, K. (1986). *Mirror of language: The debate on bilingualism.* New York: Basic Books.

Hall, G. S. (1883). *The content of children's minds on entering school.* New York: E. L. Kellogg.

Hannaford, C. D. (1995). *Smart moves: Why learning is not all in your head.* Arlington, VA: Great Ocean Publishers.

Hanson, M. F., & Gilkerson, D. (1999). Assessment: More than ABCs and 123s. *Early Childhood Education Journal, 27*(2), 81–86.

Harlan, J. D., & Rivkin, M. S. (1996). *Science experiences for the early childhood years.* Englewood Cliffs, NJ: Merrill/Prentice Hall.

Harms, T., Clifford, R. M., & Cryer, D. (1998). *Early childhood environment rating scale.* New York: Teachers College Press.

Hartup, W. W. (1989). Social relationships and their developmental significance. *American Psychologist, 44,* 120–126.

Hartup, W. W., & Moore, S. G. (1990). Early peer relations: Developmental significance and prognostic implications. *Early Childhood Research Quarterly, 5,* 1–7.

Head Start Bureau. (2001). 2001 Head Start Fact Sheet. Retrieved from www.acf.hhs.gov/programs/hsb

Healy, J. M. (1990). *Endangered minds: Why children don't think and what we can do about it.* New York: Touchstone Books.

Heath, S. B. (1983). *Way with words: Language, life and work in communities and classrooms.* New York: Touchstone Books.

Herman, J. L., Aschbacher, P. R., & Winters, L. (1992). *A practical guide to alternative assessment*. Alexandria, VA: Association for Supervision and Curriculum Development.

Herschkowitz, N., & Herschkowitz, E. C. (2002). *A good start in life*. Washington, DC: Joseph Henry Press.

Hills, T. W. (1992). Reaching potentials through appropriate assessment. In S. Bredekamp & T. Rosegrant (Eds.), *Reaching potentials: Appropriate curriculum and assessment for young children, Vol. 1*. Washington, DC: National Association for the Education of Young Children.

Hoban, T. (1986). *Red, blue, yellow shoe*. New York: Greenwillow.

Hoffman, M. L. (1988). Moral development. In M. H. Bornstein & M. E. Lamb (Eds.), *Developmental psychology: An advanced textbook* (2nd ed.). Hillsdale, NJ.: Lawrence Erlbaum Associates Publishers.

Huerta-Marcias, A. (1983). Childhood bilingualism: To switch or not to switch? In T. H. Escobedo (Ed.), *Early childhood bilingual education: A Hispanic perspective*. New York: Teachers College Press.

Hunt, J. M. (1961). *Intelligence and experience*. New York: Ronald Press.

Hyson, M. (2002). Professional development: Preparing tomorrow's teachers—NAEYC announces new standards. *Young Children, 57*(2), 78.

Hyson, M. C. (1994). *The emotional development of young children*. New York: Teachers College Press.

Hyson, M. C. (2002). Emotional development and school readiness. *Young Children, 57*(6), 76–78.

I Am Your Child Coalition. (2002). *A parent's guide to early brain development*. Retrieved from http://www.iamyourchild.org/toc.html

Isabella, R. A. (1993). Origins of attachment: Maternal interactive behavior across the first year. *Child Development, 64*, 605–621.

Isadora, R. (1989). *Ben's trumpet*. New York: Scholastic.

Isbell, R. (1995). *The complete learning center book* Beltsville, NY: Gryphon House.

Jaeger, M., & Davenport, M. R. (1996). The role of the disciplines in integrating curriculum. *The Reading Teacher, 50*(1), 64–67.

Jambor, T. (2000). Informal, real-life play: Building children's brain connections. *Dimensions of Early Childhood 28*(4), 4–8.

Jensen, M. A. (1999). Early childhood teacher education for the 21st century: Not by chance. *Journal of Early Childhood Teacher Education, 20*(2), 173–174.

Jones, E., & Nimmo, J. (1994). *Emergent curriculum*. Washington, DC: National Association for the Education of Young Children.

Kagan, S. L., & Cohen, N. E. (1997). *Not by chance. Creating an early childhood and education system for America's children*. New Haven, CT: The Bush Center in Child Development and Social Policy at Yale University.

Katz, L. B., McClellan, D. E., Fuller, J. O., & Walz, G. R. (1995). *Building social competence in children.* Greensboro, NC: ERIC Counseling and Student Services Clearinghouse & ERIC Elementary and Early Childhood Education Clearinghouse.

Katz, L. G. (1995). *Talks with teachers of young children: A collection.* Norwood, NJ: Ablex.

Katz, L. G., & Chard, S. C. (2000). *Engaging children's minds: The project approach* Norwood, NJ: Ablex.

Kaufeldt, M. (1999). *Begin with the brain: Orchestrating the learner-centered classroom.* Tucson, AZ: Zephyr Press.

Keats, E. J. (1972). *Pet show!* New York: Harper Trophy.

Kemple, K. M. (1991). Research in review: Preschool children's peer acceptance and social interaction. *Young Children, 46*(5), 47–91.

Kessler, S. A. (1991). Alternative perspectives on early childhood education. *Early Childhood Research Quarterly, 6*(2), 183–198.

Kilpatrick, W. H. (1925). *Foundations of method: Informal talks on teaching.* New York: Macmillan.

Kilpatrick, W. H. (1936). *Remaking the curriculum.* New York: Newson & Co.

Kohlberg, L. (1984). *Essays on moral development: Vol. 2. The psychology of moral development.* San Francisco: Harper & Row.

Kohn, A. (1996). *Beyond discipline: From compliance to community.* Alexandria, VA: Association for Supervision and Curriculum Development.

Kohn, A. (2000). *The case against standardized testing: Raising the scores, ruining the schools.* Portsmouth, NH: Heinemann.

Kohn, A. (2001a). Beware the standards, not just the test. *Education Week, 21*(4), 52.

Kohn, A. (2001b). Fighting the texts: Turning frustration into action. *Young Children, 52*(2), 4–12.

Kontos, S., & Wilcox-Herzog, A. (1997). Research in review: Teachers interactions with children: Why are they so important? *Young Children, 52*(2), 4–12.

Koralek, D. G., Colker, L. J., & Dodge, D. T. (1993). *The what, why, and how of high quality early childhood education: A guide for on-site supervision.* Washington, DC: National Association for the Education of Young Children.

Kostelnik, M. J. (1992). Myths associated with developmentally appropriate programs. *Young Children, 47*(4), 17–23.

Kramer, R. (1976). *Maria Montessori: A biography.* New York: Putnam.

Krashen, S. D. (1996). *Under attack: The case against bilingual education.* Culver City, CA: Language Education Association.

Ladd, G. W. (1990). Having friends, keeping friends, making friends, and being liked by peers in the classroom: Predictors of children's early school adjustment. *Child Development, 61*, 1081–1100.

Lamb, M. (1977). The development of mother-infant attachment in the second year of life. *Developmental Psychology, 13*, 639–649.

Larsen, J., & Robinson, C. (1989). Latter effects of preschool on low-risk children. *Early Childhood Research Quarterly, 4*(1), 133–144.

Lazar, I., & Darlington, R. (1982). Lasting effects of early education: A report from the consortium for longitudinal studies. *Monographs of the Society for Research in Child Development 47*, No. 2–3.

Lazerson, M. (1972). The historical antecedents of early childhood education. In The National Society for the Study of Education, *The seventy-first yearbook: Early childhood education*. Chicago: University of Chicago Press.

LeeKeenan, D., & Edwards, C. P. (1992). Using the project approach with toddlers. *Young Children, 47*(4), 31–37.

LeeKeenan, D., & Nimmo, J. (1993). Connections: Using the project approach with 2-and 3-year-olds in a university laboratory school. In C. Edwards, L. Gandini, & G. Forman (Eds.), *The hundred languages of children: The Reggio Emilia approach to early childhood education* (pp. 251–268). Norwood, NJ: Ablex.

Lewis, A. C. (2002). A second chance for policy makers. *Phi Delta Kappan, 83*(9), 648–650.

Lionni, L. (1991). *Swimmy*. New York: Knopf.

Locke, J. (1694). *Some thoughts about education*. In F. W. Garforth, Ed. (1964). Abridged Edition. Woodbury, NY: Barron.

Maldonado, N. S. (1996). Puzzles: A pathetically neglected commonly available resource. *Young Children, 51*(4), 4–6.

Mallory, B. (1992). Is it always appropriate to be developmental? Convergent models for early intervention practice. *Topics in Early Childhood Special Education, 11*(4), 245–272.

Mallory, B. L., & New, R. S. (Eds.). (1994). *Diversity and developmentally appropriate practices: Challenges for early childhood education*. New York: Teachers College Press.

Marion, M. (1999). *Guidance of young children* (5th ed.). Columbus, OH: Merrill/Prentice Hall.

Maslow, A. (1970). *Motivation and personality* (2nd ed.). New York: Harper & Row.

Masur, E. F., & Gleason, J. B. (1980). Parent-child interaction and the acquisition of lexical information during play. *Developmental Psychology, 16*, 404–409.

McClellan, D. E., & Katz, L. G. (2001). *Assessing young children's social competence*. ERIC Digest. ED4509533.

McMillan, M. (1921). *The nursery school*. New York: E.P. Dutton.

McWilliams, R. A., & Maxwell, R. L. (1999). Beyond involvement: Are elementary schools ready to be family-centered? *School Psychology Review, 28*(3), 378.

Medina, N., & Neill, D. M. (1990). *Fallout from the testing explosion. How 100 million standardized exams undermine equity and excellence in America's public schools* (3rd ed., Rev.). Cambridge, MA: National Center for Fair and Open Testing.

Meisels, S. J. (1987). Uses and abuses of developmental screening and school readiness testing. *Young Children, 42*(2), 68–73.

Meisels, S. J. (1993). Remaking classroom assessment with the work sampling system. *Young Children, 48*(5), 34–40.

Meisels, S. J. (2000). On the side of the child: Personal reflections on testing, teaching, and early childhood education. *Young Children, 55*(6), 16–19.

Mellou, E. (1995). Review of the relationship between dramatic play and creativity in young children. *Early Childhood Development and Care, 112*, 85–107.

Meyer, A. E. (1951). *The development of education in the twentieth century.* New York: Prentice Hall.

Meyer, A. E. (1975). *Grandmasters of educational thought.* New York: McGraw-Hill.

Montessori, M. (1973). *To educate the human potential.* Thiruvanmiyur, Madras 41, India: Kalakshetra Publications.

Moyer, J. (Ed.). (1995). *Selecting educational equipment and materials: For school and home.* Wheaton, MD: Association for Childhood Education International.

Murphy, D. (1997). Parent and teacher plan for the child. *Young Children, 52*(4), 32–36.

National Association for the Education of Young Children, Division for Early Childhood of the Council for Exceptional Children, & National Board for Professional Teaching Standards. (2002). *Guidelines for preparation of early childhood professionals.* Washington, DC: Authors.

National Association for the Education of Young Children. (1996). NAEYC position statement: Responding to linguistic and cultural diversity—Recommendations for effective early childhood education. *Young Children, 51*(2), 4–12.

National Association for the Education of Young Children. (1988). NAEYC position statement on standardized testing of young children 3 through 8 years of age. *Young Children, 43*(3), 42–47.

National Association for the Education of Young Children. (1996). NAEYC position statement: Technology and young children ages three through eight. *Young Children, 51*(6), 11–16.

National Association for the Education of Young Children. (1998). Accreditation criteria and procedures of the National Academy of Early Childhood Programs (Rev. ed.). Washington, DC: Author.

National Commission on Excellence in Education. (1983). *A nation at risk: The imperative for education reform.* Washington, DC: U.S. Dept. of Education.

National Council for Teachers of Mathematics. (2000). *Principles and standards for school mathematics*. Resting, VA: Author.

National Institute for Child Health and Human Development. (1998). *The NICHD study of early child care*. Washington, DC: National Institutes of Health. (NIH Pub. No. 98-4318).

Nelsen, J. (1996). *Positive discipline* (Rev. ed.). New York: Ballantine.

Nelsen, J., Erwin, C., & Duffy, R. (1995). *Positive discipline for preschoolers*. Rocklin, CA: Prima Publishing.

Nelsen, J., Lott, L., & Glenn, H. S. (2000). *Positive discipline in the classroom: Developing mutual respect, cooperation, and responsibility in your classroom* (3rd ed.). Roseville, CA: Prima Publishing.

New, R. (1990). Excellent early education: A city in Italy has it. *Young Children, 45*(6), 4–10.

Nieto, S. (1999). *The light in their eyes: Creating multicultural learning communities*. New York: Teachers College Press.

Ohanian, S. (2002). *What happened to recess and why are our children struggling in kindergarten?* New York: McGraw-Hill.

Osborn, K. (1991). *Early childhood education in historical perspective* (3rd ed.). Athens, GA: Daye Press, Ind.

Pallotta, J. (1986). *The icky bug alphabet book*. Watertown, MA: Charlesbridge Publishing.

Pallotta, J. (1989). *The yucky reptile book*. Watertown, MA: Charlesbridge.

Park, K., & Honig, A. (1991). Infant child care patterns and later teacher ratings of preschool behaviors. *Early Child Development and Care, 68*, 8–87.

Parker, J. G., & Asher, S. R. (1997). Peer relations and later personal adjustment: Are low accepted children at risk? *Psychological Bulletin, 102*, 357–389.

Parten, M. B. (1932). Social participation among preschool children. *Journal of Abnormal and Social Psychology, 27*, 243–269.

Paulson, F. L., Paulson, P. R., & Meyer, C. A. (1991). What makes a portfolio a portfolio? *Educational Leadership, 48*(5), 60–63.

Peabody, E. (1906). American preface to F. Froebel's *Mother play and nursery songs* (E. Peabody, Trans.). Boston: Lothrop, Lee, & Shepard. (Original work published 1878).

Peabody, E. P. (1886). *Lectures in the training schools for kindergartners*. Boston: Heath & Co.

Pellegrino, J. W., Chudowsky, N., & Glaser, R. (Eds.). (2001). *Knowing what students know: The science and design of educational assessment*. Washington, DC: National Academy Press.

Perez, B., & Torres-Guzman, M. E. (1996). *Learning in two worlds: An integrated Spanish/English biliteracy approach*. New York: Longman.

Piaget, J. (1952). *The origins of intelligence in children* (Margaret Cook, Trans.). New York: Norton. (Original work published 1936).

Piaget, J. (1965). *The moral judgment of the child*. New York: Norton. (Original work published 1932).

Piaget, J. (1980). Foreward. In C. Kamii & R. DeVries, *Group games in early education* (p. vii). Washington, DC: National Association for the Education of Young Children.

Piaget, J. (1962). *Play, dreams, and imitation in childhood*. New York: Norton.

Piers, H. (1993). *Taking care of your guinea pig: A young pet owner's guide*. Hauppague, NY: Barron's.

Popham, W. J. (2001). *The truth about testing: An educator's call to action*. Alexandria, VA: Association for Supervision and Curriculum Development.

Potter, E. F. (1999). What should I put in my portfolio? *Childhood Education, 75*(4), 200–215.

Puckett, M. B., & Black, J. K., (2000). *Authentic Assessment of the young child: Celebrating development and learning*. (2nd ed.). Upper Saddle River, NJ: Merrill/Prentice Hall.

Puckett, M. B. (Ed.). (2002). *Room to grow* (3rd ed.). Austin, TX: Texas Association for the Education of Young Children.

Quality counts: Building blocks for success (theme issue). (2002, January 10). *Education Week*.

Restak, R. (2001). *The secret life of the brain*. Washington, DC: The Dana Press and The John Henry Press.

Rimm-Kaufman, S. E., & Pianta, R. C. (1999). Patterns of family-school contact in preschool and kindergarten. *School Psychology Review, 28*(3), 426–439.

Rivkin, M. S. (1995). *The great outdoors: Restoring children's right to play outside*. Washington, DC: National Association for the Education of Young Children.

Rivkin, M. S. (2001). Problem solving through outdoor play. *Early Childhood Today, 15*(7), 36–44.

Rizzo, T. (1992). The role of conflict in children's friendship development. In W. A. Corsaro & P. J. Miller (Eds), *Interpretive approaches to children's socialization* San Francisco: Jossey-Bass.

Robinson, A., & Stark, D. R. (2002). *Advocates in action: Making a difference for young children*. Washington, DC: National Association for the Education of Young Children.

Roller, C. M. (1996). *Variability not disability: Struggling readers in a workshop classroom*. Newark, DE: International Reading Association.

Roopnarine, J. L., & Honig, A. S. (1985). Review of research: The unpopular child. *Young Children, 40*(6), 59–64.

Rosenthal, D. M., & Sawyers, J. Y. (1996). Building successful home/school partnerships: Strategies for parent support and involvement. *Childhood Education, 72*(4), 194–200.

Ross, M. E. (2000). Science their way. *Young Children, 55*(2), 6–13.

Rousseau, J. J. (1762). *Emile* (Barbara Foxley, Trans.). London: J. M. Dent & Sons. (Original work n.d.)

Rutter, M., Thorp, K., & Golding, J. (2000). *Twins as a natural experiment to study the causes of language delay.* Report to the Mental Health Foundation, London.

Samaras, A. P. (1996). Children's computers. *Childhood Education, 72*(3), 133–136.

Sandall, S., McLean, M. E., & Smith, B. J. (2000). *DEC recommended practices in early intervention/early childhood special education.* Longmont, CO: Sopris West; Denver: Division for Early Childhood, Council for Exceptional Children.

Schickedanz, (1989). *Much more than the ABCs: The early stages of reading and writing.* Washington, DC: National Association for the Education of Young Children.

Schweinhart, L. J., Weikart, D. P., & Larner, M. B. (1986). Consequences of three curriculum models through age 15. *Early Childhood Research Quarterly, 1,* 15–45.

Schweinhart. L. J., & Weikart, D. P. (1996). *Lasting differences: The High/Scope preschool curriculum comparison study through age 23.* Monographs of the High/Scope Educational Research Foundation, No. 12. Ypsilanti, MI: High/Scope Press.

Seefeldt, C. (1995). Transforming curriculum in social studies. In S. Bredekamp & T. Rosegrant (Eds.), *Reaching potentials: Transforming early childhood curriculum and assessment, Vol. 2* (pp. 109–124). Washington, DC: National Association for the Education of Young Children.

Seuss, Dr. (1960). *One fish, two fish, red fish, blue fish.* New York: Random House.

Shade, D. D. (1996). Software evaluation. *Young Children, 51*(6), 17–21.

Shatz, C. (1997, April 17). (panel presentation) White House Conference on Early Childhood and Learning. Washington, DC.

Shepard, L. A. (1994). The challenges of assessing young children appropriately. *Phi Delta Kappan, 76*(3), 206–212.

Shepard, L. A., & Smith, M. L. (1985). *Boulder Valley kindergarten study: Retention practices and retention effects.* Boulder, CO: Boulder Valley Public Schools.

Shepard, L. A., & Smith, M. L. (1986). Synthesis of research on school readiness and kindergarten retention. *Educational Leadership, 44*(3), 78–86.

Shepard, L. A., & Smith, M. L. (1987). Effects of kindergarten retention at the end of first grade. *Psychology in the Schools, 24,* 346–357.

Shepard, L. A., & Smith, M. L. (1989). Flunking grades: Research and policies on retention. NY: The Falmar Press.

Shonkoff, J. P., & Phillips, D. A. (Eds.). (2000). *From neurons to neighborhoods: The science of early childhood development.* Washington, DC: National Academy Press.

Shores, E. (1995). Interview: Howard Gardner on the eighth intelligence: Seeing the natural world. *Dimensions of Early Childhood, 23,* 5–7.

Small, M. F. (2001). *How biology and culture shape the way we raise our children.* New York: Doubleday.

Southern Early Childhood Association. (1999). *Developmentally appropriate assessment: A position paper.* Little Rock, AR: Author.

Soutter-Perrot, A. (1993). *Ant.* New York: American Education Publishing.

Sprung, B. (1996). Physics is fun, physics is important, and physics belongs in the early childhood curriculum. *Young Children, 51*(5), 29–33.

Steinfels, M. O. (1973). *Who's minding the children?* New York: Simon & Schuster.

Strickland, D. S., & Morrow, L. M. (Eds.). (2000). *Beginning reading and writing.* Newark, DE: International Reading Association.

Sulzby, E., & Teale, W. (1991). Emergent literacy. In R. Barr, M. L. Kamil, P. B. Mosenthal, and P. D. Pearson (Eds.), *Handbook of reading research, Vol. 2* (pp. 727–757). New York: Longman.

Swick, (1997). Involving families in the professional preparation of educators. *Clearing House, 70*(5), 265–69.

Swick, K. J., & Broadway, F. (1997). Parental efficacy and successful parent involvement. *Journal of Instructional Psychology, 24*(1), 69–76.

Sylwester, R. (1995). *A celebration of neurons.* Alexandria, VA: Association for Supervision and Curriculum Development.

Sylwester, R. (2000a). *A biological brain in a cultural classroom: Applying biological research to classroom management.* Thousand Oaks, CA: Corwin Press.

Sylwester, R. (2000b). Unconscious emotions, conscious feelings. *Educational Leadership, 58*(3), 20–24.

Sylwester, R. (Spring/Summer 2001). Caring for our youngest: Public attitudes in the United States. In R. E. Behrman (Ed.). *The future of children: Caring for infants and toddlers, 11*(1), 53–61. Los Altos, CA: The David and Lucille Packard Foundation.

Teale, W. H., & Sulzby, E. (1986). Literacy acquisition in early childhood: The roles of access and mediation in storybook reading. In D. A. Wagner (Ed.), *The future of literacy in a changing world* (pp. 111–130). New York: Pergamon Press.

Templin, M. C. (1957). Certain skills in children: Their development and interrelationships. *University of Minnesota Institute of Child Welfare Monographs,* 26.

Thomas, R. M. (1992). *Comparing theories of child development* (3rd ed.). Belmont, CA: Wadsworth.

Tomich, K. (1996). Hundreds of ladybugs, thousands of ladybugs, millions and billions and trillions of ladybugs—and a couple of roaches. *Young Children, 51*(4), 28–30.

Vavrus, L. (1990). Put portfolios to the test. *Instructor, 100*(1), 48–53.

Voltz, D. L., & Morrow, S. H. (1999). Enhancing collaborative partnerships with culturally diverse families. *Classroom Leadership Online, 2*(7). Retrieved from: www.ascdorg/readingroom/classlead/9904/2apr99.html

Vygotsky, L. (1986). *Thought and language* (A. Kozulin, Trans.). Cambridge, MA: MIT Press. (Original work published 1934).

Vygotsky, L. S. (1967). Play and its role in the mental development of the child. *Soviet Psychology, 12*, 62–76.

Vygotsky, L. S. (1978). *Mind in society* (M. Cole, S. Scribner, V. John Steiner, & E. Souberman, Trans.). Cambridge, MA: Harvard University Press.

Waite-Stupiansky, S. (1997). *Building understanding together: A constructivist approach to early childhood education.* Clifton Park, NY: Delmar Learning.

Watson, S. C. (1991). *Handbook for home visits.* Greenville, IL: Bond County Community Unit No. 2.

Wentzel, K. R. (1991). Relations between social competence and academic achievement in early adolescence. *Child Development, 62*, 1066–1078.

White, B. L. (1995). *The first three years of life* (3rd ed.). Englewood Cliffs, NJ: Prentice Hall.

Willer, B. (Ed.). (1994). A conceptual framework for early childhood professional development: NAEYC position statement. In J. Johnson & J. B. McCracken (Eds.), *The early childhood career lattice: Perspectives on professional development.* Washington, DC: National Association for the Education of Young Children.

Wolf, J. S., & Stephens, T. M. (1989). Parent/Teacher conferences: Finding common ground. *Educational Leadership, 47*(2), 28–32.

Wolfe, P. (2001). *Brain matters: Translating research into classroom practice.* Alexandria, VA: Association for Supervision and Curriculum Development.

Workman, S., & Anziano, M. C. (1993). Curriculum webs: Connections from children to teachers. *Young Children, 48*(2), 4–9.

Wortham, S. C. (1990). *Tests and measurement in early childhood education.* Columbus, OH: Merrill/Prentice Hall.

Wright, S. C., Taylor, D. M., & Macarthur, J. (2000). Subtractive bilingualism and the survival of the inuit language: Heritage versus second language education. *Journal of Educational Psychology, 92*, 63–84.

Yang, O. S. (2000). Guiding children's verbal plan and evaluation during free play: An application of Vygotsky's genetic epistemology to the early childhood classroom. *Early Childhood Education Journal, 28*(1), 3–10.

Zeanah, C. H. (2000). *Handbook of infant mental health* (2nd ed.). New York: Guilford.

ZEROTOTHREE. (2002). *Brain wonders: Helping babies and toddlers grow and develop*. Retrieved from http://www.zerotothree.org/brainwonders/index.html

Zietz, D. (1969). Child welfare: Services and perspectives. New York: Wiley and Sons.

Zigler, N. (1995). Family day home. In L. Ard & M. Pitts (Eds.), *Room to grow: How to create quality early childhood environments* (Rev. ed.). Austin, TX: Texas Association for the Education of Young Children.

# NAME INDEX

# SUBJECT INDEX